Managing and Reforming Modern Public Services

Modern Public Services

The Financial Management Dimension

PEARSON

We work with leading authors to develop the strongest
educational materials in finance, bringing cutting-edge
thinking and best learning practice to a global market.

Under a range of well-known imprints, including
Financial Times Prentice Hall we craft high quality print
and electronic publications that help readers to
understand and apply their content, whether studying
or at work.

To find out more about the complete range of our
publishing, please visit us on the World Wide Web at:
www.pearsoned.co.uk.

Managing and Reforming Modern Public Services

The Financial Management Dimension

Malcolm J. Prowle

Financial Times
Prentice Hall
is an imprint of

Harlow, England • London • New York • Boston • San Francisco • Toronto
Sydney • Tokyo • Singapore • Hong Kong • Seoul • Taipei • New Delhi
Cape Town • Madrid • Mexico City • Amsterdam • Munich • Paris • Milan

Pearson Education Limited

Edinburgh Gate
Harlow
Essex CM20 2JE
England

and Associated Companies throughout the world

Visit us on the World Wide Web at:
www.pearsoned.co.uk

First published 2010

© Pearson Education Limited 2010

The right of Malcolm Prowle to be identified as author of this work has been asserted
by him in accordance with the Copyright, Designs and Patents Act 1988.

ISBN: 978-0-273-72281-6

British Library Cataloguing-in-Publication Data
A catalogue record for this book is available from the British Library

Library of Congress Cataloging-in-Publication Data
Prowle, Malcolm.
  Managing and reforming modern public services : the financial management
dimension / Malcolm Prowle. – 1st ed.
    p. cm.
  Includes bibliographical references and index.
  ISBN 978-0-273-72281-6
  1. Finance, Public–Case studies.   2. Government spending policy–Case studies.
3. Public administration–Case studies.   I. Title.
  HJ131.P76 2009
  352.4–dc22
                                                                    2009033827

10 9 8 7 6 5 4 3 2 1
13 12 11 10

Typeset in 9.5/14 pt Arial by 35
Printed by Ashford Colour Press Ltd., Gosport

The publisher's policy is to use paper manufactured from sustainable forests.

Contents

About the author

Professor Malcolm Prowle is Professor of Business Performance at Nottingham Business School and Visiting Professor at the Open University Business School. He has more than 30 years experience of public sector financial management covering local government, central government, the health sector and further and higher education. He was educated at the Universities of Wales and Lancaster and originally trained as an accountant in local government. Subsequently he held a variety of senior financial management posts in several public sector organisations up to and including Finance Director Level. For five years he held full-time academic positions at two university business schools and has also held a number of visiting academic positions at various UK universities. For 18 years he was a senior management consultant with two international consulting firms (PwC and KPMG) where he specialised in financial management assignments with a large number of public sector and private sector clients. He has extensive experience of strategy, finance and organisational development in a wide range of public sector organisations in the UK and has also worked on various aspects of public sector reform in a number of overseas countries. He has undertaken many research projects in relation to public sector management and has published over 40 books, articles and research reports on various aspects of public sector management and has lectured widely on the subject. He has been a visiting consultant to the World Health Organization, an advisor to a House of Commons Select Committee and an advisor to two shadow ministers.

Foreword

Times are hard! And at a time when the financial pressures on public services in this and other countries are becoming intense it is both relevant and timely that this book by Malcolm Prowle is published. For despite the continuing pressures to find efficiencies and savings in the delivery of public services over the last two decades, the need to do so over the next decade, at a time when tax revenues are collapsing and demands on public services are rising means that the pressure will be greater than ever before. Effective financial management is essential, and the dearth of good up-to-date material in this key area is a significant weakness that this book aims to address.

In some senses it feels like we've been here before, in terms of the impact of a financial crisis working its way through to the whole economy, putting pressure on communities, politicians and public services. Not surprisingly, therefore, people look to past historical patterns to try and predict the future impact on public services. A little less than 35 years ago the then Local Government Minister, Tony Crossland, famously remarked 'the party's over' as the impact of a fresh financial crisis struck the country and the need to cut back on the very rapid growth that had been experienced in public services in the late 1960s and early 1970s became urgent. But simply looking at the state of financial management in public service organisations in those days, and looking at the pressures and skills required for today, just serve to remind us on how great the change has been in the intervening period.

We've seen a rapid development in the porosity of the public and private sector in terms of the delivery of public services. Private sector partnerships as opposed to simple contractual arrangements are now widespread. Back in 1976 no one would even have heard of PFI, let alone understood some of the complexities of having public assets owned by a private company delivering public services under a long-term contract. The intervening period has seen governments, both Conservative and Labour, increase their use of the market-based approach to the management and delivery of public services. The use of pricing, in both internal and external markets, has developed to an extent unheard of back then.

The pattern of public service provision in 1976, although it had undergone recent change, still followed a pattern familiar to most people. Since that time the public sector has expanded in both complexity and structural arrangements, with some parts seemingly in perpetual reorganisation. The widespread realisation that, whatever the structural arrangements, true partnership in working is needed between different public service organisations because of the tense overlap of activities, and the fact that the public need does not present itself in organisationally neat solutions, has increased immensely the demand for good financial management at both organisational and partnership level.

The move towards more market-based approaches has also given rise to a new consumerism in public services with a clear need to deliver to modern standards. The rise of targets, performance measures and inspection regimes has followed the need for government in a highly centralised economy to see that public money is well spent. Whether the organisational arrangements that have been made to try and achieve this will in the long term be seen to be effective is questionable. What is not in question, however, is just how much the public sector has changed.

Even in those areas where there might be assumed to be a level of continuity there is also major change. Public service providers work in the quasi- or non-market situation which separates payment and provision. The need to provide services on behalf of the weakest and most vulnerable communities remains a constant factor. Nevertheless, the expectation of communities has altered dramatically, and accountability now lies not just within organisations but with a much wider range of individuals than in the more deferential situation that existed back then.

Changes in financial management have run after, and sometimes failed to keep up with, this rapid pace of change in public service organisations and delivery. Twenty-five years of change at a dramatically rapid pace surely means it is now time to take stock, look back and consolidate the best financial management advice, understanding and methodology. Drawing from a wide range of examples, organisations and changes that have occurred, this book attempts to present that consolidated best practice.

Accountancy is to some extent the handmaid of economics in that it seeks to record accurately the value added by economic activity through the organisational entity. Being able to do so consistently remains a great pressure on accounting standards and practice. Not only do accountants need to make sure that in a globalised economy transnational transactions are recorded fairly and properly, and that accounts genuinely 'present fairly' irrespective of where the activity takes place, but the porosity of public service delivery between public and private and third sector organisations means that it is essential that proper financial management standards are applied to make sure that performance, cost and outcomes are properly recorded and accounted for. Where there have been chinks in the past, allowing organisations to do things 'off-balance sheet' or allowing liabilities to be generated without proper understanding of the risks that are being taken, then the opportunity has arisen, and been taken, to represent the financial outcomes of organisations in a way that does not 'present fairly' the true underlying economic activity being conducted through that organisation.

Proper, integrated and holistic financial management is the bedrock of recording transactions in organisations in such a way as to allow decision makers in those organisations, the shareholders and taxpayers supplying funds for that organisation's activities, and the users of services and products from those organisations to get an honest and transparent account of what is going on and how well it is being managed. Without the transparency and openness of information that good financial management delivers, trust is lost, confidence is undermined and society as a whole is weaker for it. In the past, research in institutional economics has shown essentially that those countries that are expected to show sustainable and continuing growth and improvement in standard of living need to have those underlying values of trust, confidence and accountability and the institutions to support them. Financial management is the foundation of recording the right information to allow communities and the economy to thrive. At a time when the world economy is under threat this book provides a valuable reminder of that essential truth.

Roger Latham

Former Chief Executive, Nottinghamshire County Council
Former County Treasurer, Nottinghamshire County Council
President of CIPFA 2009/10
Visiting Fellow, Nottingham Business School, Nottingham Trent University

June 2009

Preface

Over the last 30 years or so, public services worldwide have gone through something of a revolution and the pace of change seems likely to continue into the future. As a consequence of this level of change, the various aspects of management in public service organisations have also had to change substantially and will continue to do so.

This book is about the role and contribution of financial management in public services. The term public services organisation (PSO) is used to mean any organisation that is involved in the planning and/or delivery of public services and could involve organisations which belong to the public sector, the private sector or the third sector, and the book will be of relevance to all such organisations. The management of financial resources is often seen as one of the key aspects of management in public services since finance is the resource which binds together the activities and services of the organisation and all its resources (e.g. staffing, equipment, finance) together in a common medium, namely money. However, many people, especially non-financial managers, often have a fear of financial matters and shy away from them. On the other hand, specialist financial managers often have a tendency to over-complicate financial issues, thereby creating a mystique which other managers fail to understand. Neither of these situations are acceptable, and effective financial management is not a luxury but an essential part of public service management which aims to maximise the services delivered for the funds available.

This book has three main aims:

→ To set the context for financial management in public services by looking at the various changes in policy, configuration, culture and financing in public services which have taken place worldwide over the last 20 to 30 years. Also to consider the broad impact this has had on the practice of financial management in public services.

→ To describe, in some depth, the various aspects of financial management practice (e.g. costing, strategy, budgeting, etc.) and the ways in which they have been or can be applied in public services over this period of reform and change. The aim is to give an up-to-date working knowledge of all aspects of financial management, as it may be applied in the public services, but which is drawn from best practices in both public and private sectors.

→ To consider the forces for change in public services and their likely future impact, and then consider the possible impact of these changes on the practice of financial management.

In trying to achieve these aims, a number of over-arching points need to be emphasised. First, at the time of writing, the UK is in the midst of perhaps the worst economic recession for over 100 years and this contextual point will be referred to throughout the book. Although the situation may not be as serious in other countries the effects of this recession are being felt worldwide. In the UK the economic climate coupled with government mis-management of public expenditure has led to a situation where government borrowing and debt will reach enormous levels which will be a burden on the economy for many years to come. The consequences of this are that the pressure on public service resources will be enormous, and the public sector as a whole may have to cope with real terms cuts in resources unlike the environment of continual growth that has been in existence for many years and to which many public sector managers have become accustomed. These resource pressures will present *unprecedented* challenges to the finance profession and to the operation of financial management in public services. In particular, the search for true efficiency improvements in public services will place great burdens on service managers and finance professionals throughout public services. Thus, irrespective of what has happened in the past, it can be expected that financial management in public services will be expected to 'raise its game' substantially, in the years ahead. It is the author's view that there is plenty of scope for doing this.

Second, effective financial management is an essential aspect of the management of public services in all countries. This book focuses on public service financial management in the United Kingdom since (arguably) the UK has been in the vanguard of public service reform over the last 30 years, plus the fact that the skills and knowledge of the author are largely UK based. Furthermore, the process of delegation to the Celtic fringes of the UK has meant that there have been differences in policy between England, Scotland, Wales and Northern Ireland. Given the dominant size of England in the UK this book concentrates mainly on the English experience of public service reform. However, the approaches and methods of financial management described in the various chapters of the book should have easy applicability to public services in all countries.

Third, it must be strongly emphasised that financial management is not a stand-alone function but a component part of the overall management of public services. Furthermore, financial management has no inherent right to exist but must be judged according to the contribution it makes towards the delivery of more effective and efficient public services. Hence, it is important that in considering enhancements to financial management approaches in public services the focus is on what contribution these enhancements will make to public services themselves and not narrow (finance) professional considerations, which is sometimes the case.

Fourth, this books aims to cover both the theory and practical aspects of financial management in public services and to relate the two. Relating theory to practice has long been recognised as a fundamental part of professional education and training in a wide variety of disciplines and settings. However, the task of bringing theory and practice together is often more difficult and complex than many people realise. Consequently, the various chapters will present and discuss the key themes and issues arising from a particular topic and demonstrate how these ideas can be of benefit to busy practitioners wrestling with the demands of working with people and their problems. To this end, the book includes numerous examples of practice in public services as well as a series of case studies. The author was personally involved in the implementation of financial management developments in PSOs during the period of public service reform and all of the case studies are based on real-life situations with only minor changes to emphasise certain points of learning.

The book is aimed at five main classes of reader. First, non-financial managers and service professionals in public services organisations who require a working knowledge of each aspect of financial management. These persons may come from an administrative background or from a background of service delivery. Second, it will provide a comprehensive overview of public service financial management for specialist financial managers within public services. Third, for students who may be pursuing MBAs, MPAs, undergraduate degrees or diploma courses in public sector management or professional courses with a public sector dimension it will provide the essential knowledge required by them concerning financial management in a public service context. Fourth, non-executive directors or governors, etc. in various public service organisations. Although such people are often very experienced in commercial management issues they may feel the need for a guide to financial management in the public services. Fifth, public sector managers in overseas countries who are in the process of undertaking public sector reform and who wish to gain some practical knowledge of UK experiences.

My thanks are due to a number of people who have read drafts of the various chapters, including colleagues at the Nottingham Business School, namely Dr Don Harradine, Mr Roger Latham and Ms Rachel Edden. Also, thanks are due to Mr Stephen Gillingham of Blaenau Gwent Social Services for his assistance, and to my wife Alison Prowle for correcting my inadequate grammatical and literary skills.

Malcolm J. Prowle
Nottingham Business School
April 2009

Figures

Tables

Case studies

Terms and acronyms

3Es	economy, effectiveness and efficiency
3SOs	third sector organisations
4Ps	products, place, promotion, price
ABC	Activity-Based Costing
AME	Annually Managed Expenditure
ARR	accounting rate of return
ASB	Accounting Standards Board
BBC	British Broadcasting Corporation
BPR	Business Process Re-engineering
CAG	Comptroller and Auditor General
CBA	Cost–Benefit Analysis
CSR	Comprehensive Spending Review
CUA	Cost Utility Analysis
DCF	Discounted Cash Flow
DEA	Data Envelope Analysis
DEL	Departmental Expenditure Limits
DOF	Director of Finance
DSA	Departmental Strategic Objective
DSS	decision support system
DSO	departmental strategic objectives
DSO	Direct Service Organisation (of a local authority)
DWP	Department for Work and Pensions
ERDF	European Regional Development Fund
ESF	European Social Fund
ESS	Executive Support System
EU	European Union
FASB	Financial Accounting Standards Board
FBC	Full Business Case
FE	further education
FIS	financial information system
FM	financial memorandum
FMI	Financial Management Initiative
FRAB	Financial Reporting Advisory Board
FRC	Financial Reporting Council
FRS	Financial Reporting Standard

GAAP	Generally Accepted Accounting Principles
GDP	gross domestic product
GNI	gross national income
GO	government office
HCC	Healthcare Commission
HDU	high dependency unit
HE	higher education
HEFCE	Higher Education Funding Council for England
HEI	higher education institution
HMRC	Her Majesty's Revenue and Customs (of the UK)
HRM	Human Resource Management
I&E	income and expenditure
IASB	International Accounting Standards Board
ICT	information and communications technology
IDeA	Improvement and Development Agency (for local government)
IPSASB	International Public Sector Accounting Standards Board
IFRIC	International Financial Reporting Interpretations Committee
IFRS	International Financial Reporting Standard
IRS	Internal Revenue Service (in the United States)
IS	information system
IT	information technology
ITU	intensive therapy unit
LAA	Local Area Agreements
LEA	Local Education Authority
LSC	Learning and Skills Council
MIS	management information system
NAO	National Audit Office
NHS	National Health Service
NPfIT	National Programme for Information Technology (NHS)
NPM	New Public Management
NPV	net present value
OBC	Outline Business Case
OECD	Organisation for Economic Co-operation and Development
OFSTED	Office for standards in education
ONS	Office for national statistics
PAB	programme analysis and budgeting
PAC	Public Accounts Committee
PAF	Public Audit Forum PBB
P&L	profit and loss
PBB	priority-based budgeting

PbR	payment by results
PC	personal computer
PCT	Primary Care Trust (of the NHS)
PDCU	portable data capture unit
PEST	political, economic, societal, technological
PFI	Private Finance Initiative
PI	performance indicator
PM	performance management
PMDU	Prime Minister's Delivery Unit
PPP	Public/Private Partnerships
PRP	performance related pay
PSA	Public Service Agreement
PSC	public sector comparator
PSO	public service organisation
quango	quasi-autonomous non-governmental organisation
RAM	resource allocation model
RDA	Regional Development Agency
SLA	service level agreement
SORP	Statement of Recommended Practice
SSAP	Statement of Standard Accounting Practice
SWOT	strengths, weaknesses, opportunities, threats
TME	Total Managed Expenditure
TPS	transaction processing system
UITF	Urgent Issues Task Force
UK	United Kingdom
VAT	value added tax
VFM	value for money
WACC	weighted average cost of capital
WGA	Whole of Government Accounts
ZBB	zero-based budgeting

Acknowledgements

We are grateful to the following for permission to reproduce copyright material:

Figures

Figure 2.1 from *The Economist*, http://www.economist.com/markets/indicators/ displaystory.cfm?story_id=E1_NVNTGSG (18 March 2004), copyright The Economist Newspaper Limited, London (18 March 2004); Figure 2.2 adapted from HM Treasury, reproduced under the terms of the Click-Use Licence; Figure 2.3 from Lonti, Z. and Woods, M. (2008) *Towards Government at a Glance: Identification of Core Data and Issues Related to Public Sector Efficiency* (OECD Working Papers on Public Governance, No. 7), OECD p.39, OECD Publishing, doi:10.1787/245570167540; Figure 2.4 from HM Treasury 2008–09 projections, reproduced under the terms of the Click-Use Licence; Figure 3.2 adapted from http://www.statistics.gov.uk/cci/ nugget.asp?id=170, ONS, reproduced under the terms of the Click-Use Licence, reproduced under the terms of the Click-Use Licence; Figure 3.3 from *The Economist*; http://www.economist.com/markets/indicators/displaystory.cfm?story_id =11707320 (10 July 2008), copyright The Economist Newspaper Limited, London (10 July 2008); Figure 3.8 from The Cabinet Office, http://www.cabinetoffice.gov.uk/ cabinetoffice/strategy/assets/satisfaction.pdf, 'Satisfaction with public services: a discussion paper'; Figure 3.2 by Nick Donovan, Joanna Brown and Lisa Bellulo, November 2001, Crown Copyright; Figure 5.2 adapted with permission from Nottingham City Council; Figure 8.1 from IDeA (Improvement and Development Agency for Local Government, 2008); Figure 8.2 copyright Professor Andy Neely (2000); Figure 8.5 from *Translating Strategy into Action: The Balanced Scorecard*, Harvard Business School Publishing (Kaplan, R.S. and Norton, D.P. 1996).

Tables

Table 2.3 adapted from OECD, http://ocde.p4.siteinternet.com/publications/doifiles/ 012008061P1T027.xls, Public Finance Taxation, 2005, OECD (2008), OECD in Figures 2008, www.oecd.org/infigures; Tables 2.4 and 2.5 adapted from HM Treasury, reproduced under the terms of the Click-Use Licence; Table 2.6 adapted from House of Commons (2001); Table 3.1 adapted from United Nations: World

Population Statistics, http://esa.un.org/unpp/; Table 3.2 adapted from Office for Health Economics, http://www.ohe.org/page/knowledge/schools/addpedix/nhs_cost.cfm, Department of Health, reproduced under the terms of the Click-Use Licence.

In some instances we have been unable to trace the owners of copyright material, and we would appreciate any information that would enable us to do so.

Part 1

The organisation and development of public services

Introduction: public services and the public sector

Introduction

The twentieth and twenty-first centuries have seen substantial changes in the composition and size of the public sector and public services in most developed countries and in recent years we have also seen radical changes taking place in the organisation and funding of public services. As we move further into the new millennium, the various political, social, economic and technological trends in the world suggest that public services will continue to undergo substantial change. This will be the case in both developed countries and developing countries, although the precise nature of the changes will vary from case to case.

In this environment of ongoing and almost continual change, effective management practices are essential to ensure that public services are provided in such a way that they meet the needs of services users and are provided in an efficient manner which makes the best use of scarce public funds. As a key part of the management process, all public service organisations (PSOs) should aim to develop and apply effective approaches to financial management, and this is the focus of this book. It must be emphasised that the term public service organisation is used to mean any organisation which is involved in the planning and/or delivery of public services and includes organisations which belong to the **public sector**, the **private sector** or the **third sector**.

With regard to this book, a few important points first need to be emphasised:

→ First, one often finds books on public service management (often written by soci-ologists or political scientists rather than management specialists) which try to com-plicate and/or politicise managerial issues on the grounds that public services are 'different' and conventional managerial methods cannot be applied. The author rejects this view. Clearly public services are contextually different from other organisations, but private sector *service* organisations are also contextually different from private sector *manufacturing* organisations – and no one suggests that managerial methods are not transferable from one to the other. Thus, a key theme of this book is the need for different parts of public services to be prepared to learn from other sectors (public and private) and identify and apply best practices from those other sectors. Also, there is scope for public service organisations to learn from private sector organisations and apply their best practices, which are often well in advance of best practices in the public sector. Public sector financial management is not an isolated discipline set aside from 'conventional' financial management and should not be treated as such, other than recognising the differences of context.

→ Second, financial management is not a discipline which should exist in isolation. Clearly something like the production of annual financial accounts is an end in its own right and is required by statute. However, in other areas financial management is a contributor (and a major contributor at that) to key organisational processes such as strategy, pricing, performance improvement, etc. While this may seem obvious, in practice it is not always the case and one often sees (for example) the development of costing systems being undertaken in splendid isolation from any consideration of how that cost information is ultimately to be used.

→ Third, the development of financial management in PSOs is a dynamic rather than a static task. As this book will discuss, the environment in which public services operate has been continually changing, as has the demand for public services. Such changes are likely to continue into the future and it is thus important that financial management in PSOs keeps apace with such changes, although it has not always done so.

In this introductory chapter we will consider the following themes:

→ the distinction between the provision of and funding of public services and the con-sequent differentiation between public services and public sector;

→ how UK public services have developed over time and become more extensive and complex;

→ the configuration of public services and the various approaches to classification;

→ the importance of financial management in public service organisations.

The chapter will conclude with an outline of the structure and content of this book.

Public sector and public services: provision and financing

In considering the meaning of the terms public sector and public services it is first necessary to draw a distinction between the twin issues of service provision and service financing. This is illustrated in Figure 1.1 using health services in the UK as an example. A similar analysis can be prepared for other public services and other countries.

This figure shows that health services can actually be *provided* to patients by either public sector organisations such as NHS hospitals or private sector organisations such as private hospitals. In this context, third sector organisations (3SOs) must be regarded as being private sector but not-for-profit organisations. Also it shows that the *funds* necessary to provide health services can come from a combination of private or public sources. Private funding implies people paying out of their own pocket, usually via some form of private health insurance, while public funding suggests governmental sources. Within each of the four boxes are examples of each type.

This analysis leads us to four types of service:

→ Services which are publicly financed and publicly provided (A) – these are clearly part of the public *sector*.

→ Services which are privately financed and privately provided (D) – these are clearly *not* part of the public sector since they involve a contractual arrangement between a private individual and a private company.

→ Services which are privately financed and publicly provided (C) – these could be considered as being public services since they involve activity by a PSO.

→ Services which are publicly financed and privately provided (B) – since these involve public expenditure they can be regarded as part of public *services*.

Figure 1.1 Public sector and public services – provision and financing (UK)

		Service provision	
		Public	**Private**
Service finance	**Public**	Most NHS services (A)	NHS funds used to purchase patient care in a private hospital (B)
	Private	Private patients treated in an NHS hospital (C)	Private patients treated in a private hospital (D)

We can therefore derive the following situations:

→ **public sector** – the segments shown as A and C;

→ **public services** – the segments shown as A, B and C.

This distinction needs to be borne in mind throughout this book.

Growth and development of UK public sector

As an example, let us first consider the growth and development of public services in the UK. A hundred years ago the situation was vastly different from the way it is today.

Phases of development of public services

This upward trend in the size of UK public services needs some broad explanation and identification of the main causal factors. This is summarised in Figure 1.2.

Historical

At the start of the twentieth century, and for many centuries previous, the involvement of government and the state, in the UK and most other developed countries, was largely limited to three areas of activity:

→ **Defence of the realm** – expenditure on armed forces.

→ **Maintenance of law and order** – police, courts, prisons, etc.

→ **Trade** – regulation and promotion of trade matters.

Figure 1.2 Phases in the development of UK public services

Period	Features
Historical	• Defence • Law and order • Trade
First half of the twentieth century	• Growth in social welfare activities
Second half of the twentieth century	• Further growth in social welfare activities • Increasing involvement in economic management
Start of the twenty-first century	• Increasing state involvement in areas traditionally regarded as private • Social engineering

For example, an examination of the eighteenth-century UK prime minister, William Pitt the Younger, shows that his working life was dominated by issues of trade, war and the raising of tax revenues to finance those activities (Hague, 2005). This is very different from today where prime ministers also have to regard health, education and pensions as being key political and social issues.

Given the limited range of activities described above, it is not surprising that public services, in the UK and other developed countries, were much smaller and restricted in their scope than they are today.

First half of the twentieth century

During the first half of the twentieth century both the size and scope of public services started to grow substantially. The key factor here was the growth in the involvement of the state in promoting the welfare of its people. Partly this was for altruistic reasons, but also partly for the achievement of other aspects of government policy. For example, in the early part of the century, inadequate nutrition and housing impacted negatively on the health of poorer people in society. This in turn impacted on the productivity of employees in industry and on the effectiveness of conscripts in the army. During the First World War, recruiters uncovered the dismaying fact that almost two in every five volunteers for the British Army were entirely unsuitable for military service on the grounds of health (Wikipedia, 2009a). Not surprisingly, the government came under pressure from industrialists and generals to do something about the situation.

However, this was not always the case. In the UK, major welfare reforms took place in the early part of the twentieth century, which resulted in an increase in the size and scope of government involvement in social welfare issues. The main aspects of this were determined by two key pieces of legislation passed by the then Liberal government of the day. These were the Old Age Pensions Act of 1908, which provided for a non-contributory but means-tested pension, and the National Insurance Act of 1911, which provided a contributory but non-means-tested cover against sickness and employment for some classes of worker. Between the two world wars the development of the welfare state was somewhat limited, although there were key developments in the fields of social housing, pensions and education.

Second half of the twentieth century

In the second half of the twentieth century, there were three factors that contributed to the upward trend in public expenditure, leading to public services becoming much larger and more complex than they were historically, and having a greater direct impact on the life of the average citizen. These three factors are described next.

Increasing need for services

Once governments became involved in various aspects of social welfare they virtually committed themselves to having to respond, to a lesser or greater extent, to increases in the need for services. Unfortunately, at the time of initial involvement it was not always perceived that the needs and hence demands for services would grow substantially. Take, for example, the NHS. At the time the NHS was formed, there was a strong belief that the pool of sickness and hence the need for health services was finite and that the provision of a certain level of resources, to the NHS, would meet all the health needs of the population. With the benefit of hindsight, that view now seems naïve, and the current wisdom is that the demands for health services will be virtually unlimited.

Creeping involvement in social welfare

There is a general recognition that, in a modern state, the government needs to be actively involved in many aspects of social welfare (e.g. education, health, pensions, etc.). Politicians of the left and right may argue and debate about the extent of that involvement, but few politicians of the right would suggest that the welfare state be contracted back to pre-First World War levels.

The Beveridge Report (Beveridge, 1942) paved the way for the foundation of the modern welfare state. Beveridge made recommendations for the development of a comprehensive system of social security and the development of a national structure of health services. Following the end of the Second World War the new Labour government embarked on a huge programme of improvements in social welfare, which basically involved the implementation of the Beveridge recommendations. The social security developments were underpinned by the passing of the National Insurance Act of 1946 and the National Assistance Act of 1948. However, perhaps the flagship policy of this period was the creation of the National Health Service (NHS) in 1948, which brought into public ownership large numbers of what were previously private or voluntary hospitals. Relating back to the comments made above, however, it is interesting to note that the provision of what are now termed family health services (general practitioners, dentists, community pharmacists and opticians) all remained in the hands of private practitioners. However, even though the services were provided by these private practitioners, the funding for the services was public and the practitioners obtained most of their income through contractual arrangements with the NHS. This somewhat strange arrangement was the political compromise that had to be made by the Government to get the NHS formed.

In education the critical development was the passing of the 1944 Education Act. This laid the foundation of universal free state secondary education and provided the framework for the education services we have today.

State involvement in economic management

During the period 1935–45 there was increasing international acceptance that governments needed to have a much larger involvement in the management of their economies. This was the period of Keynes, the development of macro-economics and the use of large-scale public spending in the USA and Germany to boost flagging economies.

Also, in the period immediately following the end of the Second World War, large parts of the UK economy passed into public ownership through the nationalisation of industries such as coal, steel, electricity and gas. These policies reflected the view of the then Labour government that public ownership of such strategically important industries was essential for economic management purposes. Subsequently, all of these industries were de-nationalised through the privatisation policies followed by successive Conservative governments in the 1980s and 1990s.

It is now generally accepted that Governments should have some role in economic management. However, the extent and nature of that involvement is open to political and ideological disagreement as the debate between the merits of monetarism and Keynesianism in the 1980s illustrated. In the modern world, governments worldwide are involved in economic management in a number of ways, and the following are current examples of PSOs in the UK which are involved in and have a role in economic management:

→ **Government departments** – several departments are concerned with aspects of economic management and economic development including, for example, HM Treasury, and the Department of Business, Enterprise and Regulatory Reform.

→ **Regional Development Agencies** – these have responsibilities concerning social and economic development within UK regions.

→ **Export Credit Guarantees Department** – this facilitates the export of goods and services.

→ **Office for National Statistics** – collects and collates a wide range of economic information.

→ **Local Authority Economic Development Departments** – have substantial roles in the economic development of their areas.

Start of the twenty-first century

In 1997 a Labour government came to power after 18 years in opposition. Initially the new government abided by the public expenditure targets set by its predecessor but in subsequent years it presided over a substantial growth in the percentage of national income devoted to public service. To some extent, much of this growth in public spending might be regarded as 'more of the same'. For example, in the period between 1999–2000 and 2007–8 spending on the NHS in England grew on average by 6.4% a year in real terms, which is well in excess of the rate of NHS growth in previous decades and well in excess of the average growth in public spending (4%) for the same period (IFS, 2008). However, some available evidence (Appleby, 2007) suggests that a significant part of this growth in funding was not used wisely and led to a substantial reduction in the overall productivity of the NHS. However, much of the growth in funding clearly went on improving the range of health services and the ease of access to those services.

A considerable proportion of the growth in public expenditure has also been devoted to what might be regarded as 'new' areas of government activity. These are often controversial areas, and many people argue that the state is now getting too involved in areas of activity that have traditionally been private matters or that the state is involved in forms of social engineering. Some examples of these controversial activities include:

→ **Parenting** – concerns about the health status, educational outcomes and behaviour of many children and young people have led government and local authorities to become heavily involved in the parenting agenda, since effective parenting is seen as a key means of improvement. This can involve the provision of information, parenting training courses, etc. Traditionally this has not been an area of state involvement and parenting has been regarded as a private issue.

→ **Promotion of equality of outcomes** – most political commentators from any political party would probably accept that equality of access and opportunity (by different geographic areas, different groups in society, etc.) to services such as education, health, employment, etc. is an essential prerequisite for a fair and just society. However, the last few years have gone beyond the equality of access and opportunity to promoting equality of outcomes via state involvement or intervention. One example of this would be higher education, where a regulatory regime to monitor access has been introduced and large financial incentives have been offered to certain dis-advantaged groups in society to encourage them to enter higher education.

→ **Dilution of mission** – several examples can be quoted of situations where the key activities or mission of a PSO has been diluted or diverted as a consequence of a requirement to promote another aspect of public policy. One example of this is schools, where as well as promoting educational achievement, schools are now also asked to pursue a range of objectives concerned with, for example, healthy eating, citizenship, anti-bullying, racial awareness, etc.

Clearly such a large-scale involvement of the state in non-traditional areas has a significant financial implication, and at the time of writing the growth in public expenditure coupled with a downturn in government revenues may raise questions about the merits of such activities.

Configuration of the public sector and public services

There are three distinct ways of looking at the configuration of public services, and this is illustrated in Figure 1.3 and described below.

Organisational type

Most PSOs can be classified as belonging to one of the following organisational types:

Central government departments

These are the government departments that undertake the work of central government and support the policies of the various Secretaries of State. The main UK departments are as follows:

→ Cabinet Office
→ HM Treasury
→ Foreign and Commonwealth Office
→ Home Office
→ Department of Justice
→ Department of Health
→ Department for Schools and Families

→ Department of the Environment, Food and Rural Affairs
→ Department for International Development
→ Department for Business, Enterprise and Regulatory Reform
→ Department of Defence
→ Department of Social Security
→ Department of Culture.

In addition, associated with these departments are a series of executive agencies which undertake various operational activities on behalf of that department. Some examples of executive agencies are listed below:

Figure 1.3 Configuration of public services

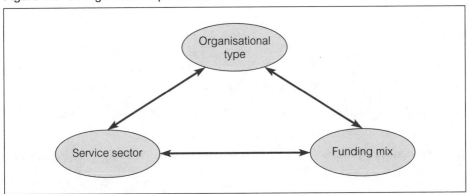

→ Jobcentre Plus – Department of Social Security;

→ Medical Devices Agency – Department of Health;

→ Highways Agency – Department of the Environment;

→ Passport Agency – Home Office;

→ Prisons Agency – Home Office.

Although these agencies operate at arms length from their sponsoring government department they are still a component of the central government sector.

Sub-national government

Many countries have a tier of government that sits below the national tier. For example, in the USA there is the State tier of government, which sits below the Federal tier. At the time the Union was formed, the State tier retained formidable powers while passing other powers (e.g. defence, foreign affairs) to the Federal tier. In other countries there are tiers of government below the central level, which may be referred to as provinces (China) or regions (India, Germany and Turkey).

In the UK there is no sub-national tier of government, with the exception of the devolved parliaments and assemblies in the Celtic fringes. Following the 1997 general election the government put forward proposals for the creation of a Scottish Parliament and a Welsh Assembly. These proposals were put to referenda and approved by the electorate of those countries and the parliament/assembly have now come into existence. Also, as part of the Northern Ireland peace process an Assembly for Northern Ireland was proposed and subsequently approved in a referendum. Clearly these assemblies and the parliament have considerable differences in organisation and constitution and, in particular, the Scottish Parliament has tax-raising powers.

Proposals were also made to establish elected regional bodies in parts of England. However, the first proposed regional assembly failed to gain majority support in a public referendum and the whole issue of English elected regional assemblies now seems dormant. Thus the UK remains one of the most centralised states in the world.

Local government

Most countries have some form of local government or municipal authorities, although this will vary from country to country. In the UK the pattern of local government varies across the country, but there are six basic types of local authority:

→ **Shire county councils** – these run services such as education, social services, consumer protection, etc.

→ **Shire district councils** – these run services such as housing, waste collection, street cleaning, etc.

→ **Metropolitan borough councils** – these councils are located in major metropolitan areas in England and deliver a comprehensive range of services.

→ **Unitary authorities** – in some areas of the country the binary structure of shire county and shire districts have been replaced by a unitary structure comprising a single unitary authority delivering a comprehensive range of services.

→ **London** – London comprises a number of London boroughs which deliver a comprehensive range of services. In addition, there is also the Greater London Authority.

→ **Parish or town councils** – these look after a limited range of services such as allotments, street lighting, playing fields, etc.

Traditionally the UK had a uniform structure of local government across the country. However, following the recommendations of the Local Government Commission, this uniform pattern began to break down. In many parts of the country the county and district local authorities have been merged to give a unitary local authority. However, in other parts both district and county authorities continue to exist.

National Health Service organisations

The configuration of health services varies greatly between countries, being part of central government in some and part of local government in others. In the UK, publicly financed health services are delivered through the National Health Service (NHS), which might be regarded as being semi-autonomous of central government. The NHS comprises the following main types of organisation:

→ **Strategic Health Authorities** – responsible for the development of coherent health strategies for large areas of the country.

→ **Primary Care Trusts (PCTs)** – concerned with local health policy and the specification of services required, and with responsibility for the commissioning of hospital-based health services. PCTs are also responsible for the management of the delivery of primary health care services.

→ **NHS Trusts** – concerned with the provision of hospital, community and ambulance services to a wide range of patients.

→ **NHS Foundation Trusts** – similar role to that of NHS Trusts except that Foundation Trusts have greater freedoms from central government to decide such matters as staff pay structures, borrowing, etc. The number of Foundation Trusts is continually increasing as NHS Trusts transfer to foundation status.

→ **Special health authorities** – these have specific functions such as, for example, the NHS Litigation Authority, which administers medical negligence issues for the NHS, and the NHS Logistics Authority, which manages the supplies function for the NHS.

Non-Departmental Public Bodies (or quasi-autonomous non-governmental organisations (quangos))

In the UK, these organisations are neither central government departments nor executive agencies. They are formally referred to as Non-Departmental Public Bodies (NDPB) but the popular term quango was developed to describe them. There are too many to provide a complete list but some examples include the following: Regional Development Agencies; Further and Higher Education Funding Councils; Countryside Commissions; English Heritage; and Housing Commissions.

Further or higher education institutions

This heading covers the following organisations which are corporate bodies in their own right, formed under the relevant education Act of Parliament:

→ higher education institutions – universities, colleges of higher education;

→ further education institutions – FE colleges, technical colleges, agricultural colleges.

Universities are sometimes referred to as being private sector organisations since some of them obtain only a small part of their total funding from government sources. However, in the view of the author, this is misleading and in terms of funding, governance and public perceptions most universities should be regarded as being PSOs.

Other PSOs

A number of other PSOs can be identified which do not fall neatly into either of the above types: police authorities, fire and rescue authorities, and probation authorities, etc.

Private sector service providers

There are a wide range of private sector organisations delivering public services directly to the public on contract to the government or other public sector bodies. Some of these organisations may be profit-driven whereas others are often described as being 'not for profit'. This does not mean they do not make a profit but that any profits made are re-invested in the business and not distributed to shareholders. Although we have included universities in the category of public sector organisations, it could also be argued that universities are really private sector 'not-for-profit' organisations who receive government funding. However, this ignores the fact that universities are now heavily regulated by government on a range of issues.

Examples of such organisations include private prisons, independent sector providers of diagnostic and surgical services, and private sector providers of child care.

Third sector service providers

The term third sector has recently come into vogue as an umbrella term to describe what might have been called voluntary sector organisations, community organisations or social enterprise organisations. Although often regarded as part of the public sector, such third sector organisations (3SOs) are technically private sector in terms of constitution and governance arrangements albeit that they operate on a not-for-profit basis.

Miscellaneous

Beyond the above there will be a large number of other organisations whose precise status is either debatable or they verge on other sectors. Examples of these include private companies owned by universities, colleges or local authorities, housing associations – these are voluntary bodies largely financed by the Housing Corporation, and general medical practitioners – these are private sector partnerships but receive the majority of their funding through contracts with the NHS.

Service sector

As an alternative to the above, PSOs could be classified according to the service sector to which they belong. Frequently, service provision cuts across organisational type and there will be established relationships between the various organisations within a particular sector. A complete sectoral analysis is difficult to produce but some examples are shown in Figure 1.4.

Funding patterns

Another approach to the classification of PSOs could be in accordance to the mix of funding they receive. PSOs can be funded from three main sources: nationally raised tax revenues and government borrowings; locally raised tax revenues; and charges for goods and services.

Each of these approaches will be discussed in more detail in Chapter 2. When trying to classify PSOs according to their funding pattern, one must first recognise that this will always be an imprecise classification. However, the following analysis is suggested:

Predominantly funded from nationally raised taxes

PSOs in this category obtain the vast majority (>90%) of their funds directly from the central government exchequer. Some UK examples of organisations falling into this category include central government departments, devolved assemblies/parliaments,

Figure 1.4 UK public sector organisations and service sectors

Sector	Organisations
Education	• Department for Schools and Families • Higher Education Funding Councils • Learning and Skills Council • Local Education Authorities • Further and higher education institutions • Private education and training providers • Third sector education and training providers
Health	• Department of Health • Strategic health authorities • Primary Care Trusts • NHS Trusts and Foundation trusts • Local authorities (Environmental Health) • Independent sector treatment centres
Economic development	• HM Treasury • Department for Business Enterprise and Regulatory Reform • HMRC • Regional Development Agencies • Learning and Skills Council • Local authorities (Economic Development Units)
Law and order	• Department of Justice • Home Office • Police authorities • Magistrates courts • Probation services
Emergency services	• Home Office • Department of Health • Ministry of Defence • Fire and rescue services • Police services • Ambulance services • HM coastguards • Armed forces • Third sector organisations (e.g. Mountain Rescue)

PCTs and NHS Trusts, economic development agencies, and education funding agencies.

Funded from locally levied taxes

PSOs in this category have powers to raise a substantial proportion of their funding through locally levied taxes. These locally levied taxes are in addition to large amounts of exchequer-based funding and other income sources. In some countries, significant funds are raised through a variety of locally levied taxes but in the UK the only two sources of this, which have already been quoted, are:

→ **local authorities** – council tax levied on inhabitants within their area;

→ **Scottish Parliament** – it has the power to levy supplementary income tax, although this power has yet to be used.

Revenue from charges

PSOs in this category obtain significant levels of funding by means of charges levied on their consumers. Some UK examples of this are as follows:

→ **Universities** – as from October 1999 universities levied a fee on students attending the institution, thus raising substantial sources of income. This is in addition to exchequer funds provided by HEFCE.

→ **District councils** – these councils rise significant amounts of income from housing rents, leisure centre charges, etc. in addition to exchequer grants and council tax.

Some international comparisons

The above sections describe the configuration of public services in the UK. Clearly in other countries there will be significant variations on that configuration and these variations will reflect a number of factors such as size, history, political ideology, culture, economic and military power, etc. The following points are illustrative:

→ **Central government departments** – all countries will have a range of central government departments (or ministries) but the number of departments and their responsibilities will vary from country to country.

→ **Sub-central government** – as noted, in the UK the only form of sub-central government is the devolved institutions in Scotland, Wales and Northern Ireland. In other countries there are tiers of government below the central level. However, the constitutional arrangements and the range of powers attributable to this tier of government will vary enormously.

→ **Local authorities** – most countries will have some form of local government structure, but the size of the local authorities and their range of powers will vary between countries.

→ **Mixed economy of provision** – in recent years the UK has seen a significant growth in the involvement of the private sector and the third sector in the provision of public services. The size of this mixed economy will clearly vary significantly between countries.

The importance of financial management in public service organisations

In Figure 1.5 the pivotal position of finance in the management of a PSO is illustrated. On the one hand the delivery of public services results in an inflow of monies to the service provider, from whatever source (e.g. taxes, charges, grants), while on the other hand the acquisition of various resources with which to deliver those services results in an outflow of monies from the service provider. Thus finance is the medium which binds together both the services delivered and the various resources need to deliver the services. Not surprisingly, therefore, the management of finance is a key management task not just for the finance professionals in a PSO but also for the service managers and professionals who deliver services and use resources (e.g. staff, equipment, etc.) with which to deliver those services.

If we turn to what sorts of persons and organisations are likely to make use of financial management information from PSOs we usually form two groups, as shown in Figure 1.6.

The first group are essentially external to the organisation and the financial informa- tion available to them is usually restricted to financial accounts (and associated annual report) produced by the PSO on an annual basis. The second group are

Figure 1.5 The role of finance in PSOs

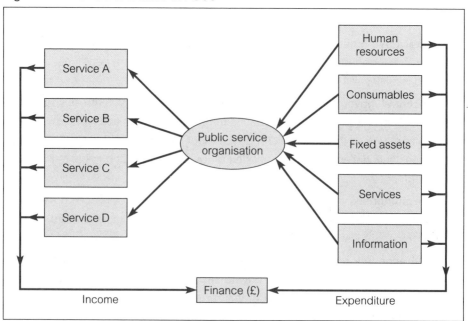

Figure 1.6 Twin aspects of accounting

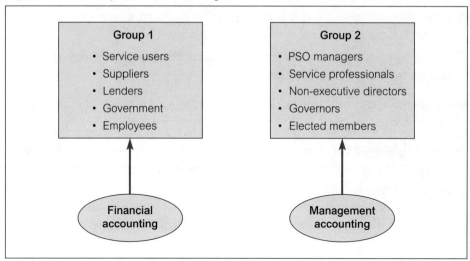

essentially internal to the organisation and a much wider range of financial information is available to them. The topic of financial accounting (and the associated issues
of accountability and governance) is discussed in Chapter 9, while several other
chapters are concerned with the different aspects of management accounting.

When we look at many PSOs today it would appear that the management tasks
facing them can be summarised as shown in Figure 1.7.

Figure 1.7 suggests that to be successful, a PSO must manage three variables
simultaneously:

Figure 1.7 Managing PSOs

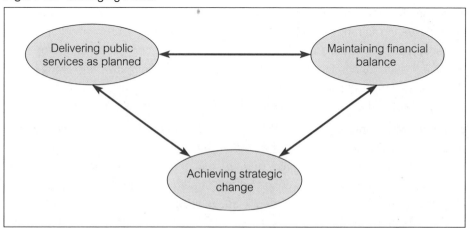

1 It must deliver on its service targets in relation to access, quality, timeliness, etc.

2 It must manage its finances in such a way as to avoid large over- or underspends against budget.

3 It must achieve 1 and 2 while at the same time transforming the delivery of services in line with its strategic plan.

Many examples can be quoted of PSOs which have to undertake all three of these tasks simultaneously:

→ **NHS Trust** – an NHS Trust failed to deliver its service targets in one year but achieved a financial balanced position. The following year it delivered on its service targets but overspent by several millions of pounds. The Trust also has a configuration of services which is unsustainable in the longer term. In future it must aim to deliver service targets, maintain financial balance *and* achieve strategic change in service provision, since the current configuration is financially non-viable.

→ **Children's Services Department** – the department must aim to achieve its strategic objectives derived from the government publication *Every Child Matters* and this must be achieved with little or no additional financial resources. However, it must also continue to deliver children's services on a day-to-day basis and to acceptable standards, while maintaining financial balance.

→ **Jobcentre Plus** – this is an agency of the Department of Work and Pensions that is concerned with paying benefits and assisting people to find work. The agency must deliver on the targets it has agreed with its parent department while maintaining financial balance. At the same time it must deliver programmes of change as part of its modernisation agenda.

Thus financial management is an essential component of management in any PSO, and consequently must be concerned with the following key issues:

→ **Identifying and managing costs** – it must be concerned with identifying the costs of delivering its range of public services because without such information it is not really possible to address issues of strategic financial planning and/or cost-based performance improvements. The reality is that in many parts of the public services the information available about the costs of delivering particular services to particular client groups in particular locations is extremely limited.

→ **Financially viable strategy** – PSOs have a strategic agenda which often implies significant change in such areas as organisational arrangements, methods of service delivery, location of service delivery, mix of resources committed to service delivery. It is also often the case that this strategic agenda has to be delivered with little or no growth in resources. Also, as already noted, this strategic agenda must be implemented while routine service delivery continues to be undertaken to agreed standards and with the resources available. To achieve this is not easy and there are a number of prerequisites for success: first, and as already noted, good quality information is needed about the current costs of service delivery; second, there is a need for effective strategic financial planning; third, effective links to the budget system are required; and, finally, effective programmes of change management must be resourced and implemented.

→ **Effective budgeting systems** – an effective budgeting system is vital in a PSO. First, the budgeting system will provide one means for implementing the strategy by ensuring that strategic changes in resource use are effected in annual budgets. Second, it will provide a means for operational performance improvement. Third, it will facilitate the effective management of resources in the organisation in accordance with plans.

→ **Balanced pricing approaches** – although most public services are financed from the proceeds of taxation and government borrowing, many services are also financed (in whole or in part) by user charges, and the prevalence of this seems likely to increase rather than decrease in the future. Thus PSOs must have pricing strategies that ensure an appropriate balance is struck between achieving financial objectives and non-financial service-based objectives.

→ **Effective performance management and improvement** – virtually all PSOs have to work in an environment where improvements in performance are required every year. Thus, financial management must be capable of making a large-scale contribution to the financially oriented performance improvement challenges facing the PSO.

→ **Effective financial reporting and accountability** – PSOs utilise large amounts of public funding and must be accountable for the use of those funds. Thus, they must have systems and processes to produce timely and accurate financial reports that comply with legislative and professional practices.

→ **Robust financial control and governance** – all of the above aspects of financial management must operate in an environment where there is confidence in the veracity of the financial information being used. There must be confidence about the way in which financial decisions are being made and the accountability for those decisions. This requires robust mechanisms to ensure effective financial control and governance within the PSO.

Expressing the above as a series of questions, we might say that financial management should assist in answering the following:

→ How can we identify, accurately, the costs of delivering our public service activities?

→ How do we prepare longer-term strategic plans for the delivery of our public services which are financially sound and achievable?

→ How can we control our costs in an effective manner while at the same time achieving our service objectives?

→ How do we achieve the required strategic change in our organisation in a financially sound manner?

→ How much should we invest in capital expenditure and in what forms and using what types of funding?

→ How should our financial management systems assist in assessing, managing and improving our organisational performance?

→ Where required, how should we set prices for our services that balance income with service take-up?

→ How do we ensure that our public service organisation has adequate financial control and financial governance arrangements?

While the above may seem obvious to many, in some PSOs and among some PSO managers and service professionals, financial management is still primarily seen as being concerned with ensuring that the organisation doesn't overspend, and the role of financial management in improving and shaping the task of service delivery, at a strategic and operational level, is not always appreciated.

Structure of this book

The structure of this book is shown in Figure 1.8. The outer circle of the figure outlines the factors which impinge on PSOs and the services they deliver. Thus, in Part 1, Chapters 2 and 3 discuss current and historical issues, while Chapter 13 in Part 4 discusses future trends and the likely ways forward.

Chapter 2 is concerned with the way in which public services are paid for. It discusses the various sources of finance for public services, the financial planning of services and the way in which resources are allocated among competing priorities.

Chapter 3 discusses the modernisation and reform agenda that has taken place in the public services of the UK and other countries over the last 30 years or so. It considers the causes of reform, the aims of reform and the various approaches that have been employed. It also considers the impact of public service reforms on the practice of financial management in PSOs.

Part 2 of the book is concerned with the six key aspects of financial management in PSOs described earlier. In Figure 1.8, costing is shown at the centre of the diagram as the key aspect of financial management. Organisations that know little about their costs and what drives those costs (as in many PSOs) are unlikely to be able to manage their organisation effectively. Chapter 4 is concerned with identifying the

Figure 1.8 Modern public service financial management

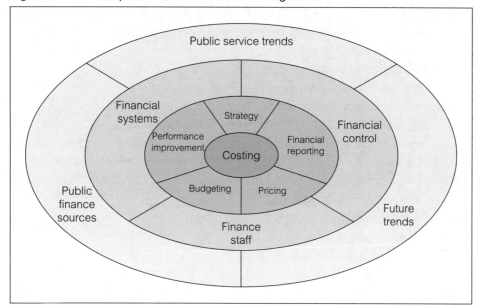

costs of delivering public services. It describes the methods through which the costs of services and activities can be established and the costing systems that assist in doing this. This is one of the key chapters in the book, since public service modernisation and reform agenda has engendered a strong and ongoing need for accurate information about the costs of public services in order that the various reforming initiatives can be implemented. Furthermore, cost information is a key element of many other aspects of financial management (e.g. pricing of public services) and this is also discussed in Chapter 4.

As already noted, much of the modernisation and reform agenda in public services has involved major strategic changes in organisational arrangements, service configurations and service delivery mechanisms. Such strategic changes have major financial implications which need to be managed effectively and Chapter 5 discusses the contribution that financial management can make to the strategic agenda. This has often been seen as a weakness in public service financial management.

Chapter 6 is concerned with budget systems and budget management in PSOs. It is often thought by many public service managers and service professionals that the main role of the budget system is in constraining expenditure within approved limits. Such a view ignores the fact that the budget system has key roles in relation to delegation and empowerment, implementation of strategy and employee motivation, and these are discussed within the chapter.

Traditionally, since most public services were funded through taxation, the role of pricing in public services was of little interest. However, pricing of public services is now far more important and has been fuelled by such developments as the commissioner/provider split, market testing, income generation, etc. Chapter 7 discusses approaches to pricing public services.

Given that, for many years now, PSOs have been subject to a regime whereby annual improvements in performance (efficiency, economy and effectiveness) are expected and even anticipated by the government, Chapter 8 discusses the role financial management can play in identifying and delivering performance improvements.

All PSOs have to produce a series of annual statutory financial statements to discharge their accountability for the use of public funds. Chapter 9 deals with the rationale and nature of such statements.

Part 3 is concerned with the environment within which the operation of financial management in PSOs is undertaken. Chapter 10 is concerned with financial information systems. It discusses the needs for financial information within PSOs and the nature and characteristics of the systems used to produce such information.

Effective financial control is needed in any PSO and this is the subject of Chapter 11. Linked to this is one of the major themes in public services over the last 15 years or so, which is the need for PSOs to improve their governance arrangements.

Chapter 12 concerns the staffing of the finance function in PSOs. The term finance function is used to cover all those involved in financial management in PSOs and not just the staff of the central finance department. The chapter considers the organisation and working practices of the finance function and the possible impact of future trends.

Finally, Part 4 of the book is concerned with the future. Chapter 13 speculates on future trends in public policy and public service reform and suggests what might be the implications for financial management of those trends.

Conclusions

Public services are a significant part of the economy in most countries but these public services have evolved over a period of years at different speeds and along different pathways. There are various ways in which the configuration of public services can be described but, once again, the detailed pattern will vary from place to place.

The management of finance is a key management task not just for the finance professionals in a PSO but also for the service managers and professionals who deliver services and use resources with which to deliver those services. However, the pattern of financial management in place will have been influenced by a range of local factors such as size, organisation, culture, etc.

Questions for discussion

→ How does the development of UK public services compare with other countries?

→ Has the involvement of the UK government become too intrusive with regard to the private citizen?

→ Is there an important role for private sector providers and third sector providers in the provision of public services?

→ How good are our current financial management arrangements and what are their weaknesses?

2

Financing public services

Learning objectives

→ To understand the nature of public expenditure and how it is financed in various countries

→ To understand the processes for planning and funding public services

→ To appreciate the ways in which financial resources are allocated between public services and different areas of the country

Introduction

Public expenditure in any country involves large sums of money and this money is used for a variety of different purposes. If we consider first the size of public services and their relation to the overall size of the economy, and express total public expenditure as a percentage of the gross domestic product (GDP) or gross national income (GNI) of that country, then we see considerable variations between countries as illustrated in Figure 2.1.

Focusing on the UK situation, we can also see the historical trends in the size of GDP committed to public expenditure as illustrated in Table 2.1.

It will be noted that the trend in UK public expenditure has been consistently upwards, reaching around 40% of GDP at the start of 1970. Since that time it has almost always been in excess of 40% of GDP and seems unlikely ever to drop back to pre-war levels. This is because since the end of the Second World War the size and composition of public services have undergone many changes in functions and organisation but have never reverted back to the limited role they had prior to the 1940s. The only exceptions to this trend are the two periods of world war (1914–18 and 1939–45) where public expenditure increased extremely rapidly as a direct result of high levels of military expenditure.

Figure 2.1 Government spending as a percentage of GDP

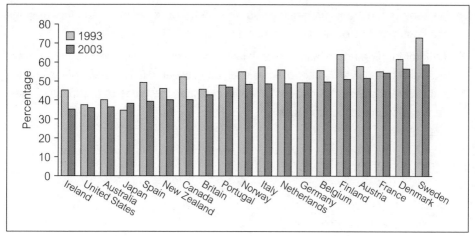

Source: *The Economist*, 18 March 2004,
www.economist.com/markets/indicators/displaystory.cfm?story_id=£1_NYNTGSG

Table 2.1 UK public expenditure and gross national income

Year	Public expenditure as a percentage of GNI
1910	12.2
1916	34.4
1930	24.4
1943	61.4
1950	33.7
1970	40.9
1980	45.4
1984	45.4
1988	37.9
1992	42.5
1996	40.5
1999	37.4
2004	41.2
2007	42.2

Source: Office for National Statistics and Institute for Fiscal Studies

In this chapter we address the following issues in relation to public services and public expenditure:

➔ the patterns and composition of public expenditure in various countries;

➔ the key sources of finance for public expenditure;

→ the role of the Private Finance Initiative (PFI);

→ the sorts of mechanisms employed at the centre of government to plan, manage and control public expenditure, focusing on the UK arrangements;

→ the total funds made available centrally for particular public services, which have to be distributed in a number of ways such as between different parts of the country and different classes of citizens. We will consider the types of approaches used for this resource allocation task.

Patterns of public spending

In 2008/9, total UK public expenditure is forecast to be £618 billion. An analysis of this expenditure is shown Figure 2.2.

In order to get some perspective about what public sector expenditure actually involves, we will divide this expenditure into a relatively small number of categories.

Figure 2.2 UK public expenditure analysis 2008–9

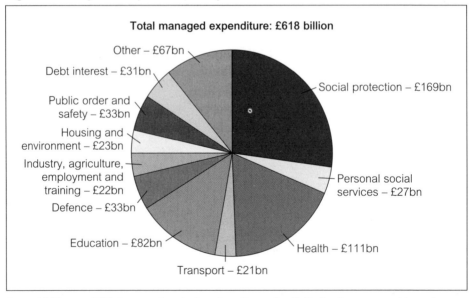

Source: HM Treasury 2008–9 near-cash projections. Spending re-classified to functions compared to previous presentations and is now using methods specified in international standards. Other expenditure includes spending on general public services: recreation, culture, media and sport; international cooperation and development; public service pensions; plus spending yet to be allocated and some accounting adjustments. Social protection includes tax credit payments in excess of an individual's tax liability, which are now counted on AME, in line with OECD guidelines. Figures may not sum to total due to rounding.

Capital expenditure

Hidden within the figures shown in Figure 2.2 is an amount of £52 billion, which represents capital expenditure. There is no single definition of capital expenditure that is acceptable in every circumstance and the precise definition will vary between different parts of public services. The basic approach is to distinguish capital expenditure from revenue expenditure according to the period of benefit (Jones and Pendlebury, 2000). The benefits flowing from revenue expenditure tend to be confined to the year in which the expenditure is incurred, but expenditure on capital expenditure is obtained over a period of several years. Thus, capital expenditure is expenditure which provides benefits for more than one year and it includes expenditure on such things as buildings, roads, equipment, vehicles, IT, etc. Often such expenditure, especially buildings and transport links, are referred to as infrastructure spending.

These figures, of course, do not include capital expenditure which has been financed through the Private Finance Initiative (PFI) and which has been used to acquire fixed assets to be used in public service delivery.

Debt interest

As will be noted later in this chapter, one of the main sources of finance for public services is borrowing by governments on domestic and international money markets. Like normal commercial loans, such government loans will be repaid over the agreed period, but the government will also have to pay interest on the loans to its lenders. The scale of UK government borrowing means that this debt interest amounts to £33 billion in 2008/9. At the time of writing, the level of government borrowing has risen substantially to cover budget deficits and to provide financial support to banks and other commercial organisations affected by the recession and 'credit crunch'. Consequently, the amount of debt interest payments can be expected to rise sharply in years to come.

Social protection

In Figure 2.2 an amount of £169 billion is shown under the heading of social protection. This is sometimes referred to as transfer payments and describes the transfer of funds from taxpayers, etc. to recipients of one of a wide range of social benefits. Examples of such transfer payments include state retirement pensions, job seekers allowance, disability living allowances, carer allowances, etc.

Current expenditure on services

The bulk of public expenditure is concerned with the running costs of delivering public services such as health, education, defence, local government, etc. This expenditure will contain a large number of elements, including salaries and wages, consumables, utility payments, rent payments, equipment, etc. The amounts shown in Figure 2.2 include expenditure by local authorities, NHS organisations and government agencies, as well as central government departments.

Devolved administrations

As discussed in Chapter 1, certain parts of the UK (i.e. Wales, Scotland and Northern Ireland) have devolved administrations that are responsible for the administration of many public services in those countries. However, funding for those services are provided by the central UK exchequer and funds are allocated to each country using an approach referred to as the Barnett formula. The figures shown in Figure 2.2 include the expenditure of the devolved administrations in the UK: Welsh Assembly – £14 billion; Scottish Parliament – £31 billion; Northern Ireland – £8 billion.

The use of this money is the responsibility of the devolved administrations themselves but the spending has been incorporated into the service categories in Figure 2.2.

Other expenditure

This substantial sum of £67 billion includes a wide range of other types of expenditure, for example the BBC – £3.5 billion, and net EU expenditures – £5.5 billion.

International perspectives on public spending

The above analysis relates to the UK. Figure 2.3 shows that in other countries, although the classes of expenditure are similar, the mix between them varies greatly.

Sources of finance for public services

There are only a limited number of ways in which public services can be financed in any country and, as an example, Figure 2.4 illustrates how public spending is currently financed in the UK.

It will be seen that there are several sources of finance for public services and these are briefly discussed below. Essentially, all of these sources of public finance are available to and used by all countries, although clearly the mix between them will vary.

Figure 2.3 International comparisons of government expenditure by function as a share of GDP in 2005 or closest year available

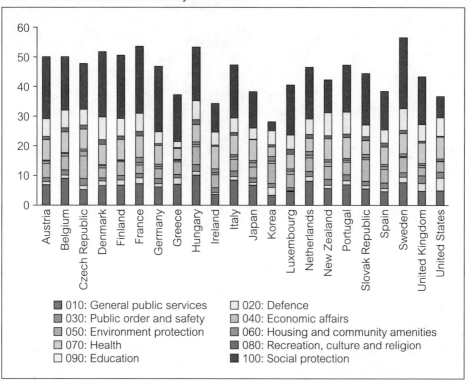

Source: OECD, *Towards Government at a Glance: Identification of Core Data and Issues related to Public Sector Efficiency* (2008)

Taxation

General principles

A tax is the imposition of a financial charge or other levy on an individual or a legal entity by a state or a functional equivalent of a state. Taxes are also imposed by many sub-national entities. Thus a tax is not a voluntary payment or donation, but an enforced contribution exacted by a state agency. Tax collection is performed by a government agency, such as the Canada Revenue Agency, the Internal Revenue Service (IRS) in the United States, or Her Majesty's Revenue and Customs (HMRC) in the UK. When taxes are not fully paid, civil penalties (such as fines or forfeiture) or criminal penalties may be imposed on the non-paying entity or individual.

Governments use different kinds of taxes and vary the tax rates. This is done to distribute the tax burden among individuals or classes of the population involved in taxable activities, such as businesses, or to redistribute resources between individuals

Figure 2.4 Sources of funding for UK public services 2008–9

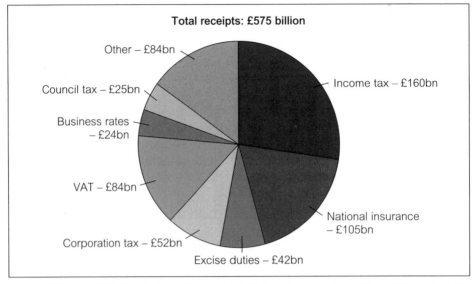

Source: HM Treasury, 2008–9 projections. Other receipts include capital taxes, stamp duties, vehicle excise duties and some other tax and non-tax receipts – for example, interest and dividends. Figures may not sum to total due to rounding.

or classes in the population. Historically, the nobility were supported by taxes on the poor; modern social security systems are intended to support the poor, the disabled or the retired by taxes on those who are still working. In addition, taxes are applied to fund foreign and military aid, to influence the macroeconomic performance of the economy (the government's strategy for doing this is called its fiscal policy), or to modify patterns of consumption or employment within an economy, by making some classes of transaction more or less attractive. A nation's tax system is often a reflection of its communal values or the values of those in power. To create a system of taxation, a nation must make choices regarding the distribution of the tax burden (who will pay taxes and how much they will pay) and how the taxes collected will be spent. In democratic nations, where the public elects those in charge of establishing the tax system, these choices should reflect the type of community that the public wishes to create. In countries where the public does not have a significant amount of influence over the system of taxation, that system may be more of a reflection of the values of those in power.

In some cases taxes are levied to finance a range of public services, and these might be termed general taxes, while the collection of a tax in order to spend it on a specified purpose, for example collecting a tax on alcohol to pay directly for alcoholism rehabilitation centres, is called hypothecation or a hypothecated tax. This practice is often disliked by finance ministers, since it reduces their freedom of action. Furthermore, it often happens that taxes or excises initially levied to fund some specific government programmes are then later diverted to the government general fund.

So what makes a good tax? The noted eighteenth-century English economist, Adam Smith, enunciated the canons of taxation in his celebrated work, *An Inquiry into the Nature and Causes of the Wealth of Nations* (Smith, 1776), which was popularly abbreviated to *Wealth of Nations*. According to Smith there are four basic canons of taxation, which are as follows:

→ **Equality** – the canon of equality arises from the idea that 'The subjects of every state ought to contribute towards the support of the government as nearly as possible in proportion to their respective abilities that is in proportion to the revenue which they respectively enjoy under the protection of the state.' This canon embodies the principle of equity or justice and lays down the moral foundation of the tax system. Thus, tax should be in proportion to the ability to pay.

→ **Certainty** – the canon of certainty is highlighted in the following statement by Smith: 'The tax which each individual is bound to pay ought to be certain, and not arbitrary. The time of payment, the manner of payment, the quantity to be paid ought all to be clear and plain to the contributor and to every other person. Where it is otherwise, every person subject to tax is put, more or less, in the power of tax-gatherer, who can either aggravate the tax upon any obnoxious contributor, or extort, by the terror of each aggravation, some present or perquisite to himself.' Certainty is needed not only from the point of view of the taxpayer but also from that of state.

→ **Convenience** – the canon of convenience states that every tax ought to be levied at the time or in the manner in which it is most likely to be convenient for the contributor to pay it.

→ **Economy** – the canon of economy dictates that every tax ought to be so contrived as both to take out and to keep out of the pocket of the people as little as possible, over and above what it brings into the public treasury of the state.

Modern economic commentators have added several more canons to Smith's four described above:

→ **Adequacy** – a tax should have the ability to produce a sufficient and desired amount of revenue to the taxing authority.

→ **Neutrality** – a tax should not encourage inefficient allocation of resources by being so extreme that taxpayers make counterproductive economic decisions.

→ **Compatibility** – a tax should be compatible with foreign tax systems (in the UK's case, with Europe's).

→ **Buoyancy** – the tax yield should automatically adjust to changes in the rate of inflation (particularly important in high inflation economies).

→ **Simplicity** – the tax system should be simple enough to be understood by the mass of the persons subject to the tax.

Few, if any taxes, would be capable of complying with all of the above canons. Consequently, there must inevitably be a balancing act between the various aims involved.

Centrally levied taxes

Taxes can be levied at central government level or at some sub-national level such as state, province, region or local authority level. A distinction must be made here between the levying of the tax (i.e. fixing the rate of tax) and the actual collection of the monies. Thus a tax might be levied at the national level of government but the proceeds of the tax might be collected at sub-national level and passed, subsequently, to central government. The reverse might also be true.

Usually, a very large proportion of public services are financed by monies made available from revenues collected by the national government, although the actual proportion will vary between countries. National government collects revenues from a variety of nationally levied taxes, such as income tax, business taxes, sales tax such as value added tax, duty on alcohol and cigarettes, duty on petrol, property taxes, etc.

Locally levied taxes

In many countries it is also common to have various forms of taxation levied at the sub-national level and these include locally levied income tax and sales tax.

In the UK there is only one operational locally based tax, known as council tax. Council tax is levied by certain local authorities in the UK and replaced the previous systems of local taxation referred to as domestic rates and its replacement, the short-lived community charge (or 'poll tax'). Council tax is effectively a tax on property values and applies to all domestic properties, including houses, bungalows, flats, maisonettes, mobile homes and houseboats, whether owned or rented. All domestic properties are allocated to one of eight bands depending on their value and one bill is sent to each household. Bills may be reduced by various discounts, reductions and benefits. The local authority concerned will levy a tax rate that, when applied to the estimated total value of domestic property in their area, will generate the amount of local tax revenues required.

Council tax is generally administered by lower tier local authorities who levy the tax to meet the costs of their own services but also incorporate an additional tax levy (termed a precept) to collect revenues on behalf of upper tier local authorities and police authorities, who also need to raise local revenues to fund their services.

Over a period of years, the proportion of local government expenditure has fallen dramatically. The implication of this is that locally elected councillors have only limited control over the total funds they can raise to deliver locally based services, and many argue that this weakens local democracy. Over the years there have been many calls (Layfield, 1976; Lyons, 2007) for the introduction of some form of local income tax, but this seems very unlikely to occur.

Mention must also be made of the national non-domestic rate (or business rates). The non-domestic rates collected by local authorities on the basis of rateable values of non-domestic properties are paid into a central government pool and redistributed to all charging authorities based on a prescribed formula. This redistributed income, together with income from council tax payers and revenue support grants from the government, is used to pay for the services provided by the local authority. Technically, this cannot be classified as a locally levied tax since the revenues receivable are not under the control of the individual local authority.

User charges for public services

Taxes may be levied on a number of bases, such as the ability to pay of the person liable for tax (e.g. income tax, corporation tax), the consumption by individuals of the goods and services being taxed (e.g. VAT, fuel duty) or the value of property (council tax). In none of these cases is the level of tax related to the cost of providing the service.

Charges for public services are different. In this case the level of charge levied will be linked to the type and volume of public services being obtained and the cost of providing that service even if the charge levied is not a full economic cost but contains some form of subsidy. There are many examples of charges for UK public services, such as NHS prescription charges, college fees, local authority leisure centre charges, public passenger transport fares, NHS private patient charges, post office charges, local authority domiciliary care charges, etc.

In considering charges for public services, it has been suggested (Jones and Prowle, 1997) that an acceptable charge might have the following features:

→ It would maximise the revenue collected.

→ It would minimise administrative costs.

→ It would avoid deterring those service users who, if not seen, will generate extra costs to the national exchequer in future years.

→ It would try to ensure that charges do not impose the heaviest burden on those who are most in need.

→ It would have exemptions designed so as to avoid accentuating the poverty trap and weakening incentives to work.

Overall charges only provide a small proportion of funding for UK public services, but again that percentage will vary greatly between sectors and individual PSOs and between different countries. At the time of writing, the parlous state of UK public finances means that it seems likely that PSOs will look to increase the funding they obtain from user charges. This is discussed further in Chapter 7 on pricing.

Borrowing

Government borrowing

It was noted earlier that UK governmental receipts (£575 billion) for 2008–9 are substantially less than government expenditures (£618 billion), and that the government will therefore be running a budget deficit. In years such as this, to make up the difference, the government must borrow funds from within the UK or overseas through the issue of government bonds. Strictly speaking, such borrowing is not really a source for public finance since the borrowing will ultimately have to be repaid and interest is payable on the loans. Hence, all borrowing really does is defer to the future the financing of public expenditure from one of the other sources of taxation or charges. Where budget deficits occur the borrowing involved will be added to the national debt, which will increase. In the event that the government has a budget surplus then the surplus could be used to reduce the national debt.

Traditionally, governments used to run up budget deficits during periods of economic recession, which would then be countered by budget surpluses during periods of economic growth. However, in recent years the present UK government has generated substantial budget deficits during a period of economic growth and the national debt is increasing at a substantial rate. At the time of writing, the economic recession in the UK is raising some alarming worries about the magnitude of future budget deficits and the impact on national debt (*Guardian*, 2009b).

Borrowing by individual PSOs

Other than borrowing by central government, individual PSOs such as local authorities, NHS Foundation Trusts and universities can also borrow funds – which of course have to be repaid with interest. Such borrowing can be used for two main purposes:

→ to finance new capital expenditure;

→ to provide working capital.

Traditionally, borrowing by PSOs was heavily controlled by HM Treasury, but in recent years attempts have been made to enable PSOs to borrow more freely, provided they comply with respective codes of practice on borrowing. For more information, refer to the *Prudential Code for Capital Finance in Local Authorities*

(CIPFA, 2003a), the *Prudential Borrowing Code for NHS Foundation Trusts* developed by Monitor (Monitor, 2009) and the *Financial Memorandum for HEI* produced by HEFCE (HEFCE, 2003).

Other sources of public finance

Various other sources of finance also exist, and in the UK these include EU grants, funds from land sales, donations, income generation (e.g. hospital shops); income from land sales, etc.

International perspectives on public service finance

Looking internationally, we find that the proportion of tax taken by different governments from their citizens varies enormously. This is shown in Table 2.2, which gives each country's total tax revenues as a percentage of its GDP.

Table 2.2 Total tax revenues as a percentage of GDP – international

	1992	1997	2002	2006	2007
Australia	26.5	29.2	30.5	30.6	–
Belgium	41.8	44.5	45.0	44.5	44.4
Denmark	46.3	48.9	47.8	49.1	48.9
Finland	44.9	46.3	44.6	43.5	43.0
France	42.0	44.4	43.4	44.2	43.6
Germany	37.0	36.2	35.4	35.6	36.2
Hungary	44.9	38.0	37.8	37.1	39.3
Italy	40.6	43.2	41.4	42.1	43.3
Japan	27.0	27.2	26.2	27.9	–
Netherlands	44.8	40.9	37.5	39.3	38.0
Norway	40.3	41.5	43.1	43.9	43.4
Poland	34.9	35.2	36.3	33.5	–
Portugal	30.8	32.7	34.5	35.7	36.6
Spain	33.8	32.9	34.2	36.6	37.2
Sweden	47.2	50.6	47.9	49.1	48.2
United Kingdom	33.8	34.9	35.2	37.1	36.6
United States	26.9	28.7	26.5	28.0	28.3
OECD – Europe	36.9	37.8	37.7	38.0	–
OECD – Total	34.4	35.4	35.4	35.9	–

Source: OECD

Table 2.3 Figure tax structures as a percentage of total tax receipts 2005

Country	Personal income tax (%)	Corporate income tax (%)	Social security contributions (%)	Taxes on goods and services (%)	Other taxes (%)
Australia	40	19	–	28	13
Canada	36	11	14	25	14
France	17	6	34	25	18
Germany	23	5	37	29	6
Italy	26	7	27	26	14
Japan	18	16	33	19	14
New Zealand	41	17	–	32	10
Norway	22	27	19	28	4
Slovak Republic	8	9	32	40	11
Sweden	32	8	27	26	7
UK	29	9	18	31	13
USA	35	11	23	18	13
EU average	**25**	**9**	**26**	**30**	**10**
OECD average	**25**	**10**	**24**	**32**	**9**

Source: OECD in figures 2008, http://ocde.p4.siteinternet.com/publications/doifiles/012008061P1T027.xls

Table 2.2 shows substantial variations between countries, with the Scandinavian countries having very high levels of taxation and the USA having very low levels. However, it should be noted that in most of the countries shown the levels of taxation have increased in recent years.

Table 2.3 shows the mix of taxation across countries. Once again, we see large variations in the mix of taxes, with some countries having a broad equivalence between direct and indirect taxes and others having large divergences between such taxes. This position reflects the differences in their economic and social policies.

The role of the Private Finance Initiative

As with government borrowing, the Private Finance Initiative (PFI) is not really a source of public finance but is often thought to be one. Like borrowing, all it does is defer to a later date the need to finance certain types of public expenditure; primarily those associated with fixed assets such as buildings.

The nature of PFI

PFI has been one of the most significant broad-based public policy developments of the last two decades and affects, substantially, the delivery of public services in most parts of the public sector in the UK. According to the government, PFI is officially

> one of the Government's main instruments for delivering higher quality and more cost-effective public services. Its aim is to bring the private sector more directly into the provision of public services, with the public sector as an enabler and, where appropriate, guarding the interest of the users and customers of public services. It is not simply about the financing of capital investment in services, but about exploiting the full range of private sector management, commercial and creative skill.
>
> (HM Treasury, 1995)

The PFI policy has been enthusiastically adopted by governments of both major political parties, but it has also generated a large amount of criticism and controversy. PFI has also been applied in a number of other countries as well as the UK.

PFI emerged as a logical outcome of the twin policies of the Conservative government – curbing public expenditure and market testing of in-house service provision against alternative private sector provision. In its simplest form, PFI involves a public sector agency contracting with a private sector organisation(s) for the provision of two main items:

→ access to fixed assets (e.g. buildings, equipment);

→ receipt of certain defined services (e.g. buildings maintenance).

Because government is able to borrow more cheaply than commercial organisations, under PFI it is not permissible for the private sector organisations to merely finance the construction of a new building and to provide and lease that building back to the public sector. A typical PFI project will be based on what is termed DBFO (design, build, finance and operate). Figure 2.5 shows the division of responsibility between the public and the private sectors using the example of a PFI hospital project.

Thus, PFI involves more than just the private sector funding of a capital asset, it also involves the private sector in the delivery of certain services surrounding that asset. A key issue here is the division between core and non-core services. Core services continue to be provided by the public sector agency but non-core services may be provided by the private partner. Figure 2.6 shows a comparison between the typical (although not universal) arrangements of core and non-core staff in a hospital PFI and a school PFI.

The division between core and non-core staff is not always precise, as illustrated by the 'grey areas' in each example. The division can vary from sector to sector, and from project to project within the same sector.

Figure 2.5 Structure of a PFI project

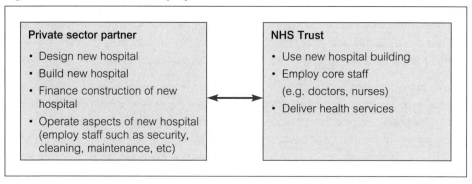

	Hospitals	Schools
Core staff	Doctors Nurses	Teachers
'Grey area'	Technicians	Supply teachers
Non-core staff	Cleaners Catering staff Maintenance staff	Cleaners Catering staff Maintenance staff

Figure 2.6 Core and non-core in PFI

Objectives of PFI

The objectives of PFI policy can be considered twofold in relation to micro-objectives and macro-objectives, as described below.

Micro-objectives

In a speech in 1994 the then Chancellor of the Exchequer (HM Treasury, 1994) reiterated that the two guiding principles of PFI were that the private sector must genuinely assume risk without a guarantee by the taxpayer against loss and that value for money must be demonstrated before any expenditure by the public sector. This suggests the following two key micro-objectives for PFI:

→ **Value for money (VFM)** – a key objective of PFI is to improve the VFM with which public resources are used to deliver public services. This may seem difficult to achieve, as the private sector has to generate a profit and rate of return (unlike the equivalent public service provider) and, as already mentioned, incurs higher borrowing costs than government. However, VFM improvement might be achieved through the PFI route in a number of ways, such as better innovation in service delivery methods; greater efficiency in the use of manpower; lower construction costs; better performance management; or better design to reduce future maintenance costs.

→ **Risk transfer** – another key objective of PFI is the transfer of certain risks from the public sector to the private sector provider. Risks such as variations in the volume of service provision are unlikely to be accepted by the private sector, but there are situations where risk transfer to the private sector can and does take place. For example, under PFI, the risks of overspends on capital projects can be transferred to the private sector partner. Other examples concern some of the long-term operating risks, such as higher maintenance costs for the facility or a shorter than predicted working life. The transfer of the risk to the private partner may have a cost, however, as it could influence the price they charge for the service.

Macro-objectives

Although governments may not wish to explicitly state this, it is well known that one key objective of PFI is to reduce up-front public expenditure. Since projects done under the auspices of PFI are financed by the private sector, the funds required do not constitute up-front public expenditure. Thus public expenditure will be lower than it might otherwise have been if the project had been financed conventionally. Also, where the government is running a budget deficit (as has been the case in the UK for several years), then again the deficit will be lower than it might otherwise have been if the project had been financed conventionally. Clearly the costs of PFI projects, rather than being met up-front, will (via the charges levied by the private sector) be spread over a period of several years and thus will be borne by future generations of taxpayers rather than the current generation. However, since those future generations will benefit from the services provided there may be some merit in this.

Another attraction of PFI was the ability to transfer outstanding borrowing liabilities for PFI projects to the balance sheets of the private sector contractors so that they would not appear on the public sector balance sheet and thus the public sector debt would appear lower. PFI projects vary and they may be classified as off-balance sheet or on-balance sheet in relation to the public sector. To understand this it is first necessary to understand the distinction between a finance lease and an operating lease. A finance lease is one that is primarily a method of raising finance to pay for assets, rather than a genuine rental of an asset. An operating lease is a lease that is not a finance lease! The key distinction between a finance lease and an operating lease is whether the lessor (the legal owner who rents out the assets) or lessee (who uses the asset) takes on the risks of ownership of the leased assets. A lease is classified as a finance lease if it transfers substantially all the risks and rewards to the lessee. All other leases are classified as operating leases.

The classification of a lease (as an operating or finance lease) also affects how it is reported in the accounts. From an accounting point of view the classification of leases as finance leases is very important. With a finance lease, assets must be shown on the balance sheet of the lessee, with the amounts due on the lease also shown on the balance sheet as liabilities. This is intended to prevent lease finance being used to keep the lease liabilities off-balance sheet.

The same is true of PFI projects. PFI projects are a form of lease and may be deemed as constituting a finance lease or an operating lease. In turn this will affect the way in which they are accounted for and on which balance sheet the outstanding borrowing liabilities for the PFI project will reside as follows:

→ **On (public sector) balance sheet** – where a particular PFI deal is structured in such a way as to be deemed a finance lease then the assets and liabilities associated with the project should be shown on the public sector balance sheet.

→ **Off-balance sheet** – where a particular PFI deal is deemed an operating lease then only the annual service charge payable by the PSO is reported in its accounts. The borrowing liabilities for the project would not be shown on the public sector balance sheet but on the private sector balance sheet of the PFI contractor, since the underlying assets and liabilities of the project are regarded as being owned by the private contractor.

Clearly it is in the government's interest to have PFI deals shown as off-balance sheet since they then do not count against government debt. In practice, just under half the PFI deals in the public sector are deemed off-balance sheet but the proportion varies by sector – for example, in the NHS the vast majority of signed PFI contracts are deemed off-balance sheet.

Outcomes of PFI

A key issue that generates great controversy concerns what has been achieved through the PFI policy. Unfortunately, there are a considerable number of difficulties involved in trying to get a robust evaluation of PFI, including the following:

→ **Validity of information** – much of the information about PFI projects derives from government sources, and in the current political climate there is always some concern about its validity and reliability. Public mistrust about government information has tended to increase in recent years along with a more general mistrust of politicians.

→ **Managerial bias** – in PFI projects VFM is judged by comparing the cost of PFI bids with a 'public sector comparator', and approval for a PFI project is only given if the PFI bids are lower. There are situations where public sector managers know that they will only get permission to construct their new building projects if the PFI scheme comes out at a lower cost. Although it is difficult to get firm evidence of this, there are frequent claims that in these circumstances there can be an incentive for managers to bias the results of any evaluation towards the PFI option.

→ **Timing** – many of the PFI projects are still in the planning stage, under construction, or only just coming on stream. In these circumstances, it is probably too early to infer anything about them.

→ **Specification changes** – PFI projects, like most large projects, are subject to continual change. Thus the project specification that was set out in the original Outline Business Case (and compared with the public sector comparator) might be very different from the final project actually undertaken.

Nevertheless, a consideration of the evidence available (Prowle, 2009a) suggests that the following tentative conclusions can be drawn about the PFI policy:

Capital formation

There can be no doubt that PFI has been responsible for large-scale capital formation in the public sector. Between 1987 and 2004 PFI raised a total of nearly £43 billion, the details of which are shown in Table 2.4.

Table 2.4 PFI in the UK – breakdown by year

Year	Number of signed projects	Capital value (£m)
1987	1	180.0
1988	0	0.0
1989	0	0.0
1990	2	336.0
1991	2	6.0
1992	5	518.5
1993	1	1.6
1994	2	10.5
1995	11	667.5
1996	38	1,560.1
1997	60	2,474.9
1998	86	2,758.0
1999	99	2,580.4
2000	108	3,934.2
2001	85	2,210.8
2002	70	7,732.5
2003	52	14,854.1
2004	45	2,809.8
N/A	10	64.6
Total	677	42,699.4

Source: HM Treasury

Table 2.5 PFI in the UK – breakdown by government department

Department	Number of signed projects	Capital value (£m)
Cabinet Office	2	347.7
HM Customs & Excise	2	170.3
Constitutional Affairs	13	306.4
Culture, Media & Sport	7	68.6
Environment, Food & Rural Affairs	13	632.7
Transport	45	21,432.1
Education & Skills	121	2,922.8
Health	136	4,901.2
Trade & Industry	8	180.8
Work & Pensions	11	1,341.0
Foreign & Commonwealth Office	2	91.0
HM Treasury	2	189.0
Home Office	37	1,095.8
Inland Revenue	8	453.8
Defence	52	4,254.8
Northern Ireland	39	528.8
Office of the Deputy Prime Minister	61	972.1
Office of Government Commerce	1	10.0
Scotland	84	2,249.3
Wales	33	551.3
Total	677	42,699.4

Source: HM Treasury

Furthermore, PFI is has been applied in most parts of the public sector, with particular emphasis on transport, health and defence. This is illustrated in Table 2.5.

Additionality of capital formation

An issue of contention is whether PFI policy has merely substituted for conventional publicly financed capital expenditure or whether PFI has generated any degree of additionality. This is difficult to assess, but evidence presented to the House of Commons (House of Commons, 2001) suggests that PFI capital spending has been additional to normal publicly financed capital spending, and has not displaced what would normally have been spent.

Construction cost over-runs

A claim often made for PFI is that it will reduce the level of construction cost over-runs that take place on public sector projects. There have been some dramatic

Table 2.6 Capital projects – cost overruns. Initial and final cost estimates of
selected publicly financed and PFI projects

Publicly financed	Initial cost (£m)	Final cost (£m)	Percentage increase (%)
Trident submarine	100	314	214
Woodhill prison	78	102	31
Limehouse link	142	293	106
Private Finance Initiative			
Norfolk and Norwich NHS Trust	90	144	60
Greenwich Healthcare NHS Trust	35	84	140
Benefits Agency computers	200	1,400	600

Source: House of Commons, 2001

cases of public procurement going wrong, both in terms of time and of cost
over-runs. This comment applies to both PFI schemes and conventionally financed
schemes, as shown in Table 2.6.

The figures in Table 2.6 suggest that significant cost over-runs can take place on
both conventionally financed and PFI projects and on the basis of these figures it is
debatable whether PFI projects have done any better than publicly financed
projects. It has been suggested that the cost over-runs on PFI projects are primarily
a consequence of changes to the project specification being made by the public
procurers, whereas for conventionally funded projects they are due to poor cost
control and project management rather than changed specifications. However, there
is no clear evidence for this.

Total project costs

Perhaps the key VFM issue in evaluation of PFI is the total project costs incurred. The
usual approach is to compare the total costs of a project (over the contract period)
under a PFI arrangement with the costs of the equivalent project through a publicly
financed route. This is the so-called public sector comparator (PSC). A considerable
number of studies on this aspect of PFI have been produced.

One study (IPPR, 2001) looked at all the publicly available evidence comparing
PFI bid costs with public sector comparators. It found that although some projects
(e.g. roads and prisons) showed significant cost advantages (of around 15%) through
the PFI approach, others, such as school and hospital schemes, demonstrated a
more marginal level of cost advantage (between 2% and 4%).

A further study (Maltby, 2003) also reviewed the evidence on cost comparisons.
Out of the 378 PFI projects completed by central and local government at the time,

only 23 projects (6%) had undergone any independent examination of value for money by official audit bodies. The study also found that the PFI picture was mixed – some deals demonstrated significant evidence of lower costs, while others, notably school PFIs, did not.

Up to the end of 2001, the National Audit Office (NAO) had reported on the VFM aspects of a small sample of PFI projects that were of particular interest but were not representative of the full range of projects undertaken. For example, the NAO did not report on projects where problems had occurred after contracts were signed (House of Commons, 2001). The NAO produced VFM reports on 15 PFI projects and, of those, seven were judged to have produced around 20% better value for money compared to the public sector comparators. However, this position is slightly skewed due to the significant contribution made by just two of the projects. If these two projects were excluded, then a more likely VFM improvement would be of the order of 10%. Subsequently, the NAO undertook a review of the PFI project at West Middlesex Hospital. Its conclusions were that, over a 35-year contract period, the PFI approach produced a cost saving of 3.5% compared to the risk-adjusted public sector comparator (NAO, 2002).

A number of academic commentators have criticised PFI, suggesting that it has not been delivering value for money in health projects and that some schemes have escalated in both cost and scale, so that greater efficiencies or levels of risk transfer have not offset the very high financing costs and the costs of private sector borrowing (Pollock, 2005). There have even been some cases where health authorities and the government have had to provide extra subsidies, and extra services have been contracted to bridge the gap. For example, the first NHS Trust to sign a PFI contract, Dartford and Gravesham, stated in its outline business case that 'at no additional cost to commissioners the scheme delivers vitally important strategic objectives'. But by the time West Kent Health Authority was asked to approve the full business case, a £2m-a-year contribution was required (on top of a new contribution from central government). This led to the withdrawal of funding for proposed community health service developments, some of which were required to provide services displaced by the PFI scheme. This conclusion seems to contradict the NAO's findings that the scheme led to better VFM than the public sector comparator (Pollock, 2005).

Risk transfer

Another suggested benefit of PFI is that the risks associated with a particular PFI project are shared between the public and private partners, on the principle that risk should be allocated to whoever is best able to manage it. Thus risk should only be transferred to the private sector to the extent that they are capable of managing it (e.g. construction risk). If they are not able to manage the risk, responsibility for these risks should remain within the public sector.

An efficiently designed PFI project contract should involve the optimum transfer of all types of risk. With this in mind, the main argument put forward by PFI proponents – that it provides value for money through the transfer of risk – would be better defined as value for money through the 'optimal allocation of risk'. It is very difficult to quantify many of the risks, and difficult to assess whether the transfer of risk can be deemed optimal. The small amount of available evidence suggests that, at least in some sectors, PFI contracts have transferred a degree of responsibility for some of the risks involved in constructing, operating and maintaining public services, and in financing the assets that support them. A survey (NAO, 2001) of public and private partners involved in 121 PFI projects prior to 2000 found that in over 95% of cases both partners agreed that the allocation of risk was either wholly or partially appropriate. However, the views of the partners varied when asked whether they believed the projects' risks had been allocated optimally: 80% of public sector partners thought the allocation of risk wholly appropriate while only 50% of the private sector partners agreed.

Service quality

Any review of the comparative merits and value for money of PFI versus public funding should take into account the services provided as well as the costs. Standards of service quality could be considered in a number of ways. For example, it could be based around the Servqual idea of five dimensions of service quality (Parasuraman et al., 1988):

→ **Tangibles** – aspects of service provision such as physical facilities, equipment condition, the appearance of its staff, etc.

→ **Reliability** – in terms of delivering the required services dependably and accurately.

→ **Responsiveness** – in meeting service user needs, helping service users providing a prompt service.

→ **Assurance** – inspiring trust and confidence among service users regarding the services being delivered.

→ **Empathy** – providing a caring and individual service to users which understands their needs.

However, assessing comparative service quality under PFI or conventional funding is difficult because of the problem of identifying whether services provided under a PFI scheme would have been better or worse than under a hypothetical publicly funded project. Some evaluations have tried to do this through attitudinal surveys, which involve asking managers whether the services have met expected requirements, and whether they have shown improvements. However, this is arguably not the same as saying whether PFI funded projects are better or worse than the equivalent publicly funded projects, and so the issue remains unclear.

Macro-outcomes

As noted earlier, up to the end of 2004, nearly £43 billion had been invested by the UK government and the private sector in 677 PFI projects. PFI approaches to project finance have also been promoted in many other countries. Thus, in financing terms, this amount of capital expenditure has been financed by the private sector and not through public sector borrowing.

Since almost half of PFI projects are off-balance sheet then clearly the government has been able to reduce the size of government borrowings and debt through the accounting treatment of PFI projects. However, the continuing ability to keep PFI projects off-balance sheet could be eliminated when the UK adopts the International Financial Reporting Standards (IFRS) in 2009/10. Under the new regime, PFI contracts will be accounted for according to IFRIC 12, issued by the International Financial Reporting Interpretations Committee (IFRIC, 2006). IFRIC 12 makes it clear that PFI investments will not score on the private sector's balance sheet, and the Treasury has accepted that this means that they must score against the capital budgets of public authorities. This will increase the amount of PFI investment recorded in the national accounts by more than £30 billion. It would also, at a stroke, eliminate one of the main advantages of PFI from the point of view of the government.

Overall findings of PFI evaluations

Political sensitivities make any evaluation of PFI a difficult task. However, a number of general conclusions can be drawn from the evidence:

→ PFI has financed large-scale capital spending on fixed assets used by PSOs.

→ There is some indication that PFI has resulted in additional capital spending, as opposed to displacement, in public services.

→ Capital cost over-runs *might* have been reduced through PFI, although the reasons for this are not clear.

→ Caution must be expressed about the results of many individual (ex-ante) PFI project evaluations because of the difficulties in accurately forecasting costs, and the incentive for managers to reduce the proposed costs of the PFI route to get a project approved.

→ Most PFI projects lack any rigorous evaluation of the impacts on service quality.

→ The various 'external' evaluations of PFI projects that have been undertaken have not reached a unanimous conclusion. In these circumstances, one has to wonder whether there is some bias at play, and whether the methodologies used by each evaluator are comparable.

→ Health PFI projects do not seem to have done as well as PFI projects in other areas. This is possibly due to the exclusion of large volumes of service activity from health PFI projects, or to the fact that health PFI projects are generally smaller in size than the average PFI project.

→ PFI has succeeded in shifting large amounts of liabilities off public sector balance sheets but high levels of risk now exist because of the possibility of major corporate failures as a consequence of the economic recession and 'credit crunch'.

The future of PFI

The demise of PFI has often been predicted but, whatever the future of PFI itself, until recently it has always seemed likely that the private sector would continue to have a major role in the financing of public service infrastructure. However, the credit crunch has had a major effect in that some of the private sector partnerships involved in PFI have been having difficulty raising the necessary capital finance for existing projects, let alone new ones. Because of this it is anticipated that the government may need to step-in to bail out certain PFI schemes which are in trouble. However, once the problems of the credit crunch have been alleviated and capital finance is more freely available, the size of UK government debt still suggests that government will need to make greater use than ever of the private sector to finance new capital expenditure and to deal with certain labour-restrictive practices in public services.

Framework of public expenditure

Accounting and budgeting for public expenditure

The government now accounts and budgets for its expenditure on the same basis as commerce and industry and most other parts of the public sector. It has moved away from a system of cash accounting to a system of accounting for resources when they are committed. Until 2000/1, expenditure was controlled and accounted for on a cash basis, but the current approach is referred to as Resource Accounting and Budgeting (RAB). Resource and capital budgets are set in terms of accruals information, which measures resources as they are consumed rather than when the cash is paid. So, for example, the resource budget includes a charge for depreciation, which is a measure of the consumption or wearing out of capital assets. Non-cash charges in budgets do not impact directly on the fiscal framework.

In considering the planning of public expenditure, the framework for public expenditure at central government level is divided between Departmental Expenditure Limit (DEL), Annually Managed Expenditure (AME), and Total Managed Expenditure (TME). These are described next.

Departmental Expenditure Limit (DEL)

Firm DEL plans are set for departments for three years as separate resource (current) and capital budgets. The resource budget contains a separate control total for 'near cash' expenditure, which is expenditure such as pay and current grants. To encourage departments to plan over the medium term, they may carry forward unspent DEL provision from one year into the next and, subject to the normal tests for accuracy and realism of plans, funds may be drawn down in future years. This end-year flexibility also removes any incentive for departments to use up their provision as the year end approaches, as this may result in less regard to value for money. There is also a small centrally held DEL reserve and support from the reserve is available only for genuinely unforeseeable contingencies which departments cannot be expected to manage within their DEL. The amount of their resource budget DEL that departments may spend on running themselves (e.g. paying most civil servants' salaries) is limited by administration budgets, which are set in Spending Reviews. Administration budgets are used to ensure that as much money as practicable is available for front-line services and programmes.

Annually Managed Expenditure (AME)

AME typically consists of programmes which are large, volatile and demand-led, and which therefore cannot reasonably be subject to firm multi-year limits. The biggest single element is social security spending. AME is reviewed twice a year as part of the Budget and Pre-Budget Report process, reflecting the close integration of the tax and benefit systems, which was enhanced by the introduction of tax credits. AME is not subject to the same three-year expenditure limits as DEL, but is still part of the overall envelope for public expenditure. Affordability is taken into account when policy decisions affecting AME are made. The government has committed itself to not taking policy measures which are likely to have the effect of increasing social security or other elements of AME without taking steps to ensure that the effects of those decisions can be accommodated prudently within the government's fiscal rules. Given an overall envelope for public spending, forecasts of AME affect the level of resources available for DEL spending. Cautious estimates and the AME margin are built in to these AME forecasts and reduce the risk of overspending on AME.

Total Managed Expenditure (TME)

Taken together, DEL plus AME sum to Total Managed Expenditure (TME). TME is a measure drawn from national accounts. It represents the current and capital spending of the whole public sector comprising central government, local government and public corporations.

Planning and financing of public services

Various mechanisms and processes exist at the national level to plan the provision and financing of public services. These are discussed below using the UK as a case study.

Comprehensive Spending Reviews

Governments have two key questions to address in relation to public expenditure:

→ What should be the total of public expenditure for each year or over a period of years?

→ How should that public expenditure be distributed between competing programmes (e.g. defence, education, health, etc.)?

Prior to 1997, public spending had been planned only a year ahead, and was announced in the annual Budget. On coming to power the new Labour government introduced the first Comprehensive Spending Review (CSR), which is now the Government's main tool for deciding how much money will go into schools, hospitals and other public services. The CSR aimed to move from the short-termism of the annual cycle and to draw up public expenditure plans on not a one-year but a three-year basis.

Under the CSR, HM Treasury sets the overall limit for public spending. The Budget preceding a Spending Review sets an overall envelope for public spending that is consistent with the fiscal rules for the period covered by the Spending Review. In the Spending Review, the Budget forecast for the Annually Managed Expenditure (AME) for year one of the Spending Review period is updated, and AME forecasts are made for the later years of the Spending Review period. In doing this, government will have to take into account the economic situation of the country. The political stance of the government in power may also have an influence, but in recent years there seem to be only slight differences between political parties in their attitudes towards levels of public spending, with opposition parties often promising to keep spending at the level of the party in power.

The CSR then allocates resources between public expenditure programmes (e.g. defence, education, transport) according to a range of factors, such as needs, gaps in service, government priorities, etc. In theory, CSRs work from a zero base. This means that that they ignore past spending plans and start from zero. All expenditure has to be justified. This could mean radical changes, with less money for low-priority departments. The CSR will indicate which programmes will see a growth in resources (and how much) and which services will lose resources, over a three-year period (although one CSR was for a two-year period only).

Budget and pre-Budget reports

The Budget is the UK's annual financial statement and includes a review of taxation levels and an announcement of spending plans. It is the responsibility of the Chancellor of the Exchequer (the Finance Minister) who works closely with his team of ministerial colleagues and senior civil servants to produce the Budget in secrecy. The Budget is traditionally delivered in Parliament some time each March.

On its election to power in 1997, the incoming Labour government introduced the idea of a pre-Budget report to Parliament. A pre-Budget report is delivered by the Chancellor to the House of Commons in the autumn of each year. It provides a progress report on what has been achieved so far, gives an update of the state of the economy and public finances, and sets out the direction of government policy in the run up to the spring Budget.

Public Service Agreements

Public Service Agreements (PSAs) were introduced as a means of helping the government to deliver on its objectives. After an initial attempt which involved great complexity, the structure of PSAs have been radically simplified.

PSAs are developed by government departments in consultation with the Treasury and the Prime Minister's Delivery Unit (PMDU). The basic aim of PSAs is to link the allocation of finance to government departments with the achievement of certain forward-looking objectives, rather than on the basis of past performance.

The process for setting PSAs is illustrated in Figure 2.7.

Figure 2.7 Setting Public Service Agreements

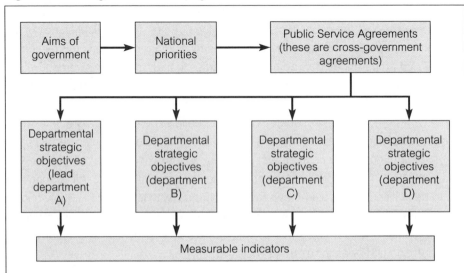

The starting point for setting PSAs is the four over-arching aims which the government has set itself:

→ sustainable growth and prosperity;

→ fairness and opportunity for all;

→ stronger communities and a better quality of life;

→ a more secure and environmentally friendly world.

In turn, each aim has a series of national priorities and one PSA underpins the achievement of each of these national priorities. However, each PSA is cross-governmental in nature and several government departments may contribute towards each PSA. The national priorities for the 'sustainable growth and prosperity' aim are shown in Figure 2.8.

Each government department will then develop its own departmental strategic objectives (DSO), the achievement of which will contribute towards the achievement of the overall PSA. However, to ensure that the whole process has leadership, one government department leads on each and every PSA. An example of the PSA structure is given in Figure 2.9 based on the Department of Work and Pensions.

In turn, these departmental strategic objectives will be cascaded down the public sector to agencies, local authorities, NHS bodies, etc., such that each will have a set of performance targets.

It remains a contentious point whether governments can expect to meet their objectives by a command and control approach of setting objectives for the whole of the public sector and monitoring results. A recent NAO report gave departments a percentage score as to how far they had met their PSAs. The average across all of them was only 45% – less than half of their targets. Only two departments (the Crown Prosecution Service and the Home Office) scored 100% and five departments scored less than 25% (Talbot, 2009).

Figure 2.8 Aims of government and national priorities

Sustainable growth and prosperity
1 Raise the productivity of the UK economy
2 Improve the skills of the population, on the way to ensuring a world-class skills base by 2020
3 Ensure controlled, fair migration that protects the public and contributes to economic growth
4 Promote world class science and innovation in the UK
5 Deliver reliable and efficient transport networks that support economic growth
6 Deliver the conditions for business success in the UK
7 Improve the economic performance of all English regions and reduce the gap in economic growth rates between regions

Figure 2.9 Structure of Public Service Agreements

Government aim	Sustainable growth and prosperity	Fairness and opportunity for all
National priority = Public Service Agreement (cross-government)	1 Raise the productivity of the UK economy	8 Maximise employment opportunity for all
Department of Work and Pensions strategic objective	Maximise employment opportunities for all	Promote equality of opportunity for disabled people
Other departments that can contribute to this PSA	HM Treasury Department for Business Enterprise and Regulatory Reform	All departments

Parliamentary estimates

Under long-established constitutional practice, each year, the government must obtain authority from Parliament to consume the resources and spend the cash the government needs to finance each department's agreed spending programmes for the financial year (April to March). Parliament gives statutory authority for both the consumption of resources and for cash to be drawn from the Consolidated Fund (the government's general bank account at the Bank of England) by Acts of Parliament known as Consolidated Fund Acts and by an annual Appropriation Act. This process is known as the 'supply procedure'. The main estimates start the supply procedure and are presented by HM Treasury at the start of the financial year to which they relate. The Treasury presents alongside the main estimates a set of supplementary budgetary information tables reconciling the estimates to departmental report tables. At various points in the year the Treasury presents new, revised and/or supplementary estimates, as appropriate, asking Parliament for approval for any necessary additional resources and/or cash or for authority to incur expenditure on new services. After the end of the financial year (around July) the Treasury presents the Public Expenditure Outturn White Paper to Parliament, providing provisional outturn figures for public expenditure by departments.

Allocating resources to public services

Having decided the levels of public expenditure to be allocated to public expenditure programmes, the next task is to distribute that funding to those agencies and organisations that will actually spend the money and deliver services. A number of general approaches to resource allocation are used and these are outlined below together with a discussion of their application.

First, however, it is useful to consider the criteria that make a good resource allocation method. The key factors suggested are as follows (Jones and Prowle, 1997):

→ **Equity** – most people accept that an approach to resource allocation should be equitable. However, equity is not an empirical concept but a moral one, and it is another matter to define equity precisely. Many would argue that equity implies that equality should be achieved by resource allocation, but this creates practical problems. For example, equality of what? Should it mean:
  • Equal range of services provided across the country?
  • Equality of access to services?
  • Equality of service outcomes?

  A further dimension to this discussion is added by the question of equality for who? Approaches to resource allocation could be concerned with equality between different geographic areas, different care groups or different social groups in the community. Equity is an extremely complex and important concept which needs precise and careful definition when evaluating approaches to resource allocation.

→ **Objectivity and transparency** – it should be possible for people examining the approach to resource allocation to understand how and why the various decisions have been arrived at and what criteria and information have been taken into account. In other words, the resource allocation decisions should be transparent. In addition, it would be desirable for the decisions to be made on objective analysis rather than subjective judgement, but this may not always be possible.

→ **Simplicity** – the chosen approach to resource allocation should be simple to understand, especially by the people most affected by it. Unfortunately, simplicity of approach often implies a lack of statistical sophistication, and there often seems to be a drive towards making resource allocation more sensitive and hence more complex. In practice, resource allocation in the public sector has tended to become increasingly complex and consequently only understood by a relatively small number of people.

→ **Stability** – an approach to resource allocation should result in a reasonable degree of stability from year to year in the funds allocated. Wide variations each year will seriously inhibit medium and long-term planning and investment.

→ **Economy** – resource allocation is not a free good and in itself consumes resources in terms of staff time, computer processing, report writing and decision taking. Clearly it is not desirable to spend a large proportion of scarce resources on the resource allocation task itself. Thus economy in resource allocation is a desirable criterion.

After reading the rest of this chapter the reader may care to reflect on the extent to which the various approaches to resource allocation meet these criteria.

The main approaches to resource allocation in relation to public services are outlined below.

Formula-based methods

In many parts of the public sector, resources are shared out between different parts of the country by means of a statistical formula designed to measure the *relative* need for resources in different areas. The key word here is relative, since such approaches do not aim to decide what level of funding is required to meet those needs in absolute terms, but how a fixed sum of resources should be shared out across the country in an equitable manner which reflects needs. Such formulae will usually contain a number of factors, such as size of client group served, level of social deprivation, etc. Two examples of formula-based approaches are as follows:

➔ **NHS** – the weighted capitation approach in the NHS uses a formula which combines data on the size and structure of the population of a PCT (plus some other needs-related factors) to identify the share of national NHS resources that each PCT should receive.

➔ **Local government** – the revenue support grant distributed to local authorities is based on the use of a complex formula which uses data on the numbers of service users (for each local government service) to identify the share each local authority should have of the total amount available nationally.

Planning and negotiation methods

With this type of approach, the level of funding to be allocated to a PSO or a particular public service is calculated through a form of service planning and negotiation exercise. Starting with past performance and past funding, an agreement will be reached about how the level of funding will change and how any additional (or reduced) funds will be used to alter volumes of service, service quality, etc. The PSAs discussed above are essentially a form of planning and negotiation where funds are allocated to central government departments on the basis of an agreement about the targets to be achieved.

Bidding methods

In some cases, certain funding is made available for a specific purpose and PSOs are invited to submit bids to access that funding. There is usually insufficient funding to meet all the bids submitted and hence there needs to be a formal selection process to identify the successful bids. This type of approach is often applied where government or a funding agency wishes to promote a new initiative.

Market methods

In some cases the allocation of resources is determined by markets and competition, albeit that these are quasi-markets involving PSOs and not open markets where private sector organisations can compete. Two examples of this are as follows:

→ **NHS Trusts** – funding is allocated to NHS Trusts (and Foundation Trusts) according to the numbers of patients treated and the national funding tariff for the condition for which the patient is being treated. In doing this, NHS Trusts are competing with one another to gain patients and thus the level of funding they obtain is dependent on how well they compete with others.

→ **Universities** – universities are also competing with one another to attract undergraduate students. However, while the success of universities in attracting students is taken account of in the HE resource allocation formula, there is not such a direct link between funding and students as there is in the NHS case.

Targets and pace of change

With many of these resource allocation approaches, it is often the case that the existing distribution of resources is often out of line with what the resource allocation model suggests it should be. In this situation, policy makers will want to change the pattern of resource distribution so that it moves towards that suggested by the model. However, it is unlikely that such a shift can be made overnight, or even in one year, and so a 'pace of change' strategy will be developed. This identifies how quickly, and realistically, the resource pattern can be changed to fit with what the resource allocation model suggests, and annual targets will be set each year to achieve that change.

Conclusions

In any country, to finance public services, funds must be raised from a limited number of sources and the mix between these sources will vary greatly. However, in all cases the sums of money involved are exceedingly large and, therefore, at the national level, governments require suitable mechanisms to plan, manage and control this money. In addition, the money set aside for particular services needs to be distributed between different parts of the country and different groups in society and appropriate mechanisms for doing this will need to be developed. However, such mechanisms will need to incorporate trade-offs between various desirable characteristics.

Questions for discussion

→ Are the sources of finance for public services too narrowly based and should there be an expansion of locally raised revenues?

→ Is the framework of PSAs developed by central government an effective approach to achieving its overall aims?

→ How well do the various approaches to resource allocation that you have encountered conform to the five criteria that were discussed in this chapter?

Public service reforms and their impact on financial management practices

---

Learning objectives

→ To understand the aims and nature of public service reforms

→ To understand the causal factors of public service reforms

→ To have a knowledge of the general themes of public service reforms

→ To appreciate the impact of public service reforms on the practice of financial management

---

Introduction

The last 20–30 years have seen immense changes in the public services of the UK and other countries. Although the detail of such changes are specific to the individual country, individual sector and individual PSO, many of the changes show clear and common trends across all parts of the public services in many countries. Differences in language and details of application and, sometimes, an inability or unwillingness by some managers to accept that they could learn something from other sectors have often disguised this fact.

These trends are important since they have, to a large degree, influenced the types of managerial practices employed in PSOs and the skills needed by public service managers. As an example, 30 years ago, very few UK civil servants would have seen a need to develop skills in financial management since it was just not relevant to the job they were doing at the time. Similarly, 30 years ago, in the UK, one would have been unlikely to find any NHS manager or headteacher who had skills and knowledge in performance management. These and other techniques are now part of the standard toolkit of public sector managers everywhere.

Figure 3.1 The public service reform agenda

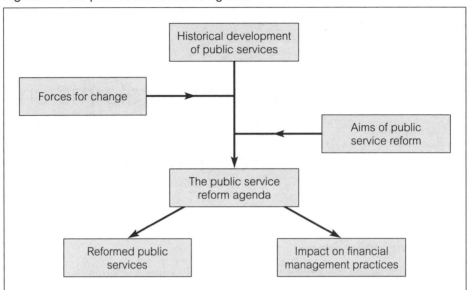

This book is concerned primarily with the practice of financial management in public services and *not* public policy, political science or public sector reforms in detail. However, in order to understand the reasons for changes in financial management practices the reader needs to have some knowledge of the reform process which has taken place worldwide over the last 20–30 years. The reader who wishes to explore the reform agenda further is referred to one of the specialist books on the subject, as listed in the section on further reading.

The structure of this chapter is outlined in Figure 3.1.

In this chapter we consider the following:

→ a brief history of public service reform in the UK;

→ forces for change – the causal factors of public service reform;

→ the aims of public service reform;

→ the public service reform agenda;

→ the impact of public service reform on financial management practice.

A brief history of public service reform in the UK

In Chapter 1 we looked at the way the UK state sector has evolved over a long period of time and the role public services played during that period of evolution. In the paragraphs below we give a brief outline of the stages in public service reform, focusing on the UK as an example.

Pre-1979

Prior to this date, most of what might be termed public service reform constituted reform of administrative practices rather than the reform of the methods of delivering front-line services. Consequently, these reforms often involved changes in the organisational structures of PSOs rather than changes in managerial and/or professional practices. An example of a structural reform would be the reorganisation of the NHS in 1974, where the existing regional hospital boards and hospital management committees were replaced by a structure of regional, area and district health authorities. These reforms involved changes to the administrative structures of the NHS but the impact at the hospital operational level was minimal.

In this period, the idea of public service management had barely been formed and there was much more use of what might be termed public 'administration'. As will be discussed later, the 1980s saw the development of public service management accompanied by a shift from administration to management. However, one aspect of this absence of strong management in public services was that the corresponding power of service professionals (e.g. doctors, teachers) over the deployment of resources and the conduct of service activities was much greater than it is today.

1979–97

This period covered the Conservative governments of Margaret Thatcher and John Major and was a period of unprecedented reform in public services. The various reforms, which will be described in more detail later, involved a wide range of themes, including the transfer of public sector activities to the private sector, structural reforms, developments in managerial processes such as the financial management initiative, competition and market testing.

In addition to such specific reforms, one over-arching theme was the idea of developing 'management' in the public services. Later in this chapter we will discuss the difference between administration and management in more detail, but prior to the 1980s, most of the language used centred around the term 'public administration', and various public sector journals and professional bodies included the term 'administration' in their titles. The 1983 Griffiths Report (Griffiths, 1983) into the NHS emphasised the need to strengthen NHS management and for NHS administrators to become NHS managers. This idea has subsequently grown substantially and, today, we rarely talk about public service administration or administrators. Consequently, the management of public services has been strengthened considerably and many would argue that increasing managerial influence and power has been achieved through a diminution of the influence and power of service professionals, such as doctors, teachers, social workers, etc.

The growth in managerialism in public services was, not surprisingly, resisted by both trade unions and professional bodies who saw their own positions being undermined. However, an important historical event was the defeat of the National Union of Mineworkers in their year-long strike in 1983–4. The miners were seen as the vanguard of the trade union movement and their defeat substantially altered the balance of power between management and unions in all sectors of the economy, including the public services. Whatever the merits of the strike it is possible that managerialism in public services and even the whole public service reform agenda may not have taken place to anything like the extent it did without this pivotal event in management–trade union relationships.

1987–today

This period covers the Labour governments of Tony Blair and Gordon Brown. To a large extent this period has involved a continuation of the reform policies of the previous Conservative administration, and policies such as market testing and the Private Finance Initiative have continued to flourish. To some degree this has been a surprise, since many people felt that a Labour government would not feel able to enthusiastically pursue such policies, as they contradicted the traditional ideology of the party.

It is clearly the case that while in office the Labour government enthusiastically pursued some programmes of public service reform, although there was strong resistance to parts of the reform agenda within the party. Arguably much of their reform agenda involved the extension or re-design of earlier initiatives such as PFI, market testing, target setting, regulation, etc., but two specific themes need to be highlighted.

The Labour government came to power with a strongly developed theme, often described as 'joined-up' government. This emphasised the need for government departments, agencies, local authorities, etc. to work together more closely in order to deliver more 'joined-up' services rather than each organisation pursuing its own service agenda. There are many aspects to this joined-up agenda, which will be discussed later in this chapter.

The second theme concerns the greater strategic focus at central government level and the development of linkages between funding and service objectives and outputs. Key aspects of this concern the introduction of Comprehensive Spending Reviews (CSRs), Public Service Agreements (PSAs) and Capability Reviews by central government departments and the preparation by departments of longer-term strategic plans.

Forces for change: causal factors of public service reform

An important question is why these waves of public service reform were initiated in the UK (and, to a large extent, many other countries as well) over this 30-year period (1979 to the current day). It cannot be an accident that such reforms occurred in many countries (including the UK) over a broadly similar timescale and so there must be causal factors at play. Let us first consider some factors that impinge on public services:

➜ demographic trends;

➜ societal trends;

➜ scientific and technological trends;

➜ macro-economic constraints;

➜ political trends.

Demographic trends

Population or demographic changes are an important factor. The data for a selection of countries are shown in Table 3.1.

This table shows substantial population growth between 1950 and 2000, albeit that some countries (e.g. China and India) have had much larger levels of growth.

Table 3.1 International population trends

	1950 (million)	2000 (million)	2025 (million)	2050 (million)	% change over 100 year period
China	545	1,267	1,453	1,417	160
Germany	68	82	79	70	3
India	372	1,043	1,431	1,614	334
Indonesia	77	205	263	288	274
Japan	82	127	121	102	24
Pakistan	41	148	246	335	717
Russia	102	147	132	116	14
USA	157	288	359	404	157
UK	51	59	67	72	41
More developed regions	812	1,195	1,277	1,275	57
Less developed regions	1,717	4,920	6,735	7,875	359
World	2,529	6,115	8,012	9,150	262

Source: United Nations, World Population Statistics, http://esa.un.org/unpp/

Furthermore, with one exception this growth in population is expected to continue in the period up to 2050, again with differential rates of growth between countries.

Since so many public services (e.g. health, education) are provided for individual citizens and the population as a whole it is self-evident that the size of the population must be an important factor in the need for services and thus a growing popula-tion probably implies a growing need for public services. Depending on the economic structure of the country, however, a growing population might also fuel increased economic growth through the productive use of its people, and this increased growth would provide greater levels of resources for public services.

The other aspect of demography concerns the structure of the population and, particularly, the age structure. One statistic that summarises the issue of the ageing population is the dependency ratio, which is the ratio of the economically dependent part of the population, comprising the sum of children (0–14 years) and the elderly (65+ years), to the working-age population (15–65 years). As the number of elderly people increases compared to the working age population then the dependency ratio increases. The trend in dependency ratios is illustrated in Figure 3.2.

It will be noted that in the countries shown the dependency rate is increasing as a consequence of the ageing population. Thus the ageing population issue is not just a UK issue but an international issue. Also, it will be noted that the increase in dependency rates is not uniform, with some countries having much higher rates of increase than others. Furthermore, this data concerns the elderly (defined as 65+), but if we focused on the very elderly in the population (80+) we would also see significant increases in the percentage of very elderly people. This scenario is the

Figure 3.2 International trends in age dependency ratios

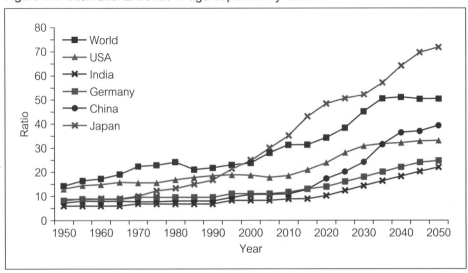

Table 3.2 Relative health services expenditure
by age group – England, 1999/2000

Age group	Expenditure per head (£)
Birth	2,655
under 5	794
5 to 15	185
16 to 44	328
45 to 64	459
65 to 74	949
75 to 84	1,684
over 84	2,639

Source: Office for Health Economics,
www.ohe.org/page/knowledge/schools/appendix/nhs_cost.cfm

consequence of medical advances, as many of the diseases that killed people at a younger age have been eradicated or inhibited.

However, it is not just the growth in the proportion of elderly in the population that is important but also the increasing costs of public service provision associated with the elderly. Consider the data shown in Table 3.2.

This data shows that, compared to the average of the population as a whole, the elderly and very elderly consume a much higher level of health service resources.

Similar pictures emerge in other areas of public policy:

→ **Transport** – access to transport makes an important contribution to older people's quality of life and older people tend to rely more heavily on public transport than other groups.

→ **Housing** – while 60% of UK people over 65 own their home outright, older people are more likely to face problems with upkeep and maintenance, and about one third of those living in unfit homes are over 60.

→ **Learning** – increasing numbers of older people are taking part in educational opportunities, with 51% of 60–69 year olds involved in learning in 2002.

It can be seen that older people place more demands on public services than the rest of the population. Thus the overall picture is one of increasing numbers of elderly people who consume a higher level of public service resources than the rest of the population.

Societal changes

The last 30 years have seen significant changes in the structure of many societies. A few examples of this from the UK are discussed below,

Figure 3.3 Divorce and marital breakdown

Source: Office for National Statistics, www.statistics.gov.uk/cci/nugget.asp?id=170

Family breakdown

The UK has seen a large-scale increase in marital and relationship breakdown. Consider the data on marital breakdown shown in Figure 3.3.

In addition to this there is also the issue of non-married cohabiting couples who break up.

These trends of marriage and relationship breakdown have led to major changes in family structures. Children in the UK are increasingly likely to live in single-parent families, with nearly a quarter of children (24%) living with just one parent in 2007 compared with 8% in 1972. The figure has crept up from 21% a decade ago and from 22% in 2001 (ONS, 2008a).

Loss of the extended family

The classic extended family consisting of three generations (children, parents, grandparents) living under the same roof, already rare in 1960, is now all but extinct. In the case of brothers and sisters there has been a marked decline both in those living nearby and those remaining in close contact (ESRC, undated).

Female employment

Worldwide, the labour market has seen dramatic changes particularly in relation to female employment. Between 1959 and 2001, female employment in the UK rose

Figure 3.4 Labour market participation by gender

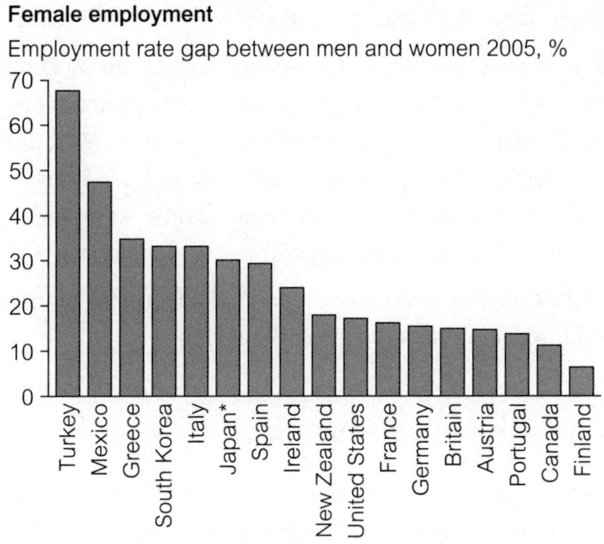

Female employment

Employment rate gap between men and women 2005, %

Source: *The Economist*, 10 July 2008, www.economist.com/markets/indicators/displaystory.cfm?story_id=11707320

from 48% to over 70% (ONS, 2002). However, the picture is not the same everywhere and Figure 3.4 illustrates large variations between male and female employment rates across a sample of countries.

More specifically, there have also been large scale increases in the involvement of mothers in the UK labour market, with more than two thirds of working-age women with dependent children now being in employment. Of working-age women with children aged under five, 57% were in employment (ONS, 2008b).

Persons living alone

More people now live alone than ever before, and by 2021 it is estimated that more than a third of all households are expected to consist of just one person (BBC, 2005). Although a large proportion of these involve the elderly, younger people are also involved and 15% of men aged 25–44 (compared to 8% of women) now live alone. These numbers are expected to rise.

Implications of societal trends

All of these (and other) social trends can have significant implications for public services:

→ Marital and relationship breakdown increases the demand for housing (including social housing) units.

→ Increases in the numbers of working mothers increases the demand for affordable child care since the loss of the extended family has substantially reduced the role of grandparents or siblings in this task.

→ Available evidence suggests that children from single parent families do badly on most indicators although there will obviously be many exceptions to this general rule. The report of the Social Justice Policy Group (SJPG, 2006) states that children from a broken home are twice as likely to have behavioural problems, perform worse at school, become sexually active at a younger age, suffer depression, or turn to drugs, smoking and heavy drinking.

→ The numbers of persons living alone has implications for housing, energy consumption and mental illness services (BBC, 1998).

Science and technological changes

Scientific and technological developments have had (and will continue to have) significant implications for public services. Two particular aspects of this should be noted.

Medical science and technological advances

It is now difficult to believe that at the time of formation of the UK NHS the commonly received view was that health service spending would flatten out as the major diseases and clinical conditions were resolved. In practice, NHS spending has grown enormously and will continue to do so. One aspect of this (the ageing population) has already been discussed, but the other factor concerns scientific and technological developments which have worldwide application. Examples of such developments include artificial joint replacements (1950s), organ transplants (1950s, 1960s), drug therapies (ongoing) and radiological imaging (CT, MRI scans) (1970s, 1980s).

The reality is that these developments start in a research phase but this soon moves into broad scale provision, and what is research today becomes commonplace tomorrow. For example, the first ever heart transplant took place in South Africa in 1967 and the patient survived 11 days. Today many thousands of people throughout the world benefit from heart transplants undertaken at many transplant centres and they may live for many decades. The economic issue is that before such scientific and technological breakthroughs were made the demand for such services was zero. The demand for heart transplants before 1967 was zero because nobody could do it. However, the existence and supply of such treatments, in turn, creates and fuels a demand that was previously non-existent.

In addition to the above well-known and well-publicised developments there are, of course, many much smaller scientific and technological developments which never make the headlines but which still have the same effect.

The key question is whether there are any limits to such developments, and, at the moment, the answer must be no. Similar developments will continue to come on stream and create demands for new services. Looking into the not too distant future, the role of genetic therapies may well become significant in the treatment of many diseases.

The IT revolution

The IT revolution is well known and understood. In the last 30 years we have seen a wide range of technological developments, such as personal computing, networks, e-mail, the Internet, etc. These developments have truly changed the world and have revolutionised many aspects of human life, including the management of public services. In particular, the Internet has become a means whereby public service organisations can find out information about the population they serve and their service needs, disseminate information about the PSO itself, communicate with a wide range of stakeholders and conduct business activities and deliver services on-line.

Macro-economic constraints

The various factors discussed above tend to increase the demands for public services and associated public expenditure. However, clearly there are limits to the amount of public expenditure that can be incurred in any country – there would still be a finite limit to the level of public expenditure even if the whole of the GDP of a country were devoted to it. In looking at how to finance any growth in public expenditure, governments can, in the main, use three approaches: rely on economic growth; increase the tax burden; use borrowing. These approaches are discussed below.

Rely on economic growth

As the size of a country's productive economy grows this will provide additional resources for public expenditure without having to increase the proportion of GDP committed to it. Thus, improved public services can be provided through the fruits of economic growth. Although most economies will go through business cycles (whereby the economy grows for a number of years but also contracts during a short recessionary period), the overall trend of most developed economies is continuously upward. However, the rate of growth in economies will vary substantially between countries. Typically, growth rates have been higher in Asian economies such as India and China and lower in the economies of the USA and the EU.

Increase the tax burden

Over and above economic growth, additional resources for public expenditure can be made available by increasing the tax burden on the population. Clearly there are both political and economic limits to increasing the tax burden, but it has often been used as a means of increasing revenues. For example, in the UK it has been calculated that in 2006/7 the Labour government took 2.1% more of national income in tax than the Conservative government did in 1996–7. It was also expected to take a further 1.3% of national income by 2009–10, increasing government revenues to 40.5% of national income (IFS, 2005). At the time of writing, the parlous state of UK public finances suggests that the tax burden will probably have to increase yet further in the future.

Government borrowing

In Chapter 2, we noted that where government revenues are projected to be less than government expenditures then the difference may be made up by government borrowing. It was also noted that it was usually the case that governments would borrow to finance budget deficits experienced during periods of economic recession, which would then be countered by budget surpluses during periods of economic growth. The impact of the severe economic recession and the 'credit crunch' has meant that UK government borrowing has now increased to rates that are just not sustainable (Prowle, 2009b).

The overall impact, therefore, is that the demands for additional public services often cannot be met just by the provision of additional resources, since, as discussed above, all the additional sources of funds are ultimately constrained. Hence the pressure for reform of public services, both historically and for the future.

Political issues

There are a number of what might be termed 'political issues' which have implications for both public services and public expenditure, and these are discussed next.

Loss of trust in the political process

Available evidence suggests a general loss of trust and confidence in the political process in the UK. The data shown in Figures 3.5 and 3.6 suggests that the UK has one of the lowest levels of trust and confidence in its political system in the European Union. This data was collected well before the recent MPs' expenses scandal.

Dissatisfaction with public services

Despite the reforms to public services that have taken place and the growth in funding allocated to public services there still appears to be a considerable degree of dissatisfaction with public services among UK citizens (Cabinet Office, 2001). Interestingly, although there appears to be something of a paradox in that while dissatisfaction with public services widely exists among the general public there is a

Figure 3.5 Electoral turnout

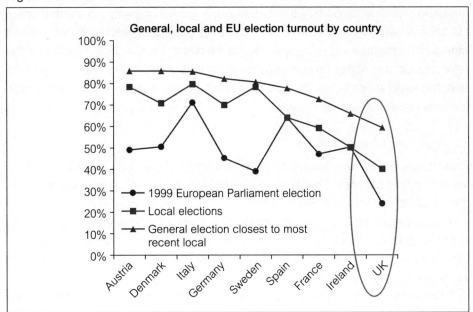

Source: European Parliament/IDEA/CoE

Figure 3.6 Confidence in Parliaments

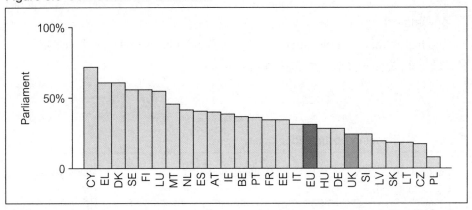

greater degree of satisfaction from those individuals who have recently made use of certain public services. Thus, for example, while there are still widespread concerns about the NHS, people who have actually been in hospital tend to be satisfied with the services received (Cabinet Office, 2001).

Reluctance to pay more tax

Polls suggest that the UK public currently have a strong aversion to paying higher levels of taxation. Most politicians interpret this as a wish not to pay higher rates of income tax and so no political party is now likely, in the foreseeable future, to raise the basic rate of income tax. As noted above, however, in reality the tax burden on UK citizens has risen sharply in recent years through a combination of new taxes and changes to existing taxes (other than raising the basic rate of income tax). Part of this reluctance to pay higher taxes seems to derive from a strongly held view that much of public expenditure is 'wasted', coupled with the level of dissatisfaction with public services referred to above.

Changing political ideologies

Political ideologies have always had a strong influence on a government's attitude towards public services. Traditionally, it is thought that the different political ideologies would be as shown in Figure 3.7.

This suggests, for example, that there is increasing enthusiasm for higher levels of public spending as we move from the political right to the political left and increasing enthusiasm for competition and private sector involvement as we move from the political left to the political right.

While these may have been traditional political ideological views regarding public services this is not necessarily the case today. Consider, for example, the following examples:

→ The use of markets and competition in public services by a Chinese communist government.

→ The high levels of public spending by the Bush administration in the USA.

→ The enthusiasm of the UK Labour government for PFI.

Figure 3.7 Changing political ideologies

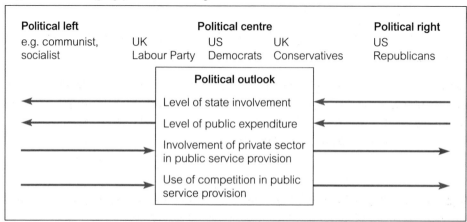

Figure 3.8 Drivers of public services reform

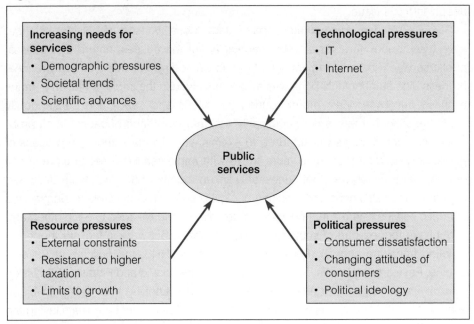

Thus, although political ideologies will have an implication for public service reform, the nature of such implications may not always be clear.

Summary

The above discussion outlined a wide range of factors with implications for public services, and the overall pressures and causes of public service reform in the UK (and worldwide) can be summarised as shown in Figure 3.8.

Aims of public service reform

Before looking at detailed aspects of public service reform it is worth spending a little time considering what the reform process was intended to achieve (the aims) and why it was pursued.

It is difficult to come up with a reasonably precise definition of public service reform that will meet all eventualities. Terms like New Public Management (NPM) and post-NPM have been developed (Christensen and Laegreid, 2007) and are in common use but these terms are not really comprehensive enough to describe the full range of reforms that have taken place. For example, NPM seems primarily concerned with marketisation and competition while post-NPM seems to be about the development of holistic or joined-up government. Hence we need to look more deeply into this issue.

Some academic commentators, particularly those working in political science, have tried to look for over-arching theories about the causes, nature and aims of public service reform and to imply that public service reform was a strongly rational process. The author of this book was actively involved in the implementation of many of these public services reforms during the 1980s and 1990s and consequently holds the view that this is not necessarily a helpful approach because, in all probability, no such theories will stand up to examination. To the author, the process of public service reform seemed more to do with implementing a set of incremental developments which were not necessarily linked together but which were designed to deal with specific concerns. Looking back, it is sometimes possible to identify sets of public service reforms that now appear to have strong linkages to each other, and might have formed part of some grand policy theme, but were in fact developed in isolation from one another. For example, in the UK NHS, the policies of Patients Choice, Payment by Results, Practice-Based Commissioning and Plurality of Provision were all implemented over a period of several years. Looking back it is possible to imagine that all four policies were part of some grand plan concerned with laying the ground for the re-introduction of the internal health market. Each policy would have a specific role in this internal health market:

→ **Patients Choice** – a factor to empower patients in making choices within the market.

→ **Plurality of Provision** – a factor to increase and diversify the supply of health services.

→ **Payment by Results** – a mechanism to provide incentives for the market to operate effectively.

→ **Practice-Based Commissioning** – a factor to disaggregate purchasing power in the health market among general practitioners.

The reality, however, is that each of these policies was developed in isolation, at different points in time and for specific purposes. It was only with the passage of time that their roles in the internal market could be discerned and utilised collectively.

An alternative approach is to suggest that public service reform does not have any grand theories but is really a set of responses to a number of broad concerns with strong political implications. Thus, it is suggested that the vast majority of what is termed public service reform can be considered in relation to the following key themes:

→ discerning the role of the state in public service provision;

→ dealing with public service monopolies;

→ improving the performance of public services;

→ changing patterns of decision making about public services;

→ improving consumer satisfaction with public services;

→ deciding how public services should be paid for.

These themes are described in the following sections.

Discerning the role of the state in public service provision

Clearly the state (or government) is an extremely important player in relation to public services, but the state can play several roles in relation to such services:

→ **The state as enabler** – the state encourages and promotes the availability of services without necessarily being a provider. An example of this is the provision of pre-school child care. The state (through local authorities) could choose to deliver child care itself or pay a private agency to deliver child care and then charge parents for their use of the service.

→ **The state as guarantor** – the state guarantees the availability of services for those unable to pay for them themselves.

→ **The state as financier** – the state pays for the provision of public services using public funds.

→ **The state as regulator** – the state regulates the provision of services by others to ensure that standards are maintained.

→ **The state as direct provider** – the state acts as a direct provider of services either itself or through one of its agencies.

In most countries the state undertakes all of these roles to a lesser or greater extent depending on the type of service and the service context. The corollary to the role of the state sector in relation to public services is the role of the non-state sector. In this context the non-state sector can be considered as involving the private sector, the community and voluntary sector, social enterprises and charities (the so-called third sector) and the individual citizen.

Much of the debate around public service reform has concentrated on the roles that the state should undertake in relation to service provision, the emphasis to be placed on each role and the roles of the non-state sector in public service provision. Thus, for example, today a significant element of public service provision (e.g. health, waste disposal) is undertaken by the private sector in a manner that would have been unthinkable 30 years ago.

Dealing with public service monopolies

Many PSOs were, in the past, often described as being state monopolies. Such organisations could hold monopolistic positions in a number of different ways:

→ A PSO being the sole national supplier of public services (e.g. the armed forces, or, historically, the various state utilities that have now been privatised).

→ A PSO being the sole supplier of public services to local residents (e.g. local authority services such as street cleaning).

→ A group of PSOs that are culturally similar with virtually sole rights to the delivery of certain services (e.g. universities).

→ A group of PSOs that are culturally similar and which have a similar range of constraints under which they must operate (e.g. NHS Trusts).

→ A group of PSOs that are culturally similar, have a similar range of constraints under which they must operate and have sole access to available public funding (e.g. schools maintained by local authorities).

There were a number of concerns about such public monopolistic arrangements, akin to the existence of private monopolies, including unresponsive services, lack of choice, and so on. Thus many aspects of public service reform are, and have been, concerned with how to deal with such monopolistic situations.

Some of these monopolistic activities have been addressed through policies such as privatisation, competition, contestability, etc., but many monopolies (e.g. local authority schools) still exist and may need addressing in the future.

Improving the performance of public services

For many years there were concerns about the performance of public services in the UK, with performance taken to mean the following:

→ **Effectiveness** – the quality and/or quantity of service provided compared to planned objectives.

→ **Economy** – the cost of acquiring resources (e.g. cost of supplies).

→ **Efficiency** – improvements in the amount of service output generated for a particular resource input (e.g. numbers of staff, use of buildings, equipment, etc.).

There is also a fourth 'E' of equity or fairness, but it is probably true to say that little attention has so far been given to the question of equity in considering the distribution of services and resources between different parts of the community. For example, the Black Report (Black, 1980) on inequalities in health showed that, across the country, there were huge inequalities in usage of and access to health services among different social classes. The report was given short shrift by the government of the day and significant inequalities still exist across the country.

Over a period of many years both the present and previous governments have undertaken a sustained drive for performance improvement in all parts of the public sector. One key aspect of this concerns restrictive practices, with many people taking the view that the public sector was rife with a large number of restrictive labour practices deriving from trade unions and/or professional bodies. Many of the reforms were concerned with loosening such restrictive practices as a means of delivering the service aims described above.

This drive for performance improvement can be shown in a number of ways, including the following:

→ **Funding allocations** – by making funding allocations to PSOs that incorporate a performance improvement element, government indicates that, in addition to the growth in funding they will allocate, they also expect the PSO to generate additional growth funding by identifying efficiency improvements in existing activities.

→ **Competition and contestability** – the role of competition and contestability in improving performance is discussed further in the next section.

→ **Performance indicators (PIs)** – the development and publication of sets of performance indicators for different service providers (e.g. NHS Trusts, schools, local authorities, etc.) is designed to identify the potential for and achievement of performance improvements in the delivery of services. In addition, the Government sometimes prepares and publishes 'league tables' so that the performance of individual PSOs can be compared with others, and this may act as a stimulus to improved performance.

→ **Value for money (VFM) audit** – the creation of the Audit Commission in 1983 with a responsibility for the audit of local authorities (and subsequently for the NHS) led to a considerable emphasis being placed on VFM audit as well as traditional probity audit. Similarly, in other parts of the public sector the National Audit Office (NAO) has been active in promoting improved VFM through its audit activities.

→ **Inspection** – many public services are subject to an independent review of the services they provide. This is discussed further in the next section.

Changing patterns of decision making about public services

There are a number of inherent tensions regarding the making of decisions about public services. Some of these are as discussed below:

→ **Localism versus centralism** – there is a constant tension between centralised decision making by central government departments and locally based decision making by, for example, local authorities, PCTs, RDAs, etc. It is sometimes suggested that decision making in the UK is far too centralised and that other countries operate more successfully with less centralised regimes. Furthermore, the local–central balance changes over time and often new governments begin with a centralised regime of targets, dictates, etc., only to later introduce a looser and more decentralised approach.

→ **Management versus service professionals** – there often exists a tension between generic public service managers and service professionals such as doctors, nurses, teachers, social workers, engineers, etc. This tension really started to become significant with the shift from administration to management that took place in public services during the 1980s. Public service reform often involved changes that affect the balance of power with regard to decision making between these two broad groups. For example, the development of practice-based commissioning in the NHS aims to give greater power to general medical practitioners over the commissioning of hospital services, at the expense of PCT managers. Similarly, the development of the lead professional budget holder in social care has also had a similar impact in increasing the power of service professionals over the use of resources.

→ **Professional versus personal** – traditionally, many decisions about services were the province of service professionals, such as doctors, teachers, social workers, etc., who would undertake an assessment of the need for a service and arrange for it to be provided and paid for with the financial resources available. Recent years have seen the development of a more personalised agenda, where the decision about what services should be provided is made by the individual consumer, who is given a personal budget to purchase the services they think they need. Perhaps the best example of this approach is the personal social care budget, where individual consumers decide what social care they wish to receive (and from what agency) within the constraints of a budget rather than have those service prescribed by a social worker. Similar personal budgets may be developed in other sectors, such as health and education.

Improving consumer satisfaction with public services

As already noted, within the UK there is often perceived to be a considerable degree of dissatisfaction with public services. A Cabinet Office study (Cabinet Office, 2001) suggested that when users of UK public services are consulted they are generally either satisfied or fairly satisfied with public services (with the exception of transport services) but when the general population is surveyed about their satisfaction with services their scores are much lower (with less than 60% fairly or very satisfied with the NHS, 39% fairly or very satisfied with primary schools and 30% fairly or very satisfied with secondary schools). While improvements in consumer satisfaction have

Figure 3.9 Satisfaction with health services

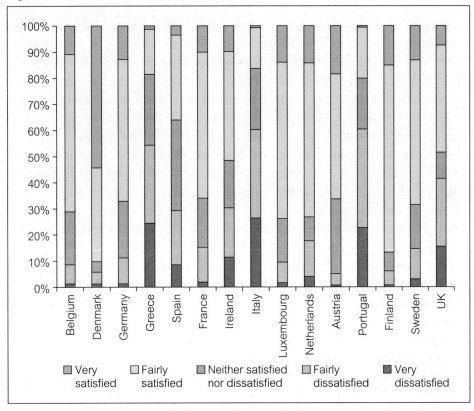

Source: Cabinet Office, www.cabinetoffice.gov.uk/media/cabinetoffice/strategy/assets/satisfaction.pdf

been achieved since that time, this is not a good situation. Moreover, low satisfaction levels are not the general rule. The same Cabinet Office study (Figure 3.9) provides data on satisfaction levels with health services across a range of countries, which suggests that the UK is among those countries with the lowest satisfaction levels.

There are a number of possible causes of consumer dissatisfaction, including poor service standards, poor communications from staff, unpleasant physical environments, lack of flexibility, long delays in receiving services, lack of 'joined-upness' in service provision, etc.

Consequently, many aspects of public service reform have focused on the achievement of greater levels of consumer satisfaction. These include consumer satisfaction surveys to identify problems, better staff training in customer care, improvements in buildings (e.g. PFI hospitals), enhanced choice for consumers (e.g. NHS Patients Choice), etc.

Deciding how public services should be paid for

A key issue is always the question of how public services should be paid for and who should pay for it. As already discussed, public services can be paid for out of public revenues (i.e. nationally raised taxes, locally based taxes or borrowings) or through charges to the consumers of those services. Most UK public services, such as education and health, are financed by means of public revenues, with a relatively small amount raised through charges to consumers. Other public services, such as public transport or leisure, have a higher element of consumer charges.

Public service reforms often involve changing the balance between tax-based funding and charges to consumers of services. For example, in recent years there has been considerable debate about the merits of extending the charging regime of the NHS to incorporate some payment for clinical services. In recent years the term 'co-payments' has been coined to describe the levying of a charge to supplement tax-based funding.

Finally, there is also the question as to whether some public services should remain public services or whether they should be transferred to the private sector and paid for, fully, by consumers in the same way as any other product. This was clearly the case with services such as water, electricity, gas and telecoms, which were privatised. An issue for the future is whether any other public services (or parts of public services) should also be privatised.

The public service reform agenda

The details of the public reforms that have taken place over the last 25–30 years vary considerably between different parts of the public sector, both in terms of their range and the detailed aspects of their implementation. Some of the key themes of the reforms that have taken place in many parts of the public services of many countries include the following:

→ Outright privatisation of public services.
→ Role differentiation – commissioner/provider separation.
→ Competition.
→ Contestability.
→ Mixed economy of provision.
→ Consumer involvement.
→ Consumer choice.
→ Inspection.

→ Improved leadership and management development.

→ Emphasis on governance and accountability.

→ Joined-up service provision.

Outright privatisation of public services

During the 1980s and 1990s, the UK government embarked on a sustained programme of outright privatisation of state-owned activities. Most of what were nationalised public utilities (and hence publicly owned) were subject to outright privatisation and converted into private sector limited companies. Examples of such privatisations include British Gas, the electricity boards, British Steel, British Coal, British Rail, the regional water authorities, etc. Consequently these former public utilities are no longer part of the public sector.

Not surprisingly, the conversion of these large-scale activities into private owner-ship led to implied reductions in public expenditure during that period. Although the pace of privatisation has subsequently decreased, a number of smaller privatisations of state activities are still taking place and may continue into the future.

Many, but not all, of these privatisations followed a similar format:

→ A private company was created to provide and manage the infrastructure for service delivery. Thus, for example, Railtrack (now Network Rail) managed the tracks and stations of the rail system, Transco managed the gas pipeline network and the National Grid managed the electricity supply network.

→ Several private companies were formed to deliver services using the service infrastructure referred to above. Thus the electricity supply companies supply electricity, the rail companies provide rail services and the gas companies pro-vide gas. In recent years there has been a trend for these companies to encroach into the traditional markets of other former public utilities (e.g. former electricity suppliers becoming suppliers of gas).

Although privately owned, these companies are subject to regulation of price and service standards by agencies such as OFGEM for the gas and electricity supply industries and OFWAT for the water industry. Whereas it seems likely that regulation of the service infrastructure companies will need to continue indefinitely, the regula-tion of service suppliers may wither away as greater competition is introduced into the market. Thus, for example, in the gas industry competition to British Gas was first introduced into the industrial gas market and subsequently also introduced into the domestic gas market.

Although often subject to heavy criticism, the privatisation programme achieved a number of things:

→ It led to the introduction of competition in industries such as gas and electricity.

→ It created utilities which undoubtedly became more consumer focused than their predecessor nationalised industries.

→ It enabled these industries to access capital from domestic and international money markets in a way that was impossible as a state-run utility.

→ The sale of these industries generated large-scale revenues for the government.

Role differentiation – commissioner/provider separation

One of the major structural reforms that has impacted on many parts of the public sector has been that of differentiating and separating the roles of the policy-making function of the organisation from that of actual service delivery – the commissioner/ provider separation.

The traditional approach to managing public services is illustrated in Figure 3.10. Under this arrangement a single integrated organisation receives funding from the government and undertakes both the policy and planning functions of public services as well as the actual delivery of those services.

Concerns were expressed that under such arrangements the integrated organisation did not pay sufficient attention to the service needs of its consumers and that the pattern of services was more influenced by the views of the providers of those services than the needs of its consumers (Enthoven, 1985). Thus, the commissioner/ provider separation splits the traditional organisation into two parts. This might involve two separate organisations or two separate units within the same organisation. The commissioner would be responsible for assessing needs and defining what type of services are to be provided, while the actual provision of those services

Figure 3.10 Traditional model of public service provision

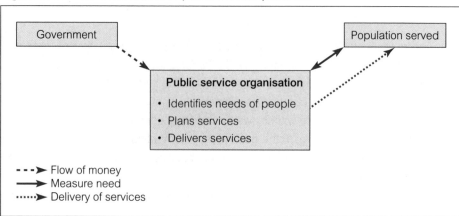

Figure 3.11 Separation of commissioner from provider

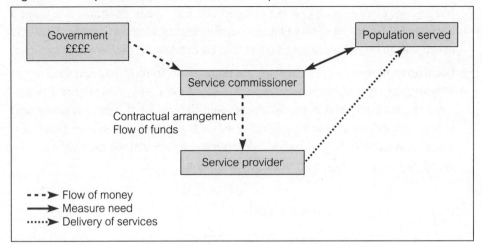

would be undertaken by a separate unit or organisation. This is illustrated in Figure 3.11.

In some situations the service commissioner may use a single provider, but in other circumstances the provision of services may be market tested, with other public, private or third sector organisations being involved. Thus, service providers must compete to win contracts – and hence funds. Under these arrangements, the service provider usually has to operate in a quasi-commercial manner and must aim to achieve tight financial and operational objectives. For example, NHS Trusts as well as achieving contract objectives in terms of quantity and quality of services must also achieve financial targets concerning rate of return on assets employed.

Some examples of where this approach has been applied in the public sector are as follows:

➔ **NHS** – within the NHS it is the PCT that is responsible for assessing the needs for health services and deciding which services should be provided, and in what volumes, and for specifying the details of service provision. The PCT would then agree a contract with a provider (an NHS Trust or some other provider) to actually deliver those services in return for payment.

➔ **Executive agencies** – within central government departments there has been a separation of the policy-making function from that of service delivery through the creation of separate executive agencies (Next Steps Agencies) with responsibility for service provision. Thus, in the Department of Work and Pensions, policy making and service planning is undertaken within the department itself, while the actual tasks of assessment, provision of advice and payment of benefits to individuals is undertaken by the executive agency, Jobcentre Plus. Jobcentre Plus is still part of the DWP but operates at 'arms length' from the main department and has its own chief executive and management. Each year, contracts are agreed between DWP and Jobcentre Plus concerning the volumes and quality standards of services to be delivered and the funds to be provided to deliver those services.

→ **Local government** – local authorities are engaged in commissioning a wide range of services (e.g. children's services, adult social care, etc.). Under this arrangement the relevant local authority department defines what types, volumes and quality of services should be provided, while the actual provision of those services is undertaken by a provider – which may be a unit of the council, a private sector organisation or a third sector organisation.

Market testing and competition

One of the key themes of public service reform (as exemplified in the term New Public Management) was that of exposing public services that were traditionally provided in-house to external competition via some form of market testing exercise. One possible outcome of such an exercise was that service provision might be outsourced to an external body, but there are also many examples of where in-house units improved their cost and quality performance to such an extent that they were successful in retaining the contract for service provision.

There have been a number of approaches to this so far in the public sector:

→ **Support services** – the Local Government (Planning and Land) Act 1981 required local authorities to set up services such as buildings maintenance as quasi-commercial units, which were then required to compete against external providers to win contracts from their parent council. The Local Government Act 1988 extended such arrangements to other services, such as cleaning, grounds maintenance, etc. Either under pressure from government or as a response to tight resource pressures other PSOs, such as the NHS or government agencies, have also exposed services such as catering, cleaning, security and maintenance to external competition.

→ **White collar services** – PSOs may also undertake market testing exercises in relation to the provision of what are generally referred to as 'white collar' services, which include services such as payroll, human resources, internal audit, IT services, etc. Alternative providers may be other neighbouring PSOs who have some slack capacity or private companies specialising in these areas. Smaller PSOs have often found it appropriate to outsource certain services to external bodies because they were just too small to run them, internally, in an efficient manner.

→ **Direct services** – PSOs may also expose to market competition the direct provision of services to the general public. Such competition may be provided by other

PSOs, the private sector or the third sector. The development of the commissioning role referred to earlier is fuelling this development and the commissioners are starting to outsource a considerable number of services based around health, children's services, drug and alcohol support, etc. to external providers.

In all of these types of market testing exercise the external competitors are chosen from other public sector organisations, private sector organisations or third sector organisations. The market testing exercise should be conducted on the basis of a systematic assessment of all of the bids (internal and external) and the final decision should be made on the basis of quality, cost and security of service being offered. In practice, however, a systematic bias towards continuation by the internal provider sometimes seeps through into the PSO's decision, especially if losing the contract means closing the in-house unit. However, in many cases the staff involved are retained by the new provider.

Market testing exercises need not just apply to in-house service provision. Where a PSO has already outsourced service provision to an external organisation they may still conduct periodic market testing exercises to ensure they are getting the best deal. One possible outcome is that the service will be re-insourced, or brought back in-house.

Market testing exercises should not be approached blindly. For such an exercise to be effective there is a need for there to be a competitive market with a sufficient number of providers. If this is not the case then the commissioner may need to encourage other organisations to enter the market before the market testing exercise is held. It is also in the commissioner's interests to maintain a competitive market since this will discourage the existing provider from 'resting on its laurels'.

Contestability

Contestability is not the same as market testing and competition. The concept of contestability was originally developed in the 1980s by the American economist William Baumol in relation to industrial markets (Baumol, 1982) and was concerned with the position and behaviour of monopolistic providers of goods and services in such markets. Baumol suggested that monopolistic providers did not need to be exposed to actual competition in order to make them responsive and competitive – the mere threat of competition might be sufficient to achieve these ends. Thus contestability is not a synonym for competition, but describes a situation whereby a provider faces a possible and credible threat of competition. In this context, contestability could involve, for example, the creation or encouragement of a credible alternative provider of goods or services. Contestability is fundamentally different to 'market testing', as it does not require every individual service to be competed.

Contestability has subsequently been extended to cover public monopolies and public service delivery. One example of this is the prison service, which although largely publicly provided has a small element of private provision. The existence and operation of this private element provides a real and credible threat that, at some future date (and if deemed necessary), more of the prison service could be transferred to private provision. This inhibits the existing public provider from displaying strong monopolistic tendencies of inflexibility, resistance to change, etc. Contestability has been applied to many other public services and may be extended even further in the future (Prowle, 2008).

Mixed economy of provision

Traditionally, most public services were delivered by the public sector. However, over the last 20 years or so there have been substantial changes in the mix of public, private and third sector provision. Such trends undoubtedly reflect changes in political perceptions of the role of the state in service provision, with an increasing emphasis on the state as an enabler rather than a direct provider. Also it must be noted that although many traditional public services are now delivered by the private or third sector they are still financed by public funds.

This enhanced involvement by the private and third sector has taken several forms:

→ **Outsourcing** – many parts of the public sector, particularly central government, local government and the NHS, have been required or encouraged to subject large parts of their in-house operations to market testing and external competition. This trend has been further emphasised by the separation of the commissioner and provider discussed earlier, where the commissioner will consider a range of public, private and third sector options for service provision. Frequently, the result of such a market testing exercise was that the in-house service retained the contract (often as a result of internal efficiency improvements). However, a significant amount of service provision has been transferred to private sector contractors via this process.

→ **Public Private Partnerships (PPP)** – the involvement of the private sector has been further extended through the application of PPPs, of which the best known is the Private Finance Initiative (PFI). The PFI involves a private sector consortium giving a PSO access to a fixed asset which it has acquired and financed as well as providing a range of services such as cleaning, maintenance, etc.

Consumer involvement

A strong theme in public service reform has been that of consulting with the actual and prospective users of services about their views. Such a consultation could be ex-ante in terms of the proposed changes to service provision or ex-post in terms of the degree of satisfaction with services received. It could take the form of consulting with individual citizens or with whole communities, and to achieve this, various techniques have been deployed, such as questionnaire surveys, focus groups, citizen's juries, etc.

It may seem strange today to imagine that 20 years ago most PSOs undertook little consultation with service users about the services being provided, but today, through consultation, the views of service users should shape services for the future.

However, the situation is not always that simple, for a number of reasons:

→ the PSO may be in breach of the law or government policy by applying the views of consumers (e.g. weekly or fortnightly refuse collection);

→ there may be insufficient resources to apply the views of consumers;

→ there may be lack of clarity about who the consumers actually are and there may be divergences of view about this – for example, in a school are the consumers the parents or the children?

Perhaps the key to this is to feedback to service users, information as to how their views have been applied or, if this was not possible, why their view could not be applied. In this way the consultation exercise will not be seen as pseudo-consultation.

Consumer choice

A natural extension to consulting with the users of services about the services they receive is to give them greater choice in the services they receive. A consideration of this idea of choice should lead one to conclude that such choice could be exercised by individuals in a number of dimensions:

→ Choice of type of service required.

→ Choice of location of service.

→ Choice of timing of service.

→ Choice of means of delivery of service.

→ Choice of provider organisation.

A key policy plank of the present government has been that of extending the choices available to individual consumers (or users) of public services. Some commentators suggest that individual choice has often been provided by public service organisations acting in a flexible and responsive manner, but that the scope for this choice and variety has been reduced by the imposition of national policy objectives and by financial constraints (Warwick University, 1995). In practice, the government's choice agenda is now being pursued largely by a combination of extending the range of alternative service providers and/or providing financial incentives to providers to compete with one another. One example of this is the policy of Patient Choice in the NHS, whereby patients choose the hospital from which they will receive their treatment from a list of possible providers (public and private). Other examples of extended individual choice include a major expansion of specialist schools and the introduction of light rail systems to improve transport choice in some parts of the country. An example of choice that goes even further is that of personal social care budgets, where the service recipient can decide not only who should be the provider of services but also what types of service they wish to purchase using their personal budgets. Examples can be quoted where individuals have used their funds for much more mundane activities, such as transport to football matches, rather than the traditional social care activities.

In spite of the present government's enthusiasm for extending choice, there is some early evidence from the NHS Patients Choice approach that, for whatever reasons, individuals are not utilising the choices available. Other criticisms of the extended choice approach include the following:

→ **Inability to chose** – many public services (e.g. health, education) are complex and the average consumer does not have the necessary skills to exercise informed choice.

→ **Lack of information** – for choice to be effective, consumers need access to good quality information about the choices available. Such information is often not available.

→ **Over-capacity and waste** – to enable choice to be exercised, there needs to be some degree of over-capacity in the supply system and this implies wastage of resources.

→ **Inequity** – for a variety of reasons (e.g. education, health) exercising choice is easier for the better off in society because of, for example, transport considerations. This may be seen as inequitable.

Inspection

There are many examples of public services that are regularly inspected by some form of government agency, which reports on the standards of service provided, areas for improvement, etc. The results of these inspections are in the public domain. Some examples of such inspection regimes are as follows:

→ **Schools** – local authority schools and some other services are subject to periodic inspection by the Office for Standards in Education (OFSTED).

→ **Health** – both public and private health care providers are inspected by the Health Care Commission (HCC).

→ **Social care** – both public and private providers of social care are inspected by the Commission for Social Care Inspection (CSCI).

The latter two agencies (HCC and CSCI) have now been merged.

However, the approach to inspection is not standardised and will vary from case to case. For example, the HCC make use of data submitted by the health providers, which is analysed to draw conclusions about the services provided. Based on the results of this analysis, the HCC will undertake a sample of on-site inspection visits of certain providers. On the other hand, OFSTED visits all education providers under its remit. However, their aim is broadly the same – to identify which organisations are doing well, what they are doing badly and how standards can be raised and performance improved.

Improved leadership and management development

At the 'softer' end of public service management there has been recognition that improvements in public services requires effective management skills, with particular emphasis being placed on leadership qualities. To promote this improvement in management and leadership there have been a number of themes, including:

→ substantial investment in leadership and management training for public service managers;

→ secondments of public service managers to other organisations;

→ recruitment of public service managers from the private sector;

→ improved appraisal procedures for public service managers;

→ some use of performance related pay for managers.

Emphasis on governance and accountability

During the 1990s there were a number of high profile 'financial scandals' in the private sector (e.g. Maxwell, BCCI) which identified the lack of awareness and ineffectiveness of many non-executive directors in those companies. These led to the publication of the Cadbury Report on Corporate Governance (and other similar reports), which was concerned with improving the accountability and governance arrangements in private companies.

Around the same time there were also a number of 'scandals' in the public sector which caused adverse publicity and many critical reports from bodies such as the Public Accounts Committee, the National Audit Office, etc. Again, these events seem to suggest a certain ineffectiveness of non-executive directors, governors, etc. in knowing what the PSO was actually doing. As a consequence there has been a great emphasis on applying the principles of corporate governance to PSOs, and this has led to developments such as the formation of audit committees, strengthened internal and external audit to provide greater assurance to non-executives and codes of practice and training for non-executives, etc.

Joined-up service provision

On coming to power, the current Labour government placed great emphasis on improvements in what was termed 'joined-up' government. This implies greater collaborative working between government departments and other PSOs in order to deliver more cohesive and coordinated services in a more efficient manner.

At the central government level a number of changes were made to foster joined-up government. These include structural changes such as the creation of Cabinet committees and inter-departmental committees of civil servants to address cross-departmental issues such as basic skills, environmental issues, etc., and the creation of Public Service Agreements covering several departments which committed those departments to a shared set of service objectives (via PSAs) aimed at fostering improvements in collaborative working between departments.

At the local level, multi-agency partnerships were created involving statutory agencies such as local authorities, NHS bodies, police authorities, etc. and third sector organisations which aimed to plan and deliver services in a more coherent and coordinated way. These partnerships have now been supplemented by the requirement to produce Local Area Agreements (LAA) which set out how the various agencies will contribute to service delivery in a coherent manner. Other developments which have fostered this joined-up working at the local level include the use of common need assessment processes, the provision of joint training for staff from the various agencies and the sharing of information resources between agencies, etc.

The impact of public service reform on financial management practices

In Chapter 1 we identified that financial management in a PSO must be concerned with the following key issues:

→ Identifying and managing costs.

→ Having a financially viable strategy.

→ Applying effective budgeting approaches.

→ Using balanced pricing approaches.

→ Having effective performance management and improvement.

→ Having effective accountability and governance.

The impact of the public service reforms has been to put much greater emphasis on the importance of all these issues. These are discussed briefly below and will be developed further, in later chapters.

Identifying and managing costs

PSOs have had to become more sophisticated at identifying the costs of their various activities and services for a number of key reasons which derive from the public service reforms:

→ The separation of the commissioner and provider now means that prospective providers have to make bids or submissions to commissioners in order to be awarded the contracts to deliver services. To do this they will have to quote a price to the commissioner, and a key input to the pricing decision will be the costs of the services they propose to undertake.

→ Market testing and competition require in-house service units to bid to retain contacts in competition with private and third sector organisations. Again, a key input to the price they quote will be the costs of the services involved.

→ One key aspect of the drive for continuous performance improvement concerns improvements in resource efficiency. In order to identify cost savings in relation to their service activities, PSOs must first be aware of their current cost structures and how their costs compare with other PSO providers.

In spite of the improvements in costing that have taken place in PSOs there is still considerable scope for improvement.

Strategic financial planning

As a consequence of the public service reforms, PSOs have had to undertake major strategic changes in the volume, type, location and configuration of the services they provide. This is necessary in order to improve their service provision and to achieve the strategic objectives they have set themselves. In order for such strategic changes to be successfully achieved, it was important that the PSO undertook robust strategic financial planning. Part of this is having an awareness of the existing costs of activities and services but also an understanding of how those costs will change as the strategic change process proceeds.

However, not all strategic changes in PSOs have been successful and often projects were completed behind schedule and over-budget. This was often a failure of effective financial planning and this is perhaps the major weakness in financial management in PSOs and one which can result in a failure to achieve strategic objectives according to planned timescales, and/or a major overspend.

Budgeting systems

PSOs have been operating budgeting systems for many years and these systems have become increasingly sophisticated over time. We have seen enhanced delegation of budget responsibility within the organisation and this has been necessary to enable PSOs to deliver more flexible, more timely and better quality services. Also we have seen improvements in the speed, accuracy and comprehensiveness of the information given to managers for budgeting purposes.

In the future, it is hoped that budget systems will evolve further in order to achieve the following:

➜ To become more capable of fostering innovation and improvement in service delivery by empowering managers and service professionals.

➜ To be more adept at implementing the strategy of the PSO and helping it achieve its strategic objectives.

➜ To be one of the main drivers for performance improvement in the PSO.

Pricing

Although pricing has not traditionally been seen as a very important activity in PSOs, it is quite likely that constraints on public funds will lead PSOs to having to undertake a greater degree of service charging. In doing this they will have to seek a balance between raising revenue and delivering other non-financial objectives. Thus more sophisticated approaches to pricing will probably be necessary.

Performance

Financial management has, and will continue to have, a strong role in helping the PSO manage its performance and achieve continuous performance improvement, particularly in relation to efficiency and economy. Some aspects of this have involved:

➜ benchmarking the PSO's unit costs of service delivery against comparable organisations;

➜ evaluating prospective improvements in performance in financial terms;

➜ changing the focus of internal audit to focus more on value for money.

Accountability and governance

The emphasis on accountability and governance, anti-fraud measures and improvements in standards in public life has placed great emphasis within PSOs on improvements in a wide range of areas, such as financial control systems, financial information systems and flows, financial decision-making processes, training requirements, etc.

Conclusions

PSOs in the UK and other countries have had to undergo major reform and modernisation over the last 20–30 years. These reforms have been wide ranging and were necessary because of factors largely outside the control of government. For such reforms to be effective it has usually been necessary for there to be significant changes in the conduct of financial management within the PSOs. For example, in the internal health market of the early 1990s the implementation of the reform and the achievement of its objectives were seriously hampered by the absence of appropriate financial management arrangements.

Questions for discussion

→ How have the services provided by your organisation changed over the last 10–20 years (volumes, types, locations, etc.)?

→ What have been the causes of these changes?

→ What models of reform have been applied to your organisation?

→ What has worked well and what has not worked well?

Part 2

Financial management of public services: key aspects

Costing and costing systems in public service organisations

Learning objectives

→ To understand the importance of costing as a key role in financial management in PSOs

→ To understand the basic principles of costing within PSOs

→ To understand how cost information can be produced in PSOs, including the use of costing systems

→ To appreciate the trends in public services and how these may affect cost structures and costing systems

Introduction

In any organisation, an understanding of its cost structure and activities, and the way in which its costs might change in response to internal or external stimuli, is critical to the effective management of the organisation.

Cost information can be used for a variety of reasons in any type of organisation, and over a period of years the topic of costing has become increasingly topical within public services. In this chapter we consider the costing approaches and systems used in PSOs to produce that information.

In this chapter we will consider the following:

→ using cost information in PSOs;

→ basic principles of costing;

→ obtaining cost information in PSOs;

→ future public service trends and their impact on costing systems;

→ developing costing systems: the way forward.

Using cost information in PSOs

At the outset, it is important to consider why cost information is so important in PSOs and why it is the bedrock of effective financial management. Cost information in a PSO is needed for a variety of different purposes, but a few of the main purposes are summarised below.

Activity analysis

PSOs will, typically, produce routine information on the overall costs incurred (and income received) by the various departments or units in the organisation. Each department or unit often undertakes a wide range of service or support activities and delivers a range of public services. However, the cost information currently available is often not sufficient to enable an analysis to be undertaken of the financial perform- ance of the various discrete activities and services within a department, such as:

→ the costs incurred by a sub-unit of a department (e.g. the MRI unit of a hospital radiology department);

→ the costs incurred undertaking particular activities which comprise service deliv- ery (e.g. client assessment in social care);

→ the costs incurred by discrete services delivered within the department (e.g. domiciliary care for the elderly);

→ the costs incurred in delivering services to particular client groups (e.g. the elderly, women) or geographical areas.

Although such cost information is important and useful at all times, it will be of particular importance if the department or unit is currently generating an overall financial deficit but is unaware of which particular activities or services are respons- ible for that deficit. Alternatively, they may wish to know which areas of activity are profitable and can be developed. In either case, an analysis will be needed of the costs (and income) that can be attributed to discrete activities of a department (see Case study 4.1).

Strategic financial planning

As will be discussed in Chapter 5, it is inevitable that over a period of time PSOs will undergo some degree of strategic change in relation to organisational structures, methods of working, staffing levels, remuneration structures, etc. Examples include reducing the numbers of campuses in an FE college, merging several departments in a local authority, changing the balance between teachers and teaching assistants

---

Case study 4.1
Analysing PSO departmental costs using an activity analysis

After generating financial surpluses for many years, Hertwell University suddenly plunged to a financial deficit of £3 million. Analysis of departmental statements indicated that the 80% of the deficit could be attributed to the School of Modern Languages and the School of Biological Sciences. Both these schools had actually been generating deficits for some years but the situation was masked (or ignored) because it had been cancelled out by the surpluses generated by other schools. Now that the surpluses in the other schools had declined the impact of the two deficit schools came to prominence.

However, within the Schools of Modern Languages and Biological Sciences it was not obvious as to what were the real causes of the financial deficit, since no analysis of the costs of the various activities in the two schools was available. The existing financial systems in the university were not capable of providing this information and so a once-off exercise was undertaken in each school to analyse the income and costs of the schools by activity. This exercise involved collecting various types of financial and non-financial data and attributing costs to activities in accordance with suitable costing methods. In summary the exercise produced the following conclusions:

- **School of Modern Languages** – the school taught language programmes in a number of languages including certain minority languages. The results of the costing exercise showed that the bulk of the deficit could be attributed to just two of those minority languages.
- **School of Biological Sciences** – the school taught a large number of different modules which taken in combination contributed to degree courses. Up to a third of these modules had only a small number of students attending and thus resulted in the school generating its financial deficit.

In the light of this information, suitable action was taken by the university authorities to resolve the situation.

---

in a school and delivering certain health services in a primary care setting instead of in hospital.

These changes may be large or small but whatever the case they are likely to have significant financial implications, and it will be necessary to undertake some degree of strategic financial planning to assess this at each stage. It would be very difficult to undertake any robust strategic financial planning in the absence of information about the existing costs of the organisation and its activities. Thus, adequate and robust cost information is a pre-requisite of effective strategic financial planning in PSOs.

As part of this strategic planning process within a PSO, new project developments may be under consideration, such as new services, short-term projects or the planned construction of new buildings, etc. Before any of these projects are initiated, good practice requires a full project appraisal, and cost information will be needed to undertake the financial aspects of that appraisal.

Budget reporting

A key component of budgetary control is the availability of actual cost information to be compared with budgeted cost. This involves the provision of cost information which shows the income and expenditure of each department or unit for a particular month in question. The topic of budget management and budgetary control will be discussed in greater depth in Chapter 6.

Pricing

Clearly, costs are an important input into pricing decisions, but they are not the only or even the most important input. Hence, to make robust pricing decisions it is essential to have a minimal level of cost information concerning the activity or service to be priced. This will be discussed further in Chapter 7.

Performance improvement and benchmarking

The issue of improving performance, at both an operational and a strategic level, is a key theme in all PSOs today, given the likely levels of public funding that will be available in the future. The process of improving performance will focus on the 3Es (economy, effectiveness and efficiency) and financial management will have a key role to play, particularly in relation to the efficiency agenda. This will be more fully discussed in Chapter 8.

A key aspect of this is the availability of information about the current costs of activities and services and how such costs may have changed over time or may compare with other similar PSOs. It is common practice for PSOs to try and compare their performance against that of other comparable PSOs (or other organisations in general) as a means of identifying potential improvements in performance. Thus, it is quite common for a PSO to compare its financial performance (e.g. cost per pupil or course, cost per mile of road maintained, cost per book issued, cost per invoice paid, etc.) against that of other PSOs and to do this it is necessary to have information about the costs of one's own organisation. Benchmarking will be discussed more fully in Chapter 8.

Basic principles of costing

In considering the issue of costing in PSOs it is important to first outline some general principles of and approaches to costing. These include:

→ cost centres and resource types;

→ period costs and product costs;

→ direct costs and indirect costs;

→ fixed costs and variable costs;

→ total costs and marginal costs;

→ actual costs and target costs;

→ traditional overhead costing and Activity-Based Costing;

→ estimating costs.

Cost centres and resource types

Costing systems operate on the basis of two concepts, that of cost centres and resource types. Within any organisation the costing system will require each and every income or expenditure transaction to have two identifier codes attached to it, namely the cost centre to which it belongs and the type of resource involved.

Cost centres

A cost centre is essentially a form of conceptual 'bucket' where costs can be collected. Examples of cost centres in a factory would be a department, a machine or a product line. In a PSO, a cost centre could be any of the following:

→ a front-line service department (e.g. a local authority care home, a hospital ward);

→ a support department (a finance department, a maintenance department);

→ a specific service (e.g. kidney dialysis services, adult education programmes, fire prevention services);

→ a geographic area of service delivery;

→ a client group (e.g. children, elderly);

→ an individual employee (e.g. a hospital consultant, a teacher).

In PSOs the costing system will enable costs to be classified against each individual cost centre via the expenditure coding system. Each cost centre will have a discrete code and each item of expenditure will be given the appropriate cost centre code. In this way an analysis of expenditure by cost centre can be undertaken. In some cases, an item of income or expenditure may be assigned to several cost centres thus facilitating different types of analysis. However, the key issue is constructing a structure of cost centres that will meet the cost information needs of the PSO. The degree of analysis of cost information will be dependent on the cost centre structure used and the extent to which costs can be disaggregated.

Resource type

In any organisation, it is possible to classify the costs of the organisation or the costs of its discrete activities according to the type of resource being utilised. Different classifications are available, but a typical example would include: income, staff costs, cost of consumables, energy costs and cost of office supplies, etc.

In most parts of the public sector it is usually the case that a broadly standard approach to costing would be applied within one sector in order to facilitate comparisons between organisations in that sector. NHS organisations undertake costing using the methods outlined in the *NHS Costing Manual* (Department of Health, 2008). Thus, NHS Trusts could compare themselves with other NHS Trusts knowing their costs had been produced to a fair degree of uniformity. However, this standard approach to costing usually only applies at a fairly high level, and at lower levels the uniformity and thus the ability to compare breaks down (Prowle, 2007).

Period costs and product costs

These two approaches to costing need to be clearly distinguished. Whereas period costing is concerned with identifying the costs incurred by different parts (e.g. departments, units) of the organisation during a *discrete time period*, product costing is concerned with identifying the costs of each of the organisation's *products*. While product is a common and understandable term in relation to private sector organisations, the term is not so clearly understood in the public services sector and needs to be discussed further.

Whereas period costing in a PSO would involve identifying the monthly costs of, for example, academic departments in a college, wards and theatres in a hospital, individual departments and sub-departments in a local authority or central government departments, product cost information would imply information about the costs of services delivered by the organisation. Examples of products in PSOs include the following:

→ costs of treating specific clinical conditions in a hospital (e.g. cancer);
→ costs of delivering certain specific courses in an FE college;
→ costs of delivering preventative services in a fire and rescue authority;
→ costs of delivering domiciliary services to the elderly;
→ costs of processing a benefit claim in Jobcentre Plus.

Figure 4.1 Product costs and period costs

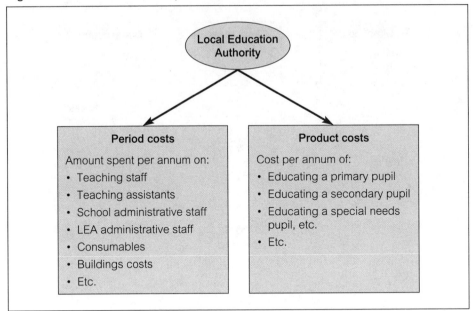

The relationship between product costs and period costs is illustrated in Figure 4.1 using a Local Education Authority.

Traditionally, product costing in PSOs has been limited but, for various reasons, PSOs have now become more sophisticated in their approach, which will necessarily involve them undertaking the following:

→ identifying their main discrete (product) service activities;

→ identifying the main cost elements associated with the delivery of each of those discrete service activities;

→ developing suitable approaches to attribute each cost element to a discrete service activity.

Direct costs and indirect costs

There is a commonly held view that the cost of a particular product or activity is a unique and precise figure. This is not the case. Cost data are derived by means of a series of costing approaches and assumptions, and different approaches and assumptions will give different costs for the same activity or product. Thus, when examining the costs associated with a particular product or activity it is vital to understand both the costing approaches that were applied and the assumptions underlying the approaches. It is therefore essential to understand the concepts of cost centres, and the direct and indirect costs associated with those cost centres.

Figure 4.2 Direct costs and indirect costs

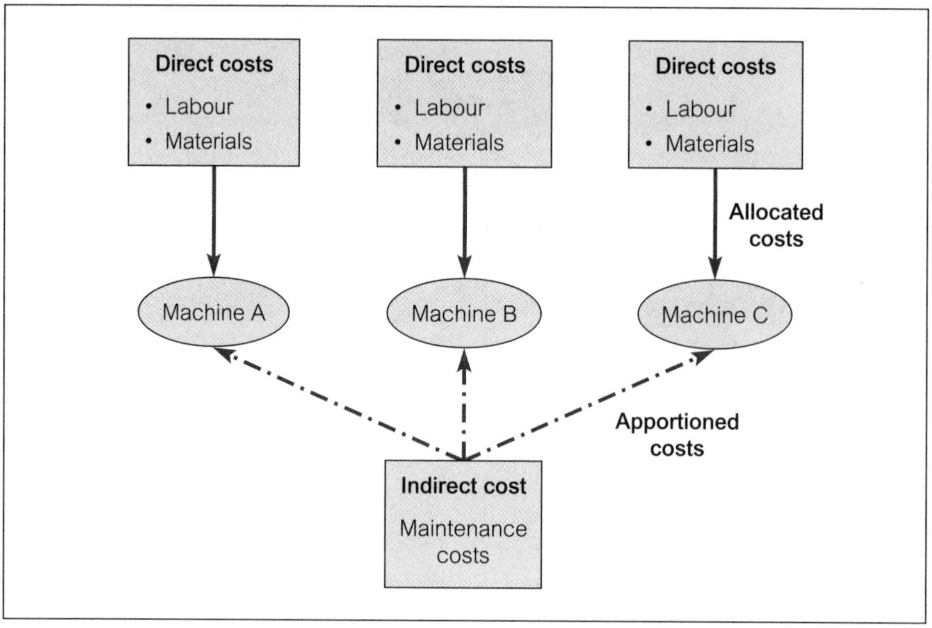

The differentiation between direct costs and indirect costs is fundamental to cost accounting practice but is frequently misunderstood, even by some accountants. Often the direct/indirect distinction is confused with the variable/fixed distinction (see below), with direct costs being seen as synonymous with variable costs and indirect costs as synonymous with fixed costs. This is a misunderstanding since the two types of cost classification are based on different principles.

The distinction between direct and indirect costs relates to the different ways in which costs are recorded against cost centres. Consider the factory-based example in Figure 4.2.

In this factory there are three machines, representing our cost centres, and management wishes to know the *total* cost of running each machine. Certain costs, such as labour and materials, are referred to as direct costs since the information systems in the factory will identify where each different cost has been incurred. Timesheets will record the labour hours/costs incurred on each machine and the stores issue system will show the materials costs consumed by each machine so these direct costs can be *allocated* to each machine. When looking at the costs of the maintenance department, no record is available of the maintenance time spent on each machine and so it is not possible to *allocate* maintenance as a direct cost to each machine. To obtain the *total* running cost for each machine it is necessary to *apportion* or spread the total costs of the maintenance department to each machine *in a reasonable manner*. The key phrase here is 'in a reasonable manner' and the basis chosen must be regarded as a proxy for the maintenance requirements of each machine. For this example we can state the following:

→ **Reasonable basis for apportionment:**
  - running hours of each machine;
  - age of each machine (in years);
  - product output of each machine.

→ **Unreasonable basis for apportionment:**
  - age (in years) of the machine operator;
  - height of each machine.

Thus, the total cost of running each machine will depend on the method of apportionment chosen for maintenance costs and different methods of apportionment will produce different total cost figures.

Let us now apply this same model to a PSO using the hospital-based examples shown in Figure 4:3.

In situation A the cost centre used is a hospital ward. In such a ward, two (of many) items of expenditure would be medical and surgical supplies (MSS) and electricity. MSS would be easily attributed to an individual ward through available supplies information systems. Hence, this cost can be regarded as a direct cost and is *allocated* to the ward. Electricity costs are also a cost of running the ward but usually the only information available concerns the electricity costs of the hospital as a whole. Hence, to obtain the total running cost of the ward it is necessary to *apportion* the total hospital electricity cost over wards using an appropriate method, for example the floor area or volume of each ward involved. Thus, the figure for the total running cost of the ward will depend on the apportionment bases chosen for indirect costs such as electricity.

In situation B, the cost centre used is now an individual patient residing in the ward and the two items of cost considered are drugs costs and, again, MSS. Drugs costs

Figure 4.3 Direct and indirect costs – hospital examples

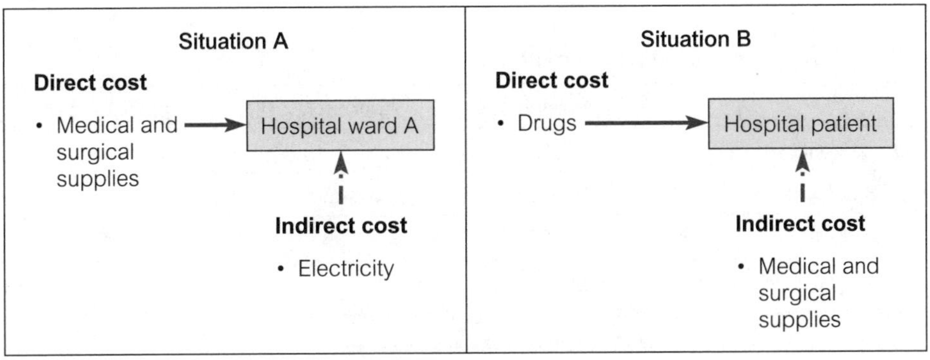

are easily attributed to an individual patient through the patient's prescription record, which is mandatory for clinical purposes. Hence, the drugs costs can be regarded as a direct cost and are *allocated* to the patient. However, it is unlikely that the ward has a system which records issues of MSS to an individual patient. Since MSS are also a cost of caring for the patient an element of this cost must be included in the total patient cost. Hence, to obtain the total cost of caring for the patient it is necessary to *apportion* the total ward MSS costs over all patients in the ward. Using an appropriate method, for example length of stay (in days).

A number of points should be emphasised regarding this example:

→ **Determinants of direct and indirect cost** – it will be noted that MSS was a direct cost to the ward cost centre but an indirect cost to the patient cost centre. Thus it is not the inherent nature of a cost type which determines whether it is direct or indirect. What determines whether a cost can be directly allocated or indirectly apportioned is the sophistication of the organisation's information systems. If the hospital had decided to install electric meters on each ward then the electricity consumed by each ward would be known exactly and electricity costs would become a direct cost of the ward instead of an indirect cost. A similar situation would occur if the hospital installed an information system which recorded MSS issues to patients.

→ **Basis of apportionment** – where cost apportionment is applied it is important to realise that there is no single correct basis of cost apportionment. As long as a particular basis of apportionment is 'reasonable' in specific circumstances then it may be used to derive total costs.

→ **Mix of allocation and apportionment** – total costs are derived from a combination of direct costs, which are directly allocated, and indirect costs, which are apportioned in some way or another. Different approaches and assumptions will give different results. Consider the simple example shown in Figure 4.4.

In each case it is the same patient, lying in the same bed, suffering from the same illness and having the same treatment. The only thing that has changed is

Figure 4.4 Variations in costing methods

	Approach 1 (£)	Approach 2 (£)	Approach 3 (£)
Drugs costs (allocated)	500	500	500
MSS costs (apportioned)	200[a]	450[b]	150[c]
Total cost	700	950	650

[a] MSS costs apportioned over patients pro-rata to length of stay
[b] MSS costs apportioned over patients pro rata to length of stay weighted by complexity of the case
[c] MSS costs shared equally over all patients irrespective of length of stay

the method of apportioning indirect MSS costs and, as shown, different methods give different costs. The position would be even more complex if we incorporated all of the costs associated with the patient.

Thus there is no single 'correct' or 'accurate' cost. The end result of a costing exercise is dependent upon the balance between allocation and apportionment of costs and the method of cost apportionment used. Two different costing methods will give two different results, both of which are reasonable. A number of important managerial issues flow from this.

The degree of costing accuracy needed by the organisation will depend on issues such as the type of organisation, its geographic location, its current efficiency level, the degree of competition it faces in the market, and so on. There is no simple answer to this question. For example, a PSO facing little competition will probably have less need for accurate cost information than a PSO facing tough competition. Thus, in designing a costing system there is always a balance to be struck between the need for accuracy of cost information and the costs of obtaining that information. Hence, a PSO must evaluate both the benefits of better cost information and the 'costs of costing'. Furthermore, although some commonality of structure is possible no standard costing system can be defined for all PSOs. PSOs vary considerably in their needs for financial information, the degree of accuracy required, and the resources they can devote to providing that information. Hence, each PSO must make its own judgement on this matter.

Fixed costs and variable costs

The distinction between a fixed cost and a variable cost is simple in principle but difficult to draw in practice. It is essentially concerned with the way in which the magnitude of a particular cost varies in relation to the activity or throughput level of the organisation. In simple terms, three different types of cost behaviour can be identified (see Figure 4.5):

→ **Variable costs** – the cost varies directly with the level of activity in the organisation. In a factory setting, direct materials may be regarded as a cost which varies directly with the level of production.

→ **Fixed costs** – the cost is unaffected by the level of activity in the organisation. In a factory setting, the rent would usually be fixed and would not vary, whatever the production level.

→ **Semi-fixed costs** – the above two examples are extremes, and in practice most cost types will be neither totally fixed nor completely variable. These are referred to as semi-fixed or semi-variable costs.

Figure 4.5 Variations in cost behaviour

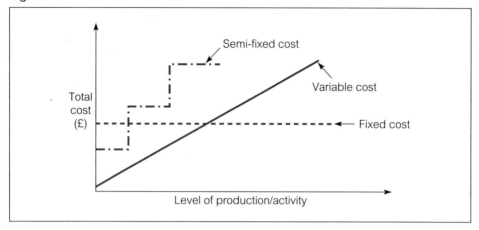

Figure 4.6 considers some possible examples from PSOs, with suggestions as to the likely cost behaviour in each case.

However, the classification of costs into variable, fixed and semi-variable costs is a simplification, and real cost profiles will be more like the ones shown in Figure 4.7.

A word of warning is needed about such a simplified approach to cost behaviour. The type of cost behaviour encountered may not always be clear and may depend on the way in which the organisation procures goods and services. For example, in Figure 4.6 it is suggested that catering is a semi-fixed cost in relation to student numbers. This is because small changes in student numbers will not result in changes to catering staff numbers (and hence pay) but will increase the cost of catering consumable. However, if the college procured catering services from a private contractor on the basis of cost per meal delivered then catering would become increasingly a variable cost since increases or decreases in student meals would lead to an immediate increase/decrease in the costs.

Total costs and marginal costs

Total cost implies inclusion of all the costs associated with a particular activity. This will incorporate both the direct costs of an activity and a share of the indirect costs apportioned to that activity. This is illustrated in Figure 4.8 by a simple example concerned with the costs of manufacturing a product.

The marginal costs are the incremental costs of producing additional units of the product and will differ from the total cost because of the issues of fixed and variable costs mentioned above. If production is increased, some costs will increase while others will remain unchanged.

Figure 4.6 Cost behaviour in PSOs

PSO	Type of cost	Activity measure	Variable	Fixed	Semi-fixed	Comments
Hospital	Drugs	Number of patients	*			
School	Teachers' pay	Number of pupils			*	Costs will not change for a certain change in pupil numbers, but ultimately a step-change will occur
University	Buildings maintenance	Numbers of students		*		Unlikely levels of planned maintenance will be affected by student numbers. Fault repairs may be affected
College	Catering	Numbers of students			*	Consumables costs will vary but staffing costs may be fixed
Ambulance service	Fuel costs	Numbers of miles run	*			
Hospital	Nursing pay	Numbers of patients			*	Costs will not change for a certain change in patient activity, but ultimately a step-change will occur
Fire authority	Equipment leasing	Number of fire incidents		*		

Figure 4.7 Profile of cost behaviour

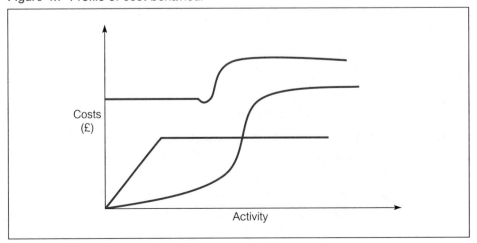

Figure 4.8 Total costing

Volume of production = 1,000 units

Costs of production:

	Total costs (£)	Unit cost (£p)
Materials	2,500	2.50
Labour	7,500	7.50
Variable overhead	2,000	2.00
Fixed overhead	1,000	1.00
Total	**13,000**	**13.00**

Thus the *total* cost of producing one unit of the product is £13.

Figure 4.9 Marginal costing

Costs of an additional 50 units of production based on total costs:

= Increased units × total unit cost

= 50 × £13.00

= **£650**

Costs of an additional 50 units of production based on marginal costs:

= Materials + labour + variable overhead + fixed overhead

= £125 + nil + £100 + nil

= **£225**

Figure 4.9 shows that the costs of an additional 50 units of production calculated on a total cost basis are £650.

However, the marginal costs of increasing production by 50 units (i.e. 5%) are only £225. The following points should be noted:

→ **Materials** – producing 50 additional units of product will result in an incremental or marginal cost in materials of £125 (i.e. 50 × £2.50).

→ **Variable overhead** – since this overhead is defined as variable it will vary directly with the level of production. Thus, increasing production by 50 units will result in an incremental or marginal cost of £100 being incurred (50 × £2).

→ **Fixed overhead** – by definition this overhead cost is fixed and will not change with increases in production. Thus the marginal cost in this area is nil.

→ **Labour** – this is the most problematic area since it is not clear what impact an increase in production of 5% will have on labour costs. Three scenarios are possible:

(1) The increase in production can be absorbed by the existing labour force and thus the marginal cost will be nil.

(2) To cope with the increase in production employees will need to work overtime at a premium. Thus, the marginal costs of increasing production will depend on the overtime hours required and the overtime premium paid.

(3) To cope with the increase in production additional employees will need to be recruited. Thus the marginal costs of increasing production will depend on the numbers and pay of additional employees needed. In this example we have assumed that the increased production can be met by the existing labour force.

This distinction between total and marginal costs is an important one and must be fully appreciated. The relevance of this distinction to PSOs can be demonstrated in the following situations:

→ **Financial forecasting** – PSOs will need to forecast the financial effect of changes in future activity levels, and to do this they will need to distinguish between fixed costs, variable costs and semi-fixed costs. For example, if a local authority children's centre planned to increase the size of its intake then estimating the incremental costs using total average costs would probably result in an overestimate since the total average cost would include a proportion of costs, such as buildings maintenance, heat and light, etc., that would not increase if the child intake was higher. Furthermore, in terms of staffing there may be some existing slack capacity and increased workload can be absorbed without any cost increases.

→ **Pricing decisions** – the distinction between marginal and total costs is important for pricing purposes. Although the general rule is that prices should be set by reference to total costs, circumstances arise where they can be set by reference to marginal costs. This is discussed in the next chapter under marginal cost pricing.

Actual costs and target costs

Actual costing is clearly concerned with establishing the actual costs incurred by an organisation in operating departments and delivering goods and services to users using the various costing methods already described.

Target costing is defined as:

a cost management tool for reducing the overall cost of a product over its entire life cycle with the help of production, engineering, research and design.

Wikipedia (2009b)

A target cost is the maximum amount of cost that can be incurred on a product and with it the organisation can still earn the required profit margin from selling that product at the market price (Wikipedia, 2009b). Target costing involves setting a target cost by subtracting a desired profit margin from a competitive market price.

Target costing is primarily used in commercial organisations. Japanese companies have developed target costing as a response to the problem of controlling and reducing costs over the product life cycle. To compete effectively, organisations must continually redesign their products (or services) in order to shorten product life cycles. The planning, development and design stage of a product is therefore critical to an organisation's cost management process. Considering possible cost reduction at this stage of a product's life cycle (rather than during the production process) is now one of the most important issues facing management accountants in industry. Examples of decisions made at the design stage that impact on the cost of a product include the number of different components, whether the components are standard or not and the ease of changing tools.

At first glance, target costing might not seem that appropriate to public services since most don't have a market price let alone deduct a profit margin to get a target price. However, this is not necessarily true for a number of reasons.

First, in some situations, PSOs work in a competitive market where there is a ruling price and so target pricing can be as applicable here as in the commercial sector, for example local authority leisure services. Second, even where there is no competitive market, PSOs have to deliver services in an environment of scarce resources. Thus, a form of target costing could be used to design services that will fit the resources available rather than the other way around. Take, for example, the costs of delivering a short course at an FE college. Using a form of target costing, the following approach could be applied:

→ Identify some comparable colleges and comparable courses.

→ Try to establish the costs of delivering comparable courses in each of those colleges.

→ Choose a target cost in line with comparable colleges but with some efficiency savings if possible and taking into account the willingness to pay of local consumers.

→ Design and develop an approach to such short courses which will meet this target cost.

Traditional overhead costing and Activity-Based Costing

Activity-Based Costing (ABC) is an approach to costing that was developed in the USA and subsequently became popular in the UK in the 1990s (Kaplan and Bruns,

1987). ABC was developed by manufacturing industry, which recognised that over a period of 40–50 years, the composition of product costs had altered substantially. The main reasons were:

→ **direct labour** – through the introduction of automation and IT the direct labour element of product costs had fallen dramatically;

→ **direct materials** – the direct materials element of product costs had remained largely unchanged;

→ **overheads** – overhead functions, such as materials handling, quality assurance and marketing, had grown substantially and the element of product cost they represented had grown to match the fall in direct labour costs.

As seen earlier, traditional approaches to costing involved the allocation of direct labour and materials costs while overhead costs were usually apportioned using an appropriate basis. The advocates of ABC recognised that applying such crude approaches to the treatment of overhead costs, which were such a high proportion of cost, was severely distorting total product costs. ABC uses a more sophisticated approach to attributing overhead costs to products, which involves identifying what activities in the organisation actually 'drive' the level of particular types of cost rather than a statistical share. It therefore aims to eliminate much of the distortion.

Using material stores costs as an example, the traditional crude approach would be to apportion the total material store costs over products pro rata to the volume or value of the products involved. On the other hand, ABC recognises that material store costs have three different elements and that a different activity drives the level of cost in each case (see Figure 4.10).

ABC would analyse the numbers of batches of materials received relating to the different products and apportion materials receipt costs pro-rata to the numbers of batches in each case. Different calculations would be needed for materials storage and materials issue.

ABC is also of great applicability in PSOs. The principles of identifying activities and establishing the cost drivers apply in public services as well as in manufacturing industry. Using domiciliary social care as an example, a simple ABC model which identifies the activities and associated cost drivers of service delivery would be as shown in Figure 4.11.

By applying the ABC approach a cost model can be developed which identifies the discrete activities involved in each specific service and the cost drivers for each of those activities. Consequently, using this model, the impact on overall costs of changing the way in which services are delivered can be assessed. Thus, ABC may assist in getting a better understanding of how PSO costs behave, although two common problems can arise:

Figure 4.10 Stores costs – traditional and ABC approaches

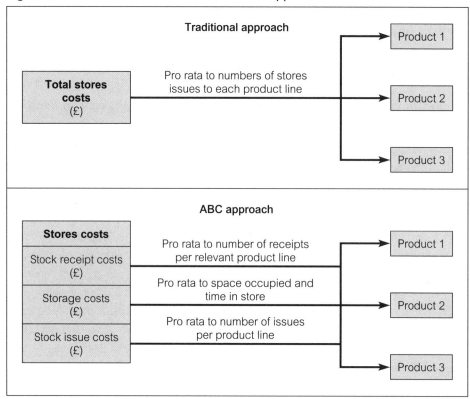

→ the lack of suitable data on activities to establish bases for cost attribution;

→ the relatively high costs associated with setting up an ABC system.

Estimating costs

There will be many instances where organisations will need to make estimates of costs. This could be the costs of undertaking a new activity or changing the level of existing activities. In estimating the costs of an activity, the purely variable costs and the purely fixed costs are easy to estimate but the difficulty comes in relation to semi-fixed costs, where the relationship between activity and costs may be unclear. There are a number of different approaches to estimating costs that can be used.

The managerial judgement approach involves managers using their judgement to classify costs as exhibiting certain behaviours. From these subjective profiles of behaviour the magnitude of semi-fixed costs can be estimated.

The engineering approach involves studying the processes that result in the occurrence of a cost and focuses on the relationships that should exist between inputs and outputs. It may also involve the use of time and motion studies (or task

Figure 4.11 Activity-Based Costing in PSOs

Domiciliary social care	
Activity	**Cost drivers**
Initial client assessment	• Numbers of clients • Complexity of client needs • Complexity of assessment process • Distance between clients
Direct services delivery	• Numbers of clients • Numbers of visits per client per day • Volume and type of services needed to be delivered (determined by need, independent living skills, etc.) • Skill level of staff used to deliver services
Record keeping	• Numbers of clients • Complexity of record keeping • Ease of record keeping
Supervision (including client satisfaction)	• Numbers of clients • Distance between clients • Numbers of staff

analysis), where employees are observed as they undertake work tasks, and activity-based approaches extend task analysis to the study of indirect activities and costs.

There are also a number of approaches to estimating costs using quantitative methods. A scatter diagram can be plotted, enabling one to visualise the relationship between cost and the level of activity and make estimates accordingly. Alternatively, the high–low method involves taking the two observations with the highest and lowest levels of activity and then calculating the cost function as being somewhere in between the two extremes. However, both these methods lack quantitative rigour and to counter this, recourse can be made to multiple regression analysis (Drury, 2004). This is a statistical technique that aims to identify a quantitative relationship between a dependent variable (i.e. costs) and one or a number of independent variables which are believed to influence that level of cost. Multiple regression equations take the following form:

$$c = m_1f_1 + m_2f_2 + m_3f_3 + m_4f_4 + \ldots + z$$

where c = cost, f = the factors that drive costs, m = the coefficient of each factor, and z = residual factor.

By collecting enough data points for each magnitude of cost (and the associated magnitude of the factors) a regression equation can be developed where the various coefficients and the residual factor can be established. This equation is then, effectively, a financial model and the estimated costs of changes in activity can be estimated by substituting suitable numbers into the regression equation and calculating the costs involved.

In public services, the multiple regression approach could be used, for example, to make estimates of changes in hospital ward costs following changes to the type and level of activity undertaken by the ward. A multiple regression equation can be identified which provides a good predictor of ward costs according to the following model:

$$
\begin{aligned}
\text{Total cost} = \ & m_1 \times \text{patient numbers on ward} \\
& + m_2 \times \text{average length of patient stay} \\
& + m_3 \times \text{average age of patients on ward} \\
& + m_4 \times \text{diagnostic mix of patients} \\
& + m_5 \times \text{severity level of patients on ward} \\
& + c
\end{aligned}
$$

Another similar study has used multiple regression analysis to forecast the drugs costs of patients in hospital (Phillips *et al.*, 1986).

Quite often much of the variation in costs can be explained by just two or three factors, with the remaining factors having only limited impact. Also, it is important to look at both the regression equation and the independent variables being used to see if they make sense. It is easy for regression equations to suggest relationships which are spurious in nature.

However, a word of warning is necessary. There are a number of reasons why these regression equations will not prove stable over time, including:

→ **learning effects** – over a period of time staff become more proficient at performing tasks with the result that the time taken and the costs involved reduce over time;

→ **practice changes** – changes in professional practices are introduced which will impact on the time taken and the costs involved;

→ **staff changes** – new staff will impact (either positively or negatively) on the time taken and the costs involved and also in the use of other resources.

Obtaining cost information in PSOs

Having discussed the potential (current and future) uses and importance of cost information in PSOs and the various principles of costing, it is now appropriate to consider the ways in which this cost information might be generated within the organisation.

Figure 4.12 Cost information in PSOs

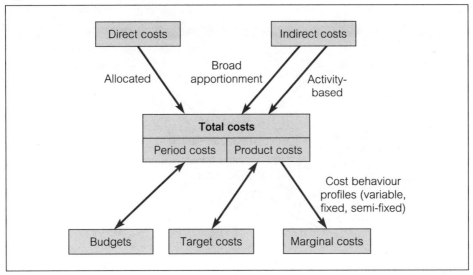

Derivation of cost information

The basic arrangement for getting cost information, incorporating the principles described earlier, is shown in Figure 4.12. The figure shows that the total (actual) costs of a unit or a product (service activity) can be obtained by a combination of allocating direct costs to the unit or product in question. Indirect costs also have to be attributed and this can be done either using broad apportionments or some form of ABC. Once established the marginal cost element of this total cost can be established by reference to the profiles of cost behaviour for each cost type (e.g. variable, fixed, semi-fixed). Also the total (actual) cost can (if desired) be compared with the relevant target cost where available. Finally, period costs can be compared to budgets.

An example of such an approach is shown in Figure 4.13 based on the establishment of course costs in a college of further education.

This costing process operates on the basis of a downward flow of costs:

→ The costs of two support departments (estates and HR) are attributed to various teaching departments in the college. This may be done using a crude overhead recovery method or some form of ABC. A proportion of these costs will go to the business department and the remainder to other teaching departments (not shown). There will be other support departments as well but for simplicity these are omitted.

→ Certain costs (administrative staff costs and consumables costs) are directly allocated to the business department and are shown alongside the indirect costs attributed to the business department.

Figure 4.13 Generating cost information in PSOs

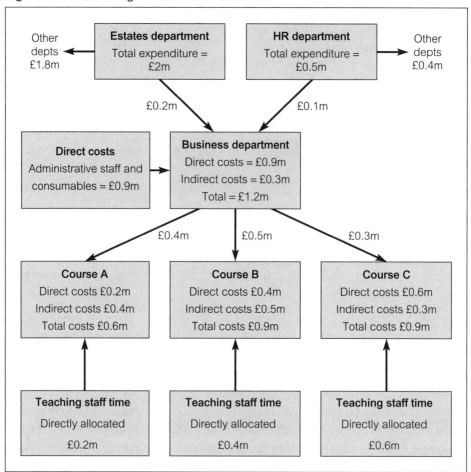

→ The total costs of the business department (direct and indirect) are then attributed to the three courses delivered by the department, again using some reasonable basis of attribution.

→ Teaching staff costs are directly allocated (via a manpower planning system) to the three courses delivered by the business department. These costs are combined with the course's share of the costs of the central business department to give a total course cost.

The results of this exercise will be information on the costs of delivering each course and from this the cost per student can be calculated. However, the costs shown have been derived from the methods of costing employed, and a different costing approach could produce different cost figures.

Approaches to deriving cost information

If a PSO has a need for a particular type of cost information then there are three main ways in which this information could be produced using the principles described above:

→ via main financial systems of the PSO;

→ via a special exercise;

→ via new financial systems.

Main financial systems

All PSOs will have main financial systems to manage the finances of the organisation. The details of such systems will be discussed in Chapter 12, but it will suffice to say here that such financial systems will record the individual financial transactions (e.g. invoice payment, employee payment, etc.) of the organisation and this will form the basis for completion of the financial accounts of the organisation and provide a range of financial information for management. The capabilities of these financial systems to produce detailed costing information will vary from place to place and no generalisations can be made. However, it is probably true to say that in most PSOs that the minimum capabilities of the main financial systems to produce cost information can be summarised as follows:

→ The direct running costs (pay and non-pay) of departments are attributed to those individual departments, with a further sub-analysis to units within those departments.

→ The costs of support services are attributed to individual support departments and such costs may subsequently be attributed to individual front-line departments using a broad-based method of apportionment.

→ Within departments, only limited information would usually be available on the costs of discrete activities and services delivered by the department. For example, FE colleges would not have routine cost information about course costs and NHS Trusts would not normally have routine cost information about disease or specialty costs.

→ Information on the depreciation costs of buildings, equipment, etc. would be limited and such costs would not usually be attributed to individual departments or activities. In the past this may not have been seen as a problem but, as noted later, the growth in the use of IT in public service provision may provoke a rethink.

The above is very much a generalisation and clearly there will be PSOs who have much more sophisticated costing systems. However, the above comments imply that the range and quality of cost information that can be generated by existing costing systems in PSOs is often somewhat limited.

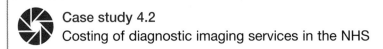

Case study 4.2
Costing of diagnostic imaging services in the NHS

Diagnostic imaging services are provided in all large acute NHS hospitals and information on the comparative costs of hospitals was required. Unfortunately the necessary cost information was not available from existing costing systems and so a specific study of the costs of undertaking these services was undertaken by using sample costing data from four large NHS Trusts. This exercise required staff to give estimates about time spent on various procedures, etc.

The results of this costing exercise are shown below by giving the calculated cost per imaging procedure for each NHS Trust and for four types of procedures.

	Trust A (£)	Trust B (£)	Trust C (£)	Trust D (£)	Weighted mean (£)
Plain X-rays	34.82	30.04	26.79	31.95	30.77
Ultrasound	21.45	23.65	49.71	42.06	29.12
CT scanning	54.33	79.81	101.20	76.71	78.43
MRI scanning	213.05	209.46	197.82	102.40	177.81

The results of this exercise show considerable variations between NHS Trusts for what were thought to be broadly similar procedures. Further examination of the costing data and other supporting data showed that the cost variations could be attributed to three main causes:

Variation in operational imaging practices
Several variations in operational practices have contributed to variations in cost:

- **Procedure mix** – the trusts involved in the project showed significant variations in the mix of procedures within a main procedure group.
- **Practice models** – there exist different models of imaging practice between trusts.
- **Outsourcing** – in one trust, a significant proportion (67%) of the conduct of MRI investigations was outsourced to a private provider.

Variations in accounting and costing practice
The following contributed to cost variations:

- **Analysis of imaging department resources** – methods of attribution of costs within the imaging department were undertaken with different degrees of sophistication.
- **Hospital overhead costs of imaging department** – the method and accuracy of apportioning hospital overhead costs to the imaging department and to its sub-sections varied between trusts in method and sophistication.

- **Equipment costs** – within trusts there are different approaches to acquiring imaging equipment (e.g. purchase, lease), which, in turn, has implications for procedure costs. Also, in some trusts, imaging equipment had been fully depreciated and so there was no depreciation cost included.

Variations in data accuracy

- **Forecasting accuracy** – variations were observed in the accuracy of estimates of staff time and consumables costs per procedure provided by the trusts for costing purposes.

Case study 4.3
Inadequate PSO costing systems

Manware County Council has operated a well-known set of financial systems for many years and these systems have been found adequate for normal management purposes. However, changes in policy and pressure on resources have meant that in the last three years there have been increasing demands for more detailed costing information within the council.

Unfortunately, the age of the main financial systems has meant that it does not have the functionality to produce the information needed by management, and the council is unwilling to replace its main systems until a shared service project (with two other councils) comes on stream in two years' time.

In the meantime, three departments of the council (schools, social services and leisure) have adopted interim solutions. This has involved developing interfaces between the main financial ledger and stand-alone departmental systems in order to download financial and other data to departmental level. This data is then analysed at departmental level and appropriate cost management reports produced. The information produced is adequate but, even with the automated interfaces, the task of producing the departmental reports is quite heavy in terms of finance staff time and thus the whole arrangement can only be regarded as an interim solution.

Special costing exercises

If the existing costing systems cannot produce the information needed or cannot be 'tweaked' to produce that information, then it may be necessary to undertake one or more discrete special exercises. Such exercises involve collecting data on activity and costs in order to undertake a one-off (or infrequent) costing exercise designed to produce the information needed.

The data for such exercise can be collected in a number of ways, including surveys of staff to obtain estimates of the time spent on activities, sample surveys of consumables used in relation to particular activities or observations of activities to identify the resources (and hence costs) used. The data obtained can then be analysed manually or by means of a spreadsheet.

Such special exercises may be time consuming and expensive to undertake and hence should be treated with caution. They may be appropriate where a one-off view of costs is appropriate, but if such cost information is needed regularly than it would be more appropriate to implement a new costing system.

New costing systems

In situations where the existing costing system is deemed inadequate and the conduct of special exercises will not give the routine cost information required by management, the only remaining alternative is to acquire some form of new costing system. There are two approaches to this:

→ Procure a completely new suite of financial systems which incorporate the costing module appropriate to the information needs of the organisation. This will be an expensive proposition and not one likely to be considered if the existing suite of financial systems is not seen as being ready for replacement. If the PSO aims to go down this route then normal systems design and procurement arrangements for IS/IT need to be applied.

→ Procure a system which would be an 'add on' to the existing financial systems and which would provide the costing analysis needed to produce the cost information required. It is quite common in large organisations such as universities or local authorities to see individual departments use such systems to take financial information from the financial ledger and undertake secondary cost analysis for the department's own purposes. Sometimes such systems may be a suitably designed spreadsheet but special proprietary systems can be purchased.

Future public service trends and their impact on costing systems

Costing systems are not static in nature but need to evolve and change in accordance with changes in the PSO and its operating environment. In the future there could be significant changes in PSO costing requirements and costing systems as a consequence of such factors (see Figure 4.14).

Figure 4.14 Trends and their impact on costing systems

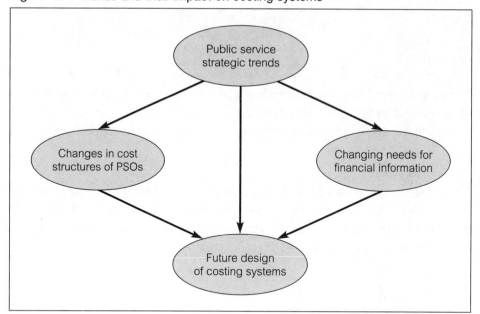

Strategic trends

A number of strategic trends can be identified, and these are outlined below.

Changes in strategic direction

In some PSOs, or parts of PSOs, we can anticipate some changes in strategic direction over the next few years. This means substantial changes in the range of service being delivered and/or the method of delivery. Examples of such strategic change may include enhanced delivery of services through partnership working at the local level, greater focus on preventative services in, for example, health care and children's social care, or privatisation of certain state activities such as some aspects of the employments and benefits service.

Changes in organisational arrangements

In many PSOs, substantial organisational change can be anticipated, including the following, particularly in relation to support service departments.

Merger
Mergers of departments within a PSO or even mergers of more than one PSO. A recent example of the former is the merger of several departments to produce

a Children's Services department in a local authority. An example of the latter is the mergers of PCTs in the NHS. Further PSO mergers are very likely.

Automation

In line with trends in many other types of organisation, substantial investment in IT can be expected alongside a rationalisation of staffing structures. This may be accompanied by greater delegation to departments, although some PSOs may possibly move in the opposite direction and re-centralise some support services.

Support services

Central support services such as finance, HR and maintenance may have to operate on a 'trading basis' with user departments for the provision of some services. This would involve some form of service agreement between the user departments and the central departments delivering the support services.

Changes in fixed asset base

A number of changes in the fixed asset base of the PSO can also be anticipated.

Rationalisation of buildings and sites

Various forms of service rationalisation may also result in a rationalisation of buildings or even complete sites. Such changes are common in many parts of the public sector, such as the university and health sectors, and will substantial alter the fixed asset base of the PSO.

Investment in IT

In recent years, PSOs have invested substantial amounts of investment in information technology. This IT investment has not only involved the development of management information systems and communication systems (e.g. e-mail, telephone systems, etc.) but has also involved the increased use of IT in the provision of information to clients and the general public and as a means of service delivery. Examples of this include:

→ residents paying council tax over the Internet rather than by post or office visit;

→ universities and colleges delivering distance learning courses over the Internet;

→ using electronic patient records in the NHS as a means of improving clinical outcomes.

All of the above involve substantial IT investment, and this can be expected to continue.

Changes in working practices

Many aspects of the working practices of PSOs have been changing in recent years, and these changes can be expected to continue.

Outsourcing/shared services

For some organisations such as small district councils the development of shared service arrangements with other councils are potentially a major source of efficiency improvement services suitable for sharing include front-line services such as regulatory services as well as traditional back-office functions such as finance, HR, etc. In addition, some PSOs have substantially outsourced several aspects of service provision (with or without PFI) and this trend is expected to continue into the future. For some PSOs this will involve a shift from staffing costs to contracted services costs.

Changes in service location

In some PSOs there will continue to be changes in the location of service provision. This could involve, for example, greater service provision in community locations such as vacant shops, hospital services delivered in primary care premises, and education and training services delivered in dispersed communities.

Skill mix changes

It seems likely that there will continue to be shifts in the mix of skills applied to the delivery of public services. This could involve better matching of staff skills to the tasks required so that overall costs are lower and over-qualified staff are not used. Past examples of this include nursing assistants on wards and teaching assistants in classrooms. Future trends of this type include the use of family support workers to undertake the roles traditionally carried out by highly qualified health visitors.

Impact on PSO cost structures

The above factors taken together could have a dynamic and substantial impact on the cost structures of various PSOs and thus in five to ten years' time their cost structure can be expected to have changed considerably. This is a critical point, the importance of which cannot be over-stated, although the overall pace of such change is unclear and will vary between sectors and individual PSOs. Consequently, the pace of change in relation to cost structures will also vary considerably but the following general trends can be anticipated.

Capital costs

The level of capital-related costs (e.g. depreciation, maintenance) can be expected to change in response to increasing levels of investment in various aspects of IT and divestment of certain fixed assets, such as buildings, as a consequence of massive under-utilisation of the estate in some PSOs and changes in the location of service delivery.

Running costs

Running costs can also be expected to change, including a shift from running costs to capital costs as a consequence of automation, changes in the mix of running costs as a result of such things as skill mix changes and an increase in the level of costs shared with other organisations due to the implementation of shared services or outsourcing.

Changing needs for cost information

Finance is a key resource of a PSO and hence good quality information on the costs and revenues of the PSO is a pre-requisite for effective decision making. Looking ahead, there are a number of areas where an improved range of financial information will be required. Some of these areas are discussed below.

Financial strategy

The accelerating pace of change and the increased uncertainty this causes will necessitate the development of effective corporate strategies in PSOs, supported by a number of resource strands including, of course, financial strands or strategies. Experience has shown that the main responsibility for the development and promulgation of such financial strategies will fall on senior finance personnel, who will cascade the development of financial strategies throughout the PSO. To do this, they will need an increased range of financial information about the various activities of the PSO.

Internal resource allocation

PSOs require robust approaches to allocating resources internally in order to achieve equity between services and client groups and to facilitate the best use of public funding. As resources become tighter, the pressures to do this are likely to increase. A key aspect of internal resource allocation is knowing what things currently cost to provide, and such information is not always easily available in a PSO. Again this suggests a need for more sophisticated costing approaches.

Departmental activity analysis

As already noted, while the costs of individual departments in a PSO are always identified it is less common for more detailed information to be available about the costs of undertaking specific activities and delivering specific services from that department. However, the resource pressures likely to impact on PSOs over the next few years suggest that a greater analysis of costs *within* departments will be required in the future.

Pricing decisions

In Chapter 7 we discuss pricing in PSOs. The key message is that pricing of public services has not had much prominence in the past but is likely to be more important in the future. Cost information, which is a key element of pricing, will therefore need to improve.

Developing costing systems: the way forward

So far in this chapter it has been argued that strategic trends will have a radical impact on the cost structure of PSOs. Changes in managerial information require-ments will also influence the needs for cost information. Thus, it is very pertinent to ask whether the current approach and current generation of costing systems in the public sector will be adequate and appropriate. The answer to such a question is probably 'no' and therefore consideration needs to be given to the design of future PSO costing systems. The following issues can be considered as a focus for development work in relation to costing systems:

→ central support service cost attribution;

→ departmental cost attribution;

→ cost behaviour classification;

→ the level of disaggregation of costing.

Central support service cost attribution

The overall financial pressures on PSOs and the need for more accurate information on the costs of activities undertaken will mean that more sophisticated arrangements are likely to be needed in the future. There are a number of issues to consider:

Cost centre hierarchies

In attributing support service costs to service departments, it must be recognised that there is a degree of inter-dependence between support service departments, and that this can affect the treatment of such costs and the hierarchy of cost centres to be used. Two broad approaches can be applied, which are illustrated in Figure 4.15.

Model A is a simple model where the costs of each central support department are attributed to a service department using some suitable basis. Model B is a more

Figure 4.15 Alternative costing hierarchies

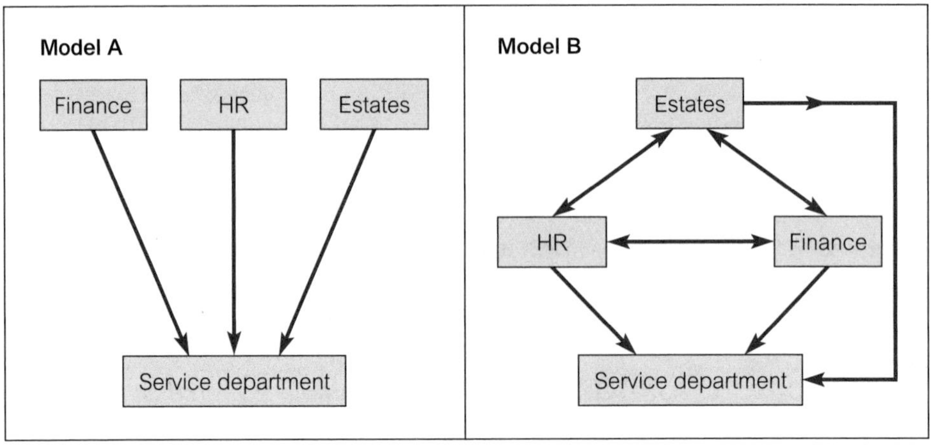

complex model which recognises that the various central support departments also service one another to some degree, and the model reflects this by attributing costs between the central support departments before attributing costs to the service department. Clearly, model A is the simplest to operate and the temptation may be to always apply such a model. However, such a simple approach can introduce large distortions into the final cost results and therefore should be treated with caution.

Improved cost drivers

An improvement to across-the-board cost apportionment would be to treat each cost element of support services separately and to attach specific cost drivers for apportioning such costs to individual departments. For example, for personnel costs the following drivers could be used:

→ recruitment costs pro rata to numbers of recruits;

→ training costs pro-rata to numbers of courses attended;

→ general personnel costs – pro rata to numbers of employees.

There will be situations where a pool of support service costs can be attributed to departments using a number of different cost drivers, but the driver actually used as a basis for attributing costs must be logically supportable. It may be that data on appropriate cost drivers may not be available and the temptation may be to use some surrogate indicator (e.g. student numbers instead of space for estate costs). This must be treated with caution, since experience has shown that the use of a surrogate cost driver can substantially impact on the distribution of cost. For example, using student numbers instead of floor area to apportion premises costs can affect the total costs by as much as 6–7%. Hence, the use of such incorrect cost drivers should be resisted; where this is not possible the costing information produced should be given a clear 'health' warning.

In practice it may not be possible to get the required range of cost drivers at first attempt. Hence, the costing approach may need to be developed on an iterative basis as further information becomes available – this is acceptable provided it is recognised that the earlier cost information has accuracy limitations.

Service level agreements

A further development which has already been mentioned is the establishment of service level agreements (SLAs) between support departments and service depart-ments which would define both the unit of service to be provided and the cost of that unit. Where it is considered applicable, a service department would be charged according to the use made of the support department's services and the support departments would be expected to pay their way by providing services to internal as well as external clients. Both a framework and rules are necessary to govern how these SLAs operate and data will need to be recorded on the use of support services by user departments. If there is an option for departments to opt out of the SLA and purchase services externally this would need to be managed carefully to avoid increasing overall PSO costs. Such approaches have successfully been implemented in other organisations including, for example, parts of the NHS and universities.

Departmental cost attribution methods

In attributing departmental costs (direct and indirect) over the lower-level cost cen-tres such as sub-units of discrete services, three main areas of cost exist for which reasonable methods of cost attribution will be required:

Staff time

A very large proportion of cost in the delivery of public services comprises staff costs. Thus, to obtain reasonably accurate estimates of the costs of delivering discrete public services within a department, reasonable estimates will be required of the commitment of staff time to those services. Unfortunately, the general rule is that it is usually difficult to get reasonable data on how public service staff use their time and often there is very strong resistance from the staff themselves to recording such information. Public service professionals such as doctors, nurses, teachers, lecturers and police officers are not used to the idea of recording how they use their time, unlike in the private sector where professional staff are used to complete timesheets each month. Thus more sophisticated methods of dis-aggregating staff time will be needed and may involve the use of programmed staff hours, or experiments may need to be undertaken (as has been done in the NHS with health care professionals) in using technology such as portable data capture units (PDCUs) to obtain good quality data on the use of staff time.

Equipment

With some public services (e.g. health) the costs associated with equipment (e.g. depreciation, maintenance) can be substantial. When such costs are a small proportion of the total costs then a broad-brush approach will suffice but when they are more significant this may introduce large distortions. Such costs will need to be attributed to specific activities reasonably accurately and methods of identifying and attributing costs to different activities and of capturing the necessary data to undertake cost attribution exercises will need to be identified. Again, mention must be made here of the increasing role (and cost) of IT in the delivery of public services.

Other costs

Apportionments are often made on the basis of staff time committed to each of the activities. However, this can easily introduce distortions where the proportion of staff time associated with an activity is not a good proxy for the proportion of other costs associated with the activity. Hence it will be necessary to consider the following: the nature of each element of cost (direct and indirect), the likely driver of that cost in relation to activities and the availability of information to enable that cost driver to be applied. Thus, judgements will need to be made about the drivers to be used and the methods of cost apportionment to be applied. A degree of pragmatism must be coupled with a minimum level of accuracy if the final results are to be meaningful and where proxy cost drivers have to be applied great care must be taken to ensure that they do not distort the resulting costs.

Cost behaviour classification

Ultimately the costing information produced will be used by departmental and corporate management to manage the organisation and to make decisions. When considering options and making decisions concerning, for example, changes in the levels of service, it is important to be able to distinguish the various costs involved according to their behavioural type, namely: variable costs, fixed costs and semi-variable costs (of different types).

Although this may not be a precise exercise, it will be important for future costing systems to be able to indicate something about the behavioural classification of different types of cost.

Level of disaggregation of costing

PSOs need to develop some clarity about what level of cost disaggregation they will need to manage their organisations effectively. Using an NHS Trust as an example, the trust will require cost information at the following levels:

→ the overall costs of a clinical directorate (e.g. surgery);

→ the costs of each medical or surgical speciality within that directorate (e.g. orthopaedic surgery);

→ the costs of treating a specific clinical condition (e.g. spinal curvature);

→ the costs of an individual surgical procedure (e.g. knee joint replacement);

→ the costs of treating knee joint arthritis in an elderly person;

→ the costs of each individual patient.

It is important that future costing systems produce the level of information needed by management, but the following points need to be borne in mind:

→ cost information can be generated at various levels of detail;

→ in general, the more detailed the cost information requirements, the more resource intensive and expensive it is to produce;

→ in general, it is cheaper to build specific costing requirements into the initial model design now than try to add-on later.

Developing costing systems: the stages

There are a number of key stages which should be followed in the development of effective approaches to costing in PSOs.

Costing strategies and policies

Before launching into any systems development, PSOs need to give substantial consideration to the development of longer-term strategies and policies for costing, including identifying longer-*term* needs for cost information, identifying future costing systems architecture and cost flow structures, reviewing strengths and weaknesses of existing information systems (financial and non-financial) – existing systems may be adequate with some 'tweaking' or establishing likely resource availability – the amount available for costing systems development is inherently limited.

Great emphasis must be made about the 'cost of costing'. Costing systems are put in place and developed in order to meet the needs of management, not to keep management accountants busy per se. As outlined in Figure 2.1, the task of management in PSOs can be reduced to three main tasks:

→ Delivering public services as planned.

→ Maintaining financial balance.

→ Achieving strategic change.

Thus, costing systems must aim to assist in the achievement of these three tasks and the sophistication of the costing systems must be geared towards this aim. It follows therefore that in considering costing system developments the PSO must carefully balance the need for cost information (to manage the PSO) against the costs associated with developing and running those systems.

Costing systems development

PSOs will need to produce a costing systems development plan, which should include the following: identification of detailed of information needs; development of detailed costing approaches and methods; enhancement of existing systems; selection of new systems; and development of an implementation plan.

Training

If the cost information produced through new systems is not fully utilised by managers and service professionals then the investment in such systems will have been wasted. Hence, it is vital to provide adequate training to all relevant staff about interpreting the cost information and how it can be used to improve decision making.

Conclusions

In conclusion, it can be confidently stated that the changes in the public service environment that will undoubtedly take place over the next few years will have a profound effect on the cost structure of PSOs. This point must continue to be emphasised. In turn this will require new approaches to costing in PSOs over and above any developments which may, at present, be taking place. Thus institutions should avoid the acquisition of new costing systems, at considerable expense, without first undertaking a strategic review of their requirements for cost information and the means of producing that cost information in the medium to longer term.

An understanding of the costs of an organisation's activities (and the factors that drive those costs) is an essential prerequisite to managing an organisation effectively. This is as true for PSOs as for any other organisation but PSOs often lack the necessary data, and examples of this have been illustrated in the text. It is therefore important that individual PSOs consider where they have information gaps regarding their cost profile and that they take steps to close that gap.

Questions for discussion

→ How much do we know about the current costs of delivering our services?

→ How much do we know about how our cost levels would change if our level of service provision changed?

→ How could we go about getting the cost information we need to manage our organisation?

→ How good are our current costing systems at proving the information we need?

5

Managing strategic change in public services: the financial management contribution

Learning objectives

→ To appreciate what major strategic change in public services involves and the financial implications of this

→ To understand the processes of managing strategic change in public services at both commissioner and provider levels

→ To understand the difference between strategic planning and strategic management

→ To appreciate the important financial management roles which should be undertaken in the strategic management of public services

→ To understand certain financial and economic techniques which can be used in relation to strategic financial management

Introduction

Strategic change is an essential aspect of public services today. Although some may look back to a 'golden age' of stability where PSOs remained unchanged for many years, the reality today is that scientific, social, economic and demographic pressures mean that PSOs must undergo a process of renewal and change. Thus, for a number of years, PSOs from various sectors have had to go through major strategic changes, involving combinations of the following:

→ changes to organisational structures;

→ changes in the location of service delivery;

→ changes in working methods;

→ changes in resource mix.

Such strategic changes are complex and time-consuming and require effective management approaches in order to make them successful. Financial management has a major contribution to make in the management of such strategic changes but, unfortunately, the tasks of strategic financial management are often the weakest aspect of financial management in public services. Examples exist where major changes in public services have resulted in one or more of the following:

→ major overspends in achieving the required strategic change;

→ a failure to achieve the intended service improvements expected from the strategic change due to insufficient funds being available as a consequence of poor financial planning;

→ a reduction in the efficiency of resource use following the change.

This chapter focuses on the important, and often under-developed, task of strategic financial management and addresses the following key issues:

→ examples of major strategic change in public services and their financial impacts.

→ the processes of managing strategic change in public services, including strategic planning, implementation of strategy and strategic monitoring – these processes are considered from the standpoint of service commissioners and service providers (public sector, private sector and third sector);

→ the financial management contribution to the strategic management of public services in both commissioners and providers;

→ relevant techniques associated with strategic financial management.

Major strategic changes in public services

Over the last 30 years, throughout the public services of most countries, a large number of major changes have taken place in the organisation and configuration of those services. These changes have had major financial implications for PSOs. In this section we examine some UK examples of such changes and their implications.

Types of strategic change

Some examples of strategic changes which have taken place in UK public services are described below in order to illustrate the scale, complexity and financial impact of such changes.

Reconfiguration of psychiatric care

During the 1980s, considerable changes were made to the configuration of services for people suffering from medium to severe psychiatric illnesses. One key aspect of this concerned the closure of large psychiatric institutions housing many hundreds of patients which were often found in isolated locations far away from local communities. These institutions were replaced by a large number of various community-based services, many of which involved patients living in small unit homes (with three to four residents) which were based in the community and provided with appropriate medical and nursing services. It was not possible to transfer all patients from the institution to the community at the same time since it took a while to develop the various community-based services. Thus, the process of change took place over several years until such time as the institution was emptied of patients. During this time the following financial issues were encountered:

→ Capital costs of constructing new community-based homes.

→ Staffing costs and running costs of providing services at the new community homes as they opened and took patients.

→ Cost savings in staffing and other costs at the institution as patients were decanted into the community. However, the cost savings made as patients left the institution were less than the costs incurred through absorbing patients into the community. This is because many of the institutional costs (e.g. maintenance costs) were largely fixed in nature and could not be saved until the institution finally closed.

→ Costs of managing the change process including the costs of retraining staff to work in new environments. These costs were very important, since many of the staff employed were more institutionalised than the patients and thus needed considerable re-training.

→ Finally, the capital receipt once the institution was closed and sold to a third party. However, this could take many years to achieve (see Case Study 5.1).

Mergers of further education colleges

During the 1990s a considerable number of mergers took place involving two (and sometimes more) FE colleges. The rationale for such mergers was usually concerned with the small size of some colleges and the diseconomies of scale they faced in undertaking some activities, but also their inability to offer a sufficiently wide range of educational programmes to their local communities. In some cases, such mergers were almost forced since one of the colleges was close to financial collapse. During the period of merger, and subsequently, the following financial issues were expected:

> ### Case study 5.1
> ### Financial implications of closing a psychiatric institution

Parkwood Hospital is a large psychiatric hospital based in its own large grounds in a rural area. At its peak the hospital held nearly 1,000 inpatients but, for various reasons, over the years this has reduced to just over 400.

The aim was to transfer patients to purpose-built smaller community homes over a three to five-year period resulting in ultimate closure of the hospital and realisation of the site. Such a change in the pattern of care had huge benefits to patients since they will reside in a more informal environment in the community but there were also implications for staff, many of whom have worked in a large institutional environment for many years.

A plan for achieving this has been prepared and associated financial modelling of the change programme undertaken. The results of this financial modelling exercise suggested that as currently configured the change project would have the following financial implications:

- Over the transitional period the overall costs of service provision would inevitably rise due to the 'double running' of services during this period.
- This 'double running' effect would ultimately disappear but the overall costs of service provision would end up at a level of cost higher than at the start of the transition. This is because of the dis-economies of scale effect.
- There would be various other non-recurring costs such as capital expenditure for new build and these would be funded by 'borrowing' until such a time that the building and its site could be sold and the capital receipts used to repay the borrowing. However, it was then noted that the hospital is in fact a listed building and was in a location where planning permission for residential development was unlikely to be obtained. Thus the level of capital receipts was likely to be much lower than was originally anticipated.
- Given the institutional background of the hospital staff, the project would require a huge change management effort and no funding for this had been included in the original plan.

In the light of the above financial assessment, it was realised that the whole project, as configured, was financially unsound. Hence the specification had to be re-thought with greater emphasis on:

- the use of non-capital community schemes by, for example, outsourcing to the third sector;
- reconsideration of staffing levels and mix in community homes;
- greater focus on change management;
- a faster timescale for closure to reduce the 'double running' effect.

→ Cost savings could be generated because of the ability to merge a number of support functions (e.g. finance, HRM, IT, senior management) currently existing in two locations into one larger and more efficient function.

→ Cost savings could be generated because of the ability to rationalise the numbers of teaching staff on identical educational programmes.

→ Redundancy costs associated with reducing numbers of teaching and support staff.

→ Incremental travel costs associated with staff travelling between two sites.

→ Costs of managing the change process.

→ Additional income generated because of the ability of the merged college to attract additional students by offering educational programmes which neither of the two separate colleges could offer. The creation of such synergies was seen as a key rationale for the merger.

→ Disposal of part of or the entire site of one of the merged colleges, thus generating a capital receipt.

→ Additional capital expenditure on buildings and/or equipment as a consequence of the merger.

Experience showed, however, that some mergers were more successful than others and the benefits and costs of merger depended on the specific situation.

Geographic reconfiguration of health services

In many parts of the country the configuration of local health services is undergoing significant and substantial change. There are a number of key drivers for such change, including:

→ a policy of trying to treat people in settings other than a secondary care hospital (which is expensive) and at settings such as primary care or at home;

→ a policy of increasing the capacity of the local health system in order to facilitate greater patient choice;

→ a policy of encouraging greater specialisation between hospitals in the same locality instead of all hospitals being a comprehensive provider of services – such specialisation might be expected to improve the clinical outcomes of treatment;

→ a drive to improve the efficiency of resource use in the NHS.

As a consequence of these, and other, drivers within a particular locality, a number of changes in the configuration of health services are planned over the next few years. These changes will not have the same pattern or pace of change in all parts of the country but some or all of the following changes can be expected:

➜ development of primary care facilities;

➜ development of intermediate care facilities;

➜ rationalisation of provision between certain hospitals;

➜ development of linkages between existing hospitals.

The changes are complex and have major financial implications, both in terms of capital costs and running costs. However, in practice, such multi-year programmes of change are often undertaken without any robust financial analysis of these.

Reconfiguration of university activities

Many universities in the UK operate from a number of geographic sites (often within the same locality but sometimes in other localities as well). In addition they undertake various research, teaching and other activities across a wide range of subject disciplines. A variety of pressures, such as government policy, reduced units of funding, changing demand from students, etc., have meant that universities have had to make substantial changes to all aspects of their organisation. Key themes are as follows:

➜ **Rationalisation of activities** – universities may make strategic decisions to specialise in certain areas of subject activity and two particular aspects of such specialisation might involve a decision to rationalise certain subjects/curricular areas and/or a decision to further specialise in certain aspects of research. Changes in student perceptions and employment prospects have meant that some subject areas in universities have had difficulty in recruiting sufficient numbers of students. Other changes in the research field have meant that some departments are struggling to earn sufficient research income. These departments, therefore, can appear financially non-viable in the short and longer term and many universities are having to consider whether such discrete and traditional departments can continue to exist. A consequence of such decisions will be the rationalisation of the current range of activities, with a consequent impact on the resource base and organisational structure of the university.

➜ **Means of service delivery** – many universities are changing the way in which they deliver educational services to students. Key aspects of this are the increasing use of electronic learning materials and the use of the Internet to deliver distance learning programmes.

➜ **Rationalisation of sites** – many universities operate from multi-site campuses, often with large distances between sites. Often some of the outlying sites are under-utilised, expensive to operate and not fit for purpose. Thus a university may choose to rationalise its estate and concentrate on a smaller number of sites.

However, this approach must be undertaken cautiously. There are often political and community pressures against site closures and the closure of certain sites may affect university student recruitment.

Sometimes the above activities take place simultaneously and so the change situation is even more complex. Significant capital investment in buildings and equipment may be involved, as well as major changes in the cost base of the university, particularly with regard to staffing costs. Finally, there will probably be some impact on the income streams of the university.

Merger of government agencies

Over the years there have been several examples of the merger of central government agencies. For example, prior to 2000 two agencies of what is now the Department of Work and Pensions were in existence:

→ **Benefits Agency** – responsible for the payment of benefits to claimants;

→ **Job Centre** – responsible for helping people back into work.

It was realised that there were strong synergies between the work of these two agencies and a decision was taken to merge them into a single agency termed Jobcentre Plus. This merger had several major implications:

→ **property** – both agencies occupied buildings in many towns and cities across the UK and merger obviously meant a rationalisation of those properties and the costs associated with them;

→ **working practices** – the merger implied a major overhaul of working practices to integrate the tasks undertaken by the two agencies;

→ **staffing** – the merger of the two agencies had major implications for the numbers, organisation and training of staff and the costs involved.

Commercialisation of public services

There are many examples of PSOs which were traditionally funded from public revenues (e.g. local authority direct service organisations) being required to be converted into organisations which operated on a (full or partial) commercial basis, in that they had to earn revenues to cover their costs. Such changes had implications for several aspects of the organisation. For example, certain business processes needed to be developed and implemented, such as marketing, product costing, billing and credit control, etc., and there would also be costs associated with acquiring the technology needed to do this. However, perhaps the most significant changes involved the culture of the organisation and the attitude and working practices of the staff, who had to be focused on the need to 'sell' their services to potential clients and ensure client satisfaction, which were areas where traditionally they had no experience.

Local authority children's services departments

Traditionally, in local authorities, services to children were provided, in different ways, by two main departments:

→ **education department** – provision of schools services, pre-school services, educational psychology services, etc.;

→ **social services departments** – the social care services for children (including child protection services) were delivered by the social services department, which also provided social care services to the elderly, disabled people, etc.

The Laming Report into the Victoria Climbie child abuse case identified a catalogue of very serious failures in the child protection system, and as a result of this the Government published a White Paper entitled *Every Child Matters* (Department of Health, 2003). The main consequence of this was that local authorities were required to form Children's Services Departments, which bought together all aspects of their services to children. This had implications in terms of the organisation and accommodation of staff in the two original departments, but perhaps the most important change concerned changes in working practices to facilitate better joint working between different types of staff. There were significant financial implications associated with such changes but often there was no clear multi-year financial strategy showing how this was to be achieved.

General nature of major strategic changes in public services

If we consider the above (and other) strategic changes that have taken place in public services, we can identify the following characteristics:

→ **Multi-year** – very few major strategic changes in public services can be achieved in a single year. More often they take several years to complete and while three to five years may be a typical timescale for completion, in some cases the period can be even longer. Thus the financial implications of such changes have multi-year effects.

→ **Complexity** – the sorts of changes discussed above are usually very complex in nature and involve significant changes over a wide variety of areas. Such changes can involve several public service agencies, several departments in the same agency and/or several professional groups. In addition, the changes can involve changes in organisational structures, changes to working practices and changes in the means and location of service delivery.

→ **Investment** – Often such major changes will involve significant capital investment in buildings and equipment and/or dis-investment in existing facilities. In addition, significant investment in new staffing resources and/or staff development may also be involved.

→ **Organisational culture** – these strategic changes can often involve significant changes in organisational cultures and to be successful new cultures need to be introduced. The example of psychiatric care described earlier involved changing the culture of service delivery from a formal and large institutional culture to one that was less formal and community based. The nature and magnitude of such cultural changes is such that often large investment in staff training and change management is required. In practice, however, ignoring the costs of change is often a common feature of strategic change in PSOs and one which contributes towards failures.

→ **Cost structure changes** – as will be seen from the examples above, these changes involve significant changes in the cost structures of organisations, both in terms of capital costs and running costs.

→ **Costs of transition** – finally, strategic changes involve getting from the current position to some future desired position. Such a transition is not a free good and there are often significant transition costs involved in these to do with redundancy payments, costs of double running, etc.

As a consequence of these issues, it is essential for success that the PSO(s) involved employ effective approaches to strategic financial management.

The management of strategic change in public services

In Chapter 1 it was suggested that the management of public services is concerned with three main objectives:

1 Delivering on service targets in relation to access, quality, timeliness, etc.

2 Managing finances in such a way as to avoid large over or under spends against budget.

3 Achieving 1 and 2 while at the same time transforming the delivery of services in line with the strategic plan.

The third item in this list concerns the management of strategic change in public services and is usually a complex task. Quite often, if the management of strategic change is not undertaken effectively then either the PSO fails to achieve its strategic

Figure 5.1 The strategic management process

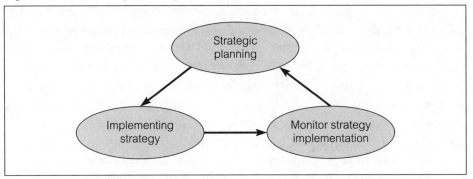

objectives and/or it fails in its operational objectives of achieving service delivery targets or financial balance. Thus, strategic management is a key element of the management process in all PSOs. Figure 5.1 illustrates its key elements.

There are three aspects of strategic management to consider:

→ strategic planning;

→ implementing strategy;

→ monitoring strategy implementation.

This distinction is important because in public services the terms strategic planning and strategic management are often used synonymously, thus failing to recognise the other two aspects.

Finance has a key role to play in all three aspects of strategic management and this chapter is primarily about the financial management role in strategic management and the contribution that can be made by the finance function to this process.

Strategic planning in public services – commissioners and providers

The terms strategy and strategic planning are, possibly, among the most misused words in the English language and there is usually considerable confusion as to what is meant by strategy. Like most aspects of management, the essence of organisational strategy is very simple and is concerned with answering three main questions in relation to the organisation:

1 Where are we now?

2 Where do we wish to get to *in the longer term*?

3 How do we get where we want to be?

These three questions can be regarded as being in increasing order of difficulty to answer. It is *relatively* easy, although time-consuming, for an organisation to establish the current situation and where it stands in relation to its external working environment. It is more difficult for it to establish where it wishes to be in the longer term in terms of its size, its range of activities, its priorities, etc. However, the most difficult aspect of strategy is establishing how to get from where we are now to where we want to be in the future. Achieving this can often require significant and radical change in an organisation and the management of such change is often difficult, particularly in the conservative culture of many PSOs.

Some form of strategic planning is usually undertaken in most medium to large organisations, in both public and private sectors. However, within public services, a broad distinction can be drawn between the following:

→ strategic planning in a service commissioner organisation;

→ strategic planning in multi-agency partnerships;

→ strategic planning in a service delivery organisation.

Strategic planning in service commissioner organisations

In Chapter 2 we discussed the commissioner/provider separation as being one of the most significant reforms that has taken place in public services over the last 30 years. In theory, at least, commissioner organisations should not be delivering services direct to service users (although this does happen in practice) but should be using the financial resources at their disposal to commission and contract services to be delivered by public sector, third sector or private sector delivery organisations. Unlike service providers, who will have large amounts of physical, human and financial resources available to them to deliver services, the physical and human resources of the commissioner organisation will be relatively limited but they will have large amounts of financial resources available to them to commission services.

Figure 5.2 shows one possible arrangement of the commissioning process in relation to public services. From this it will be seen that within commissioning there are three distinct processes with different aims and different timescales.

First, there is the commissioning (or strategic commissioning) process. This process is concerned with identifying the longer-term pattern of services needed by the population, ensuring there is a sufficient range of providers to deliver those services and establishing relationships with those providers. Second, there is the purchasing/ contracting (or operational commissioning) process, which is concerned with selecting specific providers and letting contracts for service delivery. Third, there is the construct management and compliance process.

As this chapter is concerned with strategy we will focus on the strategic commissioning process, although there are, of course, financial issues concerning operational

Figure 5.2 The commissioning process

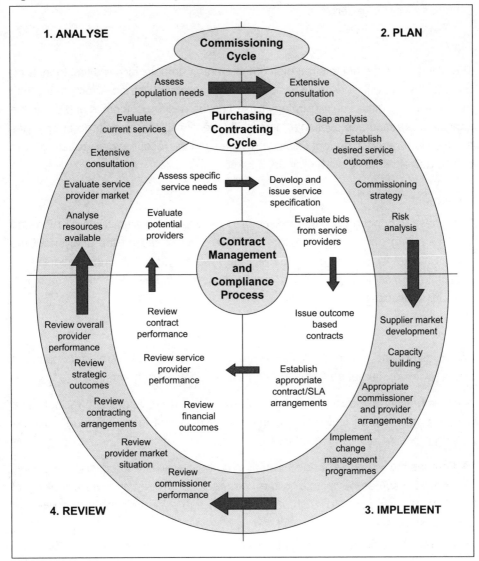

Source: Nottingham City Council

commissioning and the tendering and letting of specific contracts. From Figure 5.2 it can be seen that the strategic commissioning process is sub-divided into four phases: analyse, plan, implement and review.

Analyse

This phase involves first identifying the service needs of the client population using data which may already be available or may need to be collected and then analysing current service provision regarding volume, quality, access, etc. and the resources used to deliver those services.

Plan

The planning phase of the strategic commissioning process involves first identifying gaps in the current service provision and setting objectives as appropriate, then developing a commissioning strategy based on the desired outcomes and within the constraint of resources available, and finally identifying the magnitude of changes required compared to current service provision and the resource consequences and challenges of effecting such changes.

Implement

This phase is concerned with implementing the strategic commissioning plan and involves taking action to encourage new providers, based on the analysis of the current market for service provision, assisting with capacity building, particularly in relation to third sector organisations, and finally developing a framework for managing provider relationships.

Review

The review phase requires a review of the achievement of the strategic objectives and a review of market performance and overall contract performance.

A consideration of the range and complexity of the tasks above shows that there needs to be a strong financial management involvement in the strategic commissioning process, in a number of areas:

→ **Forecasting** – there is a need to make the best available forecasts of the likely level of resources available to the commissioner. This may involve looking at different scenarios (e.g. high, medium, low) and assessing the probabilities of each scenario.

→ **Costs** – it will be important to identify the costs of current service provision and the distribution of total resources over different services, client groups, etc. This includes both services financed from earmarked sources and services financed from general sources.

→ **Evaluation** – a key aspect of financial management is in evaluating the financial consequences of the commissioning strategy to ensure that it aligns with the likely levels of resources available. Unless the costs of the commissioning strategy can be reconciled to the likely resources available then it will lack credibility.

→ **Financial viability** – assessing the financial viability and financial management expertise of potential providers, especially the smaller third sector organisations, is important. It may also be appropriate to deliver some financial management training to such organisations to improve their managerial capacity.

→ **Financial benchmarking** – it would be beneficial to make comparisons of the unit costs of service provision with that of other local providers and providers in other areas in order to assess value for money.

→ **Review** – participate in the review of the commissioning strategy, in particular its value for money component.

Strategic planning in multi-agency partnerships

The reality now is that much of the strategic commissioning of public services is done through multi-agency partnerships rather than single commissioner organisations. To a large extent it would appear that the processes of strategic commissioning will (at a basic level) be largely the same for the individual commissioner but the practice of developing and applying those processes will be much more complex. For example, with a multi-agency partnership:

→ the assessment of population need will be more complex because of the different viewpoints of the various agencies about what constitutes need and how it should be measured;

→ the identification of the costs of current service provision and the distribution of total resources over client groups will be more difficult to undertake because it will mean integrating financial information from several agencies each with its own accounting and costing approaches;

→ the assessment of the costs of multi-agency initiatives to achieve the strategic objectives might prove to be more complex because of the different accounting and costing approaches involved.

However, none of these problems are insurmountable and solving them will no doubt, in time, become routine.

One further point that needs to be noted is that, although the commissioning strategy will be prepared on a multi-agency basis, to a large extent its implementation will be undertaken by individual agencies. This situation may change in time but, for the present, it does pose major challenges in relation to strategy implementation.

Strategic planning in a service delivery organisation

It is service delivery organisations that actually deliver services to clients and these organisations can be public sector, third sector or private sector organisations. In all three cases the organisations have a common task of needing to win contracts to deliver public services in return for an income stream. Unlike service commissioners,

Figure 5.3 Strategic business planning

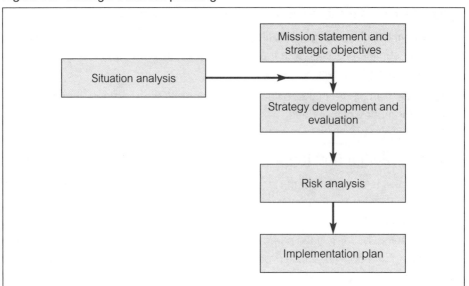

service delivery organisations have a wide range of resources (including fixed assets, manpower and finance) available to them in order to deliver services to the public. Although such service delivery organisations may be public sector, third sector or private sector in nature, in many ways they are all analogous to private sector organisations delivering products to customers, and consequently the type of strategic planning employed in such PSOs is often referred to as strategic business planning.

The classical approach to strategic business planning has a number of inter-related stages, as shown in Figure 5.3.

The various stages can be linked and summarised in terms of the three key questions already identified:

→ **Where are we now?** – situation analysis incorporating an internal appraisal of the organisation itself and the services it provides and an external appraisal of the environment (physical, social, economic, etc.) in which it operates.

→ **Where do we wish to get to in the longer term?** – this involves preparation of a mission statement and a series of strategic objectives.

→ **How do we get there?** – this involves the tasks of strategy development and evaluation, risk analysis and implementation planning.

Mission statement and strategic objectives

For a service delivery organisation this involves defining the longer-term strategic aspirations of the organisation through the derivation of a mission statement. The development of strategic objectives will involve fleshing out the mission statement into precise and quantifiable elements and such objectives provide the foundation for outlining what the organisation aims for *in the longer term*. The strategic business plan should have a series of strategic objectives which will be organisational specific but a number of over-arching objectives may also exist which should apply to the whole sector and which should be incorporated into their plan. These over-arching objectives could include:

→ **Viability** – the plan needs to ensure viability, and particularly financial viability, for the organisation. It is not sufficient for the organisation to plan to, merely, break even financially or to make small financial surpluses, since an unexpected event can still endanger the viability of the organisation if it has no financial 'cushion' to absorb the shock.

→ **Sustainability** – the plan needs to ensure that the organisation will be sustainable in the longer term given that it operates in a competitive environment. It will, therefore, have to plan to remain competitive and must try to ensure that they identify (and provide funds for) future investment in physical resources and human resources. Any organisation that does not plan for such investment will, over time, probably become less competitive and this can also endanger its sustainability.

→ **Acceptability** – it is of vital importance that the strategic business plan of the organisation is acceptable to service professionals, service users and the community at large. Looking externally, where there are strong links to the local community or region then the strategic business plan needs to be acceptable to local stakeholders such as other PSOs, the third sector, etc.

A PSO could have any of the strategic objectives shown in Figure 5.4. These examples are illustrative and not exhaustive. However, it is vitally important that strategic objectives should be capable of some quantification and measurement.

Situation analysis

Strategic business planning must be undertaken with a full understanding of one's position and what the future may hold. A key element is a SWOT (strengths, weaknesses, opportunities, threats) analysis, which comprises two distinct but related parts:

→ **An internal appraisal of organisational strengths and weaknesses** – it is essential that any internal assessment of the PSO is both systematic and honest. Experience has shown that many organisations overstate their strengths and understate their weaknesses because they find it uncomfortable to face up to reality. Examples of areas to be covered in this internal review include staff

Figure 5.4 Possible PSO strategic objectives

Local authority leisure services	Third sector organisation	Economic development agency
• Increased uptake of leisure activities • Greater diversity of participation in leisure services • Increased sporting excellence in the locality • Improved financial performance	• Greater diversity of funding • Improved client satisfaction with services • Improved access to 'hard to reach' groups • Better financial sustainability	• Increased job creation • Increased business formation • Increased volume of foreign direct investment • Improved manufacturing infrastructure

quality, equipment range and quality, buildings capacity and quality, current customer satisfaction, internal communications, service range and quality, financial position, etc.

→ **An external appraisal of opportunities and threats** – this aims to review the external environment in which the PSO operates in order to identify opportunities to seize and threats to avoid or negate. It is important to realise that some factors can represent an opportunity or a threat depending on circumstances. A number of opportunities and threats may present themselves to a PSO preparing a strategic business plan and these matters should be taken account of in the plan. One approach to this is the PEST approach, where the review of the external environment focuses on four groups of factors, namely political, economic, social, technological.

Using the external appraisal approach many specific trends can be identified, including growth in the elderly in the population, an increase in the number of competitor organisations, increasing local unemployment, likely political change in a council, new drug therapy coming on stream, large new build of housing due for completion, new commercial organisations entering the area, changes in government policies, changes in professional practices, increasing numbers of single parent families, cost pressures on commissioners, etc.

Strategy development

Within a PSO a variety of different strategies might be identified as there are usually several different routes to any destination. PSO strategies can be viewed as a series of strands which meet to provide an overall corporate strategic plan. Some of these strands are concerned with the service activities of the PSO and some with the resources it utilises. This is illustrated in Figure 5.5.

Figure 5.5 Strategic development strands

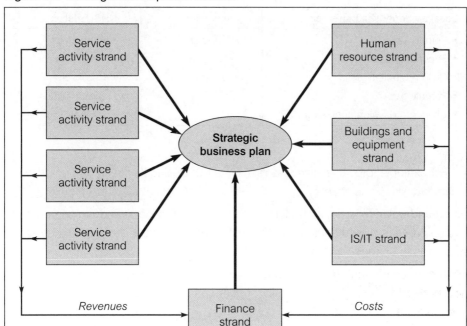

In reality, these separate strategies are best viewed as components of an overall and integrated strategic business plan, hence our reference to them as strands. Thus, within the overall strategic business plan there will be a series of business strands concerned with service activities, as well as a number of resource strands concerned with HR, buildings and equipment and IS/IT. The financial strand binds all of these together. In the absence of a robust financial strand a PSO cannot be confident that its overall strategic business plan can be afforded or that it will be able to meet its financial objectives concerning surplus/deficit, cash flow, capital financing, etc.

Some examples of service activity strands are shown in Figure 5.6, and each of these main strands can be broken down into smaller strands representing service sub-divisions.

The formulation of service strategy within a PSO will be primarily concerned with the following issues:

→ **Strand size** – what is the desired overall magnitude of each of these strands? It is often automatically assumed that a PSO should always aim to grow in size but this is not always true. Although larger size may improve competitiveness and provide economies of scale, negative points may be associated with growth.

Figure 5.6 Possible service activity strands

Local authority children's services	University	NHS Trust
• Primary education	• Teaching	• Paediatrics
• Secondary education	• Research	• General surgery
• Child protection	• Third stream	• Cardiology
• Parenting		• Orthopaedics
• Childcare development, etc.		• Urology, etc.

For example, growth in size may result in a PSO losing its caring and comfortable image with some clients.

→ **Strand balance** – although all PSOs pursue all of these strands to some extent, the process should consider the overall balance between them and whether this needs to change.

→ **Strand configuration and diversity** – within each of the strands, the PSO strategy will need to address the diversity of activities undertaken and the detailed configuration of those activities.

The various resource strands that make up the strategy are human resources, estates, IS/IT and finance. In developing a resource strategy a number of issues will need to be addressed, including the following:

→ What should be the balance between full-time, temporary and hourly-paid staff?

→ What staff remuneration mechanisms should be introduced?

→ From how many sites should the PSO operate?

→ What should be the balance between purchase and lease of equipment?

→ What role should IS/IT play in operational activities?

→ What is an appropriate balance between fixed and variable costs for the organisation?

Evaluating potential strategies

Having identified and developed some possible strategies, each must then be evaluated to establish the best way forward. There are two essential matters to consider:

→ Is it *strategically* feasible, i.e. will it enable the strategic objectives to be achieved?

→ Is it *resource* feasible in terms of the availability, to the organisation, of key resources?

Both of these are important and necessary conditions as it is possible to develop strategies that are feasible regarding the achievement of strategic objectives but not feasible in resource terms. The opposite may also be true, and strategies that are resource feasible should not necessarily be followed. Commercial organisations frequently sell off profitable and well-resourced activities, simply because they do not fit in with the strategic objectives of the organisation.

Assessing strategic feasibility

This involves identifying the strategy that has the best chance of success in terms of attaining the PSO's strategic objectives. The different evaluation approaches are summarised below:

→ **Identify competitive advantage** – this is only suitable where a PSO is in competition with other organisations (public, private or third sector) to provide some or all of its range of services. Evaluation of the possible business strategies will be in terms of whether they can give the organisation a competitive advantage over the other providers. This competitive advantage could be through lower costs, by differentiation (e.g. better quality) or by specialisation (niche market).

→ **Undertake a strategic appraisal** – this approach involves evaluating the various strategies proposed against the results of the SWOT analysis. For example, if a particular strategy utilises one of the existing strengths of the organisation then this would be a plus point for that strategy. However, if the strategy required pursuit of an activity in an area where the organisation was weak, e.g. with poorly skilled staff, then it would have to choose between not pursuing that particular strategy or taking action to reduce or eradicate the weakness, possibly through significant investment. Each of the strategies identified are judged as to whether it involves building on internal strengths or weaknesses or whether it involves building on areas identified as 'opportunities' or 'threats'. Thus, for each strategy a scorecard is compiled which assists the PSO in making an informed judgement about which is the best strategic option.

→ **Portfolio analysis** – this approach involves evaluating strategies according to their risk/return profile. In reality, different activities generate different rates of return and also have different risk profiles. Furthermore, in the 'real' world high return is usually associated with high risk. Different business strategies could be evaluated by considering their risk/return profiles, which is usually referred to as portfolio analysis. The various aspects of risk and return can be considered in relation to the mix of activities undertaken and the mix of resources needed to undertake those activities. There is no correct combination of risk and return and it is up to each PSO to choose a strategy that it judges to be the most appropriate.

It is important to emphasise that these three approaches to evaluating strategies are not mutually exclusive but can be applied individually or in combination. Furthermore, although these approaches are primarily used in commercial organisations, with a little thought they can easily be adapted for use in PSOs.

Assessing resource feasibility

Strategies must be feasible both in terms of achieving strategic objectives and in resource terms; the latter includes human resources, fixed assets, specialist supplies and finance. Some factors that may result in a strategy not being resource feasible are:

→ the unavailability of certain human resources;

→ fixed assets and specialist supplies are unobtainable;

→ the whole strategy is financially unsound;

→ redundant resources cannot be disposed of.

Although finance is not the only resource which must be considered it is perhaps the most critical. The aspect of resource feasibility is discussed further in a later section.

Strategic planning and risk analysis

Any strategic business plan should consider the potential risks faced by the organisation and the possible ways of dealing with those risks. Issues of uncertainty and risk should be addressed systematically according to the following stages:

1 **Risk identification** – identify the possible sources and causes of risk. This must be undertaken thoroughly and will require considerable thought and critical evaluation.

2 **Risk analysis** – the various risks should be analysed to assess both the probability of the risk occurring and its implications, including any possible financial implications. These tasks must be done thoroughly and objectively since there is much evidence (*The Economist*, 2004) to show that people have an inherent tendency to mis-judge both the probabilities and implications of risks.

3 **Risk prioritisation** – from the above analysis, tabulate the risks identified in terms of their order of priority to be addressed.

4 **Risk-handling strategies** – in the strategic business plan, the PSO has to consider how to respond to the risks it faces. Broadly, there are only four possible actions to take in relation to each risk factor:
   • *Minimise risk* – actions could be taken to minimise the risks faced, for example by replacing an ineffective manager or an unreliable piece of equipment, providing staff training or developing new procedures or protocols.

- *Transfer/share risk* – risks could be transferred to or shared with another organisation, for example by sub-contracting certain activities, such as IT management, to a third party, which would assume many of the risks involved.
- *Avoid risk* – the level of risk associated with certain activities may be unacceptably high and the PSO might decide to avoid such risks by not undertaking a particular activity or undertaking it in a very different way. An example might be the avoidance of certain overseas ventures where the PSO might face an unacceptable degree of risk due to currency fluctuations or insecurity of payment.
- *Retain risk* – not all risks can be transferred or completely eliminated. Thus the PSO must be clear about what level of risk it is prepared to retain and accept.

5 **Risk-coping practices** – in view of the residual risks which are inevitably retained within the organisation, it is important to have in place established practices and procedures for coping with such risks as they materialise. This could involve effective early-warning monitoring of known risk factors and having contingency plans in place to deal with their impact. These could be arrangements to hire contract personnel to replace the loss of specialist staff or arrangements to lease buildings or equipment to replace those lost through breakdown or sabotage. This would also involve putting in place financial contingency measures and provisions to deal with the impact of any risks that might occur.

Implementation plan

Strategic plans do not implement themselves. A comprehensive implementation plan needs to be prepared to ensure that the planned events actually occur. In reality the large size of many implementation plans is frequently due to the need to describe the large number of tasks that need to be undertaken to put the business plan into action. This plan will have a number of key elements, including tasks that need to be performed, individual responsibilities for ensuring that they are performed, a timetable for completing the tasks and the resources needed.

In addition, the plan may identify critical success factors and possible bottlenecks in implementation, as well as possible ways around them. The approach to these issues could adopt project management techniques.

Implementing strategy

Too often the tasks of implementing a strategy are not properly addressed and if things go wrong there can be the danger that a judgement is made that the strategy is flawed rather than that the implementation has failed. As noted above, a key component of strategy implementation is a comprehensive and robust implementation plan.

Case study 5.2
Strategic business planning in a third sector organisation

Highspring is a 3SO umbrella organisation which provides support to a wide range of other, large and small, 3SOs in its area. It has recently undertaken a strategic business planning exercise to give greater focus to its activities. Its vision statement was as follows:

> To be an organisation which fosters the development of the voluntary sector and provides high quality support to a continuously increasing number of 3SOs spread across all parts of the borough. Also to be an organisation which is seen as an equal partner with statutory agencies and which provides a channel of effective communication and advocacy between statutory organisations and 3SOs. To be an organisation which undertakes various time-limited projects which are financially sustainable and which are supportive of the activities of 3SOs and to operate through the use of effective and modern methods of management and communication and which has effective governance arrangements.

In the light of the above vision, it is suggested that the following are some strategic objectives by means of which the progress in fulfilling its vision can be assessed:

- to increase the number of 3SOs being supported;
- to increase the coverage of 3SOs supported across all parts of the borough;
- to improve the level of satisfaction with services provided to 3SOs;
- to increase the amount of statutory funding received by 3SOs for the delivery of services;
- to increase the amount of project funding received by Highspring itself while ensuring that the operation of such projects is done on the basis of at least a break-even position;
- to achieve changes in the pattern of resource use in line with the vision.

In the light of this, the organisation identified five strands of activity where development work was required. These concerned:

- member services;
- strategic liaison with local agencies and partnerships;
- innovative activities;
- special projects;
- internal working arrangements.

Detailed action plans were prepared and resource requirements identified.

Five-year financial projections were prepared which illustrated how the mix and utilisation of resources would change over the strategic period.

Figure 5.7 Strategic management approach – model A

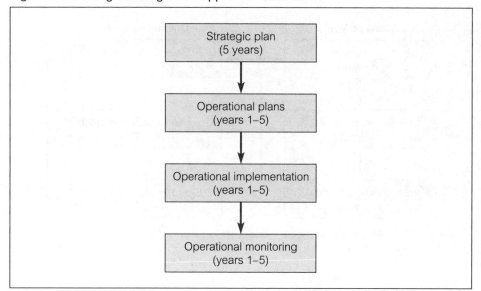

However, it is often thought that implementing a strategic plan involving consider-able change just requires the construction of a series of operational (implementation) plans and that this will result in the implementation of the strategy and the achievement of the strategic objectives. This is illustrated in Figure 5.7.

This model correctly shows that the shorter-term operational plans of an organisa-tion should be derived from the longer-term strategic plans and it also recognises that there needs to be a process of implementing and monitoring the operational plans. However, the unwritten assumption is that by implementing a series of sequential operational plans one will automatically implement the organisation's strategy. Thus, there is no concept of strategic implementation. This is an example of a theoretical model which does not fit the real world since there will be many real-life barriers to implementing the strategy. These particularly concern the failure to address issues of cultural and organisational change.

An alternative model is shown in Figure 5.8. This model also recognises that operational plans should be derived from strategic plans. However, it also recognises the underlying reality that strategic plans do not implement themselves and that too often there is a tendency to assume that once a strategic plan has been created then little more needs to be done other than to implement the operational plans. This is a huge mistake, because the implementation of strategic plans is an important and difficult task. The implementation of operational, or short-term, plans is not always that difficult since it often requires little change in operational practices in the organ-isation from those currently undertaken. However, the implementation of a strategic

Figure 5.8 Strategic management approach – model B

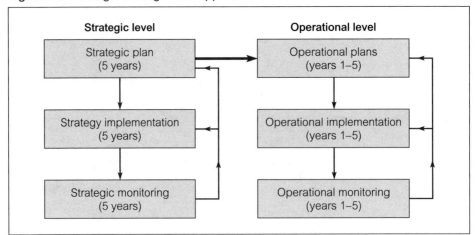

plan often raises issues of resistance to organisational change, imperfect markets for services, inability to obtain resources, etc., and these issues must be addressed as part of the process of strategy implementation. The implementation of a strategic plan will probably require substantial changes in the organisation's arrangements and operational practices. Such changes are often so radical that they may generate fierce opposition from many parts of the organisation, and the successful implementation of the strategic plan rests on overcoming this opposition. Hence the organisation needs to develop a suitable change management programme and commit sufficient resources to that programme.

From a financial management point of view, the key thing is to recognise that the process of change management has significant financial implications and is not cheap to apply. Thus, in planning for strategic change it is important to make financial provision for the process of change management, otherwise the success of the change process may be compromised.

Monitoring strategy implementation and outcomes

In implementing a programme of major strategic change it is also important that the PSO undertakes some form of strategic monitoring. This is not the same as operational monitoring, where one is monitoring the impact of annual operational plans. Strategic monitoring involves monitoring the impact of the strategy in terms of the impact on service outcomes. Furthermore, strategic monitoring may need to continue for some years after the strategic change has been fully implemented in order to judge its impact. Thus, at the time the strategic objectives are being set, PSOs need to think about how, in future years, they are going to collect the information needed to assess whether those service objectives have been met. This may require setting in train various data collection or survey exercises to ensure such information will be available when it is needed. Again, there are often substantial resource implications of setting up systems and processes to collect this data.

The results of this strategic monitoring exercise will then inform future strategic plans. While such strategic monitoring is difficult to undertake in practice, since there may be problems of data collection and evaluation methodology, these difficulties should not constitute a reason for inaction and some strategic monitoring is better than none.

The key roles of financial management in strategic management

As already noted, finance is a key resource in strategic development since it is the resource which binds together revenues from the delivery of services with the various resource costs of doing so. In this situation, it would be expected that financial management should have a very strong role to play in the strategic management of public services. Unfortunately, this has not always been the case and for many years it was not uncommon to find strategic plans of PSOs with little or no financial content at all. Often strategic objectives and strategic plans were put forward with little analysis of the resource consequences of those plans. However, the situation has improved and continues to improve and we now see much more financial content in PSO strategic plans. Nevertheless, although there has been significant improvement in the outward form of strategic financial planning, there is still scope for improvement in the substance, and specific areas where improvement is needed include:

→ setting clearer strategic financial objectives (e.g. surpluses, liquidity) which underpin the strategy;
→ more extensive and accurate information on the costs of current activities;
→ more robust resource projections which take account of risk and uncertainty;
→ robust financial evaluation of the various strategic options;
→ improved appraisal of proposed capital expenditure projects;
→ improvements in linking budgets to strategies as a means of implementation.

In any PSO, therefore, financial management and the finance function have strong roles to play in the development and implementation of strategic plans and can make important contributions in a number of areas:

→ setting strategic financial objectives;

→ financial analysis of existing activities;

→ resource forecasting;

→ financial evaluation of strategic options;

→ capital expenditure appraisal;

→ links with budgeting.

The main aspects of these are discussed below.

Setting strategic financial objectives

Along with its other planning objectives, any PSO needs to have some clear financial objectives. Just because we are dealing with public service organisations doesn't mean that financial objectives can be ignored and in the section on the strategic objectives of service providers we referred to the issues of viability and sustainability. The existence of strategic financial objectives will aid in the achievement of these over-arching strategic objectives. Usually these financial objectives will address levels of financial surplus, debt ratios, returns on investment or liquidity positions. For example, in the HE sector the HE funding councils have, in the past, suggested that university HEIs should aim, as a minimum, to generate a financial surplus equal to 3% of turnover, but in today's climate equal importance will be given to issues concerning cash flow and the generation of usable funds for investment purposes. However, it is also possible to think in terms of financial objectives which are concerned with other matters, such as the cost ratios concerning the percentage of costs represented by staff costs, the percentage of costs represented by IT costs or the percentage of costs which might be regarded as truly fixed.

The financial analysis of existing activities

As discussed in Chapter 4, an analysis can be provided of the costs and financial performance of existing service activities to identify the level of surplus/deficit being generated by each activity. At a basic level this would involve identifying the overall performance of individual departments and within that the separate financial performance of individual units and activities within that department. Such an analysis will enable the PSO to see the levels of cross-subsidy within its existing portfolio of activities and to plan accordingly for the future. Comparisons can be made of the costs of undertaking various activities in the PSO compared with other PSOs or organisations. The technique of benchmarking, which is discussed later, will facilitate this task.

In addition, a financial analysis can be undertaken to identify the distribution of resources over different types of service and different client groups. Comparisons can then be made with other areas and suitable judgements made about the appropriateness of the distribution. The techniques of programme analysis and programme budgeting discussed in Chapter 6 are of relevance here.

Resource forecasting

This task essentially involves forecasting the likely level of resources available to the PSO over a strategic period of several years and will need to assess:

→ the impact of the government's public expenditure plans as set out in the Comprehensive Spending Reviews on overall public sector funding for specific sectors;

→ the impact of public policy trends on different parts of the public sector and individual PSOs;

→ the impact of possible changes in the mechanisms of resource allocation between PSOs within the same sector – for example, the distribution of the local government revenue support grant to local authorities across the country;

→ the potential for raising revenue from locally determined taxation (council tax) for local authorities;

→ the impact of inflation on the organisation;

→ the potential for generating income through charges to clients;

→ the potential for generating any other income;

→ the level of unutilised financial balances in the PSO.

Given the level of uncertainty and risk involved it will be necessary to prepare several different resource scenarios based on different sets of assumptions and upon which different strategic planning scenarios can be built. Financial modelling is an essential tool and will be discussed further below.

Financial evaluation of strategic options

In preparing strategic business plans, PSOs must develop and evaluate a number of different strategic options and undertake an evaluation of the financial implications of those options. Options that could be evaluated include the following:

→ Reconfiguration of commissioning strategies.

→ Reconfiguration of the range and/or volume of service provision.

→ Rationalisation/amendment of methods of delivering service.

→ Rationalisation/reconfiguration of estates options.

None of these changes can be achieved in one year and thus there must be a multi-year strategy. It is completely inadequate to rely on an annual financial plan as longer-term financial plans will be needed to support strategic planning. PSOs need to develop a multi-year financial plan, and such plans should incorporate the following:

→ **Income and expenditure account** – this will show the forecast financial performance, in terms of surplus or deficit, for each year in question and, where relevant, will enable the organisation to assess the rate of return it is likely to achieve on its assets.

→ **Balance sheet** – this will show the forecast financial position at the end of each financial year in terms of assets and liabilities and, most critically, the forecast cash position.

→ **Capital programme** – this will indicate the planned pattern of capital expenditure of the PSO over the strategic period and will influence the income and expenditure account, in terms of depreciation, and the balance sheet, in terms of fixed assets.

→ **Cash flow statement** – this will show the pattern of cash inflow and outflow over the strategic period, covering both revenue and capital items.

One issue often discussed is the time period for preparing such plans – should it be three years, five years, ten years, etc.? Too often PSOs slavishly follow the requirements or guidelines of their funding body without considering their specific circumstances. While PSOs will need to meet, as a minimum, the requirements of their funding bodies there is nothing to stop them preparing forecasts for longer periods should they deem this necessary. In all of the above situations it would be beneficial if the PSOs could develop a financial planning model (or models) to assist with this.

The appraisal of proposed capital expenditure projects

A key aspect of any strategic plan concerns the level and type of capital investment to be undertaken. Like most organisations in the private sector, PSOs undertake a wide range of capital investment in new buildings, new equipment, IT and vehicles. Such capital investment can be for a variety of purposes and requires careful consideration and evaluation for a number of reasons, including:

→ **large-scale expenditure** – frequently capital projects involve large-scale expenditure running into hundreds of millions of pounds;

→ **longer-term implications** – capital investment usually has implications for the organisation for many years ahead;

→ **irreversibility** – many capital projects, once undertaken, cannot be reversed without significant additional cost;

→ **incremental revenue costs** – although some forms of capital investment can lead to lower overall revenue costs (e.g. energy conservation), many forms of capital investment lead to higher revenue costs.

Given the great emphasis placed by PSOs on the achievement of strategic object-ives it will be clear that effective decisions about capital investment will be critical to achieving those objectives. Errors in capital investment decisions can make it very difficult for those strategic objectives to be achieved. Hence, for all these reasons it is important that decisions about capital investment are rigorously appraised both in service terms and financial terms.

Financial management can contribute to decisions about capital investment in three main ways: feasibility, affordability and funding. These are discussed below.

Feasibility

This concerns the feasibility of particular capital projects in helping the PSO achieve its strategic objectives. The issue of feasibility can subsequently be broken down into two aspects:

→ **Financial feasibility** – will the project be financially feasible from the point of view of the PSO proposing to undertake the project?

→ **Economic feasibility** – will the project be economically feasible in terms of the overall benefits it would generate being in excess of the costs involved?

Both of these issues will be addressed later in this chapter, in the section on capital appraisal approaches.

Affordability

Any major investment project will have a number of financial flows, including capital expenditure, non-recurring costs, recurring running costs, depreciation costs, income streams, receipt of capital grants, financing costs of loans and repayment of loans.

All of these will have an impact on the future financial performance of the PSO as shown in its income and expenditure account. A project that is not properly finan-cially appraised could have such a negative impact on the projected (I&E) financial performance that it cannot be regarded as affordable and the capital investment appraisal should therefore involve projecting the impact, on the I&E account, of undertaking the proposed level of investment.

Identification of funding strategies

To implement its strategic business plan, the PSO will need demonstrate how it can fund its investment programme. Possible sources include borrowing, grants, internal funds, partnership arrangements with a third party or leasing.

The PSO's funding strategy will need to show the sources of funds it intends to utilise to finance its future developments and the different levels of risk attached to the different sources. For example, borrowing may run the risk of increased costs due to increased interest rates whereas grants are basically risk free. Thus, in developing a financing strategy the PSO will need to take account of the risks associated with each financing source and the overall impact on its balance sheet structure.

Linkages with budgeting systems

Chapter 6 discusses, at length, the use of budgeting systems in PSOs. One of the key points made is that there should be strong links between the strategy of the organisation and its budgeting systems. The budgeting system is one of the key mechanisms by which strategy will be implemented and it is important that the budgets for each year are drawn from the financial projections set out in the strategic plan.

Strategic Financial Planning: some relevant techniques

In the remaining sections of this chapter, we discuss some particular financial techniques which can be of relevance to the financial aspects of PSO strategic business plans:

→ cost and income benchmarking;

→ Activity-Based Costing and management;

→ financial modelling;

→ capital investment appraisal techniques.

Cost and income benchmarking

Benchmarking is a technique with a clear financial dimension that can help assess the current performance of activities in a PSO. For example, a PSO might attempt to compare its costs and income levels against benchmarks derived from the costs and incomes of other PSOs and/or other comparable organisations. Inferences could then be made about those activities.

Although the main thrust of the technique discussed here relates to the benchmarking of costs and income, for the process to be useful a wide range of information needs to be collected, including cost information, income information, information about volume of activity/workload to establish unit costs, organisational arrangements, process descriptions, etc.

In this section we explore the potential use of benchmarking in more detail.

Internal benchmarks

For activities generic to departments within PSOs a series of internal benchmarks could be developed, including average vehicle utilisation for local authority transport fleet, average class contact hours per member of academic staff in a college or average drug prescribing costs per general medical practitioner.

Sector benchmarks

Another approach might be to benchmark activities in one PSO against that in other UK PSOs in the same sector. This could be done in two distinct ways:

→ using benchmarks derived from all relevant PSOs in the sector (e.g. all local authorities);

→ using benchmarks derived from a cohort of comparable PSOs (e.g. metropolitan local authorities).

The necessary information could also be obtained in two ways:

→ **Using publicly available information** – performance could be compared against other PSOs by using information which is in the public domain, such as government statistics, annual accounts, professional associations, etc. Although some interesting comparisons can be made using this information, two key factors limit its usefulness:

  • the information is usually at too high a level of aggregation to make meaningful comparisons at an individual functional level;

  • considerable concern exists about the degree of consistency between PSOs in the methods they use to record publicly available information. This undermines the confidence in any such comparisons that may be made.

→ **Undertaking a special exercise** – the alternative to using publicly available information is to undertake a special exercise to collect information from other PSOs.

The advantage of this approach is that one can define, the type of information one wishes to collect. The major disadvantage is that experience has shown that it is often very difficult to get other PSOs to share information. The term 'commercially confidential' is often used as a reason for not sharing information. However, the following approaches can help to increase the level of cooperation:

- an offer could be made to the other PSOs to share the findings of the study on a non-attributable basis;
- an attempt could be made to undertake the exercise collaboratively with each organisation sharing the costs of the exercise and sharing the results;
- the information might be collected by a third party who keeps the results of individual PSOs confidential;
- information might be collected through face-to-face interviews rather than questionnaires. However, this approach is time-consuming.

Although this approach to benchmarking is obviously attractive the difficulties of getting comparable information should not be underestimated.

External benchmarks

Current performance at a PSO can be compared against that for a range of other organisations. This is particularly relevant for those functions which are generic and non-sector specific, such as payroll, payments, personnel administration, etc. Comparisons could be made against any of the following:

→ overseas PSOs;

→ PSOs in other sectors;

→ UK private sector organisations operating in similar business areas (e.g. private training organisations or private health organisations);

→ other UK private sector organisations.

A wide range of information is publicly available through trade associations, professional bodies, etc. However, most of the organisations involved will be considerably different from PSOs in terms of organisation, business profile, cultural background, level of technology, etc., so the comparisons should be used with caution.

Activity-based costing and management

One of the key tasks of strategic financial management described above is that of analysing the costs of existing service activities. While one must always be acutely aware of the 'cost of costing' it is equally the case that in preparing strategic plans there must be some degree of confidence about the comprehensiveness and reasonableness of the costs being produced.

As discussed in Chapter 4, Activity-Based Costing (ABC) is of great applicability in public service organisations. It is often the case in public services that the drivers of costs are not well understood and so the ABC principles of identifying activities and establishing the cost drivers are very appropriate in PSOs as a means of identifying the costs of service activities and thereby improving the management of those activities through having an understanding of what activities actually drive the costs involved.

Financial modelling

A financial model will aim to demonstrate the financial effects of possible changes in real-world situations. Clearly, the real-world situation will differ between different types of organisation and the 'real world' of a local authority is very different from that of say a hospital or a college. Thus, any model will be constructed to incorporate the essential features of the real-world situation in which the organisation operates. While important features of the real world must be included in the model, other features can safely be ignored as their impact will be insignificant.

Strategic financial planning in PSOs can be greatly assisted by the development and use of a range of computerised financial planning models, as in undertaking strategic financial planning one is not looking for precision but rather looking to evaluate and compare broad strategic options. This will involve looking for the broad-brush financial implications of these options and the degree of significance, in financial terms, between options.

Types of financial model

Different types of financial model can be developed and used for different strategic financial planning purposes. These models can be classified as follows:

Resource forecasting models

In any PSO, one of the key financial management roles is estimating or forecasting the likely levels of financial resources that will be made available to the PSO over the strategic period. Such a task is fraught with difficulties because of the uncertainties involved. Hence, a financial model could be developed which allows changes to be made to the various variables affecting resource availability (e.g. growth, inflation, methods of distribution) and the impact of those changes assessed. Also, probabilities could be attached to different levels of input for each variable such that an expected value of resources available might be obtained.

Costing models

In an earlier section it was noted that a key element of a SWOT analysis would be the production of information on the current financial performance of various PSO activities. It will therefore be necessary to establish the costs (and income) of those various activities and the development of a costing model can help with this. This model might apportion central costs over departments and sections within a department using certain pre-determined cost drivers (e.g. staff numbers, space). It would then disaggregate each element of departmental/sectional costs over individual activities in accordance with previously agreed principles. The impact of changes in assumptions about cost attribution or in levels of cost and/or activity can easily be seen using such a model.

Option appraisal models

Where a PSO is considering any form of development then a model can be developed to financially appraise the various options involved. For example, the campus expansion of a university might include expansion on existing campus, development on a greenfield site or city centre development.

A model can be developed to calculate the cost and income streams associated with each of the options, based on inputs such as increased student numbers, increased staff numbers, capital expenditure, etc., to financially appraise the outcomes of each option. Similarly, models could be used to financially appraise various options concerned with a PFI or PPP (Public/Private Partnership) development by a PSO.

Resource allocation models

As discussed in Chapter 5, PSOs have developed and used resource allocation models as a means of distributing total financial resources among individual departments and services as a prelude for departmental budget setting within the constraint of available resources. This model will have two key aspects:

→ Mechanisms for distributing the various income sources between departments and services based on the level of activity undertaken by each and the unit of funding involved. For example, an NHS Trust might distribute funds to clinical directorates on the basis of patient numbers and the national PbR (payment by results) tariff.

→ Mechanisms for recharging the costs of central support services (e.g. finance, registry) to individual departments/sections, which will usually be undertaken using a series of drivers such as staff numbers, patient numbers, space, etc.

As well as using such models to make actual allocations of funds and costs to departments, they may also be used as crude forms of financial planning models.

Financial planning models

To improve the financial analysis of their strategic business plans, in future it will probably be necessary for PSOs to develop more sophisticated financial planning models than used previously. These models can assess the financial implications of a large number of different planning scenarios by answering *what if* questions. In evaluating strategic business plans, financial planning models can take account of diverse factors and planning assumptions and assess their financial implications. Having been constructed, they could then be used to assess the financial impact of changes in planning assumptions, such as:

→ growth/contraction in client numbers;

→ change in client mix;

→ change in location of service delivery;

→ changes in levels of user charges;

→ changes in the mix of staff employed to deliver services;

→ changes in the methods of service delivery;

→ changes in levels of capital expenditure in new buildings and equipment;

→ changes in the levels of central support costs.

Financial planning models can identify any major shortfalls between the resources available and the resources needed to implement a particular strategic option, but for them to provide a realistic representation of the real world the following factors must also be incorporated:

→ **Cost and cost driver relationships** – within the model, it is necessary to establish and define which cost drivers influence which types of cost. For example, within a hospital ward costs may be driven by patient numbers, diagnostic mix, severity profile, ward procedures, etc. Also, whereas ward costs might be driven by patient numbers, other hospital costs (e.g. cleaning costs) might be driven by total people numbers, including staff, patients and visitors. Thus, it is important to identify relevant drivers and the links between changes in the drivers and changes in related costs so that they can be built into the model.

→ **Cost profiles** – within the model, profiles will need to be developed to establish the link between changes in the level of the cost driver and changes in the level of cost. These profiles will need to recognise that in relation to changes in the levels of the cost driver some costs are fixed, some directly variable and some semi-variable. In many cases, PSOs will have an unclear picture of these profiles and will need to test out different types of profile between driver levels and costs. In future, it is likely that greater precision will be needed and rough and ready calculations assuming linearity will not suffice.

→ **Resource capacity constraints** – for any planned expansion of activity (e.g. increased college student numbers) a PSO will sometimes be capable of absorbing additional activity on the basis of current resource levels while at other times additional growth will require additional resources. Hence, the model should include capacity measures for different types of resources (e.g. staff, space, equipment) which will indicate when it can absorb growth without additional costs.

Good practice in developing financial models

A number of good practice issues should be considered and applied when developing financial models:

Degree of complexity

Models must provide a realistic representation of the 'real world' and, although simplicity is desirable, the model should not be so over-simplistic as to be naïve. As already mentioned, some PSOs use their existing resource allocation models for financial planning purposes but most of these imply a linear relationship between activity levels and cost and so do not provide for realistic financial planning. Hence, to facilitate realistic financial planning, some degree of complexity is probably inherent in all but the simplest financial modelling.

Output driven

Models must be 'fit for purpose' and deliver the outputs needed. Models must be driven by business needs *not* the availability of data. Where the required data is not immediately available then specific exercises may be required to collect that data. Failing that, assumptions may have to be made which will then comprise factors of uncertainty to be considered when undertaking a sensitivity analysis.

Design principles

Financial models should incorporate certain procedures designed to facilitate good practice, such as:

→ within the model architecture, identify separate areas for input, output and calculations. Mixing them up will be a source of confusion and error;

→ models must be capable of being audited and validated by a third party;

→ models must be reasonably user friendly;

→ good model documentation must be available.

Capital investment appraisal techniques

In this section some techniques are outlined which can be used to appraise and evaluate public service capital projects. First, the basis of the technique will be described and then its applicability will be considered. The techniques discussed are:

→ financial appraisal – Discounted Cash Flow (DCF);

→ economic appraisal – Cost-Benefit Analysis (CBA).

Financial appraisal

The various approaches to capital investment appraisal are outlined below.

Payback

The payback period is both conceptually simple and easy to calculate and is commonly used in commercial organisations. The payback period is the time taken to recover the initial investment. Therefore, a £1m investment that will make a profit of £200,000 a year has a payback period of five years. Investments with a shorter payback period are preferred to those with a long period. Most companies using payback period as a criterion will have a maximum acceptable period. In theoretical terms, the payback approach has a number of weaknesses:

→ it attaches no value to cash flows after the end of the payback period;

→ it makes no adjustments for risk;

→ it is not directly related to wealth maximisation as is net present value (see below);

→ it ignores the time value of money (see below);

→ the 'cut off' period may be arbitrary.

Accounting rate of return (ARR)

The accounting rate of return (ARR) is a very simple rate of return on an investment project, which is calculated as:

$$ARR = \frac{\text{average return (over a period of years)}}{\text{project investment}} \times 100$$

In this equation, average means arithmetic mean and the return used to denote the operating profit from a particular project. ARR is most often used internally when selecting projects. While ARR overcomes some of the weaknesses of payback it still has the following problems:

→ ARR does not take into account the time value of money – the value of a cash flow does not diminish with time as is the case with NPV and IRR;

→ it does not adjust for the greater risk to longer-term forecasts;

→ it tends to favour higher risk decisions because future profits are insufficiently discounted for risk, as well as for time value, whereas use of the payback period leads to overly conservative decisions.

Discounted Cash Flow (DCF)

The main weakness of both payback and ARR is that they consider the size of the various cash flows associated with a project and ignore what is termed the time value of money, since the timing of the cash flows is not considered. Thus, they assume that £100 received or paid in year 1 is equivalent to £100 received in year 2, and so on. However, economics teaches that money has a time value as well as a magnitude and argues that £100 received in year 1 has a greater value than £100 in year 2 (which has greater value than £100 in year 3, etc.). Similarly, £100 spent in year 1 has a higher cost than £100 spent in year 2. This is for two main reasons:

→ The future is uncertain – £100 receivable today is preferable to £100 in a year's time when one may no longer be able to enjoy the benefit of that £100.

→ £100 today can be invested to produce a return which will be in excess of £100 in a year's time.

This basic principle of the time value of money leads to the Discounted Cash Flow (DCF) approach, which takes account of both the magnitude and the timing of the cash flows involved when evaluating capital projects. In PSOs it is the DCF approach which must be used for the financial appraisal of projects. Although it is not possible here to give a full explanation of the DCF approach, we will give a brief explanation of the rationale of the method. The interested reader is referred to the many excellent books on the subject (for example, Jones and Pendlebury, 2000).

With DCF, cash flows, whether they are inflows or outflows, in whatever time period they occur are converted to a common point of reference, namely a present value. Present value is essentially the converse of compound interest. Assuming an interest rate of 10%, then if £100 has a future value of £110 in a year's time the converse is that £110 receivable in a year's time has a present value of £100. Similarly £121 receivable in two years' time has a present value of £100. Thus all cash flows can be converted to a present value. When inflows and outflows are combined, the present value becomes a net present value (NPV).

Let us look at a simple practical example. An organisation is considering two possible projects involving investment in new equipment, both of which have a capital cost of £100,000. The organisation can borrow money at 10% to purchase the equipment. Both types of equipment have a four-year life and will be used to manufacture different products. There will be production costs associated with the manufacture of the products and revenues from the sales of the products. The financial implications are shown in Figure 5.9.

Three points should be noted about these results:

1 In terms of total cash flow, project Y has a larger positive net cash flow than project X.

2 However, project X has a larger net present value of cash flows than project Y. This is because the larger positive cash flows in project X occur earlier in the lifespan of the project and thus generate higher present values than cash flows occurring later in the project.

3 Project X has a positive NPV whereas project Y has a negative NPV.

DCF techniques provide two decision rules for the financial appraisal of potential capital projects:

→ In purely financial terms, projects which show a positive NPV should be undertaken while those which have negative NPVs should not be undertaken. In this case, project X should be undertaken but project Y should not.

→ Where several competing projects have positive NPVs but only one can be undertaken (e.g. because of limited investment funds available), the project with the highest positive NPV should be chosen.

The results of a DCF analysis will be significantly affected by the discount rate used in the analysis. In the above example, for simplicity, a discount rate of 10% was used.

When we look at the applicability of DCF in PSOs we can see several different applications:

→ Some PSOs, such as service providers, may find it necessary to appraise potential capital investments in a manner similar to the above. They would need to set the capital costs of a new project and the associated running costs against the income likely to be generated from the project. For example, a new piece of medical equipment would attract additional patients and hence additional funds.

→ In another PSO the generation of additional revenues may not be the main reason for capital investment. However, DCF may still be relevant in the situation

Figure 5.9 Discounted Cash Flow

	Project X			Project Y		
Year	Production costs (£)	Sales revenue generated (£)	Net cash flow (£)	Production costs (£)	Sales revenue generated (£)	Net cash flow (£)
1	−20,000	+60,000	+40,000	−20,000	+38,000	+18,000
2	−30,000	+65,000	+35,000	−30,000	+65,000	+35,000
3	−30,000	+65,000	+35,000	−30,000	+65,000	+35,000
4	−20,000	+36,000	+16,000	−20,000	+60,000	+40,000

Using DCF one obtains the following picture:

	Project X		
Year	Net cash flow (£)	Discount factor = present value of £1 in the year	Present value of cash flow (£)
0	−100,000	1.00	−100,000
1	+40,000	0.91	+36,400
2	+35,000	0.83	+29,050
3	+35,000	0.75	+26,250
4	+16,000	0.68	+10,880
Total	+26,000		NPV = +2,580

	Project Y		
Year	Net cash flow (£)	Discount factor = present value of £1 in the year	Present value of cash flow (£)
0	−100,000	1.00	−100,000
1	+18,000	0.91	+16,380
2	+35,000	0.83	+29,050
3	+35,000	0.75	+26,250
4	+40,000	0.68	+27,200
Total	+28,000		NPV = −1,120

where, for example, a PSO decides to invest large sums in computerised energy management systems. DCF can show the present value of energy savings made against the capital costs involved.

→ In some PSOs the costs of a capital investment will need to be set against the service benefits that the investment will bring. Although this will be discussed further in the next section on Cost–Benefit Analysis, it will suffice to say that DCF can be of relevance by being a technique which reduces all of the cash flows associated with projects to a single figure – namely a net present value.

Economic appraisal – Cost–Benefit Analysis

DCF is purely a technique of financial evaluation and several criticisms can be levelled at its use as a technique of investment appraisal:

→ DCF techniques use a narrow definition of cost. They consider only financial costs and ignore social costs. Social costs go beyond the financial costs to the organisation concerned and cover costs to society at large of matters such as pollution, traffic congestion, noise, etc.

→ DCF techniques do not consider the benefits of a project other than those manifested through positive cash inflows. Most public sector capital projects are not undertaken with the aim of generating additional revenues and profits but are concerned with the benefits arising from increasing the range and quality of service provision.

→ DCF techniques do not take a long-term view. They only consider projects during the period when cash flows are taking place, and not the complete lifespan of the project, which may be several decades.

Cost–Benefit Analysis (CBA) is a technique of economic evaluation designed to overcome these limitations, although within CBA the principles of discounting are utilised. CBA has been used in many parts of the public sector to assist with decisions about major capital projects, such as the Jubilee underground line and the various proposals for the siting of a third London airport. However, its application is fraught with difficulties and has many critics.

The basic methodology of CBA is summarised in Figure 5.10 and discussed below:

1 **Generate options** – it is important in project appraisal that one does not just consider a single approach to the perceived problems. Several different options and solutions must be developed in order that comparisons can be made. One of these options should be the maintenance of the status quo. The identification of options is perhaps the most difficult and creative part of CBA. It requires considerable imagination and creativity and full use should be made of techniques such as brainstorming, assessment of staff opinions, etc.

2 **List costs and benefits** – this should not prove too difficult a task. All that is required, for each option, is a full list of the potential costs and benefits. It must be emphasised that the term costs of an option means more than just the financial costs. It is intended to also cover any social costs.

Figure 5.10 Cost–Benefit Analysis

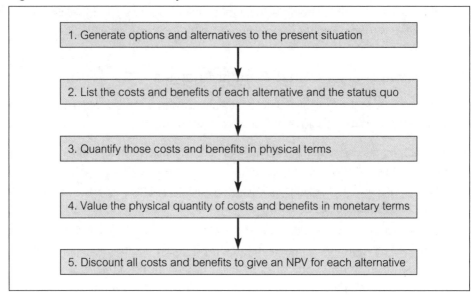

3 **Quantify costs and benefits** – given that a list of costs and benefits has been drawn up, the next stage is to try and quantify those benefits and costs in physical terms. Some public sector examples of benefits could be:
   - reductions in patient mortality rates through investment in new surgical equipment;
   - reductions in response times from investment in new police communications equipment;
   - reductions in supervisory staff numbers resulting from investment in new prisons with improved layout;
   - reductions in break-ins due to investment in school security equipment;
   - reductions in journey times resulting from investment in public transport;
   - reductions in breakdown rates resulting from investment in new ambulances.

   And some examples of costs:
   - increases in traffic noise levels resulting from investment in new roads;
   - increases in the stress levels of staff resulting from investment in new computerised equipment to replace manual procedures.

4 **Value costs and benefits** – this is perhaps the most difficult and contentious part of the CBA approach. An attempt must be made to place monetary values on all of the costs and benefits described above. In some cases (e.g. valuing any staff savings) this is relatively easy to achieve. However, in other areas it is fraught with difficulties of methodology and objectivity. How, for example, does one place monetary values on benefits such as reductions in mortality or response times, or

increases in traffic noise levels? In the past, CBA analysts have attempted to place values on benefits such as these but the approaches adopted have generated considerable controversy and often undermined the whole of the CBA approach.

5 **Discount costs and benefits** – having valued the projected costs and benefits of each option over a period of years these costs and benefits can then be discounted at the test discount rate to give an NPV of costs and benefits.

This combined NPV of costs and benefits can then be used in decision making. In terms of economic theory every project which shows a positive NPV should be undertaken but, in practice, limitations on resources available mean that choices usually have to be made. Thus, a choice between competing projects can be made on the basis of the highest NPV of costs and benefits.

CBA in its purest form has, in the past, been used in many parts of the public sector to appraise large-scale projects. With such projects there have been substantial problems and criticisms relating, particularly, to the valuation in monetary terms of benefits as reduced traffic congestion, numbers of lives saved, increased travel comfort, etc. Attempts at valuation were made but had dubious objectivity. However, there are more pragmatic approaches to CBA which can be adopted without destroying the overall philosophy of trying to compare benefits with costs. For example, the approach to capital investment shown in Figure 5.11 applies a more practical form of CBA which involves scoring and weighting social benefits and social costs rather than quantifying and expressing them in monetary terms.

→ **Identify investment objectives** – objectives must be defined which are specific, measurable, achievable, relevant and time-linked. It is important that these objectives concentrate on the end results of the proposed investment and not the means of achieving them.

→ **Generate options** – it is important that as many options as possible are generated as a means of meeting the objectives. In addition, a do-nothing option will also be needed as a basis for comparison.

→ **Identify and quantify the costs** – a thorough analysis of the costs associated with each of the options is required. For each option, an estimate of the magnitude and timing must be made for capital expenditure, running costs, any cost savings and any residual values such as scrap values.

All of these cash flows must then be discounted to a present value in line with the approach described earlier to give a net present cost for each option.

→ **Assess the benefits** – an analysis needs to be undertaken of the benefits likely to be derived from each of the options. The approach to be adopted can be summarised as follows:

Figure 5.11 Practical approach to capital investment appraisal in PSOs

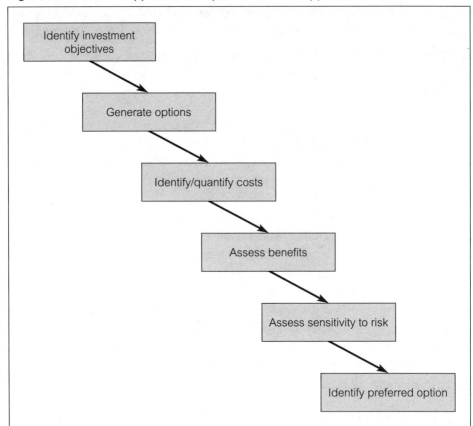

- Those benefits which can be expressed in financial terms, such as cost savings, are to be netted-off against the costs of the option.
- A series of benefit criteria needs to be identified at the outset. These criteria could include quality of care, accessibility to services and physical environment, but should be derived from the investment objectives referred to above.
- A weighting factor needs to be derived for each of these benefits criteria and will indicate its relative importance in evaluating options.
- Each of the possible investment options needs to be scored against each of the benefit criteria identified above and the individual scores weighted by the relevant weighting factor. Thus, it will be possible to derive a total weighted score for each option which will indicate the overall level of benefits to be derived.
→ **Assess sensitivity to risk** – in analysing the costs and benefits of the various options under review, certain assumptions will be made. It is important to test the impact of these assumptions on the costs and benefits of the various options, and

thus their ultimate ranking. This is usually referred to as sensitivity analysis and it may involve analysing the impact on each option of changes in benefit scores, changes in the weightings given to the benefit criterion and changes in the cost assumptions. Sensitivity analysis will provide an analysis of how robust each of the options is to changes in the basic assumptions.

→ **Identify the preferred option** – the approach suggested is to display the various options in order of benefits with the net present costs displayed alongside. The preferred option will be the one that offers the greatest ratio of benefits to costs, although making such a decision may not be easy and may require some subjective judgement.

The essence of CBA, even in this pragmatic form, is still to look at the costs and benefits impacting on all parts of society and not just the organisation itself.

In some cases the outcome of such an analysis will lead to a clearly preferred option, while in other cases the result will be less clear cut. Consider the situation shown in Figure 5.12. It will be seen that in some cases the results of the appraisal provide a clear-cut decision, while in other cases the decision is still unclear and further examination of the options will be needed.

Capital investment appraisal – technical issues

Within the public sector various guidance is available on the appraisal of capital investments in PSOs. The most important guide is probably the Treasury *Green Book* (HM Treasury, 2003). The *Green Book* focuses largely on economic appraisal but does say a little about financial appraisal as well. The guidance discusses the following points:

Timescales

The cash flows from projects will usually have a fairly limited life and thus any financial appraisal would probably not cover a period greater than 25 years. However, the economic benefits will flow for a much greater period and thus the economic appraisal may cover a much longer time period – possibly up to 100 years.

Discount rate

In the public sector the discounting calculation should be undertaken using the discount rate set out in HM Treasury guidance for public sector investments. This is currently set at 3.5% for the first 35 years of a project with a declining rate thereafter. Private sector organisations would use a discount rate that reflected the cost to them of obtaining capital resources (the weighted average cost of capital – WACC). Presumably, as private sector organisations, 3SOs would undertake a similar calculation were it necessary for them to do so.

Figure 5.12 Appraising capital projects

A public sector organisation is evaluating a capital investment project:

Scenario 1

	Option A	Option B	Option C
Weighted benefits score	11.3	13.7	14.6
NPV of costs	£250k	£240k	£230k

Decision: This decision is clear cut. Option C has both highest benefits score and lowest cost.

Scenario 2

	Option A	Option B	Option C
Weighted benefits score	11.3	13.7	14.6
NPV of costs	£250k	£240k	£240k

Decision: This decision is clear cut. Option C has highest benefits score and its costs are equal to option B, which has a lower benefits score.

Scenario 3

	Option A	Option B	Option C
Weighted benefits score	11.3	13.7	14.6
NPV of costs	£250k	£240k	£270k

Decision: Benefits score of option C is 6% greater than option B. However, its costs are 12.5% greater than option B. The options need to be looked at carefully, but the preference would probably be for option B.

Scenario 4

	Option A	Option B	Option C
Weighted benefits score	11.3	13.7	14.6
NPV of costs	£250k	£240k	£256k

Decision: Both the costs and benefits score of option C are 6% greater than option B. Hence on the basis of this appraisal there is nothing to choose between these projects. The two options need to be closely examined and a subjective decision between them will probably be needed.

Inflation

The valuation of costs or benefits should be expressed in 'real terms' or 'constant prices' (i.e. at 'today's' general price level), as opposed to 'nominal terms' or 'current prices'. If necessary, the effect of expected future inflation in the general price level can be removed by deflating future cash flows by the forecast levels of the relevant deflator. Leaving aside general inflation, perhaps of more relevance is specific price inflation, where particular prices are expected to increase at a significantly higher or lower rate than general inflation. In these cases this relative price change should be calculated. Some examples where relative price changes would be relevant to an appraisal include high-technology products, where prices may be expected to fall in real terms, and fuel prices, where the resource supply is scarce.

Risk and uncertainty

In investment appraisals, there is always likely to be some difference between what is expected, and what eventually happens, because of biases, risks and uncertainties:

→ **Bias** – there is a demonstrated, systematic, tendency for project appraisers to be overly optimistic. This is a worldwide phenomenon that affects both the private and public sectors. Adjusting for such optimism should provide a better estimate, earlier on, of key project parameters. Such adjustments for optimism may be reduced as more reliable estimates of relevant costs are built up, and project specific risk work is undertaken.

→ **Uncertainty** – in assessing uncertainty an expected value is a useful starting point for understanding the impact of risk between different options. But however well risks are identified and analysed, the future is inherently uncertain. So it is also essential to consider how future uncertainties can affect the choice between options. Sensitivity analysis is fundamental to appraisal. It is used to test the vulnerability of options to unavoidable future uncertainties. Therefore, the need for sensitivity analysis should always be considered and, in practice, dispensed with only in exceptional cases. Scenarios are also useful in considering how options may be affected by future uncertainty. Scenarios should be chosen to draw attention to the major technical, economic and political uncertainties upon which the success of a proposal depends.

As a consequence of the above phenomena, risk management strategies should be adopted for the appraisal process. Appraisers should calculate an expected value of all risks for each option, and consider how exposed each option is to future uncertainty. Before and during implementation, steps should be taken to prevent and mitigate both risks and uncertainties. It is important to be transparent with sponsors about the potential impact of risks and bias on their proposals.

Capital investment appraisal – conflicting perspectives

As already noted, financial appraisal and economic appraisal of potential capital investments have different perspectives. Financial appraisal is concerned with the

---

Case study 5.3
Public service investment appraisal – differing perspectives

Westingham is a large city suffering the usual problems of traffic congestion, noise, pollution, etc. Consequently it is investigating the feasibility of developing an urban tram system which will transport people from the outskirts of the city into the city centre. The feasibility study has taken two forms:

- a financial appraisal of the commercial feasibility of the project;
- an economic appraisal of the social desirability of the project.

The financial appraisal involves identifying the capital costs (e.g. tracks, trams) and running costs (e.g. power, staff) of the project and the revenues from passenger fares and assessing the feasibility of the project on commercial grounds. This appraisal indicated that the tram project would generate significant financial deficits each year and must, therefore, be regarded as a financially unsound project.

The economic appraisal as well as taking account of the financial costs and revenues associated with the project also took account of social costs (e.g. disruption during construction, demolition of people's houses) and social benefits (e.g. reductions in congestion, noise, pollution). This appraisal indicated that the project would generate a large net social benefit to the community.

Clearly there is a strong conflict here between the two types of appraisal. The only way in which this situation could be resolved was for there to be a public subsidy which recompenses the delivery organisation for any likely financial deficits that might be incurred.

---

financial impact on the service delivery organisation of undertaking the investment, while economic appraisal is concerned with the *broader impact on society* of undertaking the investment. These perspectives can sometimes conflict, as illustrated by the example of an urban tram system in Case study 5.3.

To some extent, these different perspectives are reflected in the respective viewpoints of the service commissioner and the service provider. Since provider organisations are quasi-commercial in nature and have business-type objectives to achieve then they are more likely to find the financial appraisal technique of DCF as being of greatest relevance to them. For example, a provider organisation needs to assess whether investment in a new piece of equipment will generating savings and/or additional income streams that will outweigh the costs of investment and, therefore, improve its financial performance. On the other hand, commissioners are more concerned with the need for a service and whether a piece of equipment will improve the quantity, quality, etc. of service provision. Hence they are likely to find the economic techniques of CBA of greatest relevance. In this case there are likely to be situations where such conflicts arise where projects which are economically desirable do not provide the delivery organisation with a financially sound case for proceeding.

Capital investment appraisal and the Private Finance Initiative

Chapter 2 noted the increasing role of PFI as a means of financing capital developments in the public sector. Consequently there is a process which PSOs must go through to obtain approval for a capital project to be financed via PFI. The precise details of PFI will vary between government departments and sectors, but in broad terms the process is as outlined below.

Outline Business Case (OBC)

An OBC must be prepared for the project. The OBC will outline the background and rationale for the project. It will identify possible options for undertaking the project and these options will be evaluated using the various techniques discussed above. A preferred option will be identified using this process. The OBC will also need to incorporate a preliminary evaluation of the preferred option using a private finance route (through the use of PFI) and a public finance route. In undertaking this evaluation a comparison of the privately financed route (PFI) and the publicly financed route will need to be made against the following criteria:

→ For the public and privately financed routes the value for money provided in the use of public funds.

→ The potential, under the privately financed route, for transferring risk to the private sector.

→ For the public and privately financed routes, the affordability of the project, to the PSO, in terms of the annual financial impact.

→ The PSO will need the approval of the relevant government department before proceeding to the next stage.

Full Business Case (FBC)

An FBC will now need to be prepared which will update the details contained in the OBC in the light of the procurement process. Approval of the relevant department will be needed before contracts can be signed.

Preparations for procurement

A number of tasks need to be undertaken following completion of the OBC but prior to commencement of the procurement process:

1 Prepare a specification of the outputs, performance standards and quality standards of the project as opposed to the physical inputs of buildings, equipment and staffing. It is this specification of service outputs that will form the basis for the tendering process.

2 The possible appointment of professional advisors.

3 The preparation of an information memorandum for possible private contractors.

4 The development of an initial contract framework for the project under a PFI arrangement.

Procurement process

This is extremely complex and only an overview will be given here. In the likely event that the proposed contract is above the EU procurement threshold then the contract will have to be advertised in the *Official Journal of the European Union* (*OJEU*). The advertisement must not be too prescriptive and must give the private sector the flexibility to come up with novel solutions based on the service outputs already specified. The next steps in this stage would be:

1 Issue the information memorandum to interested parties.

2 Create a shortlist of tenderers from those who responded to the advert.

3 Invite the shortlisted firms to tender or negotiate for the provision of services.

4 Evaluate tenders or negotiate with tenderers.

5 Select the best solution.

Contract award

Following approval of the FBC, if the best PFI solution is approved, there might be some further negotiations with the successful private contractor. Contracts can then be awarded and the project can go ahead.

Conclusion

The immense pressures on public services generated by the public service reform agenda, described in Chapter 3, have made the management of large-scale strategic change a key management challenge in PSOs. Unfortunately this task has not always been addressed adequately and has resulted in a variety of strategic failures in terms of delays, cost overruns, non-optimal service outcomes, etc. Such failures can usually be put down to a combination of poor strategic planning and poor strategy implementation.

Strategic planning in PSOs is often seen by many public service employees as being synonymous with very large strategic planning documents strong on promises and lacking in realism which are only read by only a handful of people. Furthermore, it is often the case that PSO managers fail to realise that the implementation of strategy requires large-scale changes to be made in the organisation and that these changes need to be effectively managed.

One particular weakness of strategic management in PSOs concerns the role of financial management. It is not uncommon to read large strategic plans which describe large-scale changes planned to take place in relation to public services but where there is no financial detail provided at all or the financial detail is superficial. Also, it is quite common for there to be no robust framework of financial control of multi-year change programmes with the consequence that sometimes the costs of change go out of control or strategies are not integrated into operational budgets. Finally, one sometimes sees major projects where the appraisal process is not particularly robust and the project, once implemented, fails to achieve what was expected. One well-known example of this concerns the implementation, some years ago, of the new General Medical Services (GMS) contract for family doctors. The new contract was forecast to cost substantially more but was expected to improve services to patients. In the end the project substantially exceeded the already increased budget, access to services was (arguably) poorer and patient satisfaction was lower.

In the author's view, the strategic aspects of financial management in public services are the weakest area of financial management and the one where most improvement is required.

Questions for discussion

→ In your experience, how well have major strategic change projects in public services been financially evaluated?

→ Are our strategic plans based on appropriate projections of the likely levels of resources that will be available?

→ As commissioners, do we integrate financial management into our strategic commissioning process?

→ How well do we manage the implementation of our strategy?

→ Are the changes in our proposed strategy taken account of in the budget setting process?

→ How well do we benchmark our costs against other organisations?

→ How well do we appraise proposed capital projects?

6

Budgeting systems and budget management in public service organisations

Learning objectives

→ To understand the reasons why PSOs operate budget systems

→ To understand the structure and composition of a typical budgeting system in a PSO

→ To appreciate the different types of budget that exist and variations in budgeting practice in PSOs

Introduction

In any organisation of significant size, a system of budgeting is essential and all PSOs operate some system of budgeting and budgetary control. However, in the public services a budgeting system is often seen as just a narrow instrument of financial control used by the finance director to constrain overall expenditure within pre-set limits, and it is not always fully appreciated that the budgeting system is a key management process which aims to improve the overall performance of an organisation in terms of the quantity, quality and cost of services delivered, and facilitate the implementation of strategic plans for change in the organisation.

This chapter considers the issue of budgeting systems and budget management in a PSO context, and covers the following topics:

→ the roles and purposes of a budgeting system in a PSO;

→ types of PSO budget;

→ an overview of the key elements making up a budget system;

→ resource allocation models (RAM) and the budgeting process;

➜ programme analysis and budgeting;

➜ factors to be considered when establishing budgeting arrangements.

In each case the application and operation of budget systems within PSOs will be considered alongside general principles of budgeting.

The roles and purposes of a budgeting system

Although important, the task of containing expenditure within pre-defined limits is not the only role (or even the most important role) of a budget system in a PSO. Containing overall expenditure within limits can be (and historically has been) achieved in large organisations such as PSOs without a sophisticated budget system but by means of a number of fairly crude measures, such as:

➜ freezing staff vacancies;

➜ cutting back on buildings and equipment maintenance to the bare minimum;

➜ deferral of purchases to a later date.

However, these crude approaches can have serious longer-term consequences for the organisation since ultimately key staff posts will have to be filled and maintenance will have to be undertaken. Hence, this approach cannot be seen as an effective approach to resource management, and so a proper budgeting system becomes an essential managerial tool. Let us consider some possible budget roles in PSOs.

Budgets and delegation and empowerment

Once organisations reach a certain size they become too large and complex for one individual to manage and make all the decisions. This would probably be the case in all PSOs and even most third sector organisations. Delegating certain decisions to lower levels of management is one way of resolving this problem. However, delegating the power to make decisions without also delegating the power to use resources and spend money would not be a very effective way of working. Hence, the process of delegation can be aided by utilising a system of budgets. Giving a subordinate manager a budget delegates the authority to incur expenditure up to the budget level, and in line with the strategy, without the need to refer the expenditure decision to higher authority.

Thus, in a PSO, certain budgets may be delegated from the centre of the organisation to departments and even further delegated to a particular section or unit within a department. Some examples of this are shown in Figure 6.1.

Figure 6.1 Budget delegation in PSOs

Public sector organisation	First-level budgetary delegation	Further budgetary delegation
NHS Trust	• Clinical directorates • Support directorates	• Clinical specialties • Individual wards • Individual departments
University	• Academic faculties • Support directorates	• Academic schools • Sub-units of support departments
Local authority	• Individual departments	• Sub-units of departments • Geographic areas
FE college	• Individual departments	• Individual courses

If we consider the reasons why such budget delegation might take place and why it might be a good thing, there are two points to mention:

→ First, there is a strong argument for saying that budget delegation should improve the speed of decision making in a PSO since subordinate managers do not need to obtain higher authority to implement a decision. For example, delegating certain budgets to duty social workers to enable them to make immediate decisions about crisis situations would surely lead to quicker decisions than if the social worker had to refer the case to a supervisor, with the inevitable delay this would entail.

→ Second, budget delegation may also lead to better decisions because the lower-level manager is closer to the point of action and therefore better informed about what needs to be done. For example, in a local authority DSO, the manager of street cleaning services probably has a better idea about how resources should be most effectively and efficiently deployed across various functions and geographic areas than has the general manager of the whole DSO. In this situation, the budgeting system can be seen as a means of empowering managers to improve the way in which they use the resources made available to them and to identify innovative means for improving the effectiveness and efficiency of the services they deliver.

However, the delegation of budgets must be approached with care. It would be counter-productive to delegate budgets to managers or service professionals who were unwilling to manage budgets effectively, or did not have the skills needed to manage such budgets. Whereas, in the private sector, budgetary management skills would usually be seen as a prerequisite for being an effective manager, in the public sector this is not always, and perhaps not usually, the case. Sometimes, service professionals such as doctors, nurses, teachers, social workers, etc. do not see budget management as part of their job but regard it as an administrative chore that they are required to undertake. If such a culture is prevalent in a PSO, it is easy to see how the budgetary system can become ineffective and lead to financial problems. Equally, it must also be said that, in some PSOs, finance managers are often risk averse and have a strong reluctance to decentralise budgets further down the organisation. This may be because of a perceived loss of financial control or a concern that an increasing number of budget holders will require increased support from finance staff.

Budgets and strategy

As we have already seen in Chapters 3 and 5, most PSOs have faced, and will continue to face, a situation of continual change. Such changes may be organisational, procedural, cultural, etc. Consequently, they will need to prepare strategic plans and associated financial strategies to deal and assist with these changes. It is one thing to prepare a strategic plan and another to implement that plan, and situations have arisen where PSOs have failed to implement the strategy they have prepared.

The budget system of a PSO is one key mechanism through which the expenditure priorities of future years are decided upon. Thus, the budget process should be one of the key means for facilitating the implementation of a strategic plan, by ensuring that future expenditure priorities take note of and reflect the content of the multi-year strategic plan. This is not always achieved and, as we shall discuss later, there is often a discontinuity between strategic planning and budgeting in PSOs that needs to be resolved.

Budgets and operational financial planning

Budgeting is an important element in the planning process of a PSO. Each year it is usual for a PSO to prepare an operational plan which outlines the activities to be undertaken over the year ahead and the resources to be used in undertaking those activities. In preparing this operational plan the organisation will need to take account of the resources it has available and the capacity constraints on those resources (e.g. staff, space), and will need to plan to make the best use of those resources. Thus, the budget of the organisation should be an expression of its operational plan in financial terms which indicates (in financial terms) the resources to be made available (e.g. manpower, consumables, overheads, etc.) to each department, unit and activity of the organisation, and the levels and quality of services that it aims to deliver for those resources.

Budgets and resource allocation

The overall resources available to any PSO are limited and must be shared among competing departments, units and activities within the organisation. In the section on resource allocation models we will see that there are two ways to approach this resource allocation process. One involves a type of formula-driven process while the other involves the budget system as the means of undertaking resource allocation.

Budgets and financial control

Having set a corporate plan and allocated resources accordingly, it is important that the plan is achieved. This is true in financial terms and one key role of a budgeting system in a PSO is to exert managerial control over spending to ensure that actual expenditure does not deviate too far from what was planned in the budget, both in terms of individual budgets and the PSO as a whole. This is usually referred to as budgetary control and involves periodically reporting to budget managers their actual spending in a period compared to that planned so that corrective action can be taken where needed. This process is particularly important in PSOs because many types of PSO have only limited flexibility in carrying forward unspent balances to future years.

Budgets and employee motivation

Perhaps the most commonly neglected aspect of budgeting is that of employee and managerial motivation. Much evidence exists to show that budgeting systems are not behaviourally neutral (Hopwood, 1976). The way in which budgets are set and budgetary control operated can have a considerable impact on the managerial performance of an individual manager. Thus, in setting budgets in a PSO, it is important to keep in mind the impact that the budget-setting process may have (in a positive or negative sense) on departmental and managerial performance.

Budgets and organisational demarcations

It is usually thought that the clarification of budgetary arrangements is merely a technical finance issue which can easily be resolved. However, there are situations where the attempt to clarify budget arrangements can pose awkward questions concerning various aspects of professional practice, and the budget system can aid in clarifying responsibilities and lines of demarcation. Consider the following two NHS examples taken from Prowle (1988).

Intensive therapy unit (ITU)

It is usual for an intensive therapy unit (ITU) in a hospital to have its own stock of drugs ready for administration to patients. The clarification of budgetary arrangements requires that someone should be responsible for the expenditure on this budget. Should it be the consultant anaesthetists (who usually manage the ITU) or should it be the main treating consultants? As already discussed, the person held responsible for a budget should be in a position to control the expenditure, which in this case is the prescription of drugs to patients. In this hospital, it was often the case that drugs were simultaneously prescribed to patients by both consultant anaesthetists and the main treating consultants, sometimes with detrimental effects. Trying to clarify budget responsibilities in this case implied trying to establish who is ultimately responsible for patient care while a patient is in the ITU – is the person ultimately responsible the consultant anaesthetist or the patient's own treating consultant? There were conflicting views about this which required clarification.

Therapy treatment

This example can be applied to any of the main therapy departments in a hospital, such as physiotherapy, speech therapy or occupational therapy. Under the process of clinical budgeting it is typical for consultants to be recharged the costs of therapy provided for their patients. When setting up a budgetary system it is necessary to choose the basis on which the recharge is to be made. In practice, there are two possible models:

→ Consultants to be recharged for each referral made by them to the therapy department. Thus, the recharge made would not depend on the pattern of treatment ultimately provided.

→ Consultants to be recharged according to the pattern of treatment provided. In this case the size of the recharge would depend on the treatment given to the patient.

To decide which of these models is best it is necessary to try and clarify the way in which decisions about patient care are made. The first model implies that the consultant initiates the therapy treatment but that the therapist decides the pattern of treatment. The second model implies that the consultant decides when a patient requires therapy and also decides the pattern of treatment. Obtaining an answer as to which of these patient-care models is the correct one is likely to engender a lot of inter-professional rivalry. In turn, this argument raises the question of whether it is the consultant who actually decides that a patient requires therapy. It is argued that frequently nurses and therapists initiate treatment themselves. In this case it would be inappropriate to recharge the consultant at all. Again these are issues which require clarification.

Types of PSO budget

Within any large organisation such as a PSO, a number of different types of budget will exist, although not all PSOs will have the range of budgets described below. The main ones are as follows:

Income budgets

All PSOs need income to fund expenditure and undertake service activities. In most PSOs, much of their income is raised from government sources or local taxes and income is, therefore, largely secure. However, some PSOs also receive other significant sums of income from a variety of different sources (e.g. charges, fees, contract sums, etc.) and, therefore, the PSO will need to have a range of income budgets which reflect targets for generating income from these different sources. Such income budgets may be retained and monitored centrally in the PSO and not distributed to individual departments, units or managers. Alternatively they may be delegated to departments, units or individuals in the organisation and monitored at the lower level. These income budgets will need to be carefully monitored, since shortfalls could cause severe problems in the organisation. Equally, the PSOs will need to have some form of process for dealing with shortfalls against income budgets which may arise and which may require reductions in spending or transfers from financial reserves or other programmes.

Expenditure budgets

Expenditure budgets in a PSO will be set for various departments and units within the organisation and may cover a range of items, such as permanent staffing costs, temporary staffing costs, consumables costs, travel expenses, overhead costs, equipment costs, etc.

The annual expenditure budget of the PSO is set both in total and in terms of individual departments' budgets, the former being set by reference to the total income available to the organisation from various sources. Also, it is usually the case that the overall budget for the PSO must be approved by the 'board' of the organisation and this duty cannot be delegated to lower levels.

Capital budgets

We have already seen that capital expenditure is concerned with expenditure on larger items with a working life in excess of 12 months, although the precise definition of what constitutes 'capital' will vary between sectors and between PSOs. Within a PSO there will be a variety of capital expenditure budgets related to activities such as purchase of 'front-line' equipment, purchases of other equipment (e.g. estates-related equipment), IT procurement, purchase of vehicles, buildings construction and buildings refurbishment.

Larger capital projects, for example major building construction, will take several years to complete and will involve many different stages, such as design, land acquisition, construction, fitting-out, etc. Thus, whereas most income and expenditure budgets will be for a one-year period, the capital budget for this type of major construction project will be for the total cost of the project in each year over a multi-year period. However, with multi-year projects, it will be necessary each year to produce a capital budget to show the likely level of capital expenditure and any capital receipts for that year. As is often the case, the capital project may not go according to plan for a number of reasons, such as inclement weather, technical problems, etc., and the actual capital expenditure will be different from what was anticipated. Consequently, the capital expenditure profile in later years will also have to be updated to take account of these changes.

Main elements of a budget system

Although the detailed aspects of a budgeting system will vary between different types of PSO the fundamental features will remain unchanged. Any budget system has three main components, namely: a budget framework, a budget-setting mechanism and a budget-reporting system. This framework will apply as much in a PSO as in any other type of organisation and each of these components is illustrated in Figure 6.2 and discussed below.

Figure 6.2 Elements of a budget system

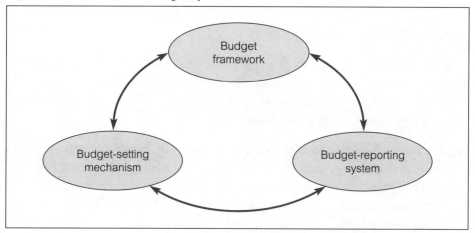

Budget framework

General principles

The role of the budget system as a means of delegation and empowerment within an organisation has already been discussed and, therefore, a budget system must reflect the framework of responsibility and accountability in the organisation. This means answering the following questions:

→ Who are to be the budget holders in the organisation?

→ What specific activities are they responsible for?

→ What items of expenditure are to be included in their budgets?

→ What items of income are to be included in their budget?

→ What workload and performance standards are required from them?

→ What powers of authority do they have in relation to their budgets? For example, are they able to switch funds between different budget categories or do they require higher approval to do this?

Answers to these questions are never clear cut and will vary. No two organisations will have the same organisational and managerial arrangements and consequently neither will they have the same budgeting framework. Furthermore, it must be recognised that many organisations, including some PSOs, do not have a rational and tidy budget framework along the lines described above. Quite often, one sees examples of individuals having responsibility for activities but having no control over resources or expenditure items with no nominated person responsible for controlling them. Thus, the framework described above must be seen as something to be aimed for and not something which already exists.

Typical PSO budget structures

In most PSOs, as with any large organisation, there will be a large number of individual budget holders, each having specific responsibilities and controlling resources. Although the precise pattern of budget holders will vary, in most PSOs these can, in general, be classified into two main types:

→ **Direct service budget holders** – these are budget holders with responsibility for direct service delivery units in the PSO. Examples include clinical directors in an NHS Trust, course or module leaders in an FE college, leaders of local authority social work teams, head teachers of schools and station managers in a fire and rescue service.

→ **Support service budget holders** – these will be the heads of the various support departments in the organisation and individual units within each support department. Examples include the personnel department, the finance department, cleaning services, security and buildings maintenance.

Let us now use a few examples to illustrate the variations in practices between PSOs in the configuration of their budget arrangements:

→ In some PSOs the buildings maintenance budget for both emergency and planned minor works might be held by a central estates manager. In other PSOs, while the budget for emergency work might still be held by the central estates manager, the budget for planned minor works might be held by individual operational managers in the organisation. In the former it is the estates manager who decides what work should be done (emergency and planned) while in the latter it is the operational managers who decides what level of planned minor works they can afford from their budgets (and on what projects). The operational manager would make a contract with the central estates department or an external contractor to undertake the work.

→ In some PSOs certain income budgets will be delegated to individual departments and units within that department. In other PSOs such delegation of income budgets will not take place and budgets will be retained centrally. For example, the income budgets for research and consultancy delegated to individual schools in a university.

→ In some PSOs, maintenance budgets for specialist equipment will be held in the central estates department, while in other PSOs the budgets will be delegated to departments who will commission and pay for maintenance work.

Degree of decentralisation

Budgets within an organisation may be decentralised to a lesser or greater degree. The example in Figure 6.3 shows the budget arrangements for the diagnostics and therapies division of an NHS Trust. In the first instance most of the budgets will be delegated to the heads of therapies and diagnostics with a small budget being retained at divisional level. The budgets may then be further delegated to individual therapies (and diagnostics) with further delegation to budget holders at the hospital and community level.

There is no one correct approach and organisations must implement the organisational and budgeting arrangements which best meet their local needs. Selecting the most appropriate budget framework in an organisation is not purely an accounting matter. Budget responsibility is a corporate topic which has financial, commercial and managerial implications.

Figure 6.3 Decentralisation of budgets

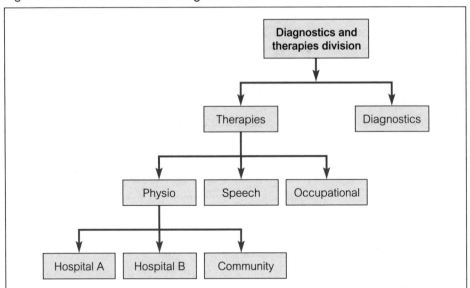

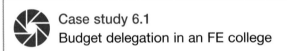

Case study 6.1
Budget delegation in an FE college

Bramwell FE College has traditionally operated a centralised budget system whereby most items of expenditure are the responsibility of the Principal or Assistant Principals in the college. The only budgets delegated to heads of academic departments are those for postage, stationery and travel expenses. The college has been considering further budget delegation to academic heads, most notably the budget for staffing. Although there are perceived to be potential advantages of such delegation in terms of better use of resources, etc., the college has decided against such a course of action for the time being because:

• it is not felt that academic heads will effectively manage their budgets and the college could end up in a financial deficit position;
• the current financial systems in the college are not believed to be capable of providing the required financial information to an extended range of budget holders;
• the small finance department cannot provide sufficient support to an extended range of budget holders;
• the college is in the middle of undertaking a process of substantial strategic change and it is felt that the delegation of budgets will hinder this change rather than facilitate it.

Budget-setting process

Whatever budget framework is adopted there will be some process or mechanism for setting the expenditure budgets for individual departments. Budgets will usually be set for a 12-month period but, as noted earlier, budgets in some PSOs may be prepared several years into the future, with the first year being firmer than the later years. This would operate as a rolling process with the outline budget for year 2 being converted into a firm budget the following year.

Overall framework

Figure 6.4 summarises the factors which may influence budget setting in a PSO. Starting with the budget for 2007/8, the budget-setting process moves towards the construction of budgets for future years. This would involve a firm budget for 2008/9 and possibly looser forms of budget for later years. In constructing such budgets

Figure 6.4 Budget-setting process – key factors

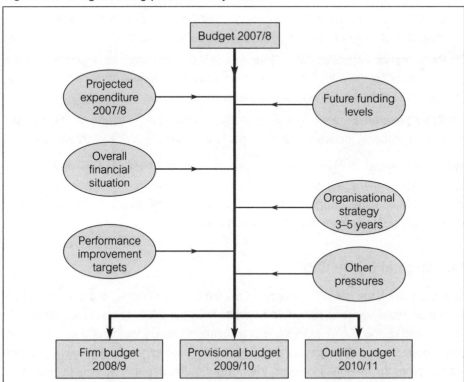

there will be a number of influencing factors, of which the following are suggested as being of greatest importance:

→ **Projected expenditure for 2007/8** – expenditure for the current year (compared to budget) is relevant since it is important to know whether the budget will be over- or underspent and whether such under/overspendings are a one-off event or have taken place over a number of years.

→ **Future funding levels** – PSOs have indications of expected funding levels for future years and the likely levels of growth (or contraction) of resources. Within those overall figures there will also be an indication of the expected levels of resources which will be available to fund specific services in future years. These resource projections will inform the budget-setting process.

→ **Overall financial situation** – this means the overall financial position of the PSO itself and includes, for example, whether it is in a position of financial surplus or financial deficit, what sort of financial reserves it has, etc.

→ **Organisational strategy** – the budget is one of the key means of implementing the overall strategy of the PSO. Thus, aspects of the strategy that require shifts in resources will need to be taken into account when setting budgets. For example, the aim may be to reduce one service and expand another or change the location where a service is delivered. These changes will have clear budgetary implications and should form part of the budget-setting process.

→ **Performance improvement targets** – most PSOs operate in a regime where it is necessary for them to demonstrate improved performance from one year to the next. This requirement will need to be factored into the budget-setting process.

→ **Other pressures** – a whole range of other factors may impinge on the budget-setting process, including political pressures, current service shortfalls, etc.

Within this overall budget-setting process a number of different models may be applied. Three of these models are briefly outlined below, but it must be recognised that in practice the budget-setting approach will probably be based, to some degree, on a combination of these broad models.

Incremental budgeting

With this model, the main determinant of the expenditure budget of a department will be the previous year's expenditure budget. Thus the 2008/9 budget will largely be determined by the 2007/8 budget, with adjustments made for the effects of inflation, new developments, changes at the margin or the need to generate across-the-board efficiency improvements. However, the budget of the department is not linked to its projected workload, planned strategic change or efficiency level, and no attempt is

Figure 6.5 Incremental budgeting

The transport unit of a public sector organisation had a budget in 2007/8 of £1.0 million. During that year, the unit was expected to cover 500,000 miles. The budget for 2008/9 is to be based on the budget for 2007/8 with the following adjustments being made:

- The organisation as a whole has to meet a 2% efficiency target in 2008/9 and this is to be applied to all units equally.
- Pay and price inflation is expected to be 4% in 2008/9.
- The unit has been told to expect a small increase in the mileage covered in 2008/9 and the costs of this are estimated to be £35,000 at 2008/9 prices.

However, it should also be noted that the unit consistently underspends against its budget and its actual mileage is consistently below plan. Also comparisons with other similar units suggests that it is not an efficient unit.

Using the incremental method of budget setting, the budget for 2008/9 would be calculated as follows:

Base budget 2007/8	£1,000,000
Deduct efficiency target (2%)	−£20,000
Base budget 2007/8 at new efficiency level and at 2007/8 prices	£980,000
Add inflation addition (4%)	+ £39,200
Base budget 2007/8 at new efficiency level and at 2009/9 prices	£1,019,200
Add amount for growth in activity in 2009 (5%)	+ £35,000
Budget 2008/9	£1,054,200

However, the following points should be noted:

- The unit has been granted additional funds for additional work in 2008/9 when it already does less mileage than planned and underspends on its budget.
- The unit has been granted additional funds for additional work when it is already seen to be an inefficient unit. This inefficiency is not questioned as part of the budget-setting process.

made to justify the historic level of the budget. Consider the simple example of a PSO transport budget, shown in Figure 6.5.

The approach to budget setting shown in Figure 6.5 is not necessarily desirable but is traditionally quite common in the public sector. The main weakness of this approach is that the base budget is not queried for appropriateness and relevance and no link exists with the overall workload, only with marginal changes in workload. Such budgets are effectively fixed budgets since they will not usually be changed in-year in response to changing departmental workload.

Figure 6.6 Workload-based budgets

The budget for the catering department of a PSO is computed as follows:

- Projected number of meals in 2008/9 = 240,000 (20,000 per month).
- Estimated cost per meal in 2008/9 = £1.50 (this equals the unit cost per meal in 2007/8 with adjustment for inflation). However, other similar units have a budgeted unit cost per meal which averages £1.30 in 2008/9.
- Notional budget for 2008/9 = 240,000 × £1.50 = £360,000.

However for the first month of the year the following results took place:

- The actual number of meals served was only 18,000.
- Actual expenditure in the month was £27,800.

Analysing the results provides the following picture:

- Notional monthly budget = 20,000 × £1.50 = £30,000.
- Workload adjusted budget for the month = 18,000 × £1.50 = £27,000.
- Budget overspend for month = workload adjusted budget − actual expenditure = £27,000 − £27,800 = −£800 (overspend).

The following comments are pertinent:

- Without the workload adjustment the budget position would have shown an underspend.
- The budget overspend in April will need to be recovered in later months.
- Although the budget is adjusted for changes in workload there is still no consideration of efficiency in relation to the unit cost per meal. The costs per meal is still high compared to other similar units and needs investigating.

Workload-based budgets

With some types of budgets, or parts of budgets, the budgeted level of expenditure can be linked to the planned departmental workload. Take, for example, the catering budget in a PSO, shown in Figure 6.6.

In Figure 6.6, the unit cost of provisions is a target cost which will apply throughout the year but which will clearly vary from meal to meal. Budgets such as these are termed flexible budgets since the overall budget will change in accordance with the numbers of meals actually produced.

However, for setting workload-based budgets there are a number of prerequisites:

→ **Measures of workload** – these are credible measures of workload on which the budgets can be based. In many public service areas such workload measures are not easy to obtain and so workload-based budgets cannot be developed. For example, consider the difficulty of identifying suitable workload measures (which could be used for budget setting) for, for example, nurses on a hospital ward or police officers.

→ **Workload data** – there would need to be reasonably accurate data on the workload of the function or department being considered. This requires the existence of suitable information systems to capture this data.

→ **Unit costs** – to set budgets there needs to be agreement as to the unit cost to be applied to different levels of workload.

Zero-based budgeting (ZBB)/priority-based budgeting (PBB)

These related approaches were developed to overcome the main weaknesses of the incremental approach, which fails to look at the base budget of a department, and the workload-based approach, which only looks at volumetric variations in workload and not the efficiency of operation. ZBB/PBB approaches are particularly applicable to central support departments in a PSO rather than to service departments. PBB is essentially a simpler and more pragmatic version of ZBB but the basic principle is the same in both cases (see Figure 6.7).

First, we need to clarify the use of the terms 'decision unit' and 'decision package':

Decision units

This is the term used to define the units in the PSO around which the budget-setting process will operate. Decision support units could be individual departments, units within a department, sub-units or geographic areas. The aim is to base budget setting on the most appropriate level in the organisation for decision making about priorities. A larger number of decision units might provide a more meaningful analysis than a small number of decision units but would also be more complex. Thus, for a university, a decision unit could be the whole university, a faculty, a department, a subject area or an individual course. Overall, a decision unit should have the following characteristics:

→ a single manager should be clearly identifiable as being responsible for its activities;

→ it must have clear and measurable objectives;

→ it must have clear and measurable outputs.

Decision packages

For the purpose of a ZBB/PBB budget-setting process these activities must be classified into what are termed 'decision packages'. This involves describing the various

Figure 6.7 Zero-based/priority-based budgeting

A PSO has four main 'decision units', namely the support departments: finance, human resources, public relations/marketing and IT. As part of a ZBB/PBB exercise the managers of each of those departments have undertaken an exercise to identify the discrete 'decision packages' within each unit.

The decision packages concern activities currently undertaken in their departments and some potential additional new activities (shaded) they wish to initiate. They have identified the costs of each decision package and benefits generated by that decision package. The decision packages in priority order are:

Finance dept	HR dept	IT	PR dept
A	V	L	H
B	W	M	I
C	X	N	
	Y	O	
	Z	P	
		Q	
		R	

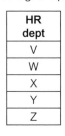
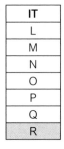

These lists of decision packages (current and planned) and associated cost/benefit information are reviewed by senior management of the PSO and ranked in order of priority for the PSO as a whole. Decision packages are then funded up to the limit of total resources available.

| H | V | W | L | M | N | I | A | X | B | O | P | Q | R | Y | Z | C |

Resource limit

Several points should be noted about the results of this exercise:

- Senior management have not altered the priorities of departmental managers, only constructed an overall ranking for the PSO as a whole.
- One current decision package has not been funded and will be discontinued.
- One new decision package has been funded and will be initiated.

activities of a decision unit as a set of decision packages which describe how the unit achieves its objectives. Thus, decision packages are concerned with identifying different ways of performing the functions of the unit and meeting its objectives. Decision packages can be of two main types:

→ **Mutually exclusive packages** – these are packages where the only alternative to undertaking and funding the package is not to undertake and fund it. There is no middle way. In public services it may be difficult to think of many such services since most services are either statutory in nature or can be provided at different levels. One example of a mutually exclusive decision package could be the provision of counselling services to employees.

→ **Incremental** – these are packages where the decision package can be undertaken at different levels, such as minimum level, current level, enhanced level, etc. Thus, health checks on patients could be provided at different levels of sophistication and thoroughness.

Under ZBB/PBB, therefore, no budget is automatically rolled forward, as is the case with the incremental approach. Expenditure budgets must be fully scrutinised and decision centre managers must indicate the decision packages they currently undertake or might wish to undertake in future, the costs attaching to each of those decision packages, and the benefits and priority of undertaking each of those decision packages.

Senior management can then scrutinise all decision units in the PSO, compare the costs with the benefits and priorities attaching to each package or activity, and where appropriate make adjustments to individual base budgets in line with overall corporate priorities and total resources available.

Whatever the merits of ZBB/PBB in principle, there are some clear practical problems:

→ Whatever the ranking process produces the reality is that some activities or decision packages must be undertaken by statute and thus there is limited discretion over this.

→ The procedures are cumbersome and time-consuming. Consequently, in some organisations the ZBB/PBB process might be applied to individual decision units every three years rather than every year.

→ It will probably be difficult to switch resources between areas of activity without retraining staff and/or making redundancies.

→ There will inevitably be strong organisation resistance to implementing the outcomes of the process.

→ The process is open to 'game-playing', whereby managers rank their weakest packages most highly thus giving them the best chance of getting across the resource threshold.

Some organisations use an approach similar to ZBB/PBB not for budget setting as such but for the purposes of identifying where reductions in expenditure might be achieved as a consequence of resource pressures. Once again, decision units are required to identify and rank those decision packages which could constitute cuts in expenditure. The packages for all decision units are submitted to senior management, who rank the proposals in order and identify the cuts to be made based on the overall priorities of the organisation.

Case study 6.2
Budget prioritisation in social care

The social services department of Dovedale County Council was faced with a severe budget deficit amounting to almost £2 million. Two approaches to resolving this budget deficit were considered:

- top-slicing all budgets in the department by 5% with each and every individual budget holder being required to identify savings of that magnitude;
- the use of a targeted approach which obtained savings of the required amount by identifying activities which are of lowest priority and greatest ease of implementation.

The second approach was adopted and departmental managers were required to put forward plans which would indicate how each manager would make savings at the following levels: 3%, 5% and 7%. In putting forward their plans, each manager also had to score the possible risk impact of each proposal (on a scale of 1–3 with 1 = low and 3 = high) against the following criteria:

- ease of deliverability;
- policy/strategy compliance (will it cause more problems in the medium term?);
- standards/vulnerability (adverse impact on discharge of statutory responsibility/professional standards as they effect vulnerable people);
- public/user risk (general impact on users and upon public perception – political test?);
- organisational risk (impact/implication for functionality of organisation);
- performance risk (adverse impact on performance measures).

The criteria were not weighted (but could have been) and an overall score was calculated.

Senior managers in the department evaluated the proposals put forward and considered the balance between the magnitude of cost savings and the various risk factors. Departmental managers were also questioned about their proposals to assess the robustness of their risk evaluations and cost estimates.

The outcome of this process was that senior management in the department identified which activities should be eliminated to achieve the savings target and an action plan was prepared. The implementation of this savings plan was closely monitored using a traffic lights system and half way through the financial year, the situation was as shown below:

- Savings achieved (green) = £1.3m
- Progress being made (amber) = £0.4m
- Difficulties being encountered and alternatives may be needed (red) = £0.3m

The overall view in the department was that although this process was laborious and time consuming, the final outcome was fairer and much more satisfactory in minimising the impact on services.

Generally, most PSOs have difficulty with the concept of ZBB/PBB. There are often difficulties in identifying clear decision packages and in identifying the objectives and impact of those packages, with consequent difficulties in ranking packages in priority order. Furthermore, some PSOs feel uncomfortable about the idea of cuts in expenditure resulting in the cessation of lower-priority activities in some departments, and PSO managers often feel happier with a situation where every department bears an equal cut. However, in an environment of limited growth in public funding this process of prioritising the various activities of the PSO will probably become increasingly important in the management of the organisation.

Mixed approaches to budget setting

These three approaches to expenditure budget setting are not mutually exclusive. For example, the provisions element of a catering budget might be a flexible or workload-based budget while the catering staffing budget might be a fixed budget established by the incremental or PBB method.

Inflation adjustments

All PSO expenditure will be affected, to a lesser or greater degree, by inflation, whether as a consequence of pay awards or commodity and service price increases. Thus, there is the issue of how to deal with this inflation during the budget-setting process. There are three basic approaches:

→ **Retain central inflation reserve** – the PSO retains a reserve of funding at the centre and releases additional funding, from that reserve, to budget holders as and when their budgets are affected by inflation. There is no guarantee that they will be fully funded for all of the impact of inflation, since the central reserve may not be large enough to do that, but they will have some degree of protection from it.

→ **Devolve to budget holders** – in this situation no central reserves are held for inflation and all funds are distributed to budget holders. The budget managers then have to manage the financial consequences of pay and price inflation using the funds available to them. Such an approach is often seen as inequitable, especially where a budget is quite small in value and has limited scope for finding savings or where a budget holder might be hit by a disproportionate amount of pay and price inflation compared to the average rate. However, this approach does give greater empowerment to budget holders to manage their resources.

→ **Combination approach** – this involves a combination of both of the above, where a small central reserve is held to provide some cushion to budget holders in difficult circumstances but the majority of inflation funding is distributed to budget holders.

Moderation of overall budgets

Overall, a PSO needs to contain its expenditure within the income available otherwise financial problems will ensue. Thus, it is vitally important in a PSO to keep a firm control of the allocation of budgets to budget holders and there needs to be an overall framework for achieving this. A simple example of a framework is shown in Figure 6.8. The following points need to be noted:

→ The sum of allocated budgets and reserves must always equate to the expected income of the PSO. However, income budgets do not necessarily remain stable

Figure 6.8 Moderation of budgets

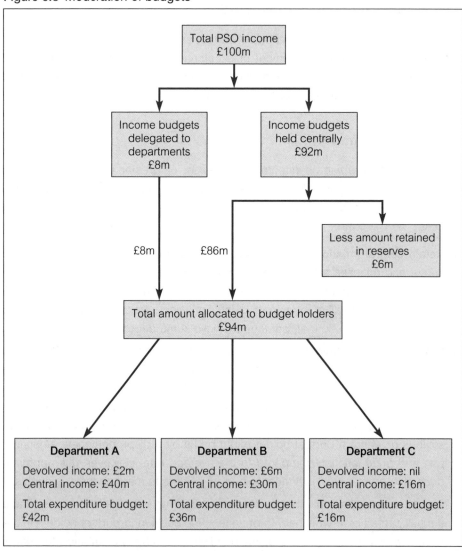

and, unlike expenditure budgets, are to a certain degree outside the direct control of the PSO. Hence, the PSO will periodically need to review its income budgets and, if necessary, amend its expenditure budgets or reserves in the light of planned changes in income. An example of this concerns university student numbers. Early in the academic year the university will need to compare actual student enrolments against the planned enrolments on which the original income budgets were based. This is because any significant shortfall in student numbers and income streams may lead to a combination of reductions in financial reserves, planned surpluses or reductions in expenditure budgets.

→ Where an individual department has a delegated income budget, the achievement of that income budget will also determine its overall expenditure budget. Any shortfall in income might lead to a reduction in an expenditure budget or depletion of accumulated reserves. However, in extreme cases it may not be possible, in the short term, for the department to reduce its expenditure budgets to the required level without damaging its operational capability. In these circumstances, financial assistance will be required from the centre over an interim period.

→ Overspendings against budgets need to be monitored since ultimately such overspendings, if they continue, will need to be financed. This can come from other budgets or from reserves.

Preparing capital budgets

As noted earlier, capital budgets will usually be prepared on a project basis. Estimates of capital expenditure on building works, engineering works and equipment will be prepared by technical specialists such as architects and engineers. Where the project extends over several years, estimates of expenditure will usually be prepared for each year based on the likely level of capital works to be undertaken in that year.

Budget-reporting system

Aims of the budget-reporting system

To manage their budgets effectively, budget managers need to be provided with information showing their progress against their budgets, whether income, expenditure or capital budgets. It is important to provide feedback on income and expenditure against budget, in order to:

→ identify problems;

→ control expenditure;

➜ focus on areas where remedial action is needed;

➜ assess managerial performance;

➜ motivate managers.

Key aspects of the reporting system

Therefore, the provision of budgeting information must be a clear part of the information and IT strategy of the organisation. Although the precise configuration of information systems will vary considerably between organisations, a number of common themes can be identified which are applicable to all budgeting information systems:

➜ **Relevance** – budget managers need relevant information. This relates to issues of responsibility and control as managers require information on those items of expenditure over which they have responsibility and can exert control.

➜ **Frequency and timeliness** – in many organisations, budget managers may receive monthly budget reports within a few days of the end of the month, but with decentralised information systems, managers can often obtain such information at any time via computer terminals within their department. However, even where such decentralised budget information systems exist, the timeliness of the information will be constrained by how frequently the budget system has been updated by the main financial feeder systems, such as payroll, payments and income.

➜ **Format** – although the precise format of a budget report will vary, it will usually show the following information:
  - total budget for the year;
  - budget for the month, which may be a simple twelfth of the annual budget or is adjusted to reflect seasonal variations in some type of expenditure, such as heating costs;
  - expenditure for the month;
  - variance for the month;
  - cumulative budget for the year to date;
  - cumulative expenditure for the year to date;
  - year-end estimated expenditure;
  - variance for the year to date.

➜ **Accuracy and content** – the information on actual expenditure included in budget reports can be of three main types:
  - cash payments actually made;
  - cash payments plus accruals of creditors, i.e. expenditure on goods and services received but not yet paid for;

- cash payments plus accruals plus commitments, i.e. goods and services ordered for which an expenditure commitment exists but which have not yet been received.

Budget reports usually include accruals of creditors but not always commitments of expenditure, although the latter is becoming more common. Budget managers obviously need to be aware of any additional expenditure commitments not included on their budget reports.

→ Support – support and advice on the content of budget reports is needed by budget managers. In some cases, departments or directorates might have their own decentralised finance officer, while in other cases support will be given by a central finance department. Provision of such support is a key role of the finance function.

Enhancements to budget reporting mechanisms

A number of enhancements to basic budget models can be identified and could be applied in some (but not all) PSOs.

Profiling of budgets

In simpler budget systems the monthly expenditure for individual budget headings is compared with one twelfth of the annual budget and variances are reported. There are in some instances where this approach will produce misleading information, for example:

→ **Heating costs** – comparing actual expenditure with twelfths of the budget will result in budget overspends in winter months and underspends in summer months.

→ **Grass cutting costs** – comparing actual expenditure with twelfths of the budget will result in budgeting overspends in summer months and underspends in winter months.

Although these are extreme examples of seasonal variations in expenditure, there are many examples where expenditure is not incurred evenly throughout the year. Hence, more advanced budget systems try to profile budgets to reflect expected expenditure for the months in question. Variations from the budget can then be regarded as real rather than seasonal variations.

Budgetary variance analysis

As noted above, a typical budgeting control report might show the variation between actual expenditure and planned budget both for the month and the cumulative position for the year. In practice, variations from budget may occur for a large number of reasons such as workload pressures, price increases or poor expenditure management.

Figure 6.9 Budgetary variance analysis

The transport unit of a PSO is comparing its actual budgetary performance with its original plan. The results for the first three months of the year are shown below:

	Planned	Actual
Mileage travelled	100,000	110,000
Fuel costs (£)	20,000	24,000
Fuel usage (gallons)	5,000	5,790
Average price per gallon (£)	4.00	4.15
Average miles per gallon	20.00	19.00

Clearly there is a budget overspend of £4,029 (£24,029 – £20,000), but this overspend can be ascribed to three main causes:

- variations in mileage travelled
- variations in fuel price
- variations in fuel efficiency.

Variance analysis permits the identification of the impact of each of these factors on the budget position as shown below:

Overall variance	£4,029
less fuel price variance =	£750
Residual variance	£3,279
less mileage variance =	£2,185
Residual variance	£1,094
less fuel efficiency variance	£1,094
Residual variance	£0

A simple budget variance does not indicate the reasons why expenditure has deviated from budget. The technique of budget variance analysis was developed in industry many years ago as a means of explaining the reasons why expenditure has deviated from budget. It has practical application in a PSO, as in the example of a PSO transport unit shown in Figure 6.9.

A standard budgetary control report would merely show that the transport unit had exceeded its budgets by £4,029 but even a cursory analysis would show that there are three factors at work here, namely the price of fuel, the mileage covered and the fuel efficiency.

Variance analysis uses this information to disaggregate the causes of an expenditure variance. It can also identify the department or individual person who should be regarded as responsible and accountable for a particular variance:

→ **Fuel price variance** – this is calculated as the difference in actual price and planned price multiplied by the planned fuel usage in gallons:

$$= (£4.15 - £4.00) \times 5,000 = £750$$

This variance is an unfavourable (overspent) variance and although fuel prices may be regarded as uncontrollable this is not necessarily the case and the variance probably lies with the procurement department of the PSO.

→ **Mileage variance** – this is calculated as the difference between actual miles (at actual fuel efficiency) and planned miles (at actual fuel efficiency) multiplied by the actual price per gallon:

$$= (110,000/19 - 100,000/14) \times £4.15 = £2,185$$

This variance is the responsibility of those departments who have requested transport services.

→ **Fuel efficiency variance** – this is calculated as the difference between planned miles (at actual fuel efficiency) and planned miles (at planned fuel efficiency) multiplied by the actual price per gallon:

$$= (100,000/19 - 100,000/20) \times £4.15 = £1,094$$

This variance is the responsibility of the transport unit itself since it is responsible for the efficiency of transport operations.

This example concerns the support function of a PSO, but with a little imagination it is easy to see how the variance analysis approach can be used to identify key variances and responsibilities for front-line services. Consider Case study 4.2, which concerned the costs of diagnostic imaging procedures in NHS Trusts. For a particular trust imaging department, the difference between planned expenditure and actual expenditure for a particular class of imaging could be analysed to produce a number of different variances:

→ **Volume variance** – resulting from the actual volume of procedures being more or less than planned.

→ **Mix variance** – resulting from the actual mix of procedures being more or less than planned.

→ **Price variance** – resulting from differences in pay and non-pay costs being different to that planned.

→ **Efficiency variance** – resulting from lesser or greater efficiency in the conduct of imaging procedures compared to that anticipated at the planning stage.

> ### Case study 6.3
> ### Ineffective budget systems in an NHS Trust
>
> Blankshire NHS Trust is a large acute NHS Trust which comprises two large hospitals. Budgets have already been formally delegated to a series of clinical directors and support service directors. The trust has recently incurred a multi-million pound financial deficit and is examining the causes of that deficit. A large part of the deficit is seen as being caused by poor budget management by the budget directors. Consequently the trust undertook a review of the operation of budgetary control in the organisation.
>
> The following key points were observed:
>
> - There is no clear link between the workload and service access targets given to clinical directors and the budgeted level of funds to deliver that workload.
> - There are concerns about the veracity of the workload data produced by the trust's information systems.
> - Sometimes, senior managers in the trust overrule clinical and support directors about certain expenditure decisions.
> - The inflation reserve is still held centrally and released to budget holders throughout the year. There are concerns that the way in which funds are released does not reflect the cost pressures incurred by the various budget holders.
> - Sometimes a budget holder holds the budget for a facility which is used by several units in the trust. No attempt is made to identify or recharge the costs incurred by the various units.
> - It is accepted that the current configuration of services in the two hospitals is financially unsustainable in the medium to longer term and rationalisation needs to take place. However, the trust has been rather slow at developing and implementing a strategy for service reconfiguration.
>
> The overall conclusion had to be that there are so many weaknesses in the existing budget system that it is not really possible to hold budget directors accountable for poor budgetary performance. Before this could be done it is necessary to remedy the weaknesses of the existing system described above.

Resource allocation models and the budgeting process

In many PSOs the budgets of individual departments are primarily expenditure budgets with little or no delegation of income budgets. Thus, after the PSO has estimated the likely level of income receivable from all sources it will set an overall expenditure budget for the whole organisation. The budget-setting process then involves setting expenditure budgets for individual departments (using one or more of the approaches outlined above) so that the total of the expenditure budgets does not exceed the total expenditure budget for the whole PSO.

The alternative approach adopted by some PSOs is to develop and use a resource allocation model (RAM). Such models will, in effect, share out the projected income of the PSO (on some suitable basis) among departments, the latter being free to set their own budgets within the total delegated income figure. The best examples of where a RAM approach is or could be applied in public services are as follows:

→ **Universities** – many universities distribute funding to academic departments using a formula-driven model based on numbers of students and subjects studied after top-slicing some of the funding to finance central support costs.

→ **Schools** – local education authorities are required to distribute funding to its schools using a formula-driven model based on the numbers of pupils and their age band.

→ **NHS Trusts** – as already discussed, NHS Trusts are largely remunerated according to the number of patients treated and the national tariff for the clinical condition of the patient. It would be an easy next step to distribute funding to clinical directorates using a formula-driven model based on numbers of patients and tariff weighting after top-slicing some of the funding to finance central support costs.

Some consider a RAM approach to be essential to the management of the organisation, as its use facilitates a devolved approach to management which enhances decision making and offers incentives to departments units to contribute to the PSO's overall strategic and financial objectives.

They also argue that the absence of such a mechanism can create a vacuum in which senior managers are unable to fully analyse the impact of both internally and externally made strategic decisions. This can lead to decisions being made on narrow departmental criteria which do not benefit the organisation as a whole and which do not facilitate the achievement of corporate objectives.

Programme analysis and budgeting

The terms 'programme analysis' and 'budgeting' are linked but are not the same thing. Let us first consider the idea of a public service programme. An example of this using an NHS Trust is illustrated in Figure 6.10.

The trust comprises a number of clinical directorates who are budget holders for the range of health services shown. Clearly, there will be financial budgets for each

Figure 6.10 Programme analysis and budgeting – NHS Trust

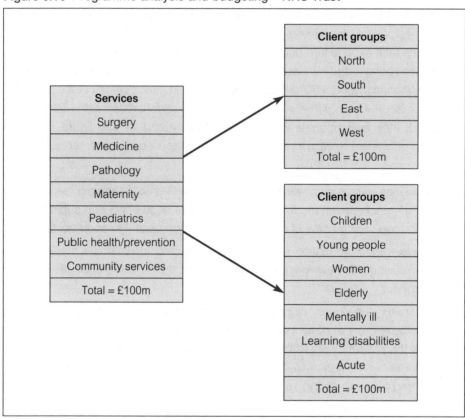

of these directorates and the actual expenditure of the trust on services such as surgery, medicine, pathology, etc. will also be known from the existing financial systems. However, the other aspect of service provision concerns the client groups who are served and who use the services shown. It is suggested that client groups can be considered in terms of identifiable groups in society (e.g. children, elderly); in terms of distinct geographic areas; or using a combination of both of these.

Thus, programme analysis would involve disaggregating the expenditure of the various services shown and assigning expenditure to one or more of the identified client groups. In this way the total expenditure of the trust would be re-classified by client group and the pattern of expenditure by societal group and/or geographic area could be observed. Alongside the costs associated with each programme or client group the following would also appear:

→ the needs of the community being served and the role of the programme;

→ the goals and objectives of the programme;

→ the outputs of the programme.

Figure 6.11 Programme analysis – multi-agency partnership

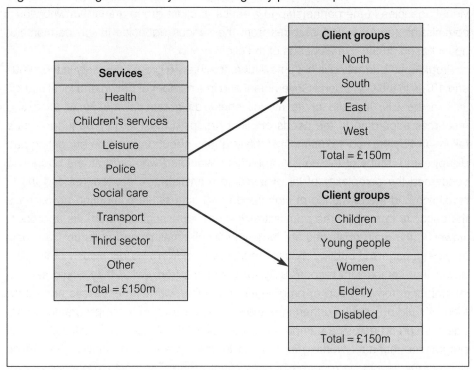

As well as undertaking a programme analysis of expenditure for one organisation (an NHS Trust) an exercise could also be undertaken on a multi-agency basis as shown in Figure 6.11. In this case the expenditure of several agencies and services is disaggregated over a series of client groups.

These patterns of client group expenditure could be compared over the same time periods or with other organisations or multi-agency partnerships to see what significant differences exist and whether they are justifiable. Such a process of disaggregation is not necessarily easy but using various cost apportionment techniques it can be achieved to a lesser or greater degree of accuracy.

Whereas programme analysis is a relatively easy (albeit time-consuming) issue, programme budgeting has far more intractable problems. Although programme analysis is limited to the production of information about client groups there is no change in the budgeting process and the authority to incur expenditure. Under a true programme budgeting system the responsibility for incurring expenditure (and the subsequent accountability) would shift from the service managers (e.g. clinical directors in the NHS Trust) to a series of client group managers who would hold the overall budget for services to the client group and would commission (and pay for) services from the clinical directorates based on the overall needs of the client group.

Similarly, in the multi-agency example, the budgetary power would shift from the individual agencies in the partnership to a series of client group managers who would commission (and pay for) services from the various agencies in the partnership, again based on the overall needs of the client group.

Programme budgeting is not a new idea. It achieved great popularity in the 1960s and 1970s in the US Federal Government and in a number of public and local authorities in the UK. In spite of its attractiveness as a rational means of allocating resources according to the needs of client groups it must largely be judged as a failure and by the mid-1970s most of the euphoria about programme budgeting had disappeared. Many of the earlier problems associated with programme budgeting concerned the complexity of the associated administrative procedures and the IT revolution and the existence of high speed and accessible computing power have the capacity to simplify the administrative burdens associated with this approach. However, the main obstacles are largely political (small p) and cultural. Traditional service managers in public services are often very powerful and jealously protect the power that comes with responsibility for resources from (what they would see as) interference from a group of programme managers with different ideas about how funds should be spent. Furthermore, the spending power of these programme managers is spread across a number of different service units and it is difficult for one programme manager working in isolation to affect the sorts of changes in service delivery that would be required by their client group. The past experience of programme budgeting suggests that it is difficult to break into the 'silo' mentality that often pervades service departments.

In recent years the emphasis on public sector partnerships, service commissioning and joined-up government has led to renewed interest in programme analysis and programme budgeting, since these approaches seem to lend themselves to the philosophy underlying partnership working with the emphasis on multi-agency delivery of services to identified client groups. As already noted, however, although modern IT can simplify much of the earlier complications of programme analysis and budgeting (e.g. programme costing) the political and cultural problems still exist. It is quite probable that considerable efforts will be put into the programme analysis of partnership activities with positive results. However, it remains to be seen whether sustainable and effective forms of programme budgeting can realistically be achieved. Only time will tell.

Variations in PSO budgeting arrangements

From the above it will be evident that within PSOs there are numerous variations and permutations relating to different aspects of budgeting systems. For example, there will be variations with regard to:

→ the degree of delegation of income budgets;

→ the degree of delegation of expenditure budgets;

→ the structure of budget managers;

→ the budgeting powers given to those managers;

→ the mechanisms for setting budgets;

→ the budget-reporting arrangements.

The view is sometimes (incorrectly) expressed that since all PSOs in a particular sector (e.g. health, local government) are in the same line of business there should be some standard budgeting arrangement which will be optimal and will apply to all PSOs. Unfortunately, life is never that simple and PSOs often differ between one another in terms of history, culture, mission, organisation, etc. Hence, what is an appropriate budgeting arrangement for one PSO will not be appropriate for another. Take, for example, the issue of delegation of budgets. It is often assumed that delegation of budgets is 'good' and non-delegation is 'bad'. However, a moment's thought will suggest that delegation of large budgets to a group of managers with limited skills in managing those budgets could prove disastrous and so should be approached with caution. Hence, budgeting arrangements must be contingent on a number of factors and it is for each PSO to decide the best arrangements for itself. Also those arrangements should not be 'set in concrete' but should be kept under review. What is optimal today may not be so in three years' time.

In considering budgeting arrangements, therefore, a PSO should take account of a number of issues, including the following:

→ The overall managerial culture of the organisation. If the organisation is centrally managed, a delegated system of budgeting will prove difficult to operate and vice versa.

→ The potential improvements in the speed and quality of decision making achievable through greater delegation of budgets.

→ The risks of loss of financial control through delegation to staff not competent to manage budgets.

→ The costs of implementing financial systems needed to support delegated budgeting arrangements.

→ The capability of the finance department to provide support to budget holders.

→ The potential loss of flexibility and efficiency caused by fragmenting budgets over a larger number of persons.

However, one common point that applies in all PSOs is that the *governing body must approve the annual budgets of the institution and this responsibility cannot be delegated*. This point is referred to again in Chapter 8 on financial control.

Conclusion

The purposes of budgeting systems are concerned with matters such as planning, control, coordination, etc. While it is clearly the case that budgeting is concerned with these matters it is suggested that the three key aspects of a modern PSO budgeting system are as follows:

→ devolving budgets to improve the speed and quality of decision making;

→ assisting with the implementation of the strategy of the PSO;

→ driving up performance of the PSO.

While there are many technical issues associated with budgeting, such as budget setting, budget reporting, etc., it must also be recognised that budgets also have strong cultural and organisational impacts within the PSO. Thus, successful implementation of improvements in budgeting requires consideration of these issues as well as technical ones.

Questions for discussion

→ Does our budgeting system reflect the pattern of authority and responsibility in the organisation?

→ How effective is our budgeting system at implementing our strategy?

→ How effective is our budgeting system at promoting improved performance?

→ How good is our budgeting system at reporting budget performance to budget holders and senior managers?

7

Pricing public services

Learning objectives

→ To understand the distinction between costs and prices

→ To understand the growing importance of effective pricing in public services

→ To understand what constitutes effective pricing practices in public services

Introduction

Private sector organisations that deliver goods and services in a market place need to set prices for those items in such a way that the organisations achieve their financial objectives. Traditionally, this has not been a major issue in public services since most public services were provided free of charge with few or no markets for public services being in existence. However, the various policy developments that have taken place in the public sector in recent years have engendered a need for pricing to be undertaken in a more rigorous manner than has traditionally been the case. Furthermore, it has been suggested that the tight constraints on centrally financed expenditure which are certain to continue for some years to come will mean that many PSOs will need to look elsewhere for additional sources of income. This implies an increased need for a wider range of user charges and more effective pricing approaches coupled to related themes such as marketing, promotion, etc. Therefore, in the future, it seems likely that public service managers will need to become much more adept at pricing – and its related issues – than they have been up to now.

In this chapter, the following issues are discussed:

→ the distinction between costs and prices;

→ business pricing and economic pricing;

→ why pricing is important in relation to public services;

219

→ the nature and structure of pricing decisions;

→ key strategic pricing factors;

→ cost inputs into pricing decisions;

→ pricing strategy and the marketing mix;

→ special factors related to pricing in PSOs;

→ individual pricing decisions: tactical considerations;

→ the financial management role in pricing in PSOs.

The distinction between costs and prices

At the outset, it is important to make a distinction between a cost and a price in relation to public services, since the two terms are often used synonymously even though they are very different concepts:

→ **Cost** – a financial expression of the resources committed by an organisation to the production, distribution, etc. of a particular product or service. Thus, if we say a particular product or service cost £45.23 this means that the manpower, material and other resources committed to making that product or service are calculated in monetary terms to be equivalent to £45.23.

→ **Price** – the amount of money that a purchaser or consumer is prepared to pay to receive a particular product or service is the price and this equates to the income a supplier finds acceptable to receive.

Although costs and costing were comprehensively discussed in Chapter 5 we need to say more about prices. The key thing to note is that a price relates to the state of the market where buyers and sellers interact and not the structure, cost profile, etc. of the supplying organisation.

Economists classify markets into a series of types where the relationship between buyers and sellers varies (Koutsoyiannis, 1975). The main ones are illustrated in Figure 7.1.

Even at the simplest level it will be seen that prices and pricing decisions in organisations are strongly influenced by the nature of the market and the players involved. At one extreme, in the competitive market position, the individual organisation will have little influence over the prices it charges for its services since these prices will be determined by the market itself. At the other extreme, with the monopolist, the organisation will have a great deal of influence over prices charged.

Because of the confusion about the difference between costs and prices, particularly in the public sector, pricing decisions are seen as primarily to do with establishing the costs of a particular product or service and deriving a price based on or

Figure 7.1 Market structures

Market type	Market features
Competitive	• Large number of suppliers • Homogeneous product • Responsive to consumer pressures
Monopolist	• Sole supplier • No real substitute product • Potential abuse of position by supplier • May abuse position and be resistant to change
Oligopolist	• Small number of suppliers (two to four) who compete • May avoid competition by forming cartels • May abuse position and be resistant to change
Monopolistic competition	• Large number of suppliers • Individual supplier products are strongly differentiated • Individual firms may behave monopolistically • May abuse position and be resistant to change
Monopsomist	• Sole purchaser but many suppliers • Potential abuse of position by purchaser • May drive suppliers out of business
Oligopsomist	• Small number of purchasers (two to four) who compete • May abuse position and be resistant to change • Non-optimal position

equal to that cost figure. Clearly the price of a product or service can be in excess of its cost (implying a surplus), can be equal to cost or can be below cost (implying a deficit). The reality is that pricing decisions are complex in nature and involve a consideration of a wide range of factors of which costs are one factor but are not the only factor or even the most important factor. In this chapter we look at all of the various factors which will (or should) be taken account of in public sector pricing decisions and then we look specifically at the financial management role in such decision making.

Business pricing and economic pricing

It is important to also make a distinction between what we have called 'business pricing' and 'economic pricing'. The basic distinction, which would not really occur in the private sector but which is of great importance with public services, is as follows:

→ **Business pricing** – these are the prices which need to be charged by an organisation to ensure its ongoing *financial* viability. Business pricing can apply to a limited company, an NHS Trust, an FE college, a local authority DSO, etc. and involves ensuring that prices are set at a level that will generate enough income to cover the financial costs of the organisation and (desirably) make some level of financial surplus.

→ **Economic pricing** – these are the prices that need to be charged to ensure that the overall social and economic objectives of the organisation are met. These social and economic objectives can be wide ranging and could include reduced traffic congestion, reduced pollution, improved health status, improved literacy, reduced crime, etc. Economic pricing has only limited applicability for private sector organisations since their main objective is financial viability and business continuity. However, it has great applicability to PSOs since they are in the business of meeting social and economic objectives through the provision of public services.

However, the needs of business pricing and economic pricing can conflict with one another. The price that a PSO would have to charge for a new service to be financially viable may be so high that the take-up of the service is inhibited (because of consumer unwillingness to pay), and this would prevent the social and economic objectives of the service being achieved. In these circumstances, the only way in which the new service could be introduced is for there to be some form of government subsidy to the service to make it financially viable. Such situations are not uncommon in the public service, as shown in Case studies 7.1 and 7.2.

Case study 7.1
Business pricing and economic pricing in public services (1)

Blankshire City Council is evaluating a major project to introduce a modern tram system for the city. Such a project is desirable since levels of traffic congestion in the city are unacceptably high and alternative public transport is inadequate. The council has undertaken a rigorous financial appraisal of the proposed project based on market research about the likely levels of tram usage at different price levels.

The results of this appraisal have shown that for the tram system to be financially viable fares for the tram would have to be set at a level of £3 for a short journey and £4.50 for a longer journey. However, the market research exercise suggests that to maximise the passenger load on the tram system fare levels should not exceed £2.50 (£3.50 for a longer journey). Fares above this level would result in a large-scale reduction in tram usage since customers would still find it cheaper and easier to use their cars. In other words, the business prices of the tram system are in excess of the economic prices.

In this situation, the council could do a number of things:

- increase car park charges in city car parks run by the council. This would make car transport more expensive and possibly permit higher fares to be charged;
- introduce a workplace parking levy which (if the costs of the levy were passed on to employees) would also make car transport more expensive and possibly permit higher fares to be charged;
- investigate differential fares whereby higher fares charged during peak periods could offset lower off-peak fares, thus encouraging greater use of the trams off-peak;
- provide a financial subsidy to the tram operators to keep tram fares down.

Case study 7.2
Business pricing and economic pricing in public services (2)

A government agency is reviewing the feasibility of developing a web-based service whereby educational providers might access high-quality teaching and learning materials in a range of subject areas on-line. This service would not be free and potential users such as schools, colleges or private learning providers would need to make payment for accessing the materials available in such a way that the project would be self-financing.

A survey of the potential value of this service suggests that it would bring huge educational benefits in terms of savings in teaching staff time, better learning outcomes, etc. However, the same survey also indicates that schools and colleges would only be prepared to pay a fairly low price for access to the service. One of the main reasons for this is that much of the teaching and learning materials are already available on a number of existing free websites and, although it is cumbersome to work in such a piecemeal manner, educational providers would not be prepared to pay much extra just to have all the materials in one place.

A financial analysis of the proposed project indicate that there were substantial costs associated with developing and maintaining the web-based service and that the price levels needed to cover the costs of the project would be well in excess of what potential users were prepared to pay. In other words, the business price is well in excess of the economic price. However, the project could proceed and the educational benefits could be realised if the government were prepared to provide a financial subsidy to the project.

Why pricing is important in relation to public services

In commercial organisations the setting of prices for products is necessary to generate revenue to cover the costs of production. However, the vast bulk of public services are provided free of charge and financed from tax-based levies. In the light of this, one might consider the underlying reasons why PSOs need to have prices for services in certain cases. There are a number of issues to consider:

→ **Conventional or required practices** – PSOs often have little or no discretion over the setting of prices for their services:

- In some cases it is a statutory requirement that the PSO levies a charge for services and the PSO may have little or no discretion about the level of charge to be levied. One example of this is NHS prescription charges, where both the level of charge and those persons in society who are required to pay it are determined by the Government. Another example is the fees charged by local authorities for planning applications, which again are centrally regulated. In both cases, it is extremely unlikely that the charge levied will bear any relationship to the cost of the activity.
- In other cases, although there may not be a statutory requirement to charge a fee it is conventional practice to do so and the PSO may have some discretion in the charge to be levied. For example, with university undergraduate tuition fees the university has discretion on the fee level up to a maximum amount prescribed by the government but is not actually required to levy such a fee. In most cases, however, universities levy a fee up to the maximum amount allowed.

In situations such as the above, the PSO has little or no discretion in the charges to be set and thus there is little in the way of a pricing decision to be made.

→ **Cost sharing** – a charge might be levied where the PSO wishes the cost of a service to be shared between itself and the consumer of the service. For example, in the provision of peripatetic music lessons in schools the school/LEA tries to share the cost with parents in such a way that demand is not seriously affected.

→ **Supplementary income generation** – in many parts of the public sector, PSOs are encouraged to raise additional income to supplement the funds received from public sources. Examples of this in PSOs include using display space for paid advertisements from commercial organisations, the operation of retail outlets in hospitals, charges for functions at PSO catering establishments and the provision of consultancy or training to other PSOs or individuals.

→ **Inhibit service demand** – in some cases, the levying of a charge on consumers is more to do with inhibiting the demand for particular services rather than for income generation. One example of this is the possible charges for refuse collection, where the aim would be to reduce the amount of refuse presented for collection and to encourage residents to undertake more recycling. Another example is where a charge might be levied to reduce frivolous demand for what otherwise might be a free service – for example, the suggested flat rate charge on patients for visiting their general medical practitioner would aim to deter patients from making visits for minor ailments or even failing to turn up for an appointment. Such approaches are already employed in some countries, such as Sweden. In both cases, the additional income generated would, of course, be a by-product but not the main purpose of the charge.

→ **Effect a policy change** – in some cases a price may be levied to affect some form of change in public policy. For example, in road pricing in cities the aim of charging drivers for using roads would be to reduce the use of the roads (and hence reduce congestion) and to encourage them to use other forms of transport such as rail, trams, buses, bicycles, etc. Clearly this is a complex issue since the charge to be levied must take account of a number of factors, including the costs of operating the road pricing system, the level of charges likely to impact on driver behaviour, the charges levied for other forms of public transport and the impact of road prices on poorer members of the community.

It is important, therefore, to be clear about the reasons why PSOs are actually levying charges for services. There is often criticism that, although charges are supposedly being levied to inhibit service demand, in reality the main purpose is to generate additional revenues in a covert manner.

Looking in detail, there are a myriad of specific examples of where PSOs provide services in return for payment and thus a price is required. A few examples of these are given in Figure 7.2.

Traditionally, the pricing of services has not been regarded as of great importance within PSOs. However, the various changes which have taken place in the public sector over the last 30 years or so have raised the importance of pricing as a managerial task and have indicated the need for improved pricing practices. Prime reasons for this include the following:

→ **Commissioner and provider separation** – in Chapter 3 we described how one of the most significant organisational changes in the public sector was the separation of the commissioning (purchaser) role from the provider role in relation to public services. One implication of this is that a provider who seeks to win contracts for service provision from commissioning organisations must be in a position to offer a price for the services required. Thus, for example, the DSO of a local authority must be able to offer a price to its client department for the services it wishes to deliver. While commissioners will not make decisions on the choice of service

Figure 7.2 Examples of pricing in PSOs

Organisation	Pricing example
Local authority	• Leisure centre usage • School hall lettings • Private road maintenance work
NHS	• Catering charges • Advertising contracts • Contract bids from NHS Trusts to PCTs
Central government	• Sale of publications • Provision of some information requests
Police/fire authorities	• Police coverage for special events
Government agencies	• Publications of the Stationery Office • Fees for new passports, driving licences, etc
University	• Research contracts • Postgraduate student fees
Further education college	• Short course fees • Room lettings

provider purely on the basis of prices, in a time of tight resource constraints prices will clearly be an important issue. This issue of identifying prices for services required by commissioning agencies is one for a range of provider organisations including public sector providers, third sector providers and private sector providers. However, whereas the setting of prices is an everyday task for most private sector providers this is not always the case for public sector and third sector providers who may need to improve their grasp of pricing practices.

➜ **Market testing and competition** – it is frequently the case in PSOs that certain services which have traditionally been delivered in-house are exposed to external competition via a market-testing exercise. Examples include catering, internal audit, security, IT, etc. Consequently the in-house unit must be prepared to offer a price for service delivery which can be compared with the prices of alternative providers. It is not sufficient for the in-house unit to offer a price equal to its current cost levels since this price might be easily undercut by competitors.

➜ **Charging and co-charging** – although PSOs are largely financed from public resources it is also the case that most PSOs do and have always levied charges on consumers for certain services. The types of charges vary greatly but do not usually represent a large proportion of PSO income. However, the situation may be changing and we are now seeing an increase in the number of what are termed co-charges or co-payments. These are charges levied on consumers for services for which consumers have already made tax-based contributions. For example, in refuse collection, where residents of an area have already made tax-based contributions via central taxes or council tax, it is possible that in the future those residents may also have to pay an additional amount for amounts of refuse over a certain limit. Clearly a pricing structure for such co-charges will need to be developed.

→ **Income diversification** – financial pressures in the public sector and the desire to diversify income streams have made increased external income generation an important objective for many PSOs. Often these PSOs wish to reduce their reliance on government funds (which are open to political machinations) and increase the proportion of their income base which comes from private sector sources. For example, some NHS Trusts generate 10% of their income from operating a private patient wing adjacent to the NHS hospital. In trying to generate such new income streams, PSOs are often trying to compete with existing private and public providers. Therefore, PSOs will need to take account of a variety of factors in order to achieve optimal pricing decisions.

→ **Increased fixed asset efficiency** – PSOs have a substantial range of expensive fixed assets, including buildings, equipment, computers, etc. It makes sense for the PSO to price activities in such a way as to maximise the use of this fixed asset base and hence improve its overall efficiency. This is sometimes referred to as 'sweating' the fixed asset base. Appropriate pricing can influence demand and hence the use made of these fixed assets.

→ **Achievement of strategic objectives** – these days most PSOs will have set themselves strategic objectives which will cover matters such as service quality, service take-up, equality of access and financial performance. However, an ineffective pricing approach can be a major contributor to a PSO failing to achieve its strategic objectives. For example,
- costs may not be fully covered;
- income may not be maximised;
- service take-up may be low;
- access to some groups may be inhibited;
- the organisation's public profile may suffer;
- financial deficits may be generated.

The nature and structure of pricing decisions

The pricing decisions that need to be made in any organisation are complex and interrelated. The key aspects of this are illustrated in Figure 7.3, with the arrows highlighting the interrelationships between the various factors.

Figure 7.3 The nature and structure of pricing decisions

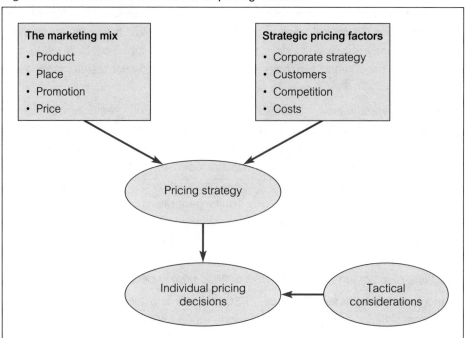

It will be noticed from Figure 7.3 that in making pricing decisions a distinction is drawn between, on the one hand, overall pricing strategy and, on the other, individual pricing decisions, which will have tactical considerations as well as being derived from the pricing strategy. Each of these aspects will be considered in turn in relation to PSOs.

Pricing strategy means having a longer-term view of the pricing of services being delivered by the PSO. It should provide the framework for pricing against which individual pricing decisions should be assessed while recognising that individual decisions will also be influenced by a series of shorter-term tactical considerations.

A strategic pricing policy will be determined by two main factors:

→ key strategic pricing factors;

→ the coordination of pricing strategy with the other elements of what is termed 'the marketing mix'.

Key strategic pricing factors

Although costs should be only one component of an effective pricing strategy, within PSOs the costs (however calculated) of a service have traditionally been the main determinant of its price. Basing pricing strategy decisions largely on the cost of provision implies an inward-looking organisation, as pricing decisions also require an external perspective. Thus, while PSOs may now have an improved understanding of their costs, to improve their pricing decisions many need to substantially improve their access to and understanding of market information. This means improving information on both customer needs and competitors.

There are four key factors, which, in combination, should be used to determine the PSO's pricing strategy for particular services:

→ strategic objectives;

→ customers/clients;

→ competitors;

→ costs.

The first three of these are discussed briefly below and the issue of costs is discussed at greater length in the next section.

Strategic objectives

In any organisation every decision taken should be in support of its overall strategy, and pricing is no exception to this. A PSO's overall strategy should, therefore, govern the approach to pricing in practice, and pricing should assist the PSO in achieving its strategic objectives.

PSOs should have a long-term vision which outlines the future direction of the organisation and what it is trying to achieve. However, PSOs are not in the world of setting simple 'bottom' line financial visions and it is likely that their vision and objectives will be characterised by an aspiration to achieve social and economic objectives and to improve the quality, access and effectiveness of service provision, etc. For example, a PSO may have, within its vision, a number of objectives such as:

→ to increase the take-up of a particular type of service provision (e.g. meals on wheels for elderly people);

→ to reduce demands on a particular service (e.g. refuse collection);

→ to increase the proportion of local ethnic minorities who use services such as adult education.

With objective such as the above, the PSO may need to balance achievement of its financial objectives (through higher prices) with achievement of its broader with social and economic objectives which may require lower prices.

The strategy of the PSO should set out how it will achieve its mission and objectives. It should be a detailed document, which contains measurable objectives over (typically) a three- to five-year period. In addition, the PSO should have an associated pricing strategy which should emphasise that pricing decisions should not made in isolation of the 'big picture' in relation to service provision. All staff involved in pricing decisions must understand the overall aims and direction of the PSO and its services, so that these decisions do not conflict with but actually support the organisation in realising its objectives and mission. Often this potential conflict only materialises some time after the (incorrect) pricing decision has been made as it becomes evident that the PSO's ability to deliver a particular strategic objective is constrained.

There is no simple solution to resolving the tensions that may appear to exist between a PSO's various strategic objectives but there are important factors which should be taken into account in trying to reach a balance:

→ All staff should be aware of the PSO's vision, mission and strategic aims and not just those which may have a direct impact on themselves or their department.

→ Strategic objectives do not all have to be implemented at the same time and pace. It may be necessary to balance a need to improve service access in a particular area in years 1 and 2 of the strategic plan with the need for a reasonable financial return from this activity which arises in years 3 to 5 of the plan.

→ In order to ensure congruence between the PSO's strategic plan and pricing decisions, internal management arrangements must be sufficiently robust.

→ Wherever possible a pricing strategy should be prepared and adopted which should seek to translate the PSO's corporate strategy into pricing aims and objectives. This should reduce the risks of inappropriate pricing decisions being made.

Customers/clients

Under this heading there are two key issues:

→ **Who are our customers?** – a PSO's pricing decisions will involve a wide range of its activities and in consequence involve many customer groups. Some of these customers will be internal to the PSO (e.g. client departments in local government) and others will be external (e.g. individuals, other PSOs, businesses, 3SOs, etc.). In developing a pricing strategy the PSO may need to disaggregate the market into a number of discrete groups and consider the likely levels of demand in each case. For example, a government agency such as the Stationery Office, which sells various government publications, might think about the various groups which purchase its products (e.g. individuals, companies, charities, other government departments and agencies, etc.) and the types and volumes of product purchased by each group.

→ **What factors influence customer purchasing decisions?** – within each of these broad customer groups will be a variety of factors that influence and determine any particular purchasing decision. Price is one of these elements, so it is important to understand how customers may react to price levels and what other factors they will take into account. The key to understanding customer purchasing decisions is the comparison between price and the perceived future benefits which will arise from their purchases. For each purchasing option it is the combination of price and benefits, rather than the price alone, on which customers' buying decisions are made. Hence, the importance of having some understanding of what customers are seeking, and the factors they take into account when making their choices. In many PSOs, a considerable time delay often exists between knowledge about customers' needs and a decision on a new product/service, etc. and, in the absence of such information, incorrect assumptions are sometimes made. Hence, PSOs need to gather information on what factors might influence the decisions of their actual or potential customers (internal or external) and this implies having close relationships with current or potential customers. If a PSO is able to provide information in response to these issues, its understanding of its customers is considerably enhanced and its pricing strategy will, therefore, become more robust. This information can be analysed to address the following questions in relation to the services offered by the PSO:

- Who are our customers – current and prospective?
- What are their needs which might be met by purchasing our services?
- What appear to be the main factors influencing their decision?
- How price sensitive is their purchasing decision?
- Are customers' needs fully met by the offer? Are there gaps and what are the implications of addressing these?
- By what means can we influence their decision?
- Are they potentially long-term customers?

Answers to these questions will influence the pricing strategy of the organisation.

Competitors

PSOs may face competition for service provision from various places, including other PSOs, commercial organisations and third sector organisations, and (as a consequence of the policy of increasing plurality of service provision) this competition is becoming increasingly complex and in many areas more intense. For example, FE colleges face competition from private training providers, NHS private patient units face competition from private hospitals, local authority leisure centres face competition from private leisure centres, local authority DSOs face competition from private companies, local authority social care services face competition from the third sector, etc.

It follows that pricing decisions must take account of this competition and there are three aspects to this, described below.

Understanding the market

We have already discussed potential market structures for the supply of services. Clearly, a PSO may be faced with a number of different market scenarios and it is therefore important that a PSO has an understanding of its market position in relation to each of its products, since this has implications for such matters as vulnerability, barriers to entry, etc.

Analysing competitors

Within a particular market, competitors will probably exist and it is therefore essential that a PSO considers this issue and asks itself the following questions:

→ What PSOs are we competing against?

→ What other organisations are we competing against?

→ What services do our competitors offer and how do they differ from ours?

→ What is their financial position?

→ What are their strengths and weaknesses?

→ What are their prices/pricing strategy?

→ Is this a key strategic market for them?

In many situations PSOs may be faced with many potential competitors and gathering information on each would not be feasible. In these cases a judgement needs to be made on whether some broad assumptions can be made about competitors based on sampling techniques. As with all data collection, knowledge from the PSO's own staff should not be overlooked but should be welcomed as a potentially rich source of information. Sources of information for the identification of competitors can include key competitors, market significance, prices charged, etc.

Assessing market position

Once an analysis of competing organisations has been undertaken, a PSO should undertake a *full and frank evaluation* of how it ranks in against them. This is partially, and necessarily, a subjective exercise and should be closely linked to the PSO's strategy, which should have identified its own strengths and weaknesses. A framework for analysing a PSO's market position with regards to its competitors is set out below:

→ **Market leaders** – these are the acknowledged dominant organisations in a particular programme or market segment. Leadership could reflect size of market share or perceived quality.

→ **Challengers** – these are 'second place' organisations, often characterised by an aspiration to become market leaders. These PSOs may well have ambitious plans for expansion.

→ **Mainstream** – often the majority of organisations in a particular market. Characteristics can include difficulties in maintaining market share and perceived significant barriers to growth (for example, if a PSO appears in the lower quartile of a national ranking).

→ **Niche players** – organisations which may operate in a particular niche or specialist market that is not currently well served.

Information on competitors can be useful for a number of purposes and in relation to pricing should be used to help develop an informed judgement of the following:

→ How will competitors react to potential pricing moves and with what consequences?

→ What aims (for example, market share, financial return) can the PSO reasonably set itself given the competitive environment in which it operates?

→ How can the PSO best insulate itself from actual or potential competitive threats?

→ Is it viable for the PSO to continue to operate in this market in the long term?

Cost inputs into pricing decisions

The costs of delivering services are clearly an important input into pricing decisions, but the key issue is 'which costs?'. There are basically three broad approaches to costing which should be considered in relation to pricing decisions: total cost pricing, contribution-based pricing and marginal cost pricing. These are described next.

Total cost pricing

A general rule when making pricing decisions is that the price should be set by reference to the total costs of the service being considered. In a PSO this can be regarded as being the sum of:

→ direct costs (e.g. labour, materials); and

→ an appropriate share of indirect costs (e.g. marketing, administration).

Before making a pricing decision it is essential for the PSO to ensure that all relevant costs are taken into account. Often, front-line service staff are conscious only of the direct costs and fail to understand the importance of incorporating a proportion of the indirect costs to ensure that the income generated will contribute to both indirect costs and surpluses. Within PSOs, the direct materials costs of products/services are often quite small but the direct costs of labour and direct overheads are quite large. PSO staff are traditionally reluctant to make any records of how they utilise their working time and so it is often difficult to estimate the staff time costs of certain services. Hence, PSOs may need to be innovative in finding means (often technological in nature) of capturing such time data. Individual PSOs may also need to devise appropriate models for apportioning indirect costs to their products or services after considering their own strategy and the behaviours they want to encourage.

Saying that price should relate to total cost does not mean that price must equate to total cost, and three scenarios are possible:

→ **Price is greater than total cost** – this implies the generation of a surplus on the activity which will be available to fund future development activities of the PSO. The amount by which price should exceed cost (and hence the element of surplus) must be set be reference to the PSO's financial strategy and the overall financial surplus the PSO wishes to achieve.

→ **Price is less than total cost** – this implies a planned deficit on the activity which is usually related to a deliberate 'loss-leader'. Again, the amount by which price should be set below total cost (and hence the element of subsidy) must be set by reference to other elements of the pricing decision such as competition and corporate objectives.

→ **Price equals total cost** – in this case there is neither a surplus nor a subsidy.

However, the pricing decision may be more complex than this and variations in pricing may be applied differentially to different types of customers and markets. Thus for one customer type the price may be set above total cost while for another customer, for strategic marketing reasons, the price may be set below total cost.

Contribution-based pricing

The concept of contribution and break-even analysis is important in making pricing decisions. It recognises that pricing decisions are dynamic and must consider the relationship between demand for a product and its price. In most situations the general economic relationship between price and demand will mean that an increase in price will mean some reduction in sales and vice versa. Contribution is the difference between sales revenue and variable costs of production. This approach involves optimising the price–volume relationship in order to obtain maximum contribution and maximum financial performance.

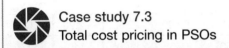

Case study 7.3
Total cost pricing in PSOs

Doitwell is a third sector organisation (3SO) which has been invited by a local authority to put in a bid to deliver advocacy services for a variety of client groups. The 3SO will be competing with the existing in-house provider and a local private provider.

The 3SO has estimated that the costs of delivering the services required to appropriate quality standards are as follows:

	£
Marginal costs of provision	50,000
Appropriate share of 3SO overheads	20,000
Total costs	70,000

The 3SO is considering making its bid at a price of £75,000. As well as covering its direct costs and overheads, this will give the 3SO a surplus of £5,000, which can be used for development purposes. The 3SO is reasonably confident that this price will fall well below that of the private provider.

However, the 3SO has heard a rumour that the bid from the in-house provider will not be a fair bid that will cover all the costs (particularly the overhead costs) incurred by the in-house unit. Since the 3SO is very keen to win the contract it has been suggested that it should submit a bid of £55,000, which will more than cover the marginal costs of the contract.

For the past two years, the financial accounts of the 3SO show that it has generated substantial financial deficits each year. It has been pointed out to the 3SO that the reasons it has incurred these financial deficits is that it has been repeatedly accepting contracts at prices which do not cover the total cost of delivering the contracted services and that its various operational activities are, in total, not generating enough money to cover its overheads. Accepting this contract for advocacy services could exacerbate the situation, rather than improve it.

Figure 7.4 illustrates this using the example of an organisation manufacturing and selling a product. Information is given about costs and sales revenues at different levels of production and sales. It can be seen from this example that maximum contribution and profit will be achieved at a sale price of £2.80 and a sales (= production) volume of 100 units.

However, although such an approach is good in theory there are practical difficulties in applying it:

Figure 7.4 Contribution-based pricing

1	Sale price per unit	£3	£2.90	£2.80	£2.20	£1.80
2	Volume of sales	50	75	100	140	200
3	Total sales revenues (1 × 2)	£150	£218	£280	£308	£360
4	Level of production (= sales)	50	75	100	140	200
5	Variable cost per unit of production	£2	£2	£2	£2	£2
6	Total variable costs (4 × 5)	£100	£150	£200	£280	£400
7	Contribution to fixed costs (3 − 6)	£50	£68	£80	£28	−£40
8	Fixed costs	30	30	30	30	30
9	Surplus/deficit (7 − 8)	£20	£38	£50	−£2	−£10

→ The above example is simple. In practice the situation will be more complex and will require sophisticated financial modelling.

→ It requires *good* data on the relationship between price and sales volume, and production levels and costs.

Very few PSOs are likely to have the data and financial modelling expertise necessary to undertake such pricing and so it is not often used in public services.

Marginal cost pricing

In *specific* circumstances it is appropriate and acceptable to base pricing decisions on the marginal costs of the product or service rather than the total cost of that product or service. The marginal costs of a product or service are the additional costs that a PSO would actually incur if they undertook the additional activity. These are synonymous with variable costs but must not be viewed as synonymous with the direct costs of an activity. For example, the staff costs associated with some sort of event may, effectively, be fixed in nature even though they are directly attributable to the activity. However, direct material costs would undoubtedly be variable costs and therefore marginal in nature. Figure 7.5 gives a simple commercial example of marginal cost pricing.

Marginal cost pricing (the setting of prices by reference to the marginal costs of an activity) must be treated with caution. If all activities were priced on a marginal cost basis there would be a risk of generating insufficient revenues to finance the indirect costs of the organisation. Thus it should only be undertaken in the following circumstances:

→ The proposed activity is for a one-off contract which is fairly short term in nature. Thus it is not applicable to ongoing activities.

Figure 7.5 Marginal cost pricing

Ambrose PLC is a British company which manufactures canned meals for sale in the UK. It manufactures and sells 1 million cans each year at a selling price of £1.10 per can. The following cost data is available:

	Total costs (£)	Cost per can (£p)
Direct material costs	400,000	0.40
Direct labour costs	200,000	0.20
Variable overhead cost	80,000	0.08
Fixed overhead cost	180,000	0.18
Total costs	860,000	0.86

Ambrose has received a request from an Australian company to supply a one-off order of 30,000 canned meals for sale in Australia. They are offering a fixed contract price of £21,000 for this contract. This equates to £0.70 per can. Clearly the offer price offered by the Australians is less than the total cost of production and less than the current UK selling price. However, when we consider the marginal costs of undertaking this contract, we see the following:

Cost type	Comments	Marginal impact	Amount (£)
Direct materials	Definitely variable	30,000 × £0.4	12,000
Direct labour	Small increase in volume so probably fixed	–	–
Variable overheads		30,000 × £0.18	5,400
Fixed overheads	Definitely fixed	–	–
Total			17,400

The contract price is greater than the marginal costs and will thus make a contribution to overheads. Thus the contract might be accepted. However, the following factors must also be noted:

- this is a once-off contract that will not be repeated;
- it represents a very small increase in total production, which could be absorbed into existing productive capacity;
- the product is being supplied to customers many thousands of miles away and so will not affect the local UK price.

→ Pricing the activity at marginal cost will not affect the price charged for the mainstream provision of the same activity. This implies that an activity might be provided in some other geographic location.

→ The proposed activity is a fairly small proportion of the existing workload of the department.

As already noted, the excess of price over marginal (variable) cost is referred to as contribution and it is important that the activity does make some contribution towards the fixed costs of the PSO. However, a judgement must be made about the size of that contribution.

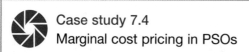

Case study 7.4
Marginal cost pricing in PSOs

The orthopaedic department of Wonderwell NHS Trust currently undertakes 300 artificial hip joint replacements during the year. The costs of this activity are £1.65 million, giving an average unit cost of £5,500. Another health purchaser, 200 miles away, has asked the hospital to quote a price to undertake a once-off contract of 30 joint replacements to help in reducing local waiting times. The following cost data is available:

Cost type	Total cost (£000)	Percentage financial impact of a 10% workload increase (estimated)	Marginal costs (£000)
Wards	200	+6	12
Theatres	300	+6	18
Drugs	60	+10	6
Diagnostics	160	+3	5
Paramedical	300	+6	18
Implants	300	+10	30
Support services	160	+5	8
Overheads	170	–	–
Total	1,650		97

The key questions to be addressed were:

- What price should the trust charge the purchaser on a full cost basis?
- What is the minimum price that should be charged on the basis of the marginal costs associated with the additional workload?
- Is the trust financially justified in bidding for the contract on a marginal cost basis?

On a total costing basis the hospital should quote a price of
30 × £5,500 = £165,000.

Using the marginal costs of undertaking the contract the quotation could be a minimum of £97,000.

It is acceptable to take the contract at marginal cost for the following reasons:

- The contract is a one-off and not ongoing. However, there are examples of NHS purchasers trying to negotiate marginal cost prices for fairly large contracts year after year. This must be avoided since marginal costs do not cover overheads.
- The contract is for a small increase in workload (10%), which can be absorbed by existing slack capacity in the trust without large incremental costs. Slack capacity can occur in physical facilities such as operating theatres and clinics or in human resources such as surgical time. If the trust is working close to full capacity then the additional work can only be done with substantial incremental cost or by displacing some other work.
- The contract price will not disturb the local price.

Pricing strategy and the marketing mix

Product pricing cannot be considered in isolation from the other factors that comprise the marketing mix, which is often described as being the 4Ps. Other than price, these are the following:

→ **products;**

→ **place;**

→ **promotion.**

However, it must also be recognised that not all of the 4Ps will have total relevance in all aspects of pricing decision making in PSO.

Products (and markets)

In a commercial organisation a key factor in pricing concerns the relationship between the products of the organisation and the market in which they are sold. A pricing policy needs to take account of the nature of a particular product or service, its position in the market and the stage in the life cycle of the product or service being considered. If an organisation has just launched a new 'product' and it is able to set the price, then the need for growth and market penetration might be important enough to justify a low or even negative financial return in the short term. As the service matures, sales growth might be seen as less important and so the price charged will be such as to produce high financial returns. Thus, in terms of marketing, an organisation can be faced with the following four possible options:

➔ **Marketing existing products in existing markets** – continue marketing existing products to existing customers or to new customers within the area or market segment.

➔ **Marketing existing products in new markets** – this is often referred to as a strategy of market development.

➔ **Marketing new products in existing markets** – this is a strategy of product development which involves developing new services and marketing them as 'add-ons' to existing customers.

➔ **Marketing new products in new markets** – the most risky and probably most time-consuming strategy, which involves both new services and new markets.

The options above are not mutually exclusive and commercial organisations might pursue several approaches simultaneously.

This approach to considering products and markets may not always be relevant in many PSOs since the nature of what they do is based on a limited number of services being made available in the locality. Thus there is no real scope for them to consider 'new' services and 'new' markets. However, for some PSOs consideration of these issues will be very relevant. Consider, for example, the case of a local authority DSO undertaking buildings maintenance. The following situations may arise:

➔ **Marketing existing products in existing markets** – continue marketing existing DSO building maintenance services to the client departments of the parent local authority.

➔ **Marketing existing products in new markets** – attempt to develop the market to provide existing DSO building maintenance services to new external clients (e.g. NHS Trust, third sector, private sector).

➔ **Marketing new products in existing markets** – develop a capability to manufacture UPVC windows and doors and promote this capability among client departments of the parent local authority who may already have an external provider.

➔ **Marketing new products in new markets** – market the provision of the UPVC capability among new external clients.

In considering any of the above, the PSO needs to bear in mind two key issues:

➔ **Client needs** – are these changing? Are client needs evolving? Is the market size increasing or decreasing? What is the client's likely level of funding availability in future?

➔ **Competition** – who is the competition? What pressures are impacting on our competitors? What are the likely reactions of competitors to any changes we might make to our range of activities?

Place (methods of service distribution)

Service delivery involves getting the *right services* to the *right place* at the *right time*. This raises two key issues:

→ the location where services should be made available to the client/customer;

→ the logistics of distributing services to the place where the customer can acquire them.

Therefore, pricing policy needs to take account of distribution policy, as the distribution channel chosen will influence the price that can be charged for a particular service. Consider, for example, the commercial example of marketing (and selling) personal computers, which may be through specialist shops or large retail chains, by mail order or direct from the manufacturer over the Internet. For the manufacturer each of these distribution options will have implications for sales volumes and revenues, costs and distribution processes. Hence each option must be fully evaluated.

Such distribution considerations are also relevant to PSOs since some public services can and may be delivered in a number of different ways, each with different logistical and cost implications – for example, at PSO main offices, at PSO outreach centres such as schools, clinics, leisure centres, etc., in the premises of other organisations (e.g. post offices in retail shops, primary care in supermarkets), by postal delivery, through the Internet, etc.

Sometimes it is the case that a PSO has no choice about where a service is delivered. For example, swimming lessons have to be delivered at a swimming pool. However, in some cases, there is a choice (e.g. adult education classes) and distribution methods need to be evaluated carefully. Often, the various options are evaluated purely on the basis of cost. This is a mistake and a full evaluation needs to be undertaken which considers likely outcomes (for example service take-up) as well as the costs related to each approach.

Promotion

Promotion concerns communicating information on services to potential and existing customers. It comprises three types of activity, each of which will have a different degree of applicability in PSOs in different situations:

→ **Advertising** – this could involve mass communication through various media (newspapers, TV, radio), which is paid for by the organisation undertaking the advertising. This may concern the organisation itself or focus on specific products and services. The potential role of the Internet in marketing organisation services is important and many organisations (including PSOs) have sophisticated web pages which help with this.

→ **Sales promotion** – a number of disparate activities concerned with promoting the organisation as a whole and/or its services and activities. Examples include exhibitions and conferences, displays, mail shots, etc.

→ **Public relations** – information which is presented to the audience, free of charge, through mass media communication such as newspapers, TV, etc. It can involve editorial comments, news stories or letters related to the organisation. However, because the channel of communication is not paid for, the organisation has less control over the style, content and presentation of the message than when promoting through other means. The main purpose of public relations activity is to keep the organisation in the audience's mind and to always present it in the most positive manner. Most PSOs employ public relations/corporate affairs personnel who maintain relations with media promote stories in the media and manage possible 'bad press' before it reaches the public domain.

The issue of advertising and promotion is often a difficult and sensitive issue in relation to public services. Consider the following two examples:

→ NHS Trusts (and especially NHS Foundation Trusts) may incur substantial amounts of expenditure on marketing and promotion in order to attract more patients under the NHS payment by results system where more patients mean more funds.

→ Colleges and universities may incur substantial amounts of expenditure on marketing and promotion in order to attract more students and hence more funding from government funding councils.

In these circumstances PSOs are merely competing with one another to gain a increased share of public funds at the expense of other PSOs and there is no increase in the overall level of publicly funded activity. There is often a view that expenditure on such advertising and promotion is a 'waste' of public resources which might be better used for service provision. However, where PSOs are exposed to competitive forces (be it from other PSOs, third sector organisations or private sector organisations) then it seems inevitable that they will undertake some degree of paid advertising and promotion. Perhaps the key issues are that the approach to advertising and promotion is properly evaluated to ensure that it is effective and that value for money is being obtained.

To summarise, in establishing prices for their services, PSOs must take account of the four elements of the marketing mix and ensure that they are properly coordinated with each other. In particular, pricing policy needs to be coordinated with promotion policy. Thus, if an organisation is launching a promotion it may offer a special pricing package to support it.

Special factors related to pricing in PSOs

Beyond the specific factors described above there are likely to be a number of other sector-specific factors which may impinge on pricing decisions in PSOs. These factors are particularly relevant to PSOs or organisations such as third sector organisations which receive large amounts of public funding. Some examples of these factors are discussed below.

Avoidance of unfair competition

PSOs particularly need to avoid any charges of unfair competition, either through accusations of forming cartels with one another in breach of anti-competition legislation or by making unilateral pricing decisions which might result in them being accused, by other organisations, of unfair competition through the use of their public subsidy.

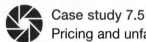

Case study 7.5
Pricing and unfair competition in public services

Summerfields NHS Trust occupies a large city centre site and manages a major laundry facility located on this site. As well as providing laundry services for itself, the trust also provides services to other NHS Trusts. In spite of this the trust laundry found itself with slack operational capacity and so decided to offer laundry services to private sector organisations at a very competitive price.

This move had serious implications for local laundry services companies who immediately complained to their national trade organisation. This organisation took up the matter with a health minister who ordered an enquiry into whether the trust was providing unfair competition to local private laundry providers.

An independent review of its pricing arrangements established that the prices charged by the trust covered the marginal costs of providing additional laundry services as well as making a reasonable contribution to its fixed overheads. Thus the charge of unfair pricing could not be substantiated.

Accountability for the use of public funds

Chief executives of PSOs are accountable for the financial health of their organisation and for their use of public funds. Failure to so account can result in public and parliamentary concerns being raised and, in extreme cases, in investigations by the National Audit Office and the Public Accounts Committee. In making pricing decisions PSOs need to ensure that they are not planning to use public funds to subsidise the delivery of private services and also that there is minimum risk to public funds should some problem arise in relation to the activities involved. Before embarking on any particular venture, PSOs need to conduct a thorough risk analysis and identify both the means of minimising any related risks and of dealing with unforeseen events.

Equity of access

The pricing of particular services may affect the degree of access available for different individuals or organisations. A price that is too high may inhibit access for certain individuals and organisations, such as the unwaged or charities.

Although these considerations may be of little relevance to commercial organisations, they will be of relevance to a PSO which receives large amounts of public funds and has a high degree of public and political accountability. Any concerns in

---

 Case study 7.6
Pricing and the achievement of strategic objectives in a PSO

Walton Further Education College has a policy of trying to widen the accessibility of its training services to all parts of the community. It delivers various management training courses to a wide range of organisations and the price charged covers the total costs of delivering the courses plus a small element of surplus.

On examining its records, the college discovered that the vast bulk of delegates on its courses were employed in either the public sector or the private sector with hardly anyone from the third sector. On investigation, it discovered that the prices charged were seen as prohibitive by third sector organisations. Examining the costings it calculated that a fairly small increase in the price charged to public and private sector organisations would allow it to offer a certain number of places to the third sector at a considerable discount.

Thus the college has widened access to its services with no financial penalty to itself.

this area may lead to substantial public disquiet and bad publicity for the PSO involved.

The pricing policy of the PSO may need to take account of the impact its prices have on access for different segments of the community. To ensure that a reasonable degree of access is provided across the whole customer base, the PSO might introduce tiered pricing, with differential prices being charged for different groups or individuals.

Social marketing

The 4Ps described earlier are also applicabile to those public services which are financed from taxation. In these cases the price can be regarded as being zero. However, the principles behind product, place and promotion still have applicability in terms of helping the PSO achieve its other service objectives of uptake, access, equity, etc. Such approaches are often referred to as social marketing.

Individual pricing decisions: tactical considerations

So far we have considered the broad pricing strategies that PSOs may wish to adopt in relation to particular markets and particular products. However, PSOs often have to make individual pricing decisions for specific services (e.g. a service contract bid) and there may be specific factors that need to be taken into account as well as the overall pricing strategy. The danger, however, is that too often specific factors are allowed to distract from the strategy to the extent that the strategic considerations no longer apply. The classic example of this is the argument that a particular bid should be submitted on a loss-leader basis since it might then generate future work and income streams. In this case the old adage 'loss-leaders lead to losses' should be borne in mind!

It is important therefore, when making pricing decisions, to strike a reasonable and realistic balance between strategic considerations and specific factors. Some examples of common pricing tactics that can be used (but only once the overall strategic pricing approach has been agreed and considered) are given below – but not all may have relevance to all PSOs:

→ **Incidental charges** – the introduction of incidental charges can sometimes generate income over and above the fixed price. For example, separating out staff travelling expenses or printing charges can be worthwhile if they are expressed as a percentage of the price ('plus travelling and subsistence expenses not exceeding 10% of the total price' or 'design and printing costs estimated at 15%

of the total price'). This can be risky if the customer is a sophisticated buyer and would seek to clarify these 'grey' additional costs.

→ **Piecemeal pricing** – rather than putting forward an overall price for a particular service, this would involve breaking up the product or service into a series of discrete elements and offering a separate price for each. Thus the client is in a position to choose what they wish to purchase. They may still purchase the total package but the ability to do it in a series of sequential steps gives them more comfort about their purchasing decision.

→ **Loss leaders** – this is a common technique designed to attract customers in the hope that they will then continue to buy from you (at a higher price) in the future. Entering any market with a price that is not viable in the long term does present risk and a PSO would need to feel very confident about future business to pursue this strategy. Under-pricing can also lead to similar moves by competitors.

→ **Premium pricing** – setting a price above that of the competition is usually associated with the product or service being perceived to be of high quality and possibly of limited appeal. If used carefully this tactic can generate significant surplus and at the same time make the customer feel that he or she is benefiting. However, there is a thin line between being desirable and being overpriced.

→ **Discounting** – discounting needs to be considered very carefully and the rationale clearly understood. PSOs need to consider why they are discounting, i.e. identify what was wrong with the original price. However, some imagination is needed.

In the real world, the dynamics of any pricing situation are often more complex than the theories outlined above. However, these examples serve to demonstrate that there is a significant range of imaginative pricing techniques and tactics that PSOs can use. The important point is that these must be set in the context of an overall pricing strategy within the overall marketing plan, and this ultimately derives from the PSO's corporate strategy.

The financial management roles in pricing in PSOs

To end this chapter, let us consider what might be regarded as the key financial management roles in pricing policy and decisions in PSOs:

→ **Costing** – although it has been emphasised in this chapter that cost is only one input into the pricing decision, it is obvious that costing is an important part of the pricing process. Finance managers must be in a position so that their costing systems are able to produce the cost information needed to inform any decisions about the pricing of the PSO's services. This cost information must be produced in a manner that is relevant to pricing decisions, with a clear analysis about how various costs would behave in relation to changes in volumes of service.

→ **Financial strategy** – as noted earlier in this chapter, the corporate strategy of the organisation is a key input into pricing strategy and individual pricing decisions. One aspect of this is the PSO's financial strategy and financial objectives. It is really difficult to have a robust pricing strategy in the absence of a financial strategy which indicates what the PSO is aiming to achieve in financial terms. Finance managers must ensure that the PSO's financial strategy is robust and comprehensive so that it can inform pricing decisions.

→ **Analysis of competitor prices** – part of the pricing process involves comparing the prices charged by competitors and possibly also their cost structures if such data is available. The advice of finance professionals may be important here to ensure that correct financial comparisons are made.

As mentioned in the Introduction to this chapter, pricing is not a topic which traditionally is seen as particularly important in PSOs and is usually not undertaken in a fairly simple manner. Even today with the growth in charging that has taken place, the fact that the bulk of public services are still tax funded means that pricing strategies and tactics are still relatively unsophisticated. However, effective pricing can provide a financial and service advantage in certain areas of activity in a PSO, even though the overall impact might be small. Furthermore, it seems likely that issues such as co-charging will lead to an increasing emphasis on pricing and so improvements in pricing methods are to be welcomed.

Conclusions

Pricing would probably still be seen as a marginal issue when considering financial management in PSOs. This is because services have traditionally been funded from taxation and so pricing has not always been seen as a key issue, and even if it was the key concern would probably have been to ensure that the price charged did not inhibit service take up.

However, times are changing and pressure on tax-based funding is likely to increase the importance of pricing within PSOs. Consequently, financial managers in PSOs need to become much more sophisticated about pricing decisions and the related topics of marketing, etc.

Questions for discussion

→ How sophisticated are our current approaches to setting prices for our public services? What are its weaknesses?

→ Do we see the setting of prices for our services as being an increasingly important task in years to come?

→ How good is the cost information we currently have as a basis for setting our prices?

Improving performance in public services: the financial management contribution

Introduction

Performance management has always been an important subject in any type of organisation. Take, for example, the military. In 1925, the future General Patton intimated to the future General Eisenhower that 'Victory in the next war will depend as much on battlefield performance as strategy'. That this clearly proved to be the case is not intended to denigrate the importance of strategy, but just to emphasise that strategy without effective implementation and performance management is sterile.

Performance management in business has also grown in importance (and continues to do so). In 1991, it was claimed that 'Within the next five years, every company will have to re-design how it measures its business performance' (Eccles, 1991). Subsequent evidence suggests that this process largely took place.

In the absence of performance management it is difficult to see how any organisation can make progress in the modern world in which it operates. All organisations will have a range of objectives, which may be short term/long term, strategic/operational, financial/non-financial, etc. In the absence of any system of performance management, an organisation will find it difficult, if not impossible, to identify how well it is performing against its pre-arranged objectives and the deviations from those objectives; communicate, internally and externally, its performance against these objectives; and provide a framework for taking action to bring the organisation back in line with its objectives.

In Chapter 3 it was noted that one of the key themes of public service reform over the last 20–30 years has been that of continuous performance improvement in the delivery of public services. Much debate has taken place concerning how much actual performance improvement has taken place and how much of this has just involved reduced costs coupled with poorer services.

Thus, performance management and performance improvement is a key managerial function in all PSOs and financial management has a key role to play in relation to public service performance improvement, although it does not have an exclusive role.

This chapter addresses the following issue:

→ systems of performance management in PSOs;

→ what constitutes performance in PSOs;

→ using performance information;

→ the role of benchmarking;

→ improving performance in public services;

→ performance management and improvement: financial management roles.

Systems of performance management in PSOs

Basic elements

In relation to organisational performance, a number of terms are often used, sometimes interchangeably. These terms include performance management, performance improvement, performance measurement, performance assessment and performance improvement. At the outset, the point needs to be made that performance management is the over-arching concept here and the other terms are components that make up performance management. Consequently, the first issue to address is what constitutes a performance management system in a PSO.

To be effective at managing and improving their performance, all organisations need some form of performance framework or system. The IDeA (IDeA, 2008) has proposed that such a system should have the elements shown in Figure 8.1.

Figure 8.1 Performance management framework (1)

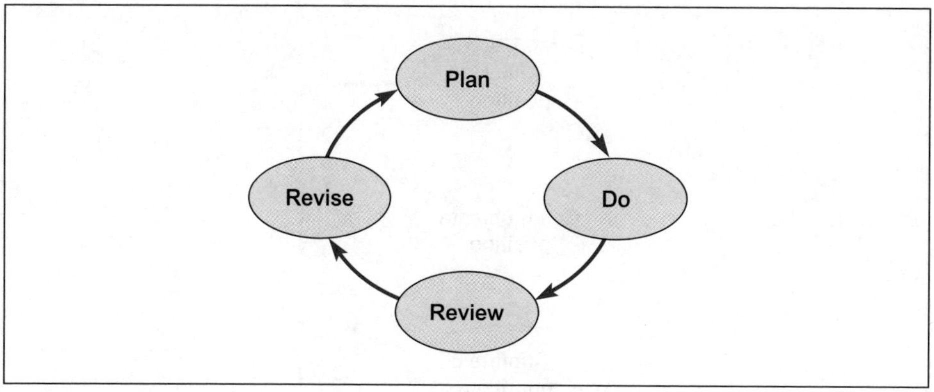

Source: IDeA (2008)

The IDeA (IDeA, 2009) goes on to suggest that effective organisations share some common characteristics:

→ real-time, regular and robust performance data;

→ a can-do culture inspired by strong leadership;

→ agreed lines of individual accountability;

→ a system of clear performance management review, combining challenge and support;

→ a transparent set of performance rewards and sanctions.

An alternative model for a performance management system is based around the well-known idea of the four CPs (see Figure 8.2).

Taken together, these models, although having some strengths, are probably incomplete and the author suggests that an effective performance management system in any organisation requires all of the following components:

1 Data on current performance.

2 A clear plan for the way ahead.

3 Measurable objectives deriving from that plan.

4 A process to measure or assess the progress being made.

5 A means for communicating the current position throughout the organisation.

6 A formal mechanism for reviewing progress.

7 A means for promoting management action in areas where performance expectations have not yet been achieved.

8 An organisational culture that promotes and rewards improved performance.

Figure 8.2 Performance management framework (2)

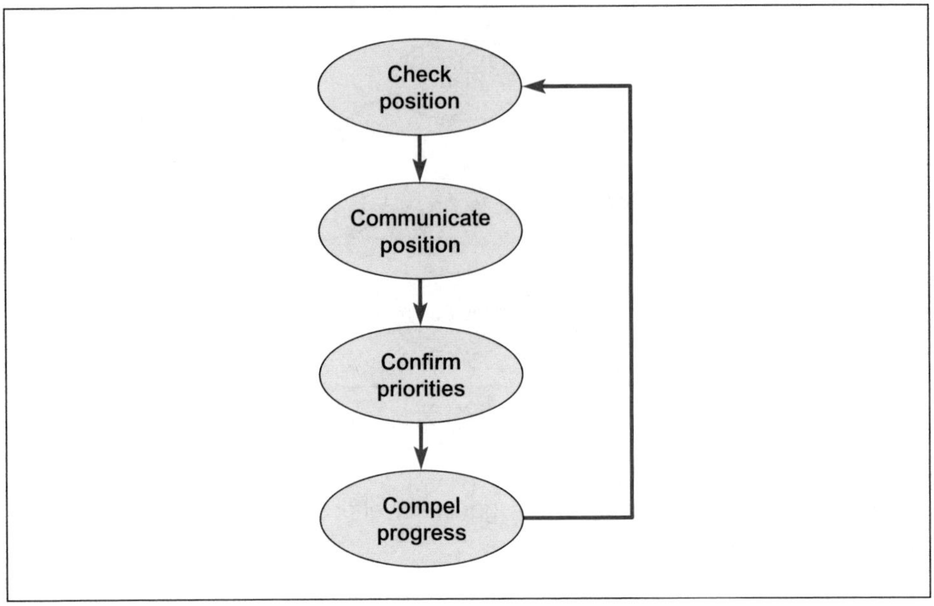

Source: IDeA (2009)

It is often the case that PSOs do not have complete performance management systems, in that some of these elements are lacking or are inadequate, and consequently the task of performance management will be difficult.

Stakeholder analysis

In designing performance management systems consideration needs to be given to what sorts of people and/or organisations might be interested in the performance of PSOs. Some possibilities include service users, prospective service users, proxies for service users, service professionals, external experts, the media, government departments and agencies, politicians, the general public, etc.

One approach would be to identify what might be the interests and influence of these groups in relation to PSO performance (Mitchell *et al.*, 1997). This involves an aspect of stakeholder analysis and one approach to this divides stakeholders into four main groups (see Figure 8.3). Stakeholder analysis then suggests that the following strategies should be adopted in relation to each quadrant:

→ **Segment A (low interest/high power)** – the strategy here is 'keep them happy and they won't bother you'. An example in this group might be Her Majesty's Revenue and Customs.

→ **Segment B (low interest/low power)** – ignore these as far as possible. An example of this group might be the suppliers of goods and services to the PSO.

Figure 8.3 Performance stakeholder analysis

		Level of interest	
		Low	High
Amount of influence or power	High	A	C
	Low	B	D

→ **Segment C (high interest/high power)** – these are the key stakeholders: consult, involve and communicate with them. Examples of key stakeholders in public services could include government departments, MPs, the media, lobby groups, etc.

→ **Segment D (high interest/low power)** – keep them in touch with what is happening at minimum cost. An example here might be neighbouring public service providers.

Some may regard such an approach as overly cynical and not particularly positive in outlook. However, it does represent an approach that keeps the task of performance management manageable in its own right. One problem is that in some PSOs (e.g. NHS Trusts) there is a large concentration of stakeholders into quadrant C, which is a scenario which might not be found in most commercial organisations. However, stakeholder analysis is a useful tool that can be applied to all types of organisations – private, public and third sector (Fletcher *et al.*, 2003).

What constitutes performance in PSOs

In this section we consider what constitutes performance in relation to public services and how that performance should be assessed or measured. The following issues are discussed:

→ sources of performance information;

→ dimensions of performance – operational and strategic.

Sources of performance information

Information about the performance of PSOs in delivering public services can be derived from a wide variety of sources. However, it is suggested that performance data and performance measures can be derived from three main sources, which are discussed below:

→ **Organisational data** – various types of data (volumes, quality, outcomes cost, etc.) that can indicate performance will be available within the organisation.

→ **Professional judgements** – issues of performance could be derived from peer reviews undertaken by service professionals within the organisation or by specialists from external organisations.

→ **Customer/client perceptions** – the views of service users or prospective service users concerning the performance of services available could be obtained by various means.

Each of the above types can be found within public services. First, a wide variety of data is produced by all PSOs and, as will be discussed later, this data can be used in isolation or in a comparative manner to assess organisational performance.

Second, judgements about performance are made by peer reviews undertaken by service professionals within the organisation, for example clinical audit procedures in the NHS. In addition there are a variety of inspections of public services carried out by external agencies which provide judgements about performance of the PSO, for example the school inspections carried out by the Office for Standards in Education (OFSTED).

Third, many PSOs undertake an analysis of the performance of their services as seen from the standpoint of service users. This analysis may be obtained by a number of means, such as surveys, focus groups, etc.

Thus, inevitably, information about the performance of PSOs will combine hard empirical data and softer information based on professional judgements or perceptions. In some cases all three types of information will point in the same direction but in other situations there may be conflicts which need to be resolved.

Dimensions of performance

Traditional approaches to performance measurement tended to focus on a fairly narrow range of issues, most notably those concerned with financial aspects such as costs, etc. While these traditional approaches sufficed at the time, they proved to have severe limitations in a world which was changing dramatically. In the commercial world, during the nineteenth and early twentieth centuries, business operated in a largely local or national context, but the development of increasingly sophisticated economies in Asia and the shift towards globalisation introduced new dynamics and risks into the business environment. In the commercial world, the development of more complex economic environments necessitated greater sophistication in relation to performance measurement. Looking beyond the operational issues, it is likely that commercial organisations will also require a number of strategic performance measures covering matters such as market share, sales growth, return on capital employed, value added, etc.

In the public service sector the increasing sophistication of consumers coupled with the increasing pressures on public funds also led to an increasing emphasis on the development of strategic management systems in the public sector and the associated development of quantitative performance measures (Elcock, 1996) against which public services could be judged. Thus, in the public sector, while there has been a continuation of the drive to have financial measures of performance (i.e. efficiency measures) there has also been a strong focus on performance measures concerned with customer or client satisfaction and inherent service quality. Examples of the latter could include the clinical outcomes of hospital procedures, educational outcomes of schools, etc. It has also been highlighted (Gaster, 1995) that in the public sector the strong political nature of much of the service delivery makes it exceedingly difficult to obtain agreement on suitable measures of quality. However, while service quality measures have progressed there remain significant difficulties in relation to such matters as conceptual design, data collection and, perhaps most significantly, the inability to recognise the differing needs of various stakeholders. It should also be noted that, in some parts of the public sector such as the NHS, certain policies (e.g. payment by results, foundation trusts) are forcing NHS Trusts to operate in a much more businesslike manner, and it seems reasonable to assume that, over a period of time, they will need to take on board some of the performance measure approaches (e.g. market share) which were traditionally the province of commercial organisations.

Performance in PSOs can have a number of different dimensions and it is important, at the outset, to try and clarify what these might be. An initial classification is to consider performance from a timescale perspective, which gives us the concepts of *operational performance* (short to medium term); and *strategic performance* (longer term). The dimensions of performance will be discussed around this framework.

Dimensions of operational performance

In public services, operational performance measurement can be considered in terms of service quality, use of resources and value for money. These are discussed below.

Service quality

Service quality is a complex issue and there a number of sub-dimensions which need to be considered:

Figure 8.4 The Servqual model

Dimensions of quality	Determinants of quality	Description of determinants
• Tangibles	• Tangibles	• The physical aspects of the service such as equipment, facilities, staff appearance
• Reliability	• Reliability	• Providing consistent, accurate and dependable service: delivering the service that was promised
• Responsiveness	• Responsiveness	• Being willing and ready to provide services when needed
• Assurance	• Competence • Courtesy • Security • Credibility	• Having the skills and knowledge to provide the service • Politeness, respect, consideration, friendliness of staff at all levels • Physical safety; financial security; confidentiality • Trustworthiness, reputation and image
• Empathy	• Access • Communication • Understanding the customer	• The ease and convenience of accessing services • Keeping customers informed in a language they understand • Knowing individual customer needs; tailoring services where practical to meet individual needs

→ **Service access** – how accessible the services are to service users in terms of time and/or distance, location, etc.

→ **Service outcomes** – these outcomes are related to the strategic objectives of the service provision and will contribute towards those strategic objectives. Examples include educational attainment outcomes (e.g. examination passes) for schools, clinical outcomes for the NHS, crime reduction for police services, etc.

→ **Service user experiences** – these measures concern the attitudes held by users of services based on their experiences. There are several aspects to this and one model for measuring them is termed Servqual (Parasuramam, 1988). It consists of several dimensions and determinants and is illustrated in Figure 8.4.

Use of resources

The second main dimension of operational performance in public services concerns the use of public resources. There are several ways of expressing this, such as:

→ **Resource utilisation** – this could include such input ratios as length of stay in hospital, staff:pupil ratio in schools, etc.

→ **Unit costs** – traditionally, unit costs of support activities in PSOs (e.g. cost per meal) have been readily available with some cost information about services. A further development would be the unit costs of service provision (e.g. cost per student for a specific course, cost per patient for a specific condition) since this could be compared with other providers.

Value for money (VFM)

'Value for money' (VFM) is a term used to assess whether or not a PSO has obtained the maximum benefit from the goods and services it both acquires and provides, within the resources available to it. VFM not only measures the cost of goods and services, but also takes into account the mix of quality, cost, resource use, fitness for purpose, timeliness and convenience to judge whether or not, together, they constitute good value. VFM is also often described in terms of the 'three Es' – economy, efficiency and effectiveness – which can be defined as follows:

→ **Economy** – this concerns the costs of acquiring the resources needed to deliver public services, for example the cost of acquiring a unit of labour for a particular skill or the cost of purchasing a unit of consumable item needed for service delivery. Improvements in economy would therefore be achieved by reducing the unit cost of acquiring these resources with no negative impact on the standards of service received.

→ **Effectiveness** – this is the extent to which a public service organisation has achieved its preordained service objectives in terms of service output. A high level of effectiveness means that the PSO has largely delivered against its service objectives. An example might be the extent to which a school has delivered educational outcomes (possibly measured as examination success rates) compared with its stated objective.

→ **Efficiency** – efficiency is basically the ratio of resource inputs to service outputs. Thus, improved efficiency could involve delivering the same level of service for less units of resource or a greater level of services for the same units of resource.

VFM is a very important concept in public services and a much-used term. However, it has a number of interpretations which are different to the above, and this often causes confusion. Also, some elements of VFM may be subjective, difficult to measure, intangible and/or misunderstood. Judgement is therefore required when considering whether VFM has been satisfactorily achieved or not. Overall, therefore, VFM is possibly best seen as a concept which requires interpretation and judgement rather than a set of performance measures.

Composite measures

Inspection bodies such as the Audit Commission and the Healthcare Commission make use of what might be termed composite measures of performance. These involved giving PSOs an overall score for their performance based on a number of different strands of performance. For example, the Audit Commission in undertaking Comprehensive Performance Assessments (now Comprehensive Area Assessments) gives local authorities an overall star rating (from zero to four stars) which indicates their judgements about performance based on annual assessments of individual services, periodic corporate assessments of the whole local authority and its use of resources.

Of particular relevance to financial management is the 'use of resources' aspects of this CPA framework, which is also applied in the NHS by means of a series of what are termed ALE scores. In this, performance regarding 'use of resources' is considered against five main criteria:

→ financial reporting;

→ financial management (including asset management);

→ financial standing;

→ internal control;

→ value for money.

Clearly, this approach involves combining judgements about the effectiveness of various financial management processes with relevant data about resource use.

Raw measures versus adjusted measures

A controversial issue in public services is the conflict between raw measures of performance and adjusted measures of performance. Raw measures are only concerned with the absolute level of performance improvement achieved by a PSO irrespective of the start point of service delivery. Adjusted measures assess the value added by the PSO after taking account of the starting point for service delivery. Two examples of this are as follows:

→ **Schools** – the quality of education in schools could be measured in terms of absolute measures by looking at the examination success rates of different schools. On the other hand, the quality of education in terms of value added would require these examination results to be compared against the socio-economic characteristics of pupils entering the school. The argument here is that schools in a deprived area are never going to achieve the same absolute examinations results as schools in a rich area but they may be achieving greater value added.

➔ **Surgical services** – the quality of surgical services could be measured in terms of absolute measures by looking at the survival rates for particular operations for different hospitals or different surgeons. On the other hand, the quality of surgical services in terms of value added would require the survival rates of individual hospitals/surgeons to be compared with the initial health status of those patients receiving the surgical intervention.

Many people argue that absolute measures give a misleading view of the performance of PSOs since they do not take account of the starting point for service delivery and the degree of difficulty involved. Others see the process of producing adjusted measures as a process of manipulation of objective data.

Dimensions of strategic performance

As well as operational performance, stakeholders will be interested in aspects of the longer-term strategic performance of PSOs. In reality, it is likely that individual service users will have little interest in such measures, whereas more sophisticated stakeholders such as government or regulatory bodies will have a strong interest.

One of the best-known models of strategic performance is known as the balanced scorecard model (Kaplan and Norton, 1996) and the structure of the original model is shown in Figure 8.5.

It will be noted that strategic performance is assessed against four main dimensions of performance, which are derived from the vision and strategy of the organisation. The original balanced scorecard model was devised, in the main, for commercial organisations but it has been adapted for PSOs with some modifications to the definition of the performance dimensions used:

➔ stakeholders (instead of customers);

➔ resource utilisation (instead of finance);

➔ management processes (for internal business processes);

➔ learning and innovation (for learning and growth).

Producing a balanced scorecard for a complex PSO is a major piece of organisational development work. The main stages in designing and implementing a balanced scorecard are as follows:

1 Establish a sound strategic foundation for the balanced scorecard.

2 Produce a multi-dimensional strategic summary.

3 Set objectives for each balanced scorecard perspective.

4 Link objectives via cause and effect.

Figure 8.5 Balanced scorecard model

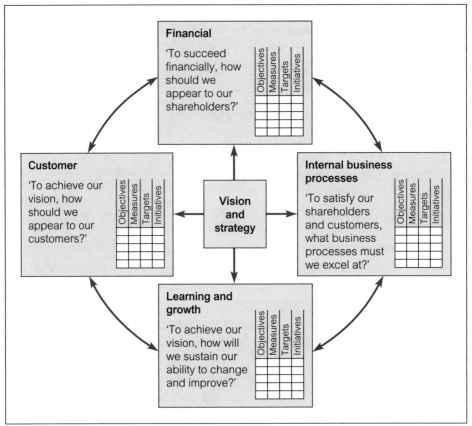

Source: Kaplan and Norton (1996)

5 Determine measures for each objective.

6 Set targets for each measure in the balanced scorecard.

7 Identify strategic initiatives to deliver targets.

8 Full implementation of the balanced scorecard.

However, it is common practice to cascade balanced scorecards down to directorate and departmental levels. This means that the scorecard can dominate the monitoring activity of managers.

An example of a balanced scorecard approach developed in an NHS Trust is shown in Figures 8.6 and 8.7.

Supporting this scorecard will be a series of initiatives designed to deliver on the targets and objectives identified.

Figure 8.6 Balanced scorecard in an NHS Trust: objectives and critical success factors

Stakeholders	Resource utilisation
Strategic objectives • Equitable and timely access to services • High quality and safe services • Engaged workforce • Improvement in health gain *Critical success factors* • Reputation/image • Stakeholder satisfaction and relationship • Service delivery and responsiveness	*Strategic objectives* • Adherence to core financial duties • Efficient use of resources • Access to and effective use of IT to improve efficiency and effectiveness *Critical success factors* • Cost control • Value for money • Efficient use of resources
Management processes	**Learning and innovation**
Strategic objectives • Management processes that support the delivery of timely and quality services • Partnership working • Robust, reliable, relevant and timely information *Critical success factors* • Interface with partners • Process efficiency and quality • Timeliness	*Strategic objectives* • Developments based on best practice and evaluation • Staff involved in modernisation of service delivery • Flexible workforce and organisation • Effective leadership *Critical success factors* • Investment in management development and training • Effective leadership • Creating and maintaining a learning organisation • Universalising best practice

Figure 8.7 Balanced scorecard in an NHS Trust: measures and targets

Stakeholders
Equitable and timely access to services • No wait over 18 months for inpatient/daycase or continuous improvement on 03/04 outcome • No wait over 18 months for 1st outpatient appointment or continuous improvement on 03/04 outcome • 10% reduction in major operations cancelled due to lack of critical care facility • 95% of patients spending less than 4 hours in A&E • Expand primary care services locally through GMS contract implementation • Develop local services to limit emergency admissions

Continued overleaf

Figure 8.7 *continued*

Stakeholders

High quality and safe services
- NICE guidance implemented within 3 months
- 15% reduction in DTOC by March 2005
- Satisfied patients (number of complaints)
- Effective PPI involvement in mental health
- CPA for serious mental illness by March 2005

Engaged workforce
- Low staff turnover rate
- Low sickness rates
- Positive staff satisfaction surveys

Preventive health initiatives and health gain
- Higher take up of immunisation services

Management processes

Partnership working
- Unified assessment summary by April 2005
- Develop a plan for increased awareness and participation in substance misuse treatment programmes by March 2005
- Develop a costed plan for CHD NSF by October 2004
- Develop a costed plan for revised Cancer Standards and NICE Improving Outcomes Service Guidance
- Implement standards 1–12 Diabetes NSF

Management processes to support delivery of timely, quality services
- Achievement of key financial deadlines
- Develop the process for producing referral/admission protocols
- Ensure effective commissioning of General Medical Services
- Full implementation of Pay Modernisation and Changing Workforce agenda
- Implement local readiness plans for Informing Healthcare
- 100% offer of flu vaccination for over 65s and at risk group
- 100% offer of pneumococcal vaccination for over 75s and at risk group
- To ensure effective Performance Management systems
- To ensure effective Governance Arrangements

Resource utilisation

Adherence with core financial duties
- Remain within resource limit (forecast outturn)
- Remain within cash limit (forecast outturn)
- Accurate forecasting
- Achievement of Public Sector Payment Requirements

Efficient use of resources
- Meet the 6 high-level prescribing targets by April 2005
- Financial plans to address variance in line with operational plans
- Sustainability Project to include review of commissioning, providing, clinical and financial performance

Figure 8.7 *continued*

Learning and innovation
Investment in management development and training • Workforce with relevant skills • Development of flexible workforce • Continued implementation and development of the OD&T Strategy and PODP process **Effective leadership** • Well developed leadership skills throughout the organisation • Developing learning organisation culture **Creating and maintaining a learning organisation** • Staff encouraged to contribute to system development • Develop a programme for team building within the IHB **Universalising best practice** • Sharing of best practice • Effective implementation of innovation

Using performance information

It is not usually the case that performance information can be used in isolation in absolute terms. For example, just stating that in a PSO the rate of client satisfaction with services is 89% or that the cost of an MRI scan is £300 in an NHS Trust tells us very little about its performance. It is more likely that the information will be used in a comparative manner, and a number of different types of comparison are possible:

1 How good is our own performance in comparison to some pre-determined object-ive (e.g. NHS waiting list targets)?

2 How good is our own performance over time?

3 How good is our own performance compared to others?
   • Other UK public sector service providers.
   • Other UK providers (e.g. private, 3SOs).
   • International comparisons.

If we applied this framework completely we would get the picture shown in Figure 8.8. The figure is based on measures of operational performance, although a similar set of comparisons may also be possible for strategic measures.

Most PSOs are unlikely to undertake the whole range of comparisons shown in this figure but they could probably do more than is currently being done. Indeed, one of the concerns is that PSOs actually limit quite considerably the extent to which they compare themselves with others:

Figure 8.8 Using PSO performance measures

	Individual PSO	Pre-determined objective	Previous year's own performance	Other UK public sector service providers	Other UK service providers	International comparisons
Service quality						
Service access						
Service outcomes						
Service user experiences						
Use of resources						
Resource utilisation						
Unit costs						

→ Many only compare their performance with other PSOs in the same sector even though the areas of comparison might have generic applicability to all sectors (e.g. costs of payroll functions).

→ Many only compare themselves within a limited geographic area. For example, Welsh local authorities tend to compare themselves only with other Welsh authorities.

→ Few will compare themselves internationally, although top universities such as Oxford and Cambridge do so because they regard themselves as working in a global HE market.

The role of benchmarking

Benchmarking is the process of comparing the cost, time or quality of what one organisation does against what another organisation does usually within their own sector. This then allows organisations to develop plans on how to make improvements or adopt best practice, usually with the aim of increasing some aspect of performance. Benchmarking may be a one-off event, but it is often treated as a continuous process in which organisations continually seek to challenge their practices.

Types of benchmarking

Benchmarking can be of several different types:

→ **Process benchmarking** – observation and investigation of business processes with a goal of identifying and observing the best practices from one or more benchmark organisations. Activity analysis will be required where the objective is to benchmark cost and efficiency; this is increasingly applied to back-office processes where outsourcing may be a consideration.

→ **Performance benchmarking** – comparison of the organisation's products and services against those of a target organisation.

→ **New product benchmarking** – the process of designing new products or upgrades to current ones. This process can sometimes involve reverse engineering, which is taking apart competitors' products to find their strengths and weaknesses.

→ **Strategic benchmarking** – involves observing how others compete. This type of benchmarking is usually not industry specific, meaning it is best to look at other industries.

→ **Functional benchmarking** – an organisation will focus its benchmarking on a single function in order to improve the operation of that particular function. Complex functions such as human resources, finance and accounting, or information and communication technology are unlikely to be directly comparable in cost and efficiency terms and may need to be disaggregated into separate processes in order to make valid comparisons.

→ **Financial benchmarking** – this involves performing a financial analysis and comparing the results in an effort to assess the organisation's overall competitiveness.

Benchmarking has become increasingly topical as a means of identifying performance improvements in relation to public services.

Benchmarking process

No single process for undertaking such specific studies has been universally adopted. The wide appeal and acceptance of benchmarking has led to various benchmarking methodologies emerging, and a possible approach is described below:

1 **Identify your problem areas** – because benchmarking can be applied to any process or function, a range of research techniques may be required, including: informal conversations with service users, employees or suppliers; exploratory research techniques such as focus groups; or in-depth marketing research, quantitative research, surveys, questionnaires, re-engineering analysis, process mapping, quality control variance reports or financial ratio analysis. Before embarking on a comparison with other organisations it is essential that you know your own

organisation's function, processes and baseline performance, against which improvements can be measured.

2 **Identify other organisations that have similar processes** – for example, if one were interested in improving types of behaviour management in schools one might try to identify other fields that have successfully addressed such behavioural challenges. Examples include the prison service, leisure organisations, colleges, etc.

3 **Identify organisations that are leaders in these areas** – look for the very best in any sector and in any country. Consult users, customers, suppliers, trade associations and magazines to determine which organisations are worthy of study. However, care is needed since, in the public services, it is easy to find claims for success which cannot be objectively justified by results.

4 **Survey organisations for measures and practices** – companies target specific business processes using detailed surveys of measures and practices used to identify business process alternatives and leading companies. Surveys are typically masked to protect confidential data by using neutral associations and consultants.

5 **If possible, visit the 'best practice' organisations to identify leading edge practices** – they may agree to mutually exchange information beneficial to all parties in a benchmarking group and share the results within the group.

6 **Implement new and improved practices** – take the leading-edge practices and develop implementation plans which include identification of specific opportunities, funding the project and selling the ideas to the organisation for the purpose of gaining demonstrated value from the process.

Improving performance in public services

Over the last 20 years or so the culture of continuous performance improvement in public services has meant that most of the easy improvements have already been achieved. Hence PSOs must now be more sophisticated in the identification of ongoing improvements. The performance of PSOs (according to the dimensions identified above) can be improved in many ways but it is useful to consider them in two main groups: strategic approaches and operation approaches.

Strategic approaches

This heading covers major changes to the way in which services are provided. Some of these are outlined below.

Service reconfiguration/transformation

Step changes in the quality and resource efficiency of public services can be achieved by major reconfigurations or transformations of public services in an area. Examples would be the reconfiguration of health services in an area, the rationalisation of schools provision as a result of falling rolls, or changes to refuse collection involving reduced collections and enhanced recycling opportunities.

Major investment in technology

Investment in technology can bring significant improvements in the quality and resource efficiency of public services. A good example would be the ability to make returns to government departments using the Internet. Such an approach should reduce costs and also give greater freedom to individuals about submitting their returns.

Changes in the skill mix

Changes in the skill mix, which often means employing less-skilled people to do the lower-skill tasks usually undertaken by more highly skilled staff can bring about improvements in performance. The less-skilled people can undertake the same work at lower cost while the higher-skilled people can concentrate on the more complex tasks, thereby improving service quality in those areas. An example here might be the employment of lower-skilled support workers who work with qualified health visitors.

Operational approaches

These are basically changes that could be made to the current operational practices in PSOs which would generate improved performance.

Process improvements

PSOs have, for some years, been copying manufacturing industry in the use of lean production methods to analyse their various operational process and make improvements. This could involve the use of techniques such as value stream mapping, identification of cost paretos, etc. However, the creation of vision and effective leadership are also core to the implementation of 'lean', as well as the use of techniques.

Improving flow

Many public service activities (e.g. teaching in a classroom) might be regarded as a form of batch production in that the services are delivered to a group of users in one location by a single service deliverer. However, other public service activities involve a flow process akin to assembly line models in manufacturing industry. One such

Figure 8.9 Flow in public services – radiological imaging

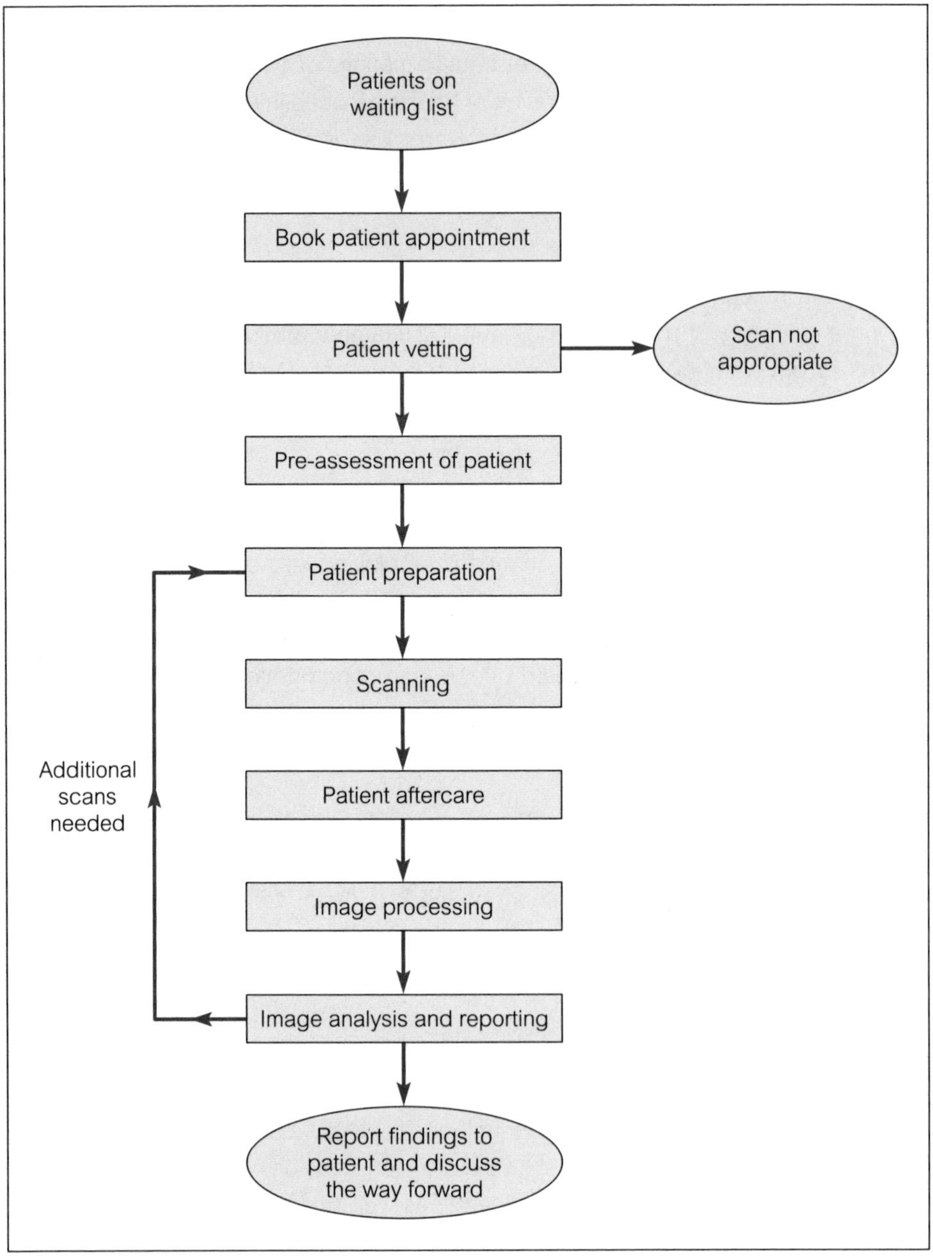

flow process in public services is the radiological imaging procedure in a hospital, which is shown in Figure 8.9.

Frequently it is the case in flow arrangements such as this that bottlenecks are experienced in various stages of the flow process and these bottlenecks result in the flow of services being halted or slowed. The consequences of this are delays in the delivery of services (e.g. scans) and possible underutilisation of resources in other stages of the flow process due to the reduction in flow. Thus, one approach to performance improvement would be to identify these bottlenecks and take remedial action to eliminate them. In this case the flow will be increased and resource utilisation improved.

The above scenarios are well known in manufacturing industry (Goldratt and Cox, 2007) but a moments thought will lead to the identification of many flow-type processes in public services where such bottlenecks might occur.

Increased staff productivity

There are a number of areas where performance improvements can be achieved by means of increasing staff productivity. Key aspects of this might include enhanced remuneration mechanisms, better supervision, outsourcing, improved recruitment and retention, and reduced sickness absence levels. Such approaches will require a number of improvements in relation to productivity measurement, leadership, better sharing of good practice and effective change management.

Enhanced procurement

Improved procurement was seen as one of the main successes of the Gershon initiatives, but there is still considerable scope for improvement. Some aspects of this which were suggested include collaborative procurement arrangements, extended use of e-procurement and collaborative IT procurement.

Fixed asset rationalisation

There is often scope for PSOs to rationalise their fixed asset base (particularly in relation to property). This would produce benefits in terms of reduced maintenance costs and the generation of capital receipts. This process might be catalysed by changes in the structure and means of service delivery achieved through service transformation/reconfiguration.

The barriers to performance improvement in public services

As always, there are a wide range of barriers to improving performance in PSOs. These can be classified as either internal or external. Some examples of these are described below.

Internal barriers

Some barriers to improving public service performance reside within the PSO itself, and examples of these include:

Case study 8.1
Improving PSO performance through eliminating bottlenecks

The cardiac surgery department of Danesfield University Hospital is under severe pressure. Although its level of resourcing seems reasonable, the department has long waiting lists of patients who require surgical treatment. Hospital management suspects that the problem is that the available resources are not being utilised in the most optimal manner, resulting in bottlenecks in the system which are inhibiting patient throughput. Consequently they have initiated a review of the department.

Cardiac surgery involves a linear flow process whereby patients move through the following stages:

- admission;
- pre-operative bed;
- operating theatre;
- intensive therapy unit (ITU);
- high dependency unit (HDU);
- post-operative bed;
- discharge.

The review team constructed a discrete event simulation model designed to simulate the flow of patients through the surgical system. The model was populated using actual data about the resources of the department and actual data on patient flows (e.g. numbers of patients, length of stay at each stage in the process).

The modelling exercise showed that there was insufficient bed capacity in the HDU to cope with the flow of patients. This was creating a bottleneck in the system which held back the flow of patients from earlier stages in the process. The model showed that the addition of one more HDU bed would free up the blockage and improve the flow of patients thus resulting in increased patient throughput. Also, it was possible to identify how resources could be moved around the department in such a way as to provide much of the funds required for the additional HDU bed without impacting on the rest of the system.

The necessary changes were implemented and found to work well. Thus the department had obtained significant increases in throughput at little additional system cost. Clearly, however, there would be some marginal costs associated with the increases in patient throughput.

→ **Incomplete PM system** – at the start of this chapter we discussed the key elements in a PM system in a PSO. It is quite often the case that a PSO will have an incomplete system, thereby inhibiting the improvement of performance.

→ **Incomplete and/or inconsistent data** – to identify and implement performance improvements, it is important to have good quality data about current performance. Often PSOs lack the necessary data (e.g. cost data) or the various data sets available may conflict with one another.

→ **Lack of managerial skills or capacity** – performance improvement is not an easy task. First, good analytical skills are required to identify changes that will make real improvements to performance, and change management skills are often required to ensure that the necessary changes are communicated within the organisation and implemented successfully. It is often the case that PSO managers are so burdened with the tasks of keeping the organisation going that they just do not have the capacity to deal with these tasks. Alternatively, even if they did have the capacity they may not possess the skills needed to deal with the issues involved.

→ **Lack of capital resources** – many performance improvements will require substantial capital investment (e.g. improved energy efficiency) and this can be hampered by a lack of access to capital resources.

→ **Internal resistance to change** – it is a well-known phenomena that PSOs attempting to improve performance suffer from internal resistance from its staff. Such resistance may be reinforced by resistance from labour unions and/or professional bodies.

External barriers

There are also barriers to performance improvement that are external to the PSO itself, and these barriers are often much more difficult to deal with than internal barriers. Some examples of external barriers include:

→ **Public opposition** – many changes to public services (whatever their merits) often result in strong public opposition. Such opposition may be genuinely based or may be based on a combination of misunderstanding and/or misinformation. Such opposition may also be fuelled by an often irresponsible and ineffective media.

→ **Lack of political support** – politicians have to be responsive to the concerns of their constituents and often such concerns will result in strong political opposition to change. Once again, these concerns may be based on a combination of misunderstanding and/or misinformation.

→ **Poor communications** – in both of the previous cases, the opposition generated may be as a consequence of poor communications by the PSO, which has failed to get its message over.

Reducing the barriers to performance improvement

There are some key things which might be done to overcome these barriers to performance improvement, including:

→ **Improved communication** – as a means of overcoming resistance from external parties, such as service users and the general public.

→ **Effective change management** – performance improvements usually involve some degree of changes in operational and managerial practices and such changes will create resistance among staff at all levels. Hence, effective programmes of change management need to be applied to overcome such resistance.

→ **Adequate information and analysis** – proposed improvements in performance need to have been subjected to robust analysis to ensure the case for change is sound. In turn this requires adequate information on which to base the analysis. This is not always the case and, not surprisingly, half-baked proposals tend to fall apart under the glare of public scrutiny.

→ **Adequate management resources** – all of the above require an adequate level of managerial resources in order to identify and implement performance improvements.

Performance management and improvement: financial management roles

Financial management has a number of key roles to play in relation to performance management and performance improvement in PSOs. This applies both to the strategic aspects of performance management as well as operational aspects.

At one level it is clear that good financial management is necessary to make improvements to the criteria that make up the composite scores of the Audit Commissions assessment of 'use of resources'. Thus, improving the use of resources will be concerned with improving the following aspects of financial management in a PSO:

→ financial reporting methods including financial reporting to the board;

→ financial and asset management practices;

→ internal control procedures within the PSO;

→ the systems and procedures for identifying and implementing value for money in the PSO.

However, at another level the contribution of financial management to performance management is based on the role it can play in relation to the areas shown in Figure 8.10.

Figure 8.10 Roles of financial management in performance management

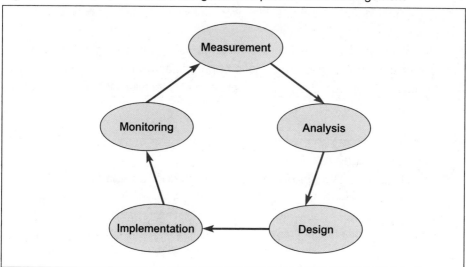

The various techniques of financial management that are of relevance here have, to a large extent, already been discussed in previous chapters. In this section we look at their applicability to performance improvement and management in PSOs.

Measurement

In financial terms, the start point of any performance improvement exercise must be identifying the costs and income associated with the particular entities or activities to be improved. For example, in order to benchmark against others we must first identify our own costs. The following are examples of the types of cost information that may be required:

→ the costs of a student place on an FE College course;

→ the costs of a child placement in care;

→ the costs of treating a patient with a particular clinical condition;

→ the costs of processing a benefit claim;

→ the costs of making an employee payment through the payroll;

→ the costs of recruiting a new employee.

More often than not this cost information will not be readily available and some form of costing exercise will need to be undertaken to identify it. In such circumstances it is likely that some form of Activity-Based Costing will be applied. However, there is a balance to be struck here in that the cost information must be of sufficient accuracy to be meaningful while not having taken an inordinate amount of time and effort to compute.

Much of the performance improvement will involve changing the relationship between costs and the other dimensions of performance. Thus, in addition, alongside the cost data, there will need to be data about the services themselves, such as types, volumes, standards, etc.

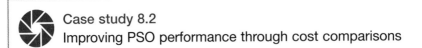

Case study 8.2
Improving PSO performance through cost comparisons

The modern languages department of Midshires University has been generating financial deficits for a number of years such that it now has an accrued financial deficit of over £1 million. The university has a major strategic problem because it portrays itself as a 'European' university and the teaching of many European (and other) languages is important for this image. However, it recognised that the deficit on modern languages is being subsidised by other subject areas. Consequently it initiated a review of the situation.

First, a costing analysis was prepared (using activity based costing), which provided a picture of the income, costs and surplus/deficits for each of the languages being taught in the department. This indicated that the vast bulk of the financial deficit was being generated by two of the six languages being taught. However, it was not clear why such deficits were being generated when other universities seemed to have no such financial problems with these languages.

Consequently, Midshires University organised a benchmarking exercise with comparable modern languages departments in five other universities. The exercise involved all the six participating universities passing a wide range of detailed financial and non-financial information to a third party who undertook an analysis of the information. For each of the six universities an analysis was produced of their performance (including financial performance) for each language area showing their own results compared to the other five institutions, suitably anonymised, plus the overall mean position.

Armed with this information, Midshires was better able to understand why it was generating such large deficits on two of the six languages taught and to take appropriate action to reduce (but perhaps not eliminate) the financial deficit. Also the fact that Midshires was able to point out that other universities were managing to avoid financial deficits through delivering courses in a different manner made it easier to implement the necessary changes.

Analysis

The analysis stage is perhaps the most complex and difficult stage of all. A considerable amount of work will need to be undertaken to analyse the financial and related non-financial data which has been obtained.

The use of financial benchmarking is well established in public services as a means of analysing and assessing comparative performance. The information needed for financial benchmarking purposes can be obtained in three ways:

Using publicly available information

Financial performance could be compared against that of other PSOs by using information which is in the public domain. Although some interesting comparisons can be made using this information, two key factors limit its usefulness:

→ The information is usually at too high a level of aggregation to make meaningful comparisons at an individual functional level.

→ Considerable concern exists about the degree of consistency, between PSOs, in the methods they use to record publicly available information. This undermines the confidence in any such comparisons that may be made.

Benchmarking clubs

In some parts of the public sector, groups of similar organisations come together to undertake collaborative benchmarking. In doing this they will exchange quite considerable volumes of financial and non-financial information about their operations and this will far exceed the detail found in publicly available sources. In this way they can make detailed comparisons of their own performance against that of very similar organisations. The detailed analysis may be undertaken by an independent third party who receives all of the information from each organisation and undertakes the required analysis. In this way, individual confidentiality of information is maintained.

Undertaking a special exercise

Another and more elaborate approach is to undertake a special exercise to collect financial and non-financial information from other PSOs. The advantage of this approach is that one can define, specifically, the type of information one wishes to collect. The major disadvantage is that experience has shown that it is often very difficult to get cooperation from other PSOs in terms of sharing information. The term 'commercially confidential' is often used as a reason for not sharing information. However, the following approaches might help to increase the level of cooperation:

→ An offer could be made to the other organisations to share the findings of the study on a non-attributable basis.

→ An attempt could be made to undertake the exercise collaboratively with each organisation sharing both the costs of the exercise and the results.

→ The information might be collected by a third party, who keeps the results of individual organisations confidential.

→ Information might be collected through face-to-face interviews rather than questionnaires. However, this approach is time-consuming.

Although this approach to benchmarking is obviously attractive the difficulties of getting comparable information should not be underestimated.

Much of the analysis of public services will involve comparisons of cost alongside comparisons of performance. One way in which this is sometimes done is for the unit costs of service provision and the quality of services (suitably measured) of a particular PSO to be ranked against the costs and performance of the benchmarked group in order to highlight how well the PSO is doing. The results can be expressed in matrix form as shown in Figure 8.11 using a local authority as an example.

In light of this information, the local authority should consider the following actions:

→ **High unit cost/low quality** – clearly this is totally unacceptable and the situation should be addressed promptly.

→ **High unit cost/high quality** – consideration might be given to the appropriateness of reducing the quality of service, with a consequent cost saving. The funds released could be invested in low-performing services.

Figure 8.11 Benchmarking public service performance

	High quality	Low quality
High unit cost	• Highways maintenance	• Adult social care
Low unit cost	• Libraries	• School catering • Refuse collection

→ **Low unit cost/high quality** – clearly this is the most desirable situation, but it should be kept under review in case it is possible to improve the situation further.

→ **Low unit cost/low quality** – consideration should be given to the scope for investing more funds, with the aim of improved quality.

It is clear, in looking at all of these scenarios, that good financial management will be important.

Where a PSO has a multiplicity of resource inputs and service outputs, a more complex approach could involve the use of Data Envelope Analysis (DEA). DEA is concerned with assessing the comparative performance of operational units in terms of efficiency where efficiency has the classic definition of outputs divided by inputs. DEA is most relevant where operational units have a multiplicity of both inputs and outputs and it is concerned with establishing the relative efficiency of those units, as follows:

$$\text{Relative efficiency} = \frac{\text{weighted sum of inputs}}{\text{weighted sum of outputs}}$$

From the viewpoint of local government, examples of operational units with multiple inputs and outputs include schools, social services day units, libraries, etc. Taking schools as an example, the inputs and outputs could be as shown in Figure 8.12.

To assess the relative efficiency of the operational units, a key task of DEA is to establish suitable weights for each of the inputs and outputs. Effectively, what DEA does is to examine each operational unit in turn and find the optimum set of weights for that particular unit. These weights are then applied to all of the operational units and the results calculated.

DEA can be used to identify how improved outputs can be generated for a fixed set of inputs (output-oriented DEA) or to establish how reduced inputs can be achieved for a fixed set of outputs (input-oriented DEA). The use of DEA involves complex statistical calculations and specialist software is usually required.

Figure 8.12 Input and outputs

Resource inputs	Service outputs
• Teaching staff	• Examination results
• Non-teaching staff	• Student destinations
• Learning materials	• Student and parental satisfaction levels
• Equipment	
• Buildings, etc.	

Design

Having undertaken the analysis of existing performance, the next stage is to design improvements that will produce genuine and significant improvements in performance. Such planned improvements may require changes to a number of aspects of service delivery, such as timing, location, method of delivery, type of resource, management, etc.

In these situations it is vitally important that the resource implications of the proposed changes are fully identified and understood before a decision is made to go ahead with them. In some situations this might be a relatively easy thing to do and will involve some relatively simple financial analysis. However, in other cases it will be much more complex and may require the development and use of decision support models to assess the financial and non-financial consequences of the proposed developments and of the various alternative options. Some examples of such models include the following:

→ **Simulation models** – simulation provides a decision maker with the equivalent of a 'flight simulator' for their operational activity. It is used to help with the design or modification of complex systems (e.g. hospitals) by experimenting with alternative combinations of resources (people, facilities, etc.), alternative service demands and alternative operating policies. Since simulated 'time' moves much faster than 'real' time, a day in a hospital could be simulated in a few seconds in the simulation model. Such models usually incorporate a costing function into their analysis.

→ **Optimisation models** – these assist in the identification of optimal solutions from a range of possibilities. Possible examples include the optimal mix of outputs of products/services within resource constraints or the optimal holdings of stocks to meet competing requirements.

→ **Systems dynamics models** – this is a branch of simulation modelling. It is an approach that is used to help provide understanding about complex systems where changes in one part of the system feedback into other parts of the system. System dynamics helps a decision maker to untangle the complexities of a system and provides a set of tools to describe and model the system.

→ **Financial planning models** – these models are designed to help with financial planning and budget setting. They enable the user to ask 'what if' questions and see the financial implications.

As discussed below, the financial aspects of such performance improvements must be identified reasonably accurately in order to incorporate them into the PSO's budgets.

Implementation

It is one thing to identify financially related performance improvements and another thing to bring them to fruition. There are many examples of viable performance improvements which were identified but where the benefits were not properly realised. This might have been through mismanagement or through some form of deliberate sabotage by vested interests.

The key tool here of financial management is the budget system of the PSO. It is quite common in the public sector for budget systems to incorporate across-the-board adjustments for efficiency improvements. However, it is also important that where specific performance improvements are identified the financial aspects of these are incorporated into the budget for the appropriate year.

Monitoring

Finally, it is clearly important to ensure that planned improvements in service performance are actually delivered. The non-financial aspects of this (e.g. quality, access) will be covered elsewhere, but it will be necessary for financial managers to monitor improvements in the use of resources and ensure that the planned improvements are achieved.

In summary, it can be seen that financial management has a very wide and important role to play in the design and implementation of public service performance improvement.

Conclusions

As will be discussed in Chapter 13, the financial and economic pressures on public services in years to come will mean that management of performance and performance improvement will be of huge importance in public services. While many public services have made substantial improvements in performance over a number of years, it does seem likely that quantum improvements in performance will be necessary over the next few years and much more radical approaches will be required. Given the importance of staffing and staff costs in the delivery of public services, key aspects of this could well include staff productivity, the various traditional practices of service professionals in public services and the potential for greater use of technology.

The need for such performance improvements means that PSOs will need to 'up their game' substantially with regard to performance management and performance improvement and robust financial management approaches will be a major component of this.

Questions for discussion

→ How much do we know about the current performance and trends in performance of our PSO?

→ Where are the gaps in our knowledge about our performance and how can we fill these gaps?

→ In our PSO, what might constitute improved performance?

→ How should we go about making improvements in performance in our PSO?

→ What are the barriers to improved performance and how can we overcome them?

Financial accounting and reporting in public service organisations

Introduction

All public and private sector organisations have a statutory duty to produce and publish a set of annual financial accounts containing certain defined financial information, relating to the organisation, for the previous 12-month period. This statutory requirement ensures that certain financial information about the organisation comes into the public domain. However, before discussing this further, we need to draw a distinction between financial and management accounting practice.

Accounting practice makes a broad distinction between two types of accounting. Management accounting is concerned with the provision of financial information within the organisation itself for the purpose of managerial decision making. Thus management accounting practice incorporates such matters as costing, budgeting, etc. On the other hand, financial accounting is concerned with the provision of financial information to various parties *external* to the organisation.

Figure 9.1 Financial accounting and management accounting compared

Theme	Financial accounting	Management accounting
Focus	External	Internal
Framework	Legislative/professional framework	User determined
Timeframe	Annual	Any period
Orientation	Historically oriented	Historical and future oriented
Disclosure	Limited disclosure of information	Wide and detailed range of information

Management accounting and financial accounting can be compared and contrasted, as shown in Figure 9.1 and described below.

→ **Focus** – as already noted, the focus of financial accounting information is parties external to the organisation, whereas the focus of management accounting information is the (internal) management of the organisation.

→ **Frameworks** – as will be seen later in this chapter, the structure and framework for financial accounting is defined by a combination of legislative statute and professional accounting requirements. This leads to financial information being prepared to a format which is in accordance with the requirements of the statutory/ professional frameworks. On the other hand, the framework of management accounting is defined largely by the management of the individual organisation concerned and it is up to the organisation to decide what information should be produced. Some caveats are needed here though. In private companies, subsidiary companies may be obliged to follow the management accounting framework laid down by the management of the holding company. The same is true in public services – for example, NHS Trusts are required to abide by the content of the national NHS Costing manual in producing cost information for internal purposes.

→ **Timeframes** – financial accounting information must be produced annually and released into the public domain. Management accounting information is produced according to the wishes of the individual organisation (e.g. weekly, monthly) and is usually kept confidential within the organisation. Combining this with the previous point, a local authority which has no discretion about the content and timing of its statutory financial accounts may, of its own volition, decide to produce weekly cost information, showing the costs of each individual DSO activity.

→ **Orientation of information produced** – financial accounting information is almost entirely historically oriented. While management accounting will have some historical orientation (e.g. unit costs for the last quarter) it will also be strongly concerned with the provision of future-oriented information and will involve various financial estimates and forecasts.

→ **Disclosure** – with financial accounting, because financial information is being released into the public domain, there are limits to the amount of information being disclosed. Thus, for example, usually only limited information on the cost structure of an organisation is released. The information disclosed is prescribed by the statutory/professional frameworks. On the other hand, with management accounting, the organisation is free to decide what information should be disclosed and to whom. Thus, disclosure is likely to be far more wide ranging, but there will still be limits to disclosure, with information being disclosed on a 'need to know' basis.

The author readily confesses to a considerable scepticism about the nature, complexity and relevance of some aspects of financial accounting in PSOs. Clearly it is important for all PSOs to demonstrate financial accountability to the taxpayer, but this duty of financial accountability can be discharged in a number of ways, possibly at less cost to the taxpayer. This issue will be returned to later in the chapter. Nevertheless, it is important to have some appreciation of the nature and methods of financial accounting and reporting in PSOs and this chapter aims to provide such an overview. However, financial accounting practice, in both public and private sectors, is very technical and complex and the reader who wishes to understand the intricacies of the subject is referred elsewhere, particularly to the mass of material found on appropriate websites of government departments and professional accountancy bodies. There is a list of websites at the back of the book.

This chapter considers the following issues:

→ the purpose of producing statutory financial accounts for PSOs – particularly in relation to accountability;
→ basic principles of financial accounting;
→ the regulatory framework for financial accounting in UK public service organisations;
→ financial accounting practices in public service organisations;
→ the relevance of financial accounting in PSOs.

The purpose of producing statutory financial accounts for PSOs

In both public and private sectors, the production of annual financial accounts is a complex and time-consuming activity with a substantial cost to the organisation both in terms of the production of the accounts and their subsequent audit. Hence, it is important that there is some clear purpose behind their production in order to justify the costs involved, even though individual organisations have no discretion as to whether or not they should produce such accounts. In most parts of the public sector (e.g. NHS, local government) the usual period for producing such accounts is for the year ended 31 March, whereas in the private sector an organisation will be able to opt for a particular accounting year end. Within the public sector, however, there are variations, since FE Colleges and HE institutions produce financial accounts based on the academic year ended 31 July.

In addressing this issue, we will consider the following:

→ Who are the users of accounts?

→ What are their information needs and how might they use financial accounting information?

Users of accounts

Accounting theory argues that financial accounts are prepared in order to put into the public domain financial information about the organisation which will be of relevance to users, and potential users, of those accounts in making decisions about the organisation – this is often referred to as the user-need theory. In saying this, it must be recognised that different users need to make different types of decision. However, this requirement must be balanced against the needs of the organisation to protect itself by not releasing information which could be damaging to itself and in not incurring excessive costs to produce the information needed. Therefore, taking the example of a limited company, the release of information for the benefit of users of accounts needs to be balanced against the release of information which benefits competitors of the company.

It follows that we first need to identify who are the users of accounts and what information they need. Users can be classified into a number of key groups, each with its own requirements for financial information, and this will vary to some extent from sector to sector. For example, the users of accounts of a public limited company might be as shown in Figure 9.2.

When we turn to PSOs, there are various ways of classifying the users or potential users of financial accounting information. Three possible approaches are described in Figure 9.3.

In the case of Professor Anthony and the ASB, even over a 30-year gap, there seems to be a fair degree of consensus about who are the potential users of PSO financial accounts. On the other hand, the FASB approach seems much more restrictive. Although there are a variety of users and potential users of such financial accounts, one of these groups is probably dominant and their needs for information have become paramount. The primary users of PSO statutory financial accounts are probably government departments and funding bodies, and their primary reasons for

Figure 9.2 Users and potential users of financial accounting information

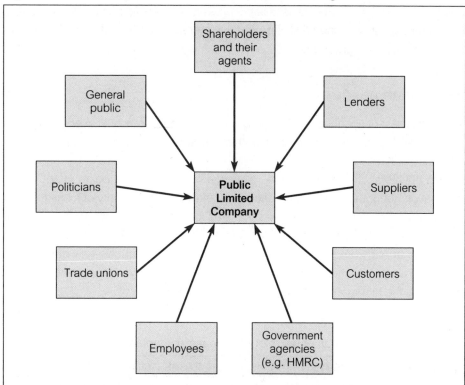

Figure 9.3 Users of public sector financial accounts

R.N. Anthony (1978)	FASAB (1994)	ASB (2007)
An academic, Professor R.N. Anthony, suggested the following major user groups: • Governing bodies • Investors and creditors • Resource providers, including fee-paying service recipients • Oversight bodies • Constituents, including taxpayers, voters and employees	The Federal Accounting Standards Advisory Board (FASAB) in the USA identified four major user groups: • Citizens – including news media, pressure groups, analysts, state and local legislatures and executives • The legislative branch – including their staff • Senior members of the executive branch • The executive branch programme managers	The ASB in its document *Statement of Principles for Public Benefit Entities*: • Present and potential investors • Present and potential funders and financial supporters • Lenders • Beneficiaries and customers • Government and their agencies including regulators • The public

needing such accounts will relate chiefly to their role in accounting for the use of public funds and their need to assess the efficiency of the service provision. Hence, this might explain why the FASB approach is more restrictive in that it only focuses on the primary user group(s).

Information needs

The key aspect of financial information given to users and potential users of financial accounts is that of relevance, but this then begs the question of what constitutes relevance?

With private sector organisations, relevance is often seen as being about having information about the future share price of a company, the security of loans made to a company, etc. However, with PSOs the situation is different since PSOs are using public funds to deliver public services and it would be useful to have some sort of framework about what financial information about PSOs might be relevant to users of their financial accounts. Again several frameworks have been developed for describing the information needs, as shown in Figure 9.4.

Figure 9.4 Possible needs of users of PSO financial accounts

Anthony (1978)	GASB (1984)	FASAB (1984)	GASB (1988)
• Financial viability • Fiscal compliance • Management performance • Cost of services provided	• Determining and predicting the flows, balances and requirements of short-term financial resources of the organisation • Determining and predicting the economic condition of the PSO and changes therein • Monitoring performance under terms of legal, contractual and fiduciary requirements • Planning and budgeting, and for predicting the impact of the acquisition and allocation of resources on the achievement of operational objectives • Evaluating managerial and organisational performance	• Budgetary integrity • Operating performance • Stewardship country • Systems and control	• Comparing actual financial results with the legally adopted budget • Assessing financial condition • Indicating compliance with finance-related laws, rules and regulations • Assisting in evaluating efficiency and effectiveness

Examination of these four sources taken over a period of 30 years suggests some common themes in that PSO financial accounts should provide information to users of accounts to help them make judgements about:

→ the legality with which public funds have been used;

→ the ongoing financial and operational viability of the PSO;

→ whether public funds have been used according to plan;

→ whether public funds have been used effectively and efficiently.

With PSOs, one of the key issues is that of stewardship since PSOs are using public funds and are acting as stewards of those public funds. Hence, they are responsible for the proper use of the funds and must be accountable for the use of those public funds. The production of statutory financial accounts is one way of discharging this accountability.

It is, of course, a debateable point as to the extent to which the content of PSO financial accounts do in fact meet all of these needs in a satisfactory manner. There are clear limits as to how far an individual PSO might go in attempting to meet the needs of its users of financial accounts:

→ **Regulatory frameworks** – the regulatory frameworks described later in this chapter place limitations on the sorts of information that PSOs might disclose in their audited statutory accounts. However, such frameworks really set a minimum level of disclosure which PSOs must adhere to in preparing their statutory accounts and PSOs are free to disclose other (non-audited) financial information alongside their statutory accounts should they think this would be helpful to users in meeting the needs described above.

→ **Commercial confidentiality** – traditionally PSOs were not seen as competing organisations, but the development of such things as market testing and com-missioning have meant that many PSOs now compete with other PSOs and with commercial organisations to win contracts and funding. The limited disclosure of financial information in the private sector has usually been justified on the basis that to disclose more information would endanger the competitive position of the organisations involved. Similar arguments are used in parts of public services (e.g. universities, NHS Trusts) to limit the amount of information that is disclosed to the minimum required by the regulatory framework.

→ **Cost of production** – these days the statutory accounts of PSOs constitute a complex set of statements and explanatory notes. The reality is that producing annual financial accounts in a PSO is a time-consuming and expensive task and one where there is no clear picture that the benefits exceed the costs. To disclose further information on a voluntary basis might add to these costs yet have no obvious benefit.

Basic principles of financial accounting

Although the financial accounts of public and private sector organisations will vary in terms of detailed content and format, in broad terms they comprise a number of different and inter-locking statements, the key ones being the income and expenditure account (or profit and loss account in the private sector), the balance sheet and the cash flow statement.

Before looking at PSO financial accounts in a little more detail it is helpful to consider the fundamental nature of, and relationship between, these three different financial statements. This is best illustrated using the example of a small hypothetical business called 'Comshare'. These same underlying principles can then be applied to the financial accounts of a PSO.

Example: Comshare

Basic financial information

Comshare commenced business on 1 April 2006. It purchases unpainted wooden toys, paints them and then sells them on at a higher price. The information available about the business is shown in Figure 9.5.

Financial statements

The organisation produces three distinct financial statements for the financial year ended 31 March 2007 and these are discussed below.

Income and expenditure (profit and loss) account

The term income and expenditure (I&E) account is more likely to be used in 'not for profit' organisations such as government agencies, NHS Trusts, etc., whereas the term profit and loss (P&L) account will be used in commercial organisations. Whichever title is used, the main function of this statement is the same.

The I&E account (P&L account) is a statement of *financial performance*. It shows the financial performance of the organisation, in terms of the surplus (or deficit) of income over expenditure, achieved over a period of a year.

The income and expenditure account for Comshare is shown in Figure 9.6.

A number of points need to be made about the structure and content of this statement:

→ **Income** – an I&E account differs from a statement of cash flows since it adopts what is termed the accounting *accruals* concept. Under this concept, income is the amount actually earned by the organisation during the year as opposed to the cash actually received. The difference between income and cash received is

---

Figure 9.5 Comshare: basic financial information

At the date of commencement of the business on 1 April 2006, Comshare had the following financial position:

	£000
Owners investment in the business	35
Loan from bank	10
This equates to:	
Cash in bank	45

During the year 2006/7, Comshare undertook the following financial transactions:

	£000
Purchase of unpainted wooden dolls	50
Sales of painted wooden dolls	65
Payment of wages	5
Cost of paint	3
Miscellaneous expenses	2
Purchase of equipment	40
New loan taken out from bank	5
Repayment of existing loan	2
Payment of bank interest	1
Owners drawings from business	2
Cash received from sales of painted dolls	61
Cash paid for purchase of unpainted dolls	48

At the end of the year, Comshare held stocks of unpainted dolls worth £3,000. There are no stocks of painted wooden dolls.

---

accounted for by amounts owing (debtors), as the data from the above example illustrates:

Sales income earned = £65,000 (shown in I&E account) *less*
Cash received from sales = £61,000 (shown in cash flow statement) *equals*
Debtors outstanding at the year end = £4,000 shown in the balance sheet

→ **Cost of purchases** – again, under the accruals concept this is the cost of purchases of wooden toys made in the year as opposed to the cash actually disbursed on their purchase. The difference between expenditure and cash spent is accounted for by amounts owed (creditors), as the data from the above example illustrate:

Purchases made = £50,000 (shown in I&E account) *less*
Cash disbursed for purchases = £48,000 (shown in cash flow statement) *equals*
Creditors outstanding at the year end = £2,000 shown in the balance sheet

→

Figure 9.6 Comshare: income and expenditure (profit and loss) account for 2006/7

	£000	£000
Sales of painted wooden dolls		65
Purchase of unpainted wooden dolls	50	
Less stocks at year end	3	
Cost of unpainted wooden dolls actually sold as painted dolls		47
Gross surplus (profit)		18
Less running costs		
Wages	5	
Paint	3	
Miscellaneous	2	
Depreciation of equipment	4	
Total running costs		14
Net surplus (profit) before finance charges		4
Less finance charges: Bank interest		1
Net surplus (profit)		3

→ **Stocks and cost of goods sold** – the business commences the year with no stocks of wooden toys but at the end of the year stocks of wooden toys amount to £3,000. Hence, the amount charged to the income and expenditure account is the cost of the wooden toys actually sold. This is derived by deducting the remaining stocks from the cost of the wooden toys purchased:

Purchases of wooden toys = £50,000 (shown in the I&E account) *less*
Stocks held at the year end = £3,000 (shown in the balance sheet) *equals*
Cost of goods sold = £47,000 (shown in the I&E account)

→ **Running costs** – various items (e.g. wages) constitute running costs, but it should be noted that purchase of equipment is not a running cost. This item is capitalised as a fixed asset and depreciation on the fixed asset is charged as a running cost (see below).

→ **Depreciation** – all organisations make use of fixed assets (or, as they are sometimes known, non-current assets) such as buildings and equipment and there are costs associated with the use of these fixed assets in the same way as wages or energy are costs. Strictly speaking, depreciation is concerned with matching costs relating to a fixed asset to the income or benefits that fixed asset generates over its lifetime. Put more simply, the use of fixed assets such as buildings or equipment means that they suffer wear and tear, and this wear and tear is as much a cost to the organisation as pay or non-pay expenditure, albeit that it involves no cash flow out of the organisation. Thus, it has to be accounted for in the I&E account under the heading of depreciation. Using the data from the above example, the depreciation charge is computed as follows:

Cost of equipment = £40,000
Useful life = 10 years
Annual depreciation charge = £40,000/10 = £4,000 per annum

This depreciation charge does not involve any cash movement into or from the organisation. Instead the surplus (profit) of the organisation is reduced by the amount of the depreciation charge and the value of the equipment is reduced in the organisation's balance sheet by the amount of depreciation charged.

→ **Interest charges** – although the business receives new loans and repays old loans during the year, these just involve adjustments to the capital of the business and are not expenses of the business. However, the interest charges on loans are an expense of the business and are charged to the I&E account. New loans and repayment of loans are shown in the balance sheet and cash flow statements below.

Balance sheet

A balance sheet is often confused with an income and expenditure statement but the two statements are very different. Whereas the income and expenditure statement is a statement of *financial performance over a period of time (one year)*, a balance sheet is a statement of the *financial position* of the organisation *at a single point in time* (usually the year end). It shows the assets owned by the organisation and its outstanding liabilities at that point in time, namely at the end of the financial year. Thus the closing balance sheet for one year becomes the opening balance sheet of the next year. The balance sheet for Comshare is shown in Figure 9.7.

A number of points need to be made about the structure and content of this statement:

→ **Fixed (non-current) assets** – the fixed assets of an organisation include land, buildings, equipment, vehicles, etc., but in this simple example only equipment is shown. The normal accounting convention (termed the historic cost convention) is that the gross cost of fixed assets is shown in the balance sheet at their original purchase price (i.e. historic cost). Depreciation (as discussed above) is calculated on this historic cost and deducted from the gross cost of fixed assets to give a net figure for fixed assets. Even within the historic cost convention, however, some fixed assets such as land and buildings may be revalued to a current value and included in the balance sheet as a revalued amount.

→ **Current assets and liabilities** – creditors, debtors and cash will be shown at actual values. Under the historic cost convention stocks are shown in the balance sheet at the lower of their original purchase price (i.e. historic cost) or their current value.

→ **Owners' investment** – at the commencement of the business this amounted to £35,000. The profits earned by Comshare (£3,000) accrue to the owners and hence increase their investment, but drawings from the business of £2,000 reduce their investment by that amount.

→

Figure 9.7 Comshare: balance sheet as at 31 March 2007

	£000	£000
ASSETS		
Fixed assets		
Equipment	40	
Less depreciation	4	
Net amount		36
Current assets		
Stocks of unpainted wooden dolls	3	
Debtors	4	
Cash	8	
Total current assets	15	
Less current liabilities – creditors	2	
Net current assets		13
Total assets		49
FINANCED BY:		
Owners of business		
Owners' initial investment	35	
Add profit for year	3	
Less owners' personal drawings	2	
Owners' capital (or stake in business)		36
Loans		
Original loan	10	
Add new loan	5	
Less repayments of existing loan	2	
Outstanding loans		13
Total financing sources		49

→ **Bank loans** – the business started the year with an outstanding loan and during the year part of this old loan was repaid while a new loan was taken out. The results of these transactions are reflected as adjustments in the balance sheet and not the I&E account, as follows:

Loans at start of the year = £10,000
less repayments = £2,000
add new loan = £5,000
Loans at end of year = £13,000

In addition, an interest payment of £1,000 was made during the year and has been charged to the I&E account as an expense to the business.

Cash flow statement
A cash flow statement is also a statement of *financial performance*, and shows whether the organisation had a net inflow or outflow of cash (as opposed to income

and expenditure) over the year. Cash flow is important since organisations generating a financial surplus in income and expenditure terms can still experience financial difficulties if their cash flow position is not also positive. An I&E can show a profit but if cash is not collected, with a resulting high level of debtors, cash flow difficulties may arise. The cash flow statement for Comshare is shown in Figure 9.8.

A number of points need to be made about the structure and content of this statement:

→ **Cash inflows** – in this example, cash receipts from sales of goods and new bank loans constitute positive flows of cash into the bank account of Comshare.

→ **Cash outflows** – in this example, negative flows of cash out of the bank account of Comshare are the result of the following:
  - *Payments* for purchases of stock items.
  - *Operating expenses* (e.g. wages, paint, expenses)
  - *Bank loans* – both interest payments and principal repayments constitute cash outflows but only the interest payments have been charged to the I&E account.
  - *Purchases of equipment* – this is not charged to the I&E account since it is not an operating expense of the business. It is reflected by changes to the fixed asset figures in the balance sheet.
  - *Owners' drawings* – this is not charged to the I&E account since it is not an operating expense of the business. It is shown as a change to the owners' capital in the balance sheet.
  - *Depreciation* – although this is a cost of production, this is *not* shown in the cash flow statement since it does not involve any flow of cash into or out of the business.

Figure 9.8 Comshare: cash flow statement 2006/7

	£000	£000	£000
Opening cash balance			45
Cash inflows			
Sales receipts	61		
New bank loan	5		
Total cash inflows		+66	
Cash outflows			
Purchases payments	48		
Wages	5		
Paint	3		
Miscellaneous expenses	2		
Bank interest	1		
Loan repayment	2		
Equipment purchase	40		
Owners' drawings	2		
Total cash outflows		−103	
Net cash outflow during 2006/7			−37
Closing cash balance			8

The regulatory framework for financial accounting in UK public service organisations

No organisation (e.g. companies, local authorities, NHS Trusts, charities, etc.) has complete freedom to decide what financial information should be disclosed in its statutory financial accounts and in what format those accounts should be prepared (however, they are, of course, free to disclose, voluntarily, more than the minimum information required). Hence, PSOs do not have freedom to decide the format and content of their annual financial accounts but must operate within a regulatory framework which defines the format of their financial accounts and the minimum information they must disclose. Such accounting frameworks are in place for all PSOs, although PSOs in different sectors will have different regulatory requirements.

Overall, the regulatory accounting framework in which PSOs must operate is complex and comprises three main aspects:

→ Accounting requirements defined by statute.

→ Accounting requirements defined by the accounting profession. These are not mandatory in law but are usually complied with.

→ Accounting requirements defined by government.

Accounting requirements defined by statute

To facilitate compliance with reporting and disclosure requirements, the regulatory framework of financial accounting must be grounded in statute. The precise statutes will vary depending on the organisations concerned. Some examples of such statutory requirements are shown in Figure 9.9.

Accounting requirements defined by the accounting profession

The accounting profession also has its own non-statutory requirements for the production of financial accounts. This can be considered twofold: domestic requirements and international requirements.

Domestic

At the domestic level the key requirements are described in Statements of Standard Accounting Practice (SSAP) and Financial Reporting Standards (FRS). Accounting standards were introduced during the 1970s in response to a series of private sector scandals concerning the way in which the statutory financial accounts of certain companies were being prepared and the inaccuracies and distortions contained in

Figure 9.9 Statutory framework for financial accounting

Sector/organisation	Statutory framework
Limited companies	The operations and accounting arrangements for such companies are governed by the Companies Act 1989, which updated and consolidated the Companies Act of 1985 and other legislation. However, subsequent changes were necessary to the Companies Act 1985 to incorporate two new EC Directives, namely the Seventh Directive (consolidated accounts) and the Eighth Directive (regulation and qualification of auditors).
Central government	Supply-financed bodies are governed by the Government Resources and Accounts Act 2000. Trading funds are covered by the Government Trading Fund Act 1973.
NHS organisations	The relevant legislation is the NHS Act 1947. This provides the statutory framework under which the Secretary of State for Health can prescribe the format and content of NHS accounts.
Further and higher education institutions	The key legislation that affects the financial reporting of further and higher education organisations is the Further and Higher Education Act 1992, which establishes the funding councils, determines the purposes for which government-based funding can be used and gives further and higher education organisations the power to raise funds through their own enterprise.
Third sector organisations	Most 3SOs are registered charities. Two Parliamentary Acts exist, both of which deal with the duty of charities to keep accounting records and be audited. These are the Charities Acts 1992 and 1993. These two Acts also detail the reporting requirements for charities of different sizes. The Charities Acts 1992 and 1993 have formed the basis for a Charities Commission publication, *Charity Accounts: The Framework*. This provides further guidance on annual reporting requirements including the contents of the annual report and financial reporting requirements.

those accounts. The aim was to develop a framework for producing such accounts and to provide for some degree of consistency of accounting practice on various issues. However, even with the advent of accounting standards there is still a fair degree of freedom for organisations to apply differing accounting practices.

Statutory financial accounts are now prepared in accordance with the require-ments of SSAPs and FRSs and these standards apply to all companies, and other kinds of entities that prepare accounts, with the intention that they show what is termed a 'true and fair view' of the financial affairs of the organisation. Currently it is the role of the Accounting Standards Board (ASB) to issue accounting standards and as such it is recognised for that purpose under the Companies Act 1985. The ASB took over the task of setting accounting standards from the former Accounting

Standards Committee (ASC). Accounting standards developed by the ASB are contained in the Financial Reporting Standards (FRSs). Soon after it started its activities, the ASB adopted the standards issued by the ASC, so that they also fall within the legal definition of accounting standards. These are designated Statements of Standard Accounting Practice (SSAPs). While some of the SSAPs have been superseded by FRSs, others remain in force.

As noted, accounting standards apply to all companies and other organisations which prepare accounts, with the intention that they provide a true and fair view of that organisation's financial performance and financial position. Thus they apply, in principle, to PSOs and PSO-owned companies, although the nature of certain standards (e.g. FRS 14 on Earnings per share) means that, although applicable, they are not relevant to PSOs.

Also to be considered are the Statements of Recommended Practice (SORPs). SORPs are recommendations on accounting practices for specialised industries or sectors such as the public sector. They supplement accounting standards and other legal and regulatory requirements in the light of the special factors prevailing or transactions undertaken in a particular industry or sector. SORPs are issued not by the Accounting Standards Board (ASB) but by industry or sectoral bodies recognised for the purpose by the ASB. To secure such recognition, SORP-making bodies are expected to meet criteria laid down by the ASB and to develop their SORP proposals in conformity with the ASB's code of practice, given in the ASB Statement 'SORPs: policy and code of practice'. A SORP is required to carry a statement by the ASB confirming, as appropriate, that the SORP does not appear to contain any fundamental points of principle that are unacceptable in the context of current accounting practice or to conflict with an accounting standard or the ASB's plans for future standards. To assist in dealing with proposals for SORPs the ASB has two specialist advisory committees: the Financial Sector and Other Special Industries Committee and the Committee on Accounting for Public-benefit Entities.

International level

It has long been recognised in the corporate sector that there is demand for a single international set of accounting standards. As both business and the financial markets become more global, one financial language aids the preparation, comparability and analysis of financial information for corporate entities. Some of the benefits for the corporate sector have been seen in merger and acquisition activity where comparable information across different countries has enhanced ease of analysis for acquirers – in both raising finance and in communications, where one accounting language has enabled companies to produce marketing material and communications that are understood globally by shareholders, analysts and other users.

Thus, at the international level, International Accounting Standards were originally prepared and issued by the International Accounting Standards Committee. One of the roles of the IASC was to promote the convergence of domestic accounting standards around the world to achieve greater harmonisation of global accounting practices particularly in relation to multi-national companies. The pressure for convergence means that, from time to time, UK domestic accounting standards may need to be amended.

The International Accounting Standards Board (IASB) is the successor to the IASC. Thirty-two IASs are still in force, having been adopted by the IASB, but the IASB now issues International Financial Reporting Standards (IFRS). The term IFRS refers to the international equivalent to the UK's Generally Accepted Accounting Principles (GAAP), which include accounting standards, Interpretations (equivalent to Urgent Issues Task Force – UITF abstracts), the IASB's Framework and established accounting practice.

Following the update in the 2008 budget, government bodies will be required to adopt International Financial Reporting Standards (IFRS) for their 2009/10 accounts and will also be required to restate 2008/9 accounts using IFRS to provide comparative information. Central government, NHS Trusts, Primary Care Trusts and NHS Foundation Trusts will all need to adopt IFRS within this same timetable. IFRS is likely to be a challenge for many public sector organisations. The implications are complex and wide ranging. IFRS is not only a technical accounting issue for the finance team and the impact of the changes will expand to encompass many areas of the organisation such as the setting and measurement of performance targets, budgeting and forecasting – as well as financial reporting. Process and systems changes are inevitable. Effective timely communication of the issues, both internally to employees and externally to stakeholders, is critical. The financial impact will vary widely from one body to another but in all cases the broader implications are wide reaching.

Another international initiative that is being pursued by the International Public Sector Accounting Standards Board (IPSASB) is the development of International Public Sector Accounting Standards (IPSASs). While IPSASs are not used in the United Kingdom, they are increasingly being adopted internationally, and also represent a very useful benchmark for the interpretation of International Financial Reporting Standards (IFRS) in a public sector context. They have informed the deliberations of the UK Financial Reporting Advisory Board (FRAB) during its review of the developing IFRS-based *Government Financial Reporting Manual*. Under a memorandum of understanding agreed in October 2008, IPSASs are now formally second in the hierarchy for the development of all financial reporting guidance for the UK public sector, encompassing government departments and their arms-length bodies, NHS Trusts, Foundation Trusts and local government.

Figure 9.10 Accounting requirements defined by government

Sector/organisation	Government requirements
Central government	Details of requirements can be found in the *Government Financial Reporting Manual* issued by HM Treasury.
NHS	With the exception of NHS Foundation Trusts, NHS organisations follow the *NHS Manual for Accounts* issued by the Department of Health. The Manual of Accounts is part of the NHS finance manual and contains detailed guidance about the preparation of financial accounts for all of the different types of NHS organisations. NHS Foundation Trusts have their own financial reporting regulations set out by foundation trust regulator, Monitor.
Higher education institutions	The Accounts Directions are issued as necessary by HEFCE to cover specific and general accounting issues for the HE sector which will impact on the annual financial statements. HEFCE also provide guidance on how to present the required information/disclosures contained in the Accounts Directions. The Accounts Directions can therefore cover very broad and very specific issues. HEFCE requires compliance with the SORP but also issues, from time to time, Accounts Directives which are mandatory on the sector. It also sets out in its Financial Memorandum that each PSO must keep proper accounting records and must submit audited financial statements to HEFCE by 31 December each year, in respect of the 31 July year end.

Accounting requirements defined by government

Various parts of government also define the accounting requirements for various PSOs. The situation regarding some sectors is shown in Figure 9.10.

At this point, reference should be made to the Financial Reporting Advisory Board (FRAB). The Board was established in 1996 to act as an independent review in the process of setting accounting standards for government during the development of resource accounting. The Board's declared role is to promote the highest possible standards in financial reporting by government and to help to ensure that any adaptations of, or departures from, GAAP are justified and properly explained. The Board's remit has grown since 1996 and now includes advising on financial report-ing across the UK (principles only in Scotland) for departments, executive agencies, executive non-departmental public bodies, trading funds and health bodies. Thus it excludes large parts of the public services which fall outside of central government such as local authorities, FE colleges, etc. The Board also advise the Treasury on the implementation of accounting policies specific to the Whole of Government

Accounts. The Whole of Government Accounts (WGA) project was concerned with putting into place procedures that could deliver an annual set of consolidated financial statements covering the whole of the public sector. The first set of WGA statements were published for the fiscal year 2006/7.

Financial accounting practices in public service organisations

Earlier in this chapter we discussed the issues of the users of PSO financial accounts and their likely information needs. In this section we will describe actual accounting practices in various parts of the public services and discuss the approach taken by PSOs towards the production of the three main accounting statements that form part of their annual financial accounts statements. As already mentioned, financial accounting practices in PSOs are complex and very technical and vary substantially in points of details between different parts of the public sector and even between different organisations within the same sector (e.g. PCTs and NHS Trusts). Thus, this section only aims to give an overview of accounting practices in different public services and the reader who requires technical details is referred elsewhere, particularly to the websites of government departments and professional accountancy bodies.

In Figure 9.11 we outline what are seen as the main purposes of each of these statements and the contribution they make towards meeting user needs.

In this section we discuss accounting practices in PSOs under three main headings which are concerned with the approach to producing the following:

→ income and expenditure statements;

→ balance sheets;

→ cash flow statements.

This section will consider the financial accounting practices in four different areas of public service, namely central government, local government, NHS and higher education.

However, before looking at these three main accounting statements, there are two other issues which need to be discussed because they have implications for the main statements. These are:

→ the approach to capital accounting in PSOs;

→ other financial statements.

Figure 9.11 PSO financial statements and user needs

Statement	Possible contribution towards user needs
Income and expenditure statement	• To provide an assessment of the financial **performance** of the PSO • To show the surplus or deficit that the organisation has incurred within the year after maintaining its capital • To provide some analysis of the cost structure of the PSO • To provide some information about the income streams of the PSO
Balance sheet	• To assess the financial **position** of the PSO • To show the liquidity of the organisation and its ability to meet payments due • To show the value of the assets of the organisation • To shown the outstanding debts of the organisation • To show the financial reserves of the organisation
Cash flow statement	• To assess the financial **performance** of the PSO • To indicate the liquidity of the PSO. Although PSOs have a lower risk of insolvency compared to the private sector (as they are funded by the taxpayer), cash flow remains an important measure • To indicate how well the cash flow has been managed and returns for surplus cash have been maximised • To indicate how well they have maintained their cash position within approved limits

Capital accounting practices in PSOs

The detailed content of the income and expenditure statement and the balance sheet of a PSO will be strongly influenced by its approach to capital accounting. The main implications are:

→ the impact on the balance sheet figures for fixed (non-current) assets and liabilities shown in the balance sheet;

→ the impact on the income and expenditure account figures for such matters as depreciation and cost of capital charges.

The approach to capital accounting in PSOs is technically very detailed and complex and the approach varies between different sectors and different parts of the same sector (e.g. PCTs, NHS Trusts). Hence, it is beyond the scope of this book to describe, in any detail, the differing approaches applied in the various PSOs and the interested reader is referred to the various technical accounting manuals that are available.

Accounting for fixed assets in PSOs is driven by two things:

→ Demonstrating compliance with UK GAAP – this leads to the need to charge depreciation, value assets fairly, etc.

→ Demonstrating that money invested in fixed assets is being used effectively and efficiently.

If we look at capital accounting practice in PSOs we see the following themes as being of most importance:

Capitalisation of expenditure

In Chapter 2 we mentioned that the basic approach to distinguishing capital expenditure from revenue expenditure concerned the flow of benefits (Jones and Pendlebury, 2000). The benefits flowing from revenue expenditure tend to be confined to the year in which the expenditure is incurred but the benefits from capital expenditure are obtained over a period of several years. Thus, capital expenditure is expenditure that provides benefits for more than one year and thus includes expenditure on such things as buildings, roads, equipment, vehicles, IT, etc. However, a question that is sometimes asked is 'what about an office stapler?' A stapler provides benefits for more than one year so should it be counted as capital expenditure and shown in the balance sheet as a non-current asset? Common sense says that the answer to this question must be 'no', but it does raise the question of how to define capital expenditure with some precision. In the NHS, capital expenditure is defined as being expenditure on a single item exceeding a prescribed limit (£5,000). In other PSOs the decision about capitalisation is more likely to be a managerial judgement.

Classification of fixed assets

In the PSO's balance sheet, fixed assets will be classified under a number of different headings. Typically a distinction will be drawn between tangible assets, intangible fixed assets and investments, but further analysis may be required according to the sector involved, with local government, for instance, requiring a split between operational fixed assets and non-operational fixed assets.

Valuation of fixed assets

A fixed asset will initially be recorded by the PSO at its original cost. Under FRS15, PSOs have the choice of valuing their tangible fixed assets at historical cost or revaluing each class of asset on a five-yearly basis and recording assets at current valuation. Typical practice might be to use the revaluation approach for long-life assets, such as land and buildings, while short-life fixed assets, such as vehicles, plant and equipment, may be held at historical cost or modified historical cost. Tangible fixed assets should be disclosed at the lower of replacement value or recoverable amount defined as the higher of net realisable value and value in use. In intervening years, assets held at modified historical cost should be indexed to bring the valuation up to today's price. Valuing assets in this way ensures that the asset value represents today's cost of replacing the assets. Some fixed assets in local government are shown at depreciated historical cost.

Calculation of depreciation

The usual practice is to calculate depreciation on a straight line basis in accordance with what is permitted under FRS15. The annual depreciation charge will be calculated using the current asset value. This will result in a higher depreciation expense being recognised in the revenue account than would otherwise have been charged. Backlog depreciation may be charged through the revaluation reserve (or donated asset reserve) to ensure that the accumulative depreciation held to date is equal to the amount of depreciation that would have been charged had the asset been consistently held at its current value.

Structure of reserves

The balance sheet will provide an analysis of the reserves of the organisation but this will differ from sector to sector. Typical reserves include revaluation reserves, donated asset reserves, the income and expenditure account and the general fund.

Cost of capital charges

In many types of PSO it is practice to make a charge on the value of the fixed assets. This is often referred to as the cost of capital charge and is designed to reflect the opportunity cost of the funds invested in the fixed assets of the PSO. Making such a charge is designed to:

→ promote an awareness of the true cost of capital;
→ improve decision making on asset acquisition and disposal;
→ promote an efficient use of assets;
→ recognise the true cost of capital.

Other financial statements

In addition to the main statements above, other statements are also produced. For example, during the year, a PSO may also generate other gains and losses in its balance sheet that are not shown in its income and expenditure account. Such gains and losses could include:

→ surplus/deficit arising from the revaluation of fixed assets;
→ actuarial gains or losses on pension fund assets and liabilities.

The Statement of Total Recognised Gains and Losses brings together these other gains and losses with the I&E account to show the movement in a PSO's net worth for the year.

We now turn to the three main accounting statements.

Income and expenditure accounts

Most PSOs which operate in a quasi-commercial basis produce formal income and expenditure statements on an accruals basis, but others produce what are referred to as operating cost statements. The comparative situation regarding income and expenditure accounts is outlined in Figure 9.12.

Balance sheets

All PSOs produce balance sheets which give details of the assets they hold, the liabilities they have and their capital. This is summarised in Figure 9.13.

Cash flow statements

All PSOs produce a cash flow statement showing the sources of cash, the applications of that cash and the opening and closing cash balances. This is summarised in Figure 9.14.

The relevance of financial accounting in PSOs

The production, audit and dissemination of statutory financial accounts is now quite a large, complex and time-consuming industry in its own right. Figure 9.15 illustrates just a few statistics about this from a random sample of PSOs.

Statutory financial reports are a substantial and complex set of documents which incur a significant cost to produce and that the audit costs associated with them are also significant. Thus, although we are not aware of any information which estimates the total costs of producing and auditing statutory financial accounts for the whole of public services, it does seem that the costs involved must be substantial, comprising as they do the costs associated with:

→ the costs of the accounts closure procedures;
→ the costs of drafting the statutory financial accounts (probably several drafts);
→ the costs of printing and disseminating the financial accounts;
→ the costs of external audit of the statutory financial accounts.

Figure 9.12 Income and expenditure accounts in PSOs

Central government

There are two aspects to reporting financial performance in central government and these concern:

- departments and supply-financed agencies;
- non-supply-financed agencies, also known as trading funds.

Basically the first group are funded through the Parliamentary Vote system (known as supply financing), whereas trading funds are funded through their own trading operations. This difference in financing regimes determines the underlying financial objectives of these different types of organisation, which in turn influences the way in which their financial statements are prepared and their performance is reported.

Departments and supply-financed agencies produce an operating cost statement, which shows how costs have been spent in supporting the provision of the department's or agency's work and the comparative expenditure on different programmes. This contrasts with most other PSOs where the income and expenditure account (or equivalent) will report the extent to which expenditure on services has been matched by the funding received, resulting in a surplus or a deficit. Supply-financed organisations will need to report their performance on a segmental basis regardless of the materiality of an individual programme. In this way the users of the accounts can assess how much is being invested in delivering projects and how much is being invested in running the department or agency.

With non-supply-financed (trading) agencies we see an income and expenditure account which is similar to that of a limited company, reporting a surplus/deficit for the year but with the expenditure being analysed in greater detail. Furthermore, with trading funds there is no notional cost of capital as there is for supply-financed bodies. Although a trading fund acts as a quasi-commercial organisation it will not have shareholders. It will also not hold specific reserves since this is not permitted under the Government Trading Funds Act 1973. There is therefore no appropriations section to the income and expenditure account.

Local government

Local authorities produce an I&E account but there are distinctive aspects to it. The I&E is split into four sections showing the following:

1. The net costs of various services provided including corporate expenditure.
2. Various other costs such as:
   - profit or loss on asset disposals;
   - precepts from other bodies;
   - surplus of deficit on trading undertakings;
   - interest payable and similar charges;
   - contribution of housing capital receipts to government pool;
   - investment losses;
   - interest and investment income;
   - pension interest costs.
3. Net cost of services plus other costs is shown as net operating expenditure.
4. How net operating expenditure is financed from: government grants, council tax and non-domestic rates.

It should be noted that a mix of reporting gross expenditure and net expenditure is adopted in local government whereas other sectors usually apply the gross principle.

Figure 9.12 *continued*

NHS

The NHS has both commissioner arms (PCTs) and provider arms (NHS Trusts and NHS Foundation Trusts). Commissioners and providers prepare a different style of financial statement although many of the underlying accounting entries that produce the statements are the same. NHS Trusts operate under a different accounting and funding regime from PCTs and it is this that drives the format and presentation of their financial statements. Also NHSFTs do not have to follow the same format as NHSTs.

PCTs operate on the boundary with central government where they interface with governmental resource accounting. Thus they produce an operating cost statement like central government organisations. The format and presentation of the operating cost statement also reflect the aims of PCTs. Although PCTs are primarily commissioning organisations they also directly provide a wide range of services themselves. This is recognised in the statement which differentiates between the PCT's commissioning and provider roles. The statement shows a net operating cost for the year. Such a cost figure does not mean that PCTs will be judged to have always incurred a deficit since they are set financial duties to ensure that their expenditure does not breach their expenditure target. This is set by the Department of Health and is known as the resource limit.

An income and expenditure account in an NHS Trust is broadly similar to the same financial statements in a limited company but there are some differences. All profits/losses on fixed assets are disclosed separately within the 'profit/loss on fixed assets line'. This is so that the users of the accounts will be able to determine from the income and expenditure account what is the surplus or deficit on providing services. Interest payable will include the same items of expenditure as for a PCT – interest on finance leases, interest paid under the Late Payment of Commercial Debts Act (1998) and the financing charge included for the unwinding of discounted provisions. Any interest paid on debt will relate to loans held with the NHS Bank. NHSFTs however may borrow more widely and have interest payable to other bodies such as commercial banks. NHS Trusts do not have the power to appropriate funds to reserves. Although there are no shareholders in the NHS, dividends are included as an expense to the NHS Trust. These are the dividends paid on its public dividend capital which is the amount of funding initially given to the trust by the Department of Health to fund its fixed assets. The public dividend capital dividends payment represents the cost of capital paid by the trust. Unlike the notional cost of capital that a PCT pays, the dividend charge is a cash payment that the NHS Trust must make.

Higher education

The I&E account provides for an analysis of income between: funding council sources, student fees, research grants, investment income and other sources. A brief analysis of expenditure is provided with any exceptional costs of restructuring being separately disclosed. Separate disclosure is made of taxation costs and any profits or losses on the disposal of assets. Finally the I&E account shows the surplus/deficit on operations after disposal of assets and tax.

Separate statements are also provided which show the impact on their surplus/deficit position of differences in approach in calculating depreciation and the impact of taxation.

Figure 9.13 Balance sheets in PSOs

Central government

With regard to departments and supply-financed agencies, the top half of the balance sheet is similar to that of a limited company. The reserves section differs in that there is no share capital, no specific revenue reserves and no retained profit. Instead the balance sheet is financed through two capital reserves – the revaluation reserve and the donated asset reserve. The general fund represents the accumulated funding for the organisation's activities. This will include both funding received for revenue and capital activities. The balance sheet of a supply-financed central government organisation will present the users of the accounts with an idea of how much has been invested in running the organisation and providing services and how much the taxpayer has spent in maintaining the net assets of the organisation.

As well as PDC, trading funds can raise finance through loans from the National Loans Fund or their parent department. Trading funds are also permitted to retain any surpluses made and use these to fund future operations. The structure of the balance sheet therefore allows the users of the accounts to assess the effectiveness with which trading funds have managed to turn public dividend capital into surpluses and how highly geared the agency is.

Local government

In the local authority balance sheet, fixed assets are separated into operational and non-operational assets as well as by their asset class. The analysis of current assets is fairly standard. The financing section of the balance sheet includes the capital adjustment account and usable capital receipts reserve which do not have equivalents in other sectors. Reserves may include earmarked reserves that can only be used for specific purposes. School funds are an example of this as any surpluses generated on school funds cannot be applied to other services. This is not the case in the NHS but may be the case in companies and central government.

NHS

The balance sheet for an NHS Trust is also similar to that of a limited company. Although the pro forma balance sheet provides a space for investments these will rarely be held since NHS Trusts are not permitted to hold investments unless prior permission has been given by the Secretary of State for Health. NHS Trusts may invest money on a short-term basis with the Department of Health who use this to make short-term loans to other NHS organisations. NHSFTs, who have greater ability to invest under the Prudential Borrowing Code for NHSFTs, may have a wider range of current asset investments. A significant element of an NHS Trust's net assets is financed through public dividend capital. Public dividend capital represents the amount of funding transferred to a trust from the Department of Health to fund its net assets and is equivalent to shareholders capital invested in a company. Dividends are paid annually on this funding and are equivalent to the notional interest recovered through cost of capital charges. Repayment of public dividend capital is accounted for as for the repayment of a loan. NHS Trusts hold a donated asset reserve to finance any donated assets held and a government grant asset reserve for any government grant funded assets received. We have seen how these reserves also exist in PCTs and in central government.

Figure 9.13 *continued*

Higher education
The balance sheet of a higher education institution gives a consolidated position with the balance sheet having separate columns for the HEI itself and any subsidiary undertakings. Particular points to note in the balance sheet are that there are separate lines for endowments (i.e. donations given to the HEI) in both assets and liabilities which show the same amounts. Also, shown in the liabilities section of the balance sheet is what is referred to as deferred capital grants. The funding councils often provide capital funds to enable HEIs to purchase buildings, equipment and other assets. When the fixed asset is purchased, the cost of the asset will appear in both the asset side of the balance sheet and on the opposite side of the balance sheet to show that the asset has been financed by a capital grant. Following the 'depreciation' principle, depreciation on the fixed asset is charged to the income and expenditure account each year to reflect wear and tear on the asset. At the same time an equivalent portion of the capital grant will be released to the income part of the I&E account (in the funding council grant section) to match the depreciation element expenditure in the depreciation heading of the I&E account. The balance of capital grants (referred to as deferred capital grants) is then shown in the balance sheet. Thus the overall impact of a fixed asset purchased through a capital grant is nil on both the I&E account and the balance sheet of the HEI. Revaluation reserves are shown and will include all changes in asset values following formal revaluations.

Figure 9.14 Cash flow statements in PSOs

Central government
The cash flow statement for a department and supply side agency is relatively simple and straightforward to understand. However, certain features which would normally be found in a cash flow statement such as equity transactions, taxation or acquisitions and disposals are not found in central government. However, some flows which are specific to central government and which are included are: • The total of any payments made to the consolidated fund in year and in previous years.   • Receipts due to the consolidated fund which are outside the scope of the department's activities.   • Financing cash flows are disclosed but the contents of the financing note are different from what would be found in company accounts.   With a trading agency, the format of the cash flow statement is more like that of a limited company. Again, as with supply-financed organisations, there are certain features such as equity transactions or taxation which are not relevant and will not be found. Trading funds are financed through loans and public dividend capital, unlike the supply-financed part of central government. This requires them to identify loans and PDC paid and received in the year. Since they retain their surpluses and are permitted to hold and invest cash balances the cash flow statement may show both invested funds and interest received.

Continued overleaf

Figure 9.14 *continued*

Local government
A local government cash flow statement is relatively straightforward. However the statement is prepared using the direct method which requires that the net cash flow from operating activities is identified by adding together all operating inflows and outflows. Other sectors use the indirect method, where the net cash flow from operating activities is obtained through the preparation of note 1. Local authorities also prepare note 1 in addition to using the direct method. Although a local authority uses the direct method to identify the net cash flow from operating activities note 1, reconciliation of operating activities to the net cash flow for the year is also produced. Using the direct method to identify the net cash flow from operating activities helps provide a clear link for the users of the accounts between the I+E account and cash flow statement. A local authority will also produce a reconciliation of cash movements to net debt/funds and an analysis of net funds. As with the NHS, this is shown in two notes and provides the users of the accounts with an understanding of how the movement in cash has reduced or increased the indebtedness of the organisation.

NHS
NHS organisations are required to publish a cash flow statement as part of their financial statements. Again there are some differences between commissioner organisations and provider organisations:

- PCTs must aim to keep their cash expenditure within a set cash limit.
- NHS organisations must keep their cash requirement from external sources within their external financing limit.

With regard to an NHS Trust, the following points should be noted:

- There is no entry for taxation as the NHS does not pay tax.
- Acquisitions will not apply to an NHS cash flow statement since transfers of services are not considered to be acquisitions.
- Dividend payments will appear in an NHS Trust cash flow statement relating to dividends paid on public dividend capital and not payments to shareholders.
- The cash flow statement separates out loans received and repaid from the Department of Health and other sources and current asset investments made and redeemed with the Department of Health and other sources. Loans and current asset investments placed with the Department of Health refers to the working capital loans and deposits scheme.

The situation with PCTs will be broadly similar to NHS Trusts but with one exception. Since PCTs are only allowed to retain cash balances in the Office of the Paymaster General no interest is received. Similarly a PCT will not report any cash flows in relation to its management of liquid resources since PCTs are not permitted to hold short-term investments.

Higher education
The cash flow statement is relatively straightforward showing cash flow movements in the period and the overall change in the cash position. However, also required is a statement which reconciles net cash flow to movements in net funds.

Figure 9.15 Costs and complexity of statutory financial accounts

PSO	Size of annual accounts and notes	Fees paid to auditors
Leeds NHS Teaching Hospitals Trust 2007/8	31 pages	£251,000
St Helens and Knowsley NHS Trust 2007/8	33 pages	£101,000
West Sussex County Council 2003/4	39 pages	£217,000
East Midlands Development Agency 2007/8	41 pages	?
University of Warwick	35 pages	£61,000

Like all public expenditure, there should be some justification for this expenditure and, based on what was discussed earlier in this chapter, it would seem that these accounts should be produced in order to provide users with relevant information in order for them to make decisions. However, when we come to consider this issue the reality is the following:

→ There is little evidence as to what classes of persons or organisations actually look at and use statutory financial accounts of PSOs.

→ It is not clear what sort of information these individuals/organisations are looking for from statutory accounts.

→ It follows that there is no evidence that the published statutory accounts meet the requirements of users in full or in part. Alternatively, it might be the case that users are looking for some fairly simple pieces of information and the complex and lengthy accounts produced are a massive and over-elaborate exercise which produce information well in excess of what is required by users.

In these circumstances it may be asked why public services have to have such a complex and extensive financial reporting requirement operated at such substantial cost when the reality is that a much simpler approach may be more appropriate. One can hypothesise a number of reasons for this, which are described in this section.

Mirroring private sector practices

The complex financial accounting and reporting requirements of PSOs appear, to some degree, designed to mirror those for private sector organisations. The reality is that accounting standards were first introduced in the 1970s as a response to series of financial scandals (e.g. Pergamon, AEI-GEC) which involved severe distortions in published financial results of companies as a consequence of subjectivities in accounting practices at the time. Subsequently, these accounting standards were extended to the public sector. During 2000 there were another series of scandals involving companies such as Enron and WorldCom which again involved severe distortions in published financial results that were caused by manipulative accounting practices. Hence, in the light of this history it is not obvious that the financial accounting regime has been totally successful in the private sector in discharging accountability and meeting user information needs.

PSOs are very different types of organisations from multi-national companies. In addition, PSOs have never had (and never will have) frauds approaching the magnitude or nature of those that took place at the multi-national companies involved in these large-scale scandals. Hence, it is not obvious why accounting practices in the public sector have to mirror those in the private sector, with all the costs and complexities this involves. For example, although the international harmonisation of accounting standards is desirable in the private sector because of the existence of multi-national companies, PSOs are, generally, domestic organisations, and it is not clear why such international harmonisation is important given the geographic, demographic, economic, social, cultural and political differences between countries. It often seems like harmonisation for harmonisation's sake.

Over-professionalisation

In the preface to this book the point was made that financial management (and we include in this external financial reporting) should be judged according to the contribution it makes towards the delivery of more effective and efficient public services. It might be thought that the complexity of PSO financial accounts is more to do with the views and influence of the accounting and audit professions than it is to making such a contribution.

Financial accountability in PSOs has to be discharged, but there are many ways to do this and it is not obvious that producing long and complex financial statements is the best way to do this – particularly in the light of the probable costs involved with the current approach and the lack of evidence that it involves effective financial accountability.

Overall, it seems that it might be more important to get the views about what information should be produced (and audited) in PSOs' statutory accounts from: service users, taxpayers, politicians as well as the public sector accounting profession, etc. and to construct a user-relevant public service accounting framework rather than the current expensive and over-elaborate approach which is derived from private sector practices.

Conclusions

It is obviously important for PSOs to discharge accountability to taxpayers and others for their use of public funds and to provide financial information about the organisation which meets the needs of stakeholders and users. At present, the main way in which this is done is through the production and subsequent audit of a complex set of statutory financial accounts. Although financial accounts should be produced to meet the information needs of users, there is no real evidence that this is actually achieved under the current arrangements. Meanwhile, the cost of producing and auditing these accounts is substantial. Consequently, perhaps the whole financial reporting arrangements of the public sector should be re-thought to identify more appropriate arrangements.

Questions for discussion

→ How effective are current PSO financial accounting approaches at meeting the needs for financial information of users of accounts?

→ Are the costs associated with producing the current complex range of financial accounts for PSOs justified by the benefits produced?
Might not a simpler form of accounts be more cost-effective?

→ Does the current framework of PSO financial accounts provide for accountability for the use of public funds?

→ Do the Whole of Government Accounts add anything meaningful to the range of information currently found in the public domain?

Part 3

The operation of financial management in public service organisations

Information systems and financial management in public service organisations

Learning objectives

→ To understand the general nature of information systems in organisations

→ To appreciate how information systems can produce information for relevance to the application of financial management

→ To appreciate how financial management approaches can contribute to decisions about the acquisition of information systems (IS) and information technology (IT)

Introduction

Financial information of various sorts is essential for the operation of effective financial management in PSOs. Most PSOs have a wide range of information systems concerning their activities and their resources. One aspect of this concerns those systems which (in conjunction with other information systems) produce financial information.

This chapter is about the relationship between financial management and information systems. From a financial management perspective there are two key aspects to this:

→ The way in which information systems can produce the financial information needed by PSOs for the operation of effective financial management.

→ The financial management aspects of decisions about the acquisition of information systems and information technology. Such decisions are extremely important since in many (if not most) PSOs the costs of IS/IT are of a very significant magnitude and often represent an increasing proportion of PSO expenditure.

This chapter discusses the following issues:

→ the general structure of information systems;

→ management information systems within PSOs;

→ financial information systems in PSOs;

→ key characteristics of financial information systems in PSOs;

→ the financial management involvement in the acquisition of IS/IT;

→ key management challenges in relation to IS/IT in PSOs.

The general structure of information systems

Figure 10.1 outlines the general structure of the information system used in any organisation. In looking at this diagram, we need to be clear about the use of terminology. It is quite common to hear certain terms used incorrectly, or some terms used synonymously even though they mean different things. At the outset, therefore, it is useful to list a few terms and define how each of them is to be understood in relation to Figure 10.1:

→ **Data** – this is the raw material of information systems and constitutes the input into such systems. Some examples of data could be payroll data, sales data, expenditure data, stores issues data, staff timesheets, etc.

→ **Information** – information is the output of an information system after the raw data has been processed and analysed. Some examples could be total payroll expenditure each month, sales value each month, numbers of service users by geographic location, etc.

→ **Information systems (IS)** – an information system is the means by which raw data is processed and analysed to produce the output of information. An IS has the structure and key elements shown in Figure 10.1.

Figure 10.1 Structure of an information system

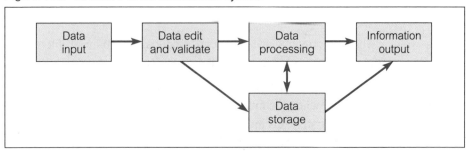

→ **Management information system (MIS)** – information from an organisational IS can be used in a number of ways by a variety of people, such as customers and service users, suppliers, employees, politicians, etc. An MIS is basically an information system where the system output is primarily for the managers of the organisation, who are required to make managerial decisions on the basis of that information.

→ **Information technology (IT)** – information systems could be manually based, computer-based or some combination of both. Where they are computer-based, the term IT refers to the technological infrastructure (hardware, software and communications) on which the information system operates.

→ **Information and communications technology (ICT)** – modern IT systems are often inextricably bound to the communications systems used in the organisation, such as e-mail, Internet, etc. Thus, the term ICT can be used to describe the technology infrastructure which is concerned with communications and information provision.

Management information systems within PSOs

By definition, the purpose of an IS is to produce information and an MIS produces information for management decision purposes. Such information can be used to assist planning, controlling and decision making in the organisation. However, the provision of management information will consume scarce organisational resources and so it is essential in judging whether certain information should be provided that a judgement is made about the costs and benefits involved.

MIS in any organisation can be classified in a number of different ways and these are described below.

Functional

Individual MIS can be used to support specific management functions in an organisation. Looking at a PSO, the following are examples of systems we could encounter:

→ **Activity-related systems** – for example, patient administration systems (NHS), student information systems (HE and FE), benefit claimant systems (Jobcentre Plus), etc.

→ **Resource-related systems** – for example, human resource systems, physical asset systems, financial systems, etc.

Degree of system integration

MIS can be of two broad types with numerous variations in between. At one extreme individual MIS can stand alone, as illustrated in Figure 10.2.

Figure 10.2 Discrete systems

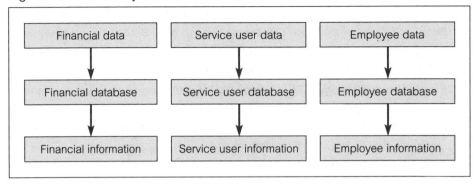

Figure 10.3 Integrated systems

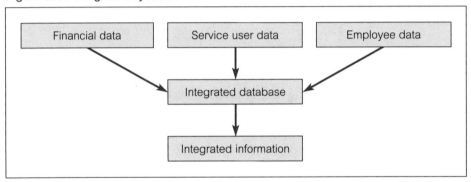

Such systems ensure that information is available for each discrete area but there is no sharing and integration of different types of information. The alternative is that systems can be integrated, as shown in Figure 10.3.

With this approach, separate sources of data are integrated into a single database, which allows integrated information to be drawn from related sets of data.

In an organisation such as a local authority which provides a multiplicity of services and thus has a multiplicity of services users, this can be taken further, as illustrated in Figure 10.4.

With this arrangement it is possible to interrogate the integrated database and identify relationships between the different sets of data. This would facilitate, for example, greater integration of service provision, greater efficiency of service provision, reduction of inequalities, etc. Thus, for example, it would be possible to identify:

➔ which types of schoolchildren make the greatest use of library services;

➔ which types of recipients of social care are most likely to also receive housing benefit;

Figure 10.4 Integrated service database

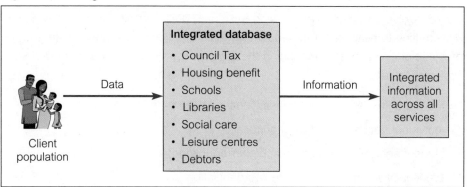

→ whether persons who are debtors to the council in one area of activity also owe money in other areas of council activity.

With the growth of multi-agency partnerships in the public sector, it seems likely that pressure will grow to develop databases that are fully integrated across agencies as well as within agencies.

System level

MIS can also be classified in terms of the level of the organisation at which it operates. This is illustrated in Figure 10.5.

Figure 10.5 System levels

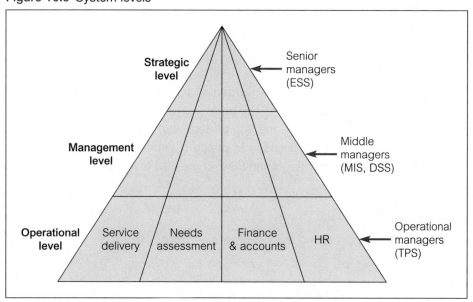

Operational-level systems

These involve transaction processing systems (TPS) and aim to track the flow of daily routine transactions. Consequently, the information they produce is largely the province of operational managers in the organisation. Some PSO examples of such systems include:

→ individual tax records and transactions in HMRC;

→ individual patient records in a hospital;

→ student achievement records in higher education;

→ creditor payments systems in any organisation.

Management-level systems

As the name suggests, these systems are concerned with providing middle managers in the organisation with information to assist with their monitoring, controlling and decision-making activities. This involves summarising data held in one or more TPS and producing reports – which may be issued on a daily, weekly, monthly or yearly basis. It may also involve the use of decision support systems (DSS) to analyse data to help make better decisions. Some PSO examples of such systems include:

→ the budgetary control system in any PSO;

→ service activity systems (e.g. student numbers, patient numbers, claimant numbers);

→ waiting list systems (e.g. NHS).

Strategic-level systems

These are often termed an executive support system (ESS) and they are aimed at senior managers in the organisation. They draw upon summarised MIS and DSS, and external events, and may involve the use of data and graphs of most importance to senior managers. Their purposes is to match changes in the external environment with existing organisational capabilities. Some PSO examples of such systems include:

→ longer-term expenditure trends;

→ performance benchmarked against other comparable PSOs;

→ market share of local market (e.g. for FE course provision).

Figure 10.6 gives a PSO example of MIS at all three levels.

Figure 10.6 Example of system levels in a PSO – hospital drugs

Level	Examples
Operational	• Details of drugs prescribed to an individual patient
Managerial	• Summary of monthly/annual drugs expenditure by: – type of drug – type of patient
Strategic	• Trends in drugs expenditure over a period of years • Level of drugs expenditure as a percentage of total patient costs • Drugs spending compared to other hospitals

Financial information systems in PSOs

This section considers a subset of MIS in PSOs, called a financial information system (or FIS). We consider the nature and role of an FIS in PSOs.

Nature of financial information systems

The overall structure of an FIS is illustrated in Figure 10.7. In organisations of any kind there will be a series of what are termed financial feeder systems. These are the systems which undertake the basic financial transactions of the organisation, such as payments of wages, receipt of income, etc. These systems are essentially a part of the transaction processing systems described earlier.

Financial data from these feeder systems will then be aggregated and stored within some form of what might be termed a financial ledger or a financial database. This aggregated financial data on income and expenditure will usually be organised around a series of expenditure codes, which will comprise:

→ a cost centre identifier (e.g. hospital ward, day centre, college department, etc.);

→ the income or expense type (staff costs, utilities, fee income, etc.).

In this way, the financial database/ledger will contain aggregated data about the income and expenditure of the organisation by cost centre and expense code. In addition, within the financial database/ledger other inputs might be made by a series of manual inputs or automated journal transfers.

This cost and income information may be manipulated within the financial reporting system to produce the range of cost information needed by managers in the PSO. Thus, for example, within the FIS the costs of support services may be attributed

Figure 10.7 Overall structure of a financial information system

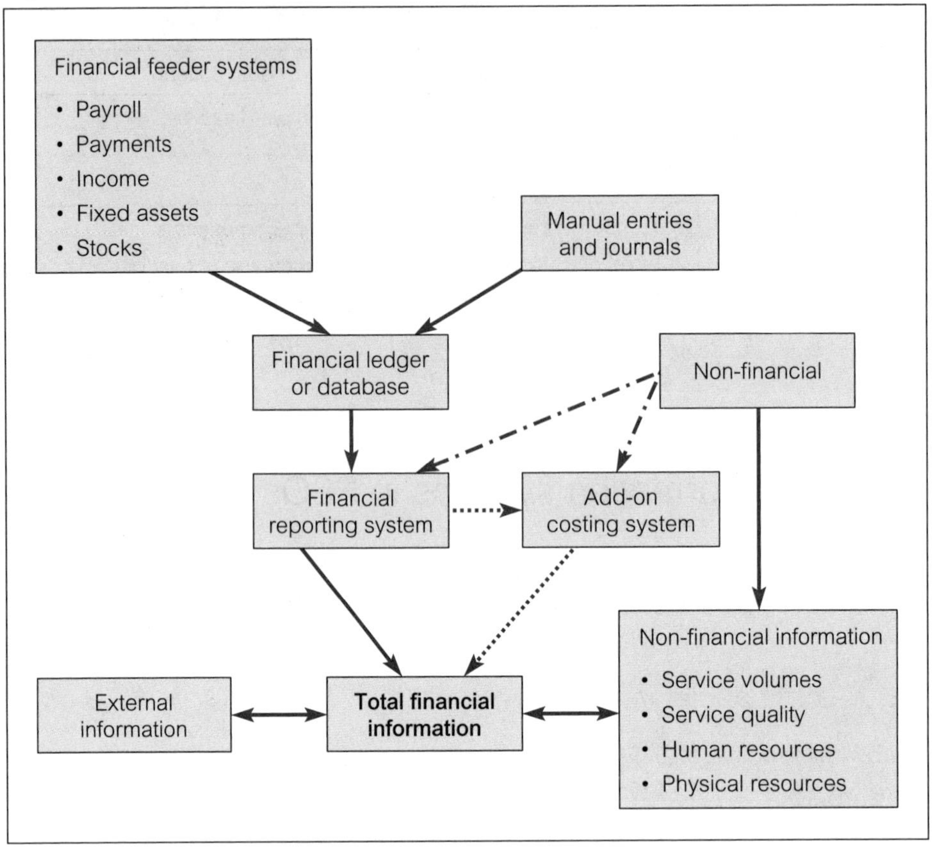

to front-line service departments on the basis of non-financial data provided. In Chapter 4 it was mentioned that some PSOs also use 'add-on' costing systems which take financial information from the main financial reporting system and manipulate it (using non-financial data) to produce the financial information required by managers at all levels in the PSO.

Thus, from the financial reporting system (and any add-on systems), financial reports can be produced which will contain selected information about the income and expenditure of specific parts of the organisation. These reports will be made available to the relevant managers and this corresponds to the management-level information described in the previous section. As shown in Figure 10.7, this financial information will be used alongside a range of relevant non-financial information in order to draw conclusions, identify findings and take appropriate management actions. This is the managerial level of the FIS referred to under managerial level systems.

Finally, the financial and non-financial information from within the PSO can be used alongside, and integrated with, other external information to provide a range of strategic level financial information, such as cost and income trends, comparator unit costs, etc. This is the strategic level of the MIS referred to under strategic level systems.

Key characteristics of financial information systems in PSOs

In considering financial information and financial information systems in PSOs, the following characteristics are seen as important.

Relevance

It is axiomatic that the financial information made available to managers in the organisation must be of relevance to them in doing their jobs. This means that the information provided must be pitched at the right level in the organisation and reference should be made to the systems levels discussed above. Failure to do this can mean that either incorrect decisions are made or information is just not used and this indicates a waste of scarce resources.

Reliability

The information produced must be reliable in terms of its accuracy and, if predictions are involved, the reasonableness of those predictions. Failure to do this will result in a lack of trust by managers in these formal systems and, in such circumstances, it is common for them to set up and maintain their own informal systems to run alongside the formal systems.

Comprehensibility

Managers need to understand what the financial information provided actually represents. For example, do the financial figures represent cash payments, cash payments plus creditors or cash payments plus creditors/commitments? Where outturn projections are made they need to understand the basis on which these projections have been made.

Timeliness

The information provided must be delivered in a timely manner. Information for a particular accounting period must be provided as soon as possible after the end of that period and delays of several weeks are unacceptable. Often there are trade-offs to be made between timeliness and reliability and finance managers sometimes hold back the issue of financial information on order to improve its accuracy. While this is a laudable aim a reasonable compromise between timeliness and accuracy is needed.

Flexibility

Circumstances change and budget managers often require financial information in a different format or a different degree of analysis. Within reason, financial systems need to be flexible in order to respond to changing needs.

Economy

Finally the provision of financial information, in itself, absorbs resources. Thus, the provision of financial information must be undertaken on as economic a basis as possible while ensuring that managerial needs are being met to a reasonable standard.

Case study 10.1
The effective implementation of new financial systems in a PSO

Oakdale University has recently made a major change to its financial information systems by choosing to replace its existing piecemeal systems with a well-known integrated proprietary system. The new system emphasises the following features:

- increased direct input of data by user departments with the consequent reduction of workload in the central finance department;
- reduction in central finance department costs;
- faster and more flexible information for budget managers.

Acquisition of the new integrated system involved a substantial up-front investment with ongoing and substantial development costs each year. Unfortunately the whole process of selection and implementation of a new system has been badly handled, with the following consequences:

- data is still being sent to the central finance department for input, with the consequence that there have been no savings in finance department costs;
- budget managers are generally very dissatisfied with the new system, which they see as being an inferior service to the previous system;
- it is difficult to relate financial information to activity information in the organisation.

Because of the substantial investment costs involved, it is difficult to show that this investment has provided value for money.

Developing financial information systems in PSOs

At the outset, the point must be made that FIS are but a part of the larger MIS that exists within any PSO and financial information will be inextricably linked to other information within the organisation. Consequently, the requirement for FIS must be derived, at least in part, from the overall information systems strategy of the organisation. This point cannot be emphasised too strongly since it is not unknown for FIS in PSOs to be developed in isolation from other aspects of MIS in the organisation.

The development of financial information systems in a PSO can be a complex, time-consuming and expensive task to undertake. It is not unusual for things to go wrong for a variety of reasons and this can result in a combination of delays in implementation, costs being substantially over budget and users being dissatisfied. Addressing the issues described in the following six stages should reduce the risks of such problems taking place, although it is, of course, impossible to eradicate all such risks.

Stage 1: Analysis

This is a very important part of the development of an FIS and involves looking at the organisation or system and finding out how financial and other information is currently being handled. It is equally important to look at the organisational context and see how that might change in the future. This will give an indication of how the needs for financial information may change over time.

Stage 2: Feasibility study

The aim of a feasibility study is to see whether it is possible to develop a suitable FIS at a reasonable cost. At the end of the feasibility study a decision is taken on whether to proceed or not. A feasibility study contains the general requirements of the proposed system.

Stage 3: System design

The key areas that need to be considered in the conceptual design stage are essentially outputs, inputs and file design. At this point, decisions have to be made about how the various software and hardware needed to implement the conceptual design is to be acquired and whether this should involve, for example:

➔ acquisition of software/hardware or computer services from an external supplier;

➔ acquisition of a commercial software package which is broadly capable of delivering the conceptual design or the design of a bespoke system which would fully deliver it.

Stage 4: Systems testing

Any new system needs to be thoroughly tested before being introduced. First, the system should be tested with normal data to see if it works correctly. Second, the system should be tested with data containing known errors to try and make it fail ('crash'). Finally, the system should be tested with very large amounts of data to see how it can cope. It is important that processing time and response rates remain acceptable with varying amounts of data.

Stage 5: Systems implementation

New financial information systems can be implemented in one of two main ways:

→ **Direct running** involves the replacement of an existing FIS by the immediate implementation of a new FIS. Usually such a change would take place at the end of a financial year and although the old system would probably be kept running for a while in order to deal with transactions relating to the financial year just ended, it would not take financial data and produce financial information for the new financial year. This approach poses great risks for the organisation should the new FIS develop faults, and to go down this road the organisation needs to be very sure about the robustness of the new system. The author has personally been involved in a direct running implementation in a PSO which went seriously wrong.

→ **Parallel running** involves implementing the new FIS but keeping the existing system running (probably for several months) until there is confidence that the new system is working satisfactorily. Such an approach is time-consuming since it can involve massive duplication of data input, financial reconciliations, etc.

Stage 6: Documentation

User guides for the new FIS should be written in plain English rather than technical language. The guide should cover how to run the system, how to enter data, how to modify data and how to save and print reports. The guide should include a list of error messages and advice on what to do if something goes wrong.

The financial management involvement in the acquisition of IS/IT

IS/IT is an expensive resource in most PSOs and is becoming increasingly so with the shift towards greater use of IS/IT for a variety of different reasons. This section is concerned with the role of financial management in the acquisition of IS/IT. However,

Figure 10.8 Procuring IS/IT

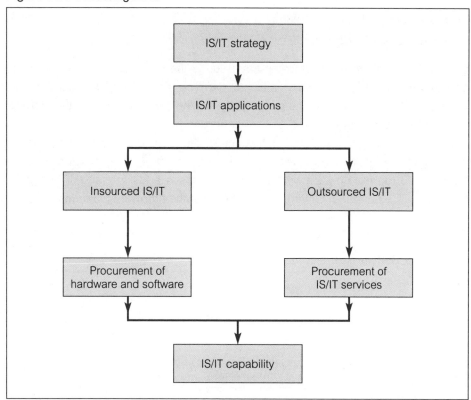

it first considers procurement pathways for IS/IT before moving on to financial considerations.

Procurement pathways for IS/IT

In acquiring IS/IT there are basically two paths to be followed, as shown in Figure 10.8.

Procuring software and hardware

Where IS/IT is largely insourced, it is nearly always the case that the procurement process should be software driven rather than hardware driven. The need for new software can take a variety of forms and does not always imply a completely new development – often all that is needed is some modification or enhancement to existing software. Basically, software can be developed in five main ways:

→ acquisition of standard packaged software;

→ in-house tailored package;

➔ external tailored package;

➔ in-house bespoke development;

➔ external bespoke development.

Whichever approach is adopted the key issue is the extent to which the software acquired will do the job for which it is intended and the extent to which it will meet the needs of its future users. The process of planning new software can therefore be summarised as in Figure 10.9.

Unless there are good reasons to the contrary the process of hardware acquisition will follow that of software acquisition. In some cases the existing hardware will be adequate to run the new software but in other cases additional and/or enhanced hardware will be needed. Other than ensuring that the hardware platforms acquired

Figure 10.9 Software development

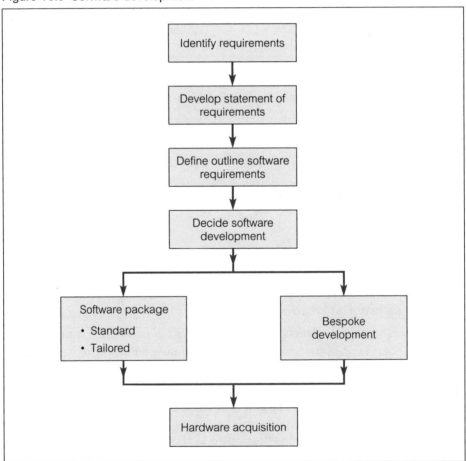

can effectively support the software chosen there are two strategic issues to consider here:

→ **Sizing and architecture** – 'right-sizing' is the term given to choosing the most appropriate hardware platform for a given application. It is important when procuring a particular piece of hardware to ensure that it will align with any proposed changes in the organisation's overall systems architecture.

→ **Procurement source channels** – hardware can be purchased from a number of different sources and the choice of procurement channel should take account of not just the immediate purchase but the longer-term hardware needs of the organisation and the potential for obtaining effective procurement and good value for money.

Procuring IS/IT services

The alternative to procuring software and hardware is to procure IS/IT services from a third party on a contractual basis. The procurement of IS/IT services involves three main issues:

→ deciding what IS/IT services should be outsourced and what should be retained in-house;

→ arranging to enter into contractual relationships with an appropriate IS/IT supplier;

→ managing the supplier relationship.

Outsourcing decisions

Outsourcing decisions are, rarely, all-or-nothing decisions and a PSO needs to decide what IT services it wishes to outsource and what are to be retained in-house. A general rule is that a PSO should think carefully about outsourcing those IS/IT applications which are seen as strategically important or where there are overwhelming concerns about data confidentiality (which there often are in many parts of the public sector, such as the NHS, police, etc.). Beyond that, PSOs must consider all outsourcing options on their merits. However, as already noted the pressure to find PFI solutions means that many PSOs may be forced to adopt IS/IT outsourcing more often than may be warranted by its merits.

Having decided to outsource a particular IS/IT service the PSO needs to take steps to enter into contractual arrangements for the provision of those services. This can be a complex process with several stages to be followed:

Tendering

In the public sector, the scale of IS/IT provision means that much of the tendering for IS/IT services will be governed by EU procurement rules for public sector purchasing.

PSOs must be aware of these rules and must comply with them. Having identified organisational needs and developed a statement of requirements, the PSO will need to place appropriate advertisements requesting details from potential suppliers as to ways in which they might meet those needs and to tender for the provision of services.

Evaluation and choice

The PSO needs to apply a formal evaluation process against which potential suppliers should be judged. This process will use certain criteria and tenders should be judged against those criteria. Possible criteria could include the experience of the supplier organisation, the financial stability of the supplier organisation, the extent to which suppliers meet the essential features of the service specification, the extent to which suppliers meet the desirable features of the service specification, the cost, etc.

At this point the PSO might choose a preferred supplier or may reduce the long list of suppliers to a shortlist and then ask for further information before making a final decision about the preferred supplier.

Negotiation

The purchaser should not feel bound by the tender details submitted by suppliers, and having identified a preferred supplier the PSO may wish to enter into further negotiations with that supplier. It is important that the PSO has a 'hard-nosed' attitude to such negotiations since the supplier will inevitably wish to sell more than the purchaser wishes to buy. Also the purchaser should apply the well-known tools of effective negotiation, such as only dealing with the supplier representative with negotiating authority and, if necessary, halting negotiations to allow the suppliers to reconsider their position.

Contract

It is important that at the end of the procurement process an effective contract is formed between supplier and purchaser. In drawing up a contract, the purchaser should consider the following points:

→ standard supplier contracts should be avoided;

→ legal and commercial advice should be taken where appropriate;

→ the contract adequately specifies the services to be delivered;

→ the contract specifies the penalties for contract failure and the arbitration procedures in the event of a dispute;

→ the supplier should be required to provide accurate and timely statistics on the delivery of service.

Financial management aspects of IS/IT procurement

There are a number of key areas where there should be strong financial management involvement in any decisions made.

Financial planning and control of in-house developments

Many public sector IS/IT developments have gone well over budget, or were late coming on stream. A couple of examples of larger projects that have gone over budget are:

→ the Libra project for magistrates courts – the initial budget of £184 million rose to £557 million;

→ the Passport Agency's computerised passport processing system incurred additional costs of £12 million.

In addition, there have been numerous smaller projects where cost overruns have occurred. In general terms, it would appear that these cost overruns arise from three main causes:

1 Poor planning.
2 Poor project management.
3 Inadequate consultation with users resulting in the need for remedial works.

These general issues can often be reflected in financial management terms and shows that there is a need for robust financial planning of the costs of the proposed development of a project plan which includes high quality financial projections of costs and/or indications of the levels of uncertainty surrounding each cost element. In addition, financial systems need to be in place which not only record the costs that have actually been incurred on the IS/IT development but also keep a running total of the likely overall costs based on the best forward estimates available. If this basic advice is followed, no project should get to completion with such large cost overruns.

Procurement of IS/IT

As discussed above, PSOs often have to make decisions about the procurement of commercial hardware/software for operation in-house and/or outsourced IS/IT services. As with all such procurement decisions there is a need for strong financial management involvement, particularly in relation to IS/IT, because of the large-scale financial and non-financial impacts such decisions might have for the organisation. Key financial management issues include:

→ Assessment of the financial viability of potential provider organisations to ensure continuity of service.

→ Robust assessment of *all* of the costs involved in the various options being considered.

→ A systematic evaluation process to compare costs against outcomes and benefits for each option.

→ Assessment of the financial aspects of proposed contracts.

→ Assessment of payment arrangements.

Promoting VFM in IS/IT developments

Financial management has a number of key roles to play to ensure that a PSO is achieving VFM in its use of IS/IT. A number of aspects of this which should be noted include:

→ Consider the potential role of the internal auditor in reviewing the robustness of and compliance with established management systems concerned with the procurement of IS/IT.

→ Consider the use of performance indicators concerning IS/IT in public services (Public Audit Forum, 2008). Examples of these concern unit costs, user satisfaction, etc.

→ Ensure there is careful control over the size of any in-house IS/IT development team. Where such teams exist they are often looking for projects to make use of the resources available and such projects may have only marginal benefits to the PSO. Projects should be user-need driven and not resource-availability driven.

Key management challenges in relation to IS/IT in PSOs

Management information is vital for the effective management of any organisation and PSOs are no exception to this. At the same time, the design of MIS is a complex issue with many factors and modern MIS requires sophisticated IT, which is often expensive and has significant risks attached to it. Thus, the issue of IS/IT represents some major challenges for PSOs and some of these are discussed below.

Strategic challenges

IS/IT poses huge strategic challenges for all types of PSO. Consideration needs to be given as to whether (and if so, how?) IS/IT can support the future direction (vision and objectives) of the PSO. If it can then a number of questions need to be answered:

→ What new technology do we need and how does it help the organisation deliver its vision and objectives?

→ What changes will be required in employee and management behaviour for the systems to be effective?

→ Will the changes brought about by the introduction of IS/IT be accepted by its users (employees, service users, citizens, etc.)?

These are formidable challenges and failure to achieve the necessary organisational change and gaining acceptance of the new systems can impose significant costs on the project. As a consequence of such additional costs the overall VFM of the project can be called into doubt.

The NHS National Programme for Information Technology (NPfIT) is the world's largest civilian IT project. It aims to improve patient care by enabling clinicians and other NHS staff to increase their efficiency and effectiveness by giving them access to patient information safely, securely and easily. However, the project has been besieged by problems (Randell, 2007) and while some of these problems have been technical in nature there are also significant issues of user acceptance and behavioural change. This has added significantly to the costs of the project and affected its potential VFM.

Investment challenges

As already noted, for most PSOs, investment in IS/IT is likely to be substantial. One of the key challenges therefore concerns how PSO managers can make IS/IT investments that deliver value for the organisation. This involves considering which IS/IT investments are necessary, productive and give high-value returns. Thus, managers need to determine how much they should spend on technology and how to measure returns in IT in the same way as other investments. Quite often, PSOs have no clear-cut way of doing this.

System integration challenges

The issue of systems integration was discussed earlier in this chapter. Multiple systems that cannot share information make it difficult for managers to obtain information for operating the whole organisation. However, systems serving specific functions can be integrated to provide organisation-wide information. This can be done on a fairly narrow intra-organisational basis (e.g. an individual local authority integrating its information systems), on a domestic basis (e.g. the NPfIT project discussed above) and even internationally (e.g. police departments across Europe integrating their systems to provide information on any EU citizen). Clearly, there are substantial benefits to be obtained from such systems integration but also substantial risks (which increase in line with the scale of integration). There are also security and ethical challenges, which are discussed next.

Security and ethical challenges

IS/IT in any sector, but particularly the public service sector, poses major security and ethical challenges which are extremely politically controversial. Numerous losses of information by government departments and employees in various ways (e.g. loss of discs or laptops) have engendered concerns among the public about these issues. A few of the key themes to be addressed under this heading include:

→ the importance of developing MIS that people can understand and control, and that have tight security;

→ controlling threats to individual privacy;

→ minimising the incidence and impact of computer crimes;

→ minimising the incidence and impact of system disruption by outsiders.

Conclusions

MIS and its associated IT will be vitally important for PSOs in the future. In particular, effective financial information systems will be needed to produce the financial information needed to manage the organisation. However, IS/IT is expensive and PSOs do not have a good track record of procuring IS/IT and getting VFM for public funds, particularly at the central government level. Hence, there must be strong financial discipline and financial management involvement in any such procurement decisions.

The importance of IS/IT to the future of public services cannot be over-emphasised. On the one hand, IS/IT will make huge contributions to improving the management of public services, including improved financial management. On the other hand, IS/IT will also have an increasing involvement in the delivery of public services.

Investment in IS/IT involves large sums of money and that investment will have large-scale implications (financial and non-financial) for PSOs for many years ahead. Hence, robust evaluation (including financial evaluation) of proposed IS/IT investments is essential.

Questions for discussion

→ How well integrated are the various MIS in our PSO? What benefits could be derived from greater integration?

→ To what extent do the financial information systems in our PSO meet the key characteristics described earlier?

→ Do the financial information systems in our PSO need replacing or improving? How should we go about this?

→ How satisfied are we that we are getting VFM from our IS/IT investments? How might we improve it?

11

Financial control and governance in public service organisations

Learning objectives

→ To understand the nature and importance of financial control in PSOs

→ To understand the structure and role of the various audit functions in PSOs

→ To understand the structure and purpose of corporate governance in PSOs

→ To understand the impact on audit of PSO corporate governance requirements

Introduction

Given that PSOs are dealing with large amounts of public funds and that they are operating in a largely political environment, there needs to be a high degree of confidence in the way in which their financial affairs are being conducted. Furthermore, all other aspects of financial management in PSOs (e.g. costing, pricing, strategy) must operate in an environment where there is confidence in the veracity of the financial information being used. Hence, PSOs require robust systems of financial control supported by effective audit and assurance arrangements. Furthermore, because of these political factors and the fact that public money is involved, it is likely that the financial control arrangements in a PSO will be much stricter than in many commercial organisations.

In this chapter we will discuss the following key issues:

→ financial control frameworks in PSOs;

→ audit arrangements in PSOs;

→ corporate governance arrangements in PSOs;

→ audit implications of PSO governance requirements.

Figure 11.1 Financial control framework

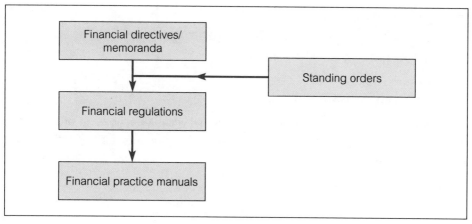

Financial control frameworks in PSOs

All PSOs require a framework of financial control in which to conduct their financial affairs. Usually this framework has four main components, as shown in Figure 11.1. These components will be discussed in this section.

Financial directives/memoranda

Several terms may be used to describe this but basically such documents aim to provide guidance on minimal statutory requirements for financial control on which the PSO must base its detailed financial procedures. These will be prescribed by government itself or some agency of government and will vary from sector to sector. Some examples of the issues that could be covered in this framework include:

→ respective roles of government (or agency) and the PSO;

→ financial management arrangements, value for money and provision of information;

→ accounting arrangements;

→ audit arrangements;

→ borrowing constraints.

Standing orders

All PSOs require a framework for the overall conduct of business in the organisation and this is provided by the standing orders of the organisation. Standing orders will cover a wide range of matters, including:

→ appointment of the chair/vice chair;

→ conduct of board meetings;

→ arrangements for delegation to officers or other agencies;

→ tendering and contract arrangements.

Financial regulations

PSOs usually have a financial procedures manual which describes, in broad terms, the way in which the organisation will control and manage its financial affairs. This manual will cover such matters as:

→ financial planning;

→ accounting arrangements;

→ treasury management;

→ income.

In the appendix to this chapter we provide a typical list of what might be included in a set of PSO financial regulations.

Financial practice manuals

Following on from the financial procedures there will be detailed financial practice manuals which lay down, in considerable detail, how the content of the financial procedures are to be applied. They will indicate the various processes and systems to be followed, the records to be kept and the persons who can authorise various transactions. Examples of the types of procedure notes that will be needed include ordering goods and services, payment of creditors, collection of income, payment of salaries and wages, stock control, fixed assets, budgetary control, etc.

It is one thing to draft and get approval for the documents described above but it is another thing to ensure that the staff of the PSO comply with the practices outlined in these documents. However, it is not uncommon to find PSO staff (particularly service professionals such as doctors, nurses, lecturers, etc.) who have only a cursory awareness and knowledge of these procedures. When such documents are prepared there needs to be appropriate dissemination and training. It is the role of internal audit to evaluate the robustness of systems of financial control in the organisation and to monitor compliance with them. This will be discussed in a later section.

Audit arrangements in PSOs

In a perfect world there would be no need for audit as all governance and operational management would be conducted according to accepted best principles and practices. All decisions would be perfect and all processes would be performed with 100% accuracy, using perfectly designed procedures.

The real world is not like this and audit, defined generally as 'a check or examination', is, therefore, necessary to reassure the many different stakeholders that their diverse interests in an organisation or operation are being properly observed. There is always a balance, often in reality a tension, between the amount of 'auditing' and its cost, both in terms of the direct costs of running an 'audit operation' and the extra workload this audit activity may create for operating departments. Theoretically, there is a break-even level at which the marginal cost of additional audit equates to the benefits it produces and any additional audit effort will cost more than the additional benefits produced. Thus there is a balance to be struck. The level of audit required will also differ depending on the type of organisation, its objectives and its sources of funding. For example, PSOs in the UK do not, in general, have shareholders and therefore external auditors of PSOs do not need to reassure shareholders that their interests are being safeguarded by proper financial reporting. In this last respect the well-publicised external audit failures in a number of US multi-nationals, in recent years, has highlighted the issue of 'who audits the auditors?'

Different stakeholders in relation to public services will have different needs, and this immediately generates the fundamental division of audit between 'internal' and 'external'. Internal audit aims to provide reassurance for those governing and managing an organisation that everything is in order internally and, whenever appropriate, also aims to assist management. This can be particularly important when management and other changes are taking place. In the public sector external audit is aimed particularly at providing reassurance to external stakeholders that funding is being applied for the designated purposes.

The issue of audit sometimes causes confusion among non-financial staff in the public sector because of the wide range and diverse nature of audit activities to which PSOs can be subjected. That is, PSOs could at various times be subjected to several different types of audit:

→ internal audit;
→ external audit;
→ other audit.

Each of these types of audit will be discussed in turn.

Internal audit arrangements

In this section consideration is given to the role of and approach to internal audit in PSOs.

Internal audit – the roles

Reference was made earlier to financial procedures and one section of those procedures usually requires the Director of Finance to ensure that an adequate internal audit service is in place. In practice, an internal audit service may be provided in three main ways:

→ internal audit staff directly employed by the PSO;

→ by staff of a public sector audit consortium (a shared service);

→ by means of a contract with a private firm of auditors.

The scope and objectives of internal audit will vary from organisation to organisation. However, best professional practice suggests that the role of internal audit can be summarised as being to review, appraise and report to management on:

→ the soundness, adequacy and application of financial and other management controls;

→ the extent of compliance with, relevance and financial effect of established policies, plans and procedures;

→ the extent to which the organisation's assets and interests are accounted for and safeguarded from losses of all kinds arising from fraud and other offences, or waste, extravagance, inefficient administration, poor value for money or other causes;

→ the suitability and reliability of financial and other management data developed within the organisation.

A number of points should be emphasised regarding the above roles:

→ Internal audit should not just be concerned with the effectiveness of financial controls in the organisation but should also review the effectiveness of non-financial managerial controls.

→ As well as being concerned with the effectiveness of systems, internal audit should also review the robustness of the policies and plans of the organisation. Thus internal audit should be looking at, for example, the business plan and financial strategy of the organisation.

→ Internal audit should be concerned with reviewing financial information in the organisation but also should look at non-financial information as well. Thus, it should be reviewing the suitability and reliability of activity, human resource and fixed asset information in the organisation.

→ Internal audit has a clear role in identifying ways in which the organisation can improve its use of resources or VFM.

These comments are important because some internal audit sections still restrict themselves to the audit of financial systems and fail to undertake much broader roles. Failure to do this must raise question marks about the value for money being given by the internal audit itself.

Internal audit – approach

A large component of modern internal audit is undertaken using a systems-based approach. Thus, instead of manually checking large volumes of financial transactions such as payment vouchers to assess their accuracy and correctness, internal auditors concentrate on the underlying systems and procedures in place. A systems-based approach would work as follows:

1. The auditor examines the system involved and assesses the strengths and weaknesses making up the system. Such systems could include the payroll system, the income collection system, the ordering system, the medical records system or the manpower recruitment system. A key element of this would involve considering the potential risk of failure in a system and the consequences should such a failure occur.

2. The auditor test checks a small number of transactions processed through the system to reveal if they had conformed to the procedures laid down. The number of items checked depends on the evaluation of the strengths and weaknesses of the system.

3. Where weaknesses in a system or non-compliance with the requirements of that system are identified the internal auditor would report to management and recommend a course of action to be undertaken. Traditionally, internal auditors have reported to and been accountable to the Director of Finance of the organisation, as part of this role is ensuring effective financial control in the organisation. This has changed in that the principles of corporate governance indicate that internal audit may be seen as part of a wider reporting relationship to board level in the organisation via the audit committee.

4. Some months later the internal auditors will follow-up to see if their recommendations have been implemented.

It is important to emphasise that internal audit cannot look at everything and cannot guarantee finding systems weaknesses or detecting fraud. Internal audit has limited resources and must focus those resources on what are regarded as the areas of greatest risk in the organisation. Thus, internal auditors will need to assess the risks associated with different activities and systems in the organisation and focus its efforts on those areas of greatest risk. In assessing risks, internal audit will look at a number of factors, including:

→ the magnitude of a system or activity in terms of numbers of transactions or expenditure;

→ the dependency of the organisation on particular systems and activities and thus the risks of a breakdown in system control;

→ the effectiveness of the management of a particular system or activity and the degree of organisational change taking place in that area;

→ the inherent weaknesses in a system and its controls.

Thus the modern role and approach of internal audit in evaluating systems is very different from the traditional role and approach.

A growing trend in internal audit which will probably impact on PSOs in years to come is the concept of risk self-assessment. Under this approach it is line managers, rather than internal auditors, who will assess the various risks being faced by the organisation and the strengths and weaknesses of the existing control framework. Managers will then propose and implement new controls where these are perceived to be necessary to deal with unacceptable risks. Under a system of risk self-assessment the role of the internal auditor will become one of training line managers in the tasks of risk assessment and control design, and undertaking quality assurance of the work being done by those line managers. Clearly, such an approach has a strong emphasis on placing responsibility for managerial control on line managers and empowering them to take appropriate action.

External audit arrangements

In this section consideration is given to the role, approach and organisation of external audit in the public sector.

External audit – the role

Whereas internal audit is a tool of management whose reporting relationships are determined by the management itself, external audit is independent of the organisation and provides an external view. In the private sector external auditors formally report to the shareholders of the company. In the public sector, although external auditors will submit copies of their reports to the organisation itself, their primary function often involves reporting to the relevant Secretary of State on the financial management and control of the organisation.

The main roles of the external auditor can be described under three main headings, namely:

→ To examine the adequacy of financial control systems and procedures in the organisation and the extent of compliance with those procedures. In doing this the external auditor will wish to rely upon the work of the internal auditor in this area.

→ To examine the annual financial accounts and underlying financial records and systems of the organisation to establish whether or not those accounts give a fair representation of the financial performance and position of the organisation. Put simply, can the information in the accounts be relied on?

→ To examine the way in which the organisation has used the resources at its disposal to establish the extent to which value for money has been achieved.

External audit – approach

In limited companies the primary role of the external auditor is to comment on the accuracy or otherwise of the company's published accounts. To assure themselves about the accuracy of these accounts the external auditor must 'go behind the books' and examine the systems and records on which the accounts are based. If the external auditor cannot state that the accounts show a true and fair view then the accounts will be suitably qualified. In the public sector the external auditors must issue a number of key documents:

→ to the organisation itself: a management letter;

→ to the Director of Finance: a letter setting out any weaknesses revealed in internal audit;

→ exceptionally, to the Secretary of State, the auditor may also issue a report directly where there are serious matters of concern.

Arrangements for external audit in the public sector

Currently the arrangements for external audit of PSOs show considerable variations in practice. Figure 11.2 shows the current arrangements for external audit of the main PSOs in England and Wales and indicates whether the individual PSO involved has any discretion over the choice of external auditor.

Slightly different arrangements apply in Scotland and Northern Ireland where the Accounts Commission for Scotland and the Northern Ireland Audit Office operate.

National Audit Office

The head of the National Audit Office (NAO) is the Comptroller and Auditor General (CAG) who has the statutory role, on behalf of Parliament, of auditing the accounts of all government departments and a wide range of accounts of other publicly financed

Figure 11.2 Public sector external audit arrangements

Public sector organisation	External auditor	Discretion
Central government departments	National Audit Office	None
Executive agencies	National Audit Office	None
Quangos	National Audit Office	None
Local authorities	Audit Commission	Limited
NHS organisations	Audit Commission	Limited
Further education colleges	Private auditor	Yes
Higher education institutions	Private auditors	Yes

bodies. The CAG is an officer of Parliament who reports to the Public Accounts Committee, and is independent of the executive arm of government. Dismissal from post can only be by a resolution of both houses of parliament. Not surprisingly, many of the reports of the NAO can be extremely critical of the Government of the day.

The NAO, is responsible for auditing Appropriation Accounts within government departments and, ultimately, for certifying the correctness of those accounts when they are laid before Parliament. In discharging the duties, the NAO must be satisfied about the adequacy of systems of financial control operating in the PSO. Aside from being the primary external auditor of government departments, agencies and quangos, the NAO also undertakes various types of review in other parts of the public sector. For example, it undertakes value for money audits testing the economy, effectiveness and efficiency of government department activities and also undertakes investigations into matters of public concern on behalf of the Public Accounts Committee.

The Audit Commission

External audit of NHS organisations and local authorities is the responsibility of the Audit Commission which, although a public sector organisation, is largely independent of central government. In practice, the Audit Commission discharges its external audit duties in two ways:

→ Much of the audit workload is undertaken through the District Audit Service, the operational arm of the Audit Commission.

→ The balance is undertaken through firms of private sector auditors who are contracted to the Audit Commission to undertake these external audit duties.

Irrespective of who actually conducts the audit, audit fees are based on a common scale of fees negotiated centrally by the Audit Commission. Both types of auditor are required to work to the Audit Commission's Code of Practice.

Private audit

Private audit means audit services provided by a firm of accountants and auditors. Private audit of PSOs may take place in two ways:

→ The Audit Commission may run a competitive tendering process in which District Audit and private firms compete to win audit contracts. The various local authorities and NHS organisations that are to be audited are involved in the selection process.

→ HE and FE institutions are free to choose who should be their external auditor and usually will choose a private firm. They may also use the same firm of accountants as internal and external auditors. However, in choosing an auditor they must refer to guidance provided by the various funding councils.

Internal and external audit compared

There is often confusion about the respective roles and reporting relationships of internal and external audit and so some clarification is needed. First, there are some similarities between the role of the external auditor and the internal auditor. Both are concerned with evaluating systems of control in the organisation and duplication of effort should be avoided because the external auditor will usually place great reliance on the work done by and the findings and recommendations made by the internal auditor. External auditors will thereby contain their effort within the minimum audit fee. However, one major difference concerns the statutory accounts of the organisation. The external auditor has a clear role in assessing the veracity of the accounts of the PSO and the underlying financial systems that generate those accounts. The internal auditor has no such role. It is also suggested that the role of internal audit is wider. External audit concentrates primarily on financial control, whereas internal audit should be less financially oriented and should be concerned with all aspects of management planning and control, financial and non-financial, in the organisation.

Second, with regard to reporting relationships, external audit is external to the PSO and usually reports to the relevant Secretary of State on the financial affairs of the organisation. However, internal audit is internal to the organisation and while internal auditors may be independent of individual senior managers the function is not independent of the PSO as a whole and internal audit is sometimes referred to as a tool of management.

Other audit bodies

There are some additional audit activities which may impinge on PSOs to a lesser or greater extent, and these are outlined in this section.

Education funding council audit

The further and higher education funding councils both have their own audit sections. These audit sections undertake various reviews of further and higher education institutions respectively. These reviews are in addition to the internal and external audit arrangements of the institutions themselves.

European Court of Auditors

Sometimes PSOs may receive funds from the European Commission to undertake specific projects in specialist fields. They will be required to prepare financial statements and certify that the funds have been spent for the approved purposes. Although it is not a common event, the organisation may be visited by an auditor of the European Court of Auditors, who will be concerned with verifying the correctness of the financial statements submitted.

Specialist audit activities

In describing the roles of the different types of auditor, reference was made to a number of general audit activities, such as assessing the strengths and weaknesses of the financial control systems. In addition, three specialist audit activities are undertaken by either external or internal auditors:

→ value for money audit;

→ information systems audit;

→ capital audit.

Value for money audit

Auditors have a clear role in evaluating the extent to which PSOs achieve value for money (VFM) in their use of public resources and for identifying ways of improving VFM. The term VFM is shorthand for the three Es of economy, effectiveness and efficiency in resource use. There are clear definitions in each case:

→ **Economy** – concerns the amount paid by the organisation for the acquisition of real resources. It includes the cost of obtaining supplies and employing staff.

→ **Effectiveness** – concerns the output of the organisation and the extent to which the organisation has achieved its pre-determined service objectives.

→ **Efficiency** – concerns the amount of resources used to produce a certain level of service output, or the so-called input–output ratio. Examples include patient throughput per bed and cost per surgical procedure. Cost-effectiveness is often used to mean efficiency but it should be noted that the term 'cost-efficiency' is meaningless.

It has also been suggested that a fourth 'E' of equity is also important to consider.

Internal auditors have a key role in VFM audit and will conduct such audits in two main ways:

→ **Systems reviews** – examine and evaluate certain management systems and make recommendations that will improve VFM. An example might be a review of the estates maintenance system which could produce a recommendation for improving the targeting of resources.

→ **In-depth reviews** – review a specific activity or department, in-depth, and recommend improvements in operational practices.

VFM audit could comprise up to 40% of the external audit effort. The Audit Commission undertakes a series of national VFM studies into particular issues and the external auditors look at the potential to apply the results locally. Such national studies can be concerned with aspects of professional practice such as nurse management, maternity services, school management, etc. In addition external auditors undertake a series of local VFM studies.

The skills of the VFM auditor are very different to those of the general auditor. Often VFM auditors have a background away from general audit, such as management consultancy, buildings management and IT management.

Information systems audit

In most organisations, the last 30 years or so have seen an increasing use of computers in financial and management systems to the point where the vast bulk of systems are now computerised. The extensive use of computers in information management creates considerable risk of loss or fraud for the organisation. Consequently auditors, both internal and external, must continually pay attention to a number of different aspects of computerisation. The various IS audit roles can broadly be classified as follows:

→ **System design** – where the organisation is planning to design new or amended computerised systems which will contribute to the financial management of the organisation, the auditor will need to be involved at an early stage to ensure that the planned system will incorporate sound financial control principles and enable the auditor to undertake audit checks once it is up and running.

→ **System operation** – when computer systems are operational, the auditor will wish to review and be assured that financial control is maintained. This will include the physical security of computers and their environment, controls on the ability to input data and access to information held on files, maintenance of 'audit trails' and reconciliation between the input and output of data – for example, ensuring that the total of creditor invoices submitted for payment equates to the total of cheques drawn.

→ **VFM of information systems** – the computer auditor will wish to be involved in assessing the organisation's achievements in value for money from information systems and information technology. This should include a review of the benefits actually achieved compared with the planned benefits.

Capital projects audit

Traditionally, PSOs have spent large sums each year on major capital buildings projects. Clearly, they need to be assured that its contracts meet the specifications and tender terms and prices. Internal and external auditors have a strong role here. Some of the matters which they will examine concern the following:

→ the adequacy of the planning procedures leading up to the commissioning of capital schemes and adherence to those procedures;

→ the appropriateness of and adherence to procedures for letting contracts;

→ procedures for authorising variations to contracts;

→ procedures for approving the final accounts of contractors;

→ post-project appraisal, including value for money.

The nature of much of this work is extremely technical. The internal auditors involved in this often have a building or engineering background, rather than accountancy.

However, capital project audit may be of declining importance. The emergence of the Private Finance Initiative (PFI) means that a very large proportion of public sector capital expenditure will be financed and built by the private sector. Hence, it is the private company that needs to assure itself that its contracts meet the specifications and tender terms and prices. Public sector auditors will be concerned with ensuring that PSOs have correctly followed the established PFI procurement procedures and that the correct accounting treatment has been applied to capital projects financed under the PFI.

Corporate governance arrangements

Background

Corporate governance is a topic which originated as a substantial issue in the private sector but, like accounting standards, soon evolved into the public sector and is now a key feature of public sector management. Although the term 'corporate governance' has been used in a variety of contexts in recent years, particularly in relation to the boards of companies listed on a stock exchange, many of the issues also have significant implications for the boards of privately owned companies and PSOs. Indeed, governance is at the heart of the role of boards in any organisation and so an understanding of the issues involved is of great importance.

Twenty years ago the term 'corporate governance' was virtually unheard of. The issues involved probably came to the fore in the USA in the early 1980s during the heyday of corporate takeover activity. Perceiving little support from their shareholders, numerous company boards began to introduce protective practices to ward off undesirable takeover bids. While sometimes effective in their primary aim, these measures were seen by some shareholders as acting against their best interests and highlighted the tensions that must inevitably exist between directors and shareholders. As a consequence, corporate activity in the USA has been placed under a more intensive media spotlight. Board decisions were more public and annual meetings gained a high profile as shareholder activists raised questions about board decisions.

In the UK, the corporate governance debate came into the spotlight due to several high-profile corporate failures – such as Polly Peck and BCCI. In these cases, directors were not only seen as acting against the shareholders' interests, they were also seen as acting in dereliction of their duties to the company. A perceived growing public distrust of the corporate sector meant that action was needed, lest a legislative response was found to counter public disquiet. The corporate failures in the late 1980s generated a number of initiatives to improve the corporate governance of both private and publicly funded organisations. The Cadbury Committee, established in May 1991 by the Financial Reporting Council, the London Stock Exchange and the accounting profession, was the first of these and helpfully incorporated its recommendations into a code of practice (Report of the Committee on the Financial Aspects of Corporate Governance, December 1992). This code highlighted the following issues:

→ the responsibilities of executive and non-executive directors for reviewing and reporting on performance to shareholders;

→ the case for establishing audit committees;

→ the principal responsibilities of auditors;

→ the links between shareholders, boards of directors and auditors.

Beyond the detail, the Cadbury Report states that 'Corporate governance is the system by which companies are directed and controlled' and hence emphasises the structures and processes of accountability of directors to shareholders. Placing accountability at the heart of corporate governance inevitably led the general debate to the issue of to whom are directors accountable. An expanded definition of accountability suggests that the structures and processes chosen by directors should take into account parties other than shareholders. More subtle than suggesting direct accountability, this definition places an increased emphasis on these interested parties. The subsequent debate – on the so-called stakeholders – has widened the scope of corporate governance yet further.

The implementations of the Cadbury and Greenbury Committees and how they were implemented, was reviewed by the Hampel Committee *Final Report* (1998), which also re-examined the role of directors, auditors and shareholders. The report led to the Financial Reporting Council publishing its combined code in July 2003, covering topics such as responsibilities of directors, their remuneration, relations with shareholders and accountability and audit.

This set of reports was further augmented in September 1999 by probably the most important of all such governance reviews, namely the Turnbull Report (ICEAW, 1999), which produced guidelines on internal control. The recommendations of this report have had far-reaching implications for governance of both private and public sector institutions, as they define and expand the responsibilities of company directors. Issues covered include:

→ the type of risks that need to be controlled;

→ what control systems are necessary to cover such risks;

→ how to keep control systems up to date;

→ the responsibilities of directors.

The basic approach in the report was, therefore, one of risk assessment and installing mechanisms to cover such risks. Most PSOs took this approach very much on board – although some would say 'gone overboard' – with detailed guidance and requirements on risk management.

In January 2003, another important report on the governance of companies, entitled 'Review of the role and effectiveness of non-executive directors', prepared by Derek Higgs for the Government, was published. However, the recommendations of this report appear to have little direct bearing on the public sector, other than to stress the importance of corporate governance as an issue. The report's main thrust was to considerably strengthen the role of non-executive directors, recommending that at least half the board, excluding the chairman, should be independent non-executive directors, which is always the case in PSOs. Such directors are also to be appropriately remunerated.

A report on audit committees prepared for the FRC (Financial Reporting Council) by Sir Robert Smith, entitled 'Audit committees – combined code guidance' was also published in January 2003 at the same time as the Higgs Report.

In addition, a key report for the public sector was that of the Committee on Standards of Conduct in Private Life, chaired by Lord Nolan. Its first report, issued in May 1995, identified six principles:

→ selflessness;

→ integrity;

→ objectivity;

→ openness;

→ honesty;

→ leadership.

The Nolan Committee's report has been assimilated by the public sector, while other high-level reports have simultaneously influenced the corporate governance climate.

Corporate governance in PSOs

It first needs to be stressed that instances of financial difficulty or irregularity in PSOs have been of a completely different and lesser order to the problems encountered in the large corporate institutions mentioned above. However, owing to the use of public (taxpayers') money and the transparent and high-profile accountability through to Parliament and its select committee system, relatively minor problems which would go unnoticed in the corporate sector can become national scandals if they occur in the public sector. Nevertheless, corporate governance is still an extremely important issue in the public sector.

PSOs do not have shareholders but they do have boards of directors or governors which incorporate people who are involved on a non-executive basis. There are two key roles for such non-executive persons:

→ to discharge their duty of accountability to various stakeholders including the general public;

→ to effect appropriate direction and control over the activities of the PSO.

It is therefore suggested that there are three key issues of concern and these are described below.

Governance arrangements

This is the means by which boards/governors maintain sustainable organisations, which are accountable to stakeholders, capable of delivering value and worthy of marketplace trust. Consequently, it is important to improve the effectiveness of board operations and performance through:

→ assessing compliance with governance codes and advice on regulatory changes;

→ analysing the effectiveness and accountability of boards, sub-committees and individual directors;

→ identifying changes regarding performance reviews and remuneration structures.

Risk management

The organisation-wide application of risk management in PSOs, supported by a framework which delivers aggregated risk information, should aid in protecting and creating value through informed risk taking. Thus, PSOs need to develop an appropriate framework for their risk management activity through:

→ assessing the effectiveness and value delivered by current risk management activity, its alignment with business strategy, consistency with organisational risk appetite, and the ability to identify, assess and monitor the risks that really matter;

→ developing appropriate reporting structures and procedures for risk along supported by appropriate roles, responsibilities and accountabilities;

→ improving management and employee attitudes to risk and risk taking to deliver improved decision making.

Assurance

Boards seek assurance over the management of risk through day-to-day operations, oversight functions and internal audit functions. Thus, boards need assurance about their risk management and internal control systems through:

→ establishing 'three lines of defence' against the risks faced by their organisations (business operations, oversight functions and internal audit);

→ using leading-edge tools and technology to deliver low-level compliance work, cut costs and improve analysis;

→ providing resourcing flexibility in terms of costs, skills and geographical reach.

The various reports described earlier have all influenced corporate structures in PSOs, and the minimum governance structure which must be in place usually requires only three formal committees: the board of governors/council; an audit committee; and a remuneration committee for senior executives. Most PSOs will also have a finance committee, employment committee, or finance and general purposes committee.

As with all systems, governance structures are only as robust as the individuals operating them and, while a robust structure goes a long way to establishing a well-run and resilient PSO, instances have been reported where a strong chief executive has acted as de facto chief executive and chairman, or the chairman has interfered excessively in the executive management of a PSO and acted as de facto chief executive. Many of the improprieties in PSOs which have made headlines in the past couple of decades have had as their root cause the merging or blurring of responsibilities at chairman/chief executive level.

Audit implications of PSO governance requirements

This section describes a number of important implications for the audit arrangements of corporate governance issues.

Audit committees

Most PSOs have now created audit committees. All audit matters, including audit plans and audit findings, should be considered in detail by the audit committee and the committee may cultivate a relationship with the chief internal auditor separate from the relationship with the director of finance. Membership of the audit committee is an important matter. Maintaining a high level of independence may preclude executive directors and, generally, audit committees will comprise only non-executive directors, although executive directors may be in attendance for some or all issues.

Internal auditors

An important source of information and assurance for boards and audit committees is the internal audit function. In the author's opinion, many organisations select their internal audit providers on the basis of cost alone, without taking sufficient account of quality or value for money. Boards should ensure that the PSOs internal audit programme is based on the organisation's own risk assessment, informed by the external auditor's views on areas for review. However, some internal audit reviews are under-resourced, and their scope is too limited to offer adequate assurance to the board. This may not always be obvious to the board or audit committee, which believes that it is receiving a higher level of assurance than is in fact the case. Once an internal audit programme has been approved, it should be managed and delivered. Audit committees should not approve variations to a programme that is underway, for example by dropping some projects simply to compensate for cost overruns on others. Where internal auditors lack the capacity to undertake a particular project in full and to budget additional resources should be procured. Audit committees should ensure that they understand the value that they are receiving from internal audit work and should assess the effectiveness of internal audit on an annual basis.

Conclusions

All PSOs need robust systems of financial control in which to conduct their financial activities. Also, it is important that there are robust audit arrangements to ensure compliance with procedures, veracity of information and VFM in the use of resources. Efforts must continue to be made to improve these arrangements, particularly in the light of the financial austerity which public services will face for the foreseeable future.

The concepts of corporate governance have become increasingly important in public services, with a wide range of initiatives to try and improve corporate govern-ance arrangements. Unfortunately, at the time of writing, there have been a number of major corporate failures in the banking and financial services sector worldwide and this must raise questions about how effective corporate governance in the private sector has really been. We have also recently seen some serious 'scandals' in public services, most notably in relation to the NHS, and again this must raise questions about the robustness of the corporate governance that has taken place. It has been the author's long-held view that all the guidelines, training courses, regulations, good practice manuals, etc. are of limited use. PSOs need to recruit to their boards/ governing bodies people of independent mind who are prepared to ask searching questions of managers and service professionals and not desist until they have satis-factory answers. Unfortunately, there is often a suspicion that these are the sorts of people PSOs avoid when making such appointments, because of the difficult con-sequences that may ensue.

Questions for discussion

→ How effective are the financial control arrangements of our PSO?

→ Are PSOs over-audited compared to private sector organisations, taking account of the relative risks involved?

→ Are the corporate governance arrangements in our PSO really effective? How might they be improved?

Appendix 11.1
Model content of a PSO's financial regulations[1]

Financial planning
→ Budget objectives
→ Resource allocation
→ Budget preparation
→ Capital programmes
→ Overseas activity

Financial control
→ Budgetary control
→ Financial information
→ Changes to the approved budget
→ Virement
→ Treatment of year end balances

Accounting arrangements
→ Financial year
→ Basis of accounting
→ Format of the financial statements
→ Capitalisation and depreciation
→ Accounting records
→ Public access
→ Taxation

Audit requirements
→ General
→ External audit
→ Internal audit
→ Fraud and corruption
→ Value for money
→ Other auditors

[1] Source: CIPFA (2003b) *A Model Set of Financial Regulations for Further and Higher Education Institutions*. Chartered Institute of Public Finance and Accountancy.

Treasury management

→ Treasury management policy

→ Appointment of bankers and other professional advisors

→ Banking arrangements

Income

→ General

→ Maximisation of income

→ Receipt of cash, cheques and other negotiable

→ instruments

→ Collection of debts

→ Student fees

→ Student loans

→ Emergency/hardship loans

Research grants and contracts

→ General

→ Recovery of overheads

→ Costing/transparency

→ Grant and contract conditions

Other income-generating activity

→ Private consultancies and other paid work

→ Short courses and services rendered

→ Off-site collaborative provision (franchising)

→ European Union and other 'match funding'

→ Profitability and recovery for overheads

→ Deficits

→ Additional contributions to departments

→ Additional payments to staff

Intellectual property rights and patents

→ General

→ Patents

→ Intellectual property rights

Expenditure

→ General
→ Scheme of delegation/financial authorities
→ Procurement
→ Purchase orders
→ Tenders and quotations
→ Post tender negotiations
→ Contracts
→ EU regulations
→ Receipt of goods
→ Payment of invoices
→ Staff reimbursement
→ Institution of credit cards
→ Petty cash
→ Other payments
→ Late payments rules
→ Project advances
→ Giving hospitality

Pay expenditure

→ Remuneration policy
→ Appointment of staff
→ Salaries and wages
→ Superannuation schemes
→ Travel, subsistence and other allowances
→ Overseas travel
→ Allowances for members of the governing body
→ Severance and other non-recurring payments

Assets

→ Land, buildings, fixed plant and machinery
→ Fixed asset register
→ Inventories
→ Stocks and stores

→ Safeguarding assets

→ Personal use

→ Asset disposal

→ All other assets

Funds held on trust

→ Gifts, benefactions and donations

→ Student welfare and access funds

→ Trust funds

→ Voluntary funds

Other

→ Insurance

→ Company and joint ventures

→ Security

→ Students Union

→ Use of the institution's seal

→ Provision of indemnities

The organisation and staffing of the public service finance function

Introduction

The term finance function is used to cover both the PSO's central finance department plus financial activities undertaken by finance staff outposted in various departments or directorates. High-quality finance function staff are critical to the operation of financial systems and the conduct of effective financial management and control in the PSO, and in this chapter we deal with the organisation and staffing of the PSO finance function itself.

This chapter considers the following issues:

→ the configuration of the PSO finance function;

→ the roles and responsibilities of the PSO Director of Finance;

→ staffing of PSO finance departments;

→ strategic trends in the PSO finance function;

→ organisational change in the PSO finance function.

The configuration of the PSO finance function

There are two key aspects concerning the configuration of the PSO finance function, namely the activities of the finance function and the organisation of those activities.

Finance function activities

Although details will vary between PSOs, finance functions will usually control and be responsible for the following:

Payroll

The payment of salaries, wages and other benefits to employees. Sometimes this activity will be undertaken by the human resources department although the finance function will still have responsibilities in relation to the financial control of this operation.

Travel expenses

The payment of travel and subsistence expenses to employees including, in some cases, international payments and payments in advance.

Payments

Payments to suppliers and contractors for goods and services received, including payments for utilities. Integral to this function will be the processes of ordering goods and services and the confirmation of the receipt of those goods and services. Also included will be payments made to contractors in relation to capital projects. Effective liaison between the finance function and the procurement function will be necessary.

Income collection

The collection of income from a range of different sources. Key finance function activities might include issuing invoices for the income due, credit management, and recording and banking of payments made. However, some of these activities might be undertaken within user departments but within a framework of financial control. Two important features of this are prompt and accurate billing and rapid collection.

Financial control

This involves creating the basic financial control framework for the organisation to ensure that income due is collected, expenditure is controlled, the assets of the organisation are protected and proper financial practices are applied. Integral to this will be the formulation of procedures, the conduct of training and the monitoring of compliance with those procedures.

Financial accounting and reporting

This involves maintaining the basic accounting records of the organisation during the year and preparing the annual statutory accounts and statements of the organisation.

Management accounting

This includes a variety of activities, such as the provision of financial information and advice, development of a financial strategy, budgetary control, costing and pricing and investment appraisal, all of which require liaison with departmental line managers.

Treasury management

This involves liquidity control and managing cash balances and other aspects of working capital, such as creditor and debtor levels. This mirrors the commercial world where company failures can arise due to cash flow problems rather than poor profitability.

Internal audit

As noted in Chapter 11, internal audit provides a continuous examination of the application of standards of financial control and value for money. In practice the internal audit function may not report to the director of finance but may report to another individual in the organisation.

Finance function organisation

All (or most) of the above activities will be found, to some extent, in all PSO finance departments, although their precise size and organisation will vary according to the organisation. Thus the structure and organisation of finance functions will vary from place to place. Typically, however, a PSO finance function will have sections concerned with the following:

→ financial services (payroll, payments, etc.);

→ financial accounting (e.g. maintaining the financial ledgers, undertaking financial reconciliations, preparing financial accounts);

→ management accounting (e.g. provision of financial information to managers, provision of advice);

→ internal audit.

However, two particular organisational themes which must be mentioned concern decentralisation and outsourcing. In a later section we will also consider various strategic trends with implications for the future organisation of the PSO finance function.

Decentralisation

In the past, PSO finance functions used to operate as a centralised model where all of the activities noted above were undertaken in a central finance department. However, as a consequence of improved IT systems and changing management ideas most PSOs have taken steps to devolve certain finance activities (and possibly HR and other activities) to operational departments. Accompanying this devolution of responsibilities has been the outplacement of certain finance staff who hitherto had been based in the central finance department. These outposted staff might retain a direct managerial link to the finance department but work closely with staff in the department where they are based. It is also possible that they might be managerially accountable to the head of the department they are working in while retaining professional accountability to the Director of Finance (DOF).

The most common finance activities to be devolved and outposted have been management accounting and the provision of financial advice to departmental managers. However, it is also possible for activities such as payments or income collection (and the associated finance staff) to be outposted and, as noted earlier, modern financial systems facilitate such an arrangement. However, other tasks such as financial accounting are likely to remain centralised.

Outsourcing/shared services

Most finance function activities have traditionally been undertaken in PSO premises by the PSO's own staff. However, in recent years there has been an increasing trend towards outsourcing certain activities to a private company or the provision of shared services with another PSO. Examples include:

➔ **Payroll** – the bulk of the payroll function could be outsourced to an external contractor or shared service provider. However, the need for some form of internal payroll liaison function would remain and the DOF would retain responsible for the security of payroll systems including such external services.

➔ **Internal audit** – many PSOs have outsourced their internal audit service to private accountancy firms or a shared service provider.

We will return later to possible trends in outsourcing of finance activities.

The roles and responsibilities of the PSO Director of Finance

In a PSO, the title Director of Finance (DOF) is often given to the most senior finance manager in the organisation. However, other titles may still be used, such as finance manager, head of finance, etc.

As noted in Chapter 1, there are significant variations in overall organisational arrangements between PSOs. Thus, in some PSOs, the DOF will be directly accountable to the chief executive of the PSO, while in other PSOs the DOF will be accountable to another senior manager (e.g. Director of Resources, encompassing finance, IT and HR) who will report to the chief executive. Also, in smaller organisations the DOF role itself may also be combined with other roles to create posts such as Director of Finance and Information or Director of Finance and Legal Services, etc.

Whatever the organisational arrangements, there are certain roles and responsibilities which attach to the post of DOF and these are now substantially greater than they were (say) 10–15 years ago. These roles and responsibilities will be summarised in the following sections.

Financial control

The DOF must ensure that adequate standards of financial control operate in the organisation. This will need to cover the areas outlined above including, for example, payments to staff and suppliers, the control of expenditure, the collection of income and the management of investments. Linked to this, the DOF may be responsible for ensuring access to an adequately skilled and resourced internal audit function. Finally, the DOF is usually personally responsible for reporting to the Board (or equivalent forum) on the adequacy, or otherwise, of financial control in the organisation and the remedial action required.

Financial services

The DOF is usually responsible for ensuring there are effective and efficient financial services, such as payroll, payments, income collection, etc. However, it is not obligatory for all such services to be directly managed by the DOF and, for example, payroll may be managed by the HR department or contracted out to an agency or contractor while creditor payments may be managed by the procurement department. Irrespective of who actually manages the various financial services, the DOF is always responsible for ensuring that adequate standards of financial control prevail.

Financial systems

The DOF is responsible for ensuring that there are adequate and robust financial systems which record details of the income, expenditure, assets and liabilities of the organisation. These are needed for two main purposes:

→ to prepare the annual statutory accounts of the organisation;

→ to provide ongoing financial information throughout the year for PSO managers.

Financial information and advice

This must be provided by DOF and the staff of the finance function. This advice could be at an operational level concerning, for example, budgetary trends or at a strategic level covering, for example, the financial implications of a major capital investment or the implementation of a new pay structure. The DOF and finance staff are responsible for the provision of this information and advice to managers throughout the organisation and at a more personal level, the DOF will usually provide financial information and advice to the board about all aspects of the PSOs activities.

Strategic development

In addition to managing their ongoing day-to-day activities, all PSOs will have a strategic agenda, which can take a variety of forms such as:

→ site rationalisation;

→ organisational restructuring;

→ pay restructuring;

→ expansion of service provision;

→ capital investment (including PFI);

→ expansion of commercial activities.

All these trends have major strategic financial implications and must be considered carefully. The DOF has direct responsibilities for the financial appraisal of any proposed strategies in addition to making a general contribution as a senior manager.

Corporate management

The DOF is usually a member of the PSO senior management team and thus has corporate responsibilities for the management and performance of the organisation. In this role the DOF must be able to contribute towards all matters that affect the organisation, including public and press relations, management of change, perform-ance review and strategic development. These matters must not be regarded as the exclusive province of a single senior manager.

Consequently, the DOF requires a wide range of skills and competencies and traditional financial and accounting skills form only one part of the required skill set for a DOF in today's PSO. These skills can be summarised as:

→ technical financial and accounting skills and knowledge;

→ knowledge of the particular service sector;

→ strategic vision;

→ inter-personal and communication skills;

→ team working skills.

Staffing of PSO finance departments

The staff of a PSO finance function can be classified into three main types:

→ professional accounting staff;

→ technical staff;

→ support staff.

These roles and responsibilities are described next.

Professional staff

The senior positions in the finance function will usually be occupied by people who are professionally qualified accountants. It is now increasingly unusual to find a DOF or deputy DOF who is not a professionally qualified accountant and even in central government departments, which have not traditionally had professionally qualified accountants in senior posts, most departments have a DOF (or equivalent) who is professionally qualified. However, in the private sector it is not unusual to find that the finance director of a large company is not always a qualified accountant but may have business qualifications such as an MBA or DBA. In future, it is possible that such business qualifications might also be seen as more relevant than professional accounting qualifications in PSOs for DOF posts. The onus here is for professionally qualified accountants to demonstrate that they have the strategic vision needed to ensure the PSO is effective and efficient.

A professionally qualified accountant is usually a member of one of the six UK chartered accounting bodies:

→ Chartered Association of Certified Accountants (ACCA);

→ Chartered Institute of Public Finance and Accountancy (CIPFA);

→ Chartered Institute of Management Accountants (CIMA);

→ Institute of Chartered Accountants in England and Wales (ICAEW);

→ Institute of Chartered Accountants in Scotland (ICAS);

→ Institute of Chartered Accountants in Ireland (ICAI).

At the risk of over-simplifying, it is probably preferable that professional accounting staff in the PSO are, or should be, largely concerned with issues of strategic financial management and the provision of financial information and advice to managers. They should not be involved in the operation or maintenance of routine financial systems and bookkeeping since this would not be making the best use of their skills developed through long and costly training as professional accountants.

Beyond the senior posts the numbers of professional accounting staff in PSO finance functions will vary according to the size and type of the organisation involved. However, there are sometimes concerns within PSOs that there is an inadequate number of professional staff available to provide the financial advice needed by managers. This is especially the case in PSOs where the budget system is heavily devolved and there are a large number of budget holders needing advice about their budgets. This situation often creates a tension with service professional staff, who often view the employment of an additional accountant as being in place of extra nurses, teachers, etc. However, the reality is that the PSO must employ sufficient professional accounting staff to be able to effectively manage its financial resources.

Technical staff

Below the professional accounting staff level there will be technical accounting staff. Some of these staff may hold qualifications such as the Association of Accounting Technicians while others may hold their posts by virtue of many years' experience. These staff are often the bedrock of PSO finance departments. They undertake the various finance function activities, such as paying the bills, running the payroll, collecting income and maintaining accounting records.

Support staff

Finally, there are a variety of other staff in support roles, such as clerical officers, secretaries and receptionists. Their roles are integral to the operation of the finance function, but outside the scope of this book.

Strategic trends in the PSO finance function

There are a number of strategic trends in PSOs which will effect the organisation, staffing and working arrangements of the PSO finance function in the medium term. The precise timing of these changes will vary from place to place.

The main trends which are foreseen are described in the following sections.

Strategic pressures

PSOs will need to continue to be more strategically focused in order to deal with the ongoing challenges of matters such as effectiveness, choice, efficiency, flexibility, etc. Finance is a key resource and therefore there will be an expectation for the finance function to contribute to this strategic agenda by providing managers with information and advice which has a strategic dimension. As we have seen in earlier chapters, the development and operation of financial models, dealing with a range of scenarios for strategic planning, will be of great relevance.

Commercialisation

There are several particular trends which require PSOs, and particularly their finance functions, to operate in a more commercial manner than hitherto. There are two aspects to this.

First, there is a continuing need for PSOs to work more closely with commercial organisations and to have an understanding of how commercial organisations operate. Some aspects of this include:

→ the need, by PSOs, to develop increasing links with the business community through for example, greater partnership working, economic development, etc.;

→ the application of outsourcing of services to the commercial sector;

→ the use of commercial partnerships, PFI, etc.

Second, there are now many aspects of a PSO's activities which require a commercial outlook within the organisation itself. For example, the development of PFI projects and the selection of preferred bidders require a good degree of commercial acumen. In addition, many PSOs now have to deliver services in what is, in effect, a form of competitive market. For example, NHS Trusts operate in an environment of payment by results and local authority leisure centres have to compete with private providers. Again, a good commercial outlook is necessary.

Commercial financial skills will be very important in relation to the above and thus it is important that the PSO functions have the necessary commercial skills and acumen to operate in a more commercial environment.

Standards of governance, accountability and financial control

The importance of maintaining high standards of governance, accountability and financial control were discussed in Chapters 9 and 11. This is manifested in a number of ways, such as increased emphasis on corporate governance, application of rules on business conduct and improved standards of internal audit. For the future, there seems no likelihood of there being any diminution of the expected standards and, if anything, standards will need to improve.

Developing financial skills in managers

A key means of improving financial management in PSOs is to improve the financial skills among non-financial managers, within both service departments and other support departments. This is not always an easy task since many PSO managers have moved into managerial posts after having held posts delivering front-line services such as nursing, teaching, social work, town planning, etc. In fact some of these managers may still undertake professional duties, as in the case of NHS clinical directors. Consequently, they do not always have a great interest or even empathy with financial management issues, often seeing it as an 'administrative' task for which they are not really suited.

It is inevitable that it will fall to the DOF and finance function staff to take on board the task of developing financial awareness and financial skills throughout the PSO. This will require appropriate planning and adequate resources to be effective.

Resource pressures

As already discussed, the current state of the UK economy means that, for the foreseeable future, the level of growth available to public services will be very limited. Continual cost pressures in service delivery will affect the work and organisation of the entire PSO. Some examples of such cost pressures include:

→ growth in demands for services from the elderly;

→ shortfalls in funding to cover nationally agreed pay awards;

→ additional costs arising from pension provision;

→ costs of maintaining the estate and of updating IT.

The finance function itself will be under pressure to reduce costs and, as an overhead to the main functions of the PSO, may be required to generate a disproportionate level of cost savings, while maintaining or even improving the quality of services provided by the department. Many finance departments are now being benchmarked, which involves comparing their performance with other finance departments in the public and private sector on matters such as:

→ cost per invoice paid;

→ percentage of manual cheques issued;

→ percentage of journal vouchers raised manually.

Organisational change in the PSO finance function

In response to the above trends, significant changes in the organisation of PSO finance functions can be forseen. The processing work of finance departments is likely to be radically restructured to allow time to be released to enable DOFs and their senior staff to become more strategically focused.

Changes in organisational arrangements

A number of changes in the organisational arrangements of the traditional PSO finance function will almost certainly result from the strategic trends referred to above. To some extent these changes will be seen in all PSOs, but the pace of change will differ from sector to sector. The three possible changes are listed below.

Decentralisation versus centralisation

We have already discussed past trends of decentralisation of certain finance functions and department staff to operational departments. Such trends were popular with departmental managers and were seen as successful. An issue for the future is whether further decentralisation of finance staff will take place (which might be the case in PSOs where little decentralisation has taken place up to now) or whether some degree of re-centralisation will occur. With support from modern web-based information systems coupled with user support there is often a case for arguing that the same level and quality of service can be provided to operational managers by a central finance team but at lower cost. Such things often go in circles and the pressure on resources coupled with IT developments has now created something of a trend for re-centralisation of activities in some parts of the public services. The final outcome of these trends remains to be seen.

Outsourcing/shared services

In theory, the economies of scale afforded by outsourcing or shared service arrangements should facilitate a reduction in the unit cost of certain aspects of service delivery (e.g. cost per invoice paid). Thus an increased use of outsourcing or shared services can be anticipated. Groups of PSOs may form consortia to organise the delivery of certain financial services for all members of the group – as has already happened in the NHS. The development of local strategic partnerships concerned with joined-up service delivery might also be a means for facilitating shared financial services.

Organisational structures

Over the last 10–15 years a worldwide trend that happened in many different types of organisation was the removal of certain tiers of hierarchical management. This was because many middle management posts did little more than supervise lower level members of staff and pass information from a lower tier to a higher tier within the organisation. This trend also occurred in PSOs and their finance departments with the net effect of removing certain tiers and producing flatter and leaner organisational structures and lower costs. The need for close supervision was reduced by improved training and development among lower levels of staff and an improved internal audit process while substantial investment in modern IT systems facilitated the direct flow of information within the organisation. This process of rationalising the organisational structure of the finance function was further facilitated by the outsourcing of certain activities and the grouping together of others.

In many ways it seems likely that much of the 'fat' has now been stripped out of PSO finance departments and any further 'stripping out' is limited. However, further outsourcing of some activities is possible, as is some recentralisation. Also there will be ongoing pressures to provide better strategic financial advice to line managers. Overall, it seems likely that organisational structures in PSOs will be in a state of flux for some years to come, with different models being applied in different places.

Increasing investment in IT

No function is immune from the impact of IT. There are a number of aspects of the finance function where IT investment can lead to improved services at lower cost. Some examples are as follows:

→ **Direct input of pay** – where such systems are implemented, payroll data can be directly input by line managers using a computer terminal rather than paper details being sent to a central payroll section for input to the payroll system. This would reduce the number of staff needed in payroll sections.

→ **Direct payments** – the traditional ordering and payment process is for a PSO to place a paper order with a supplier, for the supplier to supply the goods/services and issue an invoice and for that invoice to be paid. This is a cumbersome process both in terms of paperwork and staff time. The whole process can be streamlined by investment in modern systems which operate along the following lines:

(1) Once the quantity of goods held in stock falls below a pre-determined re-order level, the system automatically issues an order to a supplier.

(2) The order is processed by the supplier whose own system automatically issues the goods.

(3) The supplier's system automatically requisitions payment for these goods from the PSO's bank account.

For this approach to work the PSO must have established links with relatively few suppliers and have made the necessary investment in IT. This simplification of ordering and creditor payments processes will lead to staff reductions in the finance and supplies functions.

→ **User-friendly financial systems** – investment in financial models and expert systems which can easily be operated by managers may reduce the need for financial analysis and advice from financial managers, leading to a reduction in the skills base and numbers of those financial managers.

All these developments have major implications for financial control, internal audit and financial management in PSOs, but do not produce any insurmountable problems. However, there may be significant capital investment requirements and cultural change issues in the PSO.

Changing skill mix

The various changes described above are likely to lead to significant changes in the staffing of finance departments, as follows:

→ **More professional/technical staff** – meeting the challenges of providing more strategic and commercial information in a decentralised management structure, and the need for better financial control in an IT environment, is likely to require a greater range of specialist financial and business skills from more professional and technical staff. Linked to this will be greater investment in training and development to enable those staff in the finance department to maintain their skills.

→ **Fewer support staff** – the impact of IT and market testing is likely to lead to a lower number of support and clerical staff in finance departments.

As a consequence of these changes, it is likely that future finance departments will have a considerably different skill mix from that at present.

Case study 12.1
Improving a PSO finance function

Groomfield College is a large college delivering both further and higher education. For some years the college has had a poor financial track record generating, at best, small financial surpluses and often deficits. The governors of the college have been getting increasingly concerned about this matter as well as having concerns about critical audit reports and receiving financial reports which were confusing even to those governors who were qualified accountants.

They commissioned an external review of the college and this review made a number of points:

- The college principal had little understanding of finance and financial management.
- The college DOF (Director of Finance) had spent most of his working life in this one organisation and had risen through the ranks.
- Senior and middle managers in the college had little understanding of finance and financial management and little sympathy with its aims.
- College management was heavily centralised with much of the budget being held by the principal or his deputy.
- Financial systems in the college were hopelessly outdated because the college was unwilling to invest in what it saw as 'administrative' functions.
- The finance department was totally centralised and not highly regarded in the college. The DOF had low visibility in the college and the department had put locks on the door to stop other college staff from visiting the finance department.
- The college had high unit costs of service delivery.
- The college had a strategic plan but there was no financial articulation of this plan.

In the light of this report the principal and the DOF took early retirement and a new principal and DOF were appointed. The new DOF concentrated on a number of things, including:

- the provision of vision and leadership for the finance function;
- ensuring he was highly visible in the organisation and people were aware of what he was trying to do;
- investment in new financial systems;
- getting his staff and himself to liaise with college managers with the aim of improving their understanding of finance;
- providing greater access to financial advice – the locks were removed!
- devolving the budget to college managers with accountability for performance;
- developing a financial strategy and encouraging an environment of continuous performance improvement.

Five years later, the college is now a successful organisation with effective financial management.

Conclusions

This book strongly argues that effective and efficient public services require public service organisations with strong and effective finance functions. This in turn requires finance departments with the necessary staff skills both in terms of professional/ technical skills and inter-personal skills. The latter are important because in many PSOs, financial management is seen, by many staff, as an administrative issue which is nothing to do with them. Finance staff with the right inter-personal skills can both educate and influence non-financial managers in a way that improves the overall standards of financial management in the organisation.

Questions for discussion

→ Do you think you fully understand all of the roles of the finance function?

→ How good a job do you think your finance function is doing? Why do you say this?

→ How do you see your particular finance function evolving in the next few years? Do you think this is the right way to go?

Part 4

The way ahead

The future of public services: the implications for financial management

Introduction

As noted in Chapter 1, this book is concerned with financial management in public services. Its focus has been on how public services have changed radically over the last 30 years and how financial management methods have had to change to cope with the challenges involved.

In this final chapter we look to the future. Changes in the nature, organisation, funding, etc. of public services will have implications for the conduct of financial management. In turn, public services themselves will have been influenced and impacted on by a range of external forces.

This chapter considers the following:

→ forces for change which may impact on public services;

→ the possible implications of these forces for public services;

→ the challenges for financial management that these changes would cause.

Forces for change

In looking ahead at the possible future of public services there are many different frameworks which could be applied. The PEST approach (described in Chapter 5 on strategic planning) has been chosen as a means of examining the forces with potential implications for public services. The term PEST is an acronym for political, economic, social, technological. The forces for change will be discussed under these headings.

Political forces

There are three types of potential political force that can be looked at:

→ global political forces;
→ European political forces;
→ domestic political forces.

However, when considering potential political forces the point should be made that it is impossible to separate them from the current economic climate and economic forces impacting around the world. Consequently, it is very dangerous to speculate about the political changes that might take place in the future, because of the huge degree of economic uncertainty.

Global political forces

At the time of writing (2009), we are in the midst of a severe economic recession which is affecting all countries across the world, including developed countries, transition countries and developing countries. Clearly, each country will formulate its own public policies but the global impact of the recession means that international cooperation will be needed to overcome the problems being faced.

There are three particular policy themes that may occur in many parts of the world:

Trade protectionism
Some countries when faced with economic downturn and increasing unemployment may resort to some form of economic protectionism in order to stem the flow of inputs into their country and protect domestic jobs. It is beyond the scope of this book to discuss whether such approaches would be a correct response to the pressures being faced.

Policing
During a severe economic recession, tensions between different parts of the community are likely to increase and could spill over into community disturbances of one sort of another. The likely severity of such disturbances is impossible to predict.

Former cabinet minister Hazel Blears has already warned that the recession could fuel racial tensions (*Daily Telegraph*, 2009) and this prediction was made before the severity of the current recession was known. Furthermore, a recent and unexpected 25% increase in personal thefts and a 4% rise in domestic burglaries in the official quarterly crime figures seemed to confirm predictions that the recession and rising joblessness will fuel a rise in property crime (*Guardian*, 2009a). It seems likely that emphasis will need to be placed on effective policing and this could have resource implications for policing and security services.

Defence

Global recessions like the one currently being faced may create a strong degree of uncertainty and concern within some countries. In such circumstances it would not be surprising if those countries decided to bolster their defence capabilities by increasing expenditure on defence at the expense of other public services.

European political forces

The situation with regard to Europe is currently unclear. At the time of writing we await the result of a probable second referendum in Ireland on ratification of the Lisbon treaty. If assent is given to this treaty then it is probable that the EU will go down the track of greater integration and this could apply to public policy in many different areas. Clearly, if this is the case it could involve a much greater involvement by the EU in the formulation of public policy in many areas and this will have implications for PSOs in the UK. If the Lisbon Treaty is not approved by the Irish people then the future of the EU seems even more unclear.

Domestic political forces

There are a number of domestic political issues which need to be highlighted:

Change of government

At the time of writing there is a strong possibility that the Labour government (which has been in power for 12 years) will be forced from power in 2010. What form of government might replace the current administration is uncertain. Furthermore, even though a new government may have its own distinctive ideas about public services, the parlous economic condition of the country will mean that there will be strong constraints on its actions. A similar situation may arise in the USA where the Obama administration, although committed to major health service reform, may find its actions constrained by the state of the US public finances.

Devolution

There will probably be continued pressure for further devolution of powers to the devolved administrations of Scotland, Wales and Northern Ireland. Whether this leads to full independence in any of these countries remains to be seen but it does seem likely that the divergence between England and the rest of the UK in various aspects of public policy may remain and even enlarge.

Greater localism

Greater devolvement of decision-making power to local or regional levels is frequently discussed by all political parties. Although devolution in Scotland, Wales and Northern Ireland was achieved, similar devolution to the English regions was rejected by the public and such a policy seems unlikely to be revived in the near future. Furthermore, the Lyons Report (Lyons, 2007) on the future of local government in the UK called for 'greater flexibility for local authorities and the space for local decisions on priorities, with a reduction in centrally determined and monitored targets'. However, although there have been many similar calls for greater devolvement to local government over the years, centralised control has actually increased. Hence, the nature of the UK political system means that such greater localism seems unlikely.

Economic forces

The global economic situation is, arguably, the force that will have the greatest influence on public policy and public expenditure in years to come in all countries. At the time of writing, the UK economy has just, formally, entered a period of economic recession, defined as a reduction in economic output for two successive economic quarters. However, this recession may be different from others because of the impact of the credit crunch and the globalisation of the economies of the world. The so-called 'credit crunch', which is in fact both a squeezing of business credit and a contraction in banks' liquidity positions, has as its genesis the losses incurred by several US and UK banks in the US sub-prime mortgage market, with the consequent and uncertain exposure to risk of financial institutions worldwide. There are many consequences of this. Many banks have had serious liquidity problems and when this has become public knowledge has led to a run on the bank. In general, banks have become very risk averse about lending to business and individuals as well as to other banks. The second factor is the global impact of the recession. The comment used to be made that 'When America sneezes, the rest of the world catches a cold' but having said that, until fairly recently, the impact of a recession on one country on other countries was fairly limited. However, the globalisation of business and finance has significantly altered that. Today we have huge international trade flows between countries, large-scale movements of populations and global movement of capital. Thus, a recession in one country, particularly if it is a large country, will have an impact on other countries. The combination of these three factors of recession, credit crunch and globalisation is virtually unprecedented and creates great uncertainty.

Any economic recession can play havoc with the public finances of a country since a recession usually results in reduced tax revenues and increased needs for public spending (e.g. unemployment benefit). However, policy makers would usually have aimed to generate budget surpluses during a period of economic growth in order to offset budget deficits during a period of recession. This would also be seen as part of the normal business cycle. However, in the UK, for a number of years the government has been running large budget deficits during a period of economic growth. These deficits have been financed by borrowing, thus increasing the borrowing requirement. The impact of the recession (e.g. reduced tax revenues and increased demands for public spending) coupled with the costs of bailing out the failing banking system have meant that government borrowing and government debt have grown enormously. This impact of the recession coupled with the mismanagement of public finances over a period of years now puts the UK in a dangerous position. The most recent demonstration of this is the 2009 Budget Report presented to the House of Commons by the Chancellor of the Exchequer in April 2009.

By the Chancellor's own admission, government borrowing will soar to £175 billion this year (falling to £173 billion the year after). This would be the worst budget deficit since the Second World War, at more than 12% of expected national income. Meanwhile, the national debt will soar to 79% of GDP over the next five years. The government says things will improve from 2011, but it is assuming that after a contraction of 3.5% in the size of the economy this year, and GDP growth of 1.25% the year after, the economy will rebound at 3.5% in 2011. Many independent commentators regard this scenario as pretty optimistic, and so the economic situation could become much worse than that predicted by the government.

The state of government finances has serious implications for public expenditure levels in the future. By HM Treasury's own admission, four-fifths of this record borrowing will be 'structural' and therefore impervious to economic recovery, whenever it comes and however strong it is. This means tax increases and/or cuts in public expenditure, and the problem is so great that the IFS (IFS, 2009) suggests that whoever takes office in the general election after next will still have to find another £45 billion a year, in today's money, by the end of their parliament to eliminate this deficit, funded from tax increases and cuts in non-investment spending. Therefore the UK will need to make major cuts in public expenditure. These would not just be reductions in the level of growth in public expenditure that are often portrayed as 'cuts' in the media, but reduction in public expenditure, from present levels, in real terms after removing the effects of inflation). This would imply reductions in the levels and/or standards of current public services. Moreover, since large parts of public expenditure (e.g. debt interest, payments to the EU) are immune to cuts, the burden will fall on the remainder of public expenditure. However, nothing will happen immediately (until after the next general election) at which point the Government plans a big 'efficiency' drive to save about £9 billion (which makes one wonder why these efficiencies couldn't have been released anyway without the pressures of economic recession).

However, there is an even worse scenario (Prowle, 2009b). Government borrowing is now so high that there is some doubt about the willingness of investors to purchase UK government bonds. At the time of writing, the UK still possesses the prestigious triple-A rating, but in evidence before the Treasury Select Committee, the Head of European corporate ratings at ratings agency Standard & Poors confirmed the UK's status on the assumption that 'up to approximately 20% of GDP in the form of bank assets could be problematic in the future'. Twenty percent of UK GDP would equate to £280 billion. However, it has since emerged that the Treasury is preparing to ring-fence about £400 billion of 'toxic' bank debt – or 29% of GDP – to draw a line under the financial crisis. Royal Bank of Scotland is said to want to use the scheme for £200 billion alone. Questioned about the UK, the Standard & Poors spokesman told MPs: 'We are looking at the ratings on an ongoing basis. If there were major shocks or changes we would look at the rating again.' A ratings downgrade could be devastating for the UK. A loss of credit worthiness would imply the government being unable to borrow to finance its budget deficit or being forced to pay much higher interest rates. There has already been some difficulty in this area, with sales of some government bonds being under-subscribed or requiring a generous premium for them to be fully sold. There are two implications which flow from this: either the government will just not be able to raise money on the money markets and so will need to make emergency cuts in public spending or they will need to pay premiums to raise funding and this will mean yet higher levels of debt interest with the consequent impact on the rest of public expenditure.

Overall, this suggests that there are really stormy waters ahead, with the probability of major real terms cuts in public expenditure (which would be unprecedented in modern times). The overall impact of this would pose huge challenges to public services and it is self-evident that decisions about public spending will be painful.

Societal forces

In Chapter 3, a number of UK societal trends were identified as having had, over a number of years, a significant impact on the demands for public services, both in terms of volume and type. The main factors identified were:

→ ageing population;

→ prevalence of family breakdown;

→ loss of the extended family;

→ number of persons living alone.

Taken as a whole, some commentators would refer to these changes as constituting an implosion of our society. Looking ahead it does not seem likely that any of these forces can or will be alleviated, given the constraints of our democratic political system, and so the demands for public services which derive from these factors are likely to remain the same or even increase. This does not mean, of course, that the type of service provided will remain unchanged.

Furthermore, relating to the economic conditions that are likely to exist for the foreseeable future, it seems likely that this will directly increase the needs for public spending (e.g. unemployment benefits) but might also contribute to, for example, higher levels of family breakdown, which will in turn further increase the demands for public services.

Technological forces

It must be assumed that technological development will continue maybe at the current rate or even at an accelerated rates. Such technological developments could happen in a large number of fields, including pharmaceutical developments, health diagnostic and treatment developments, communications, information systems, automated systems (e.g. energy management), transport developments, etc.

While some of these developments may have the effect of reducing the running costs of delivering public services, it is more likely that they will actually increase the running costs, albeit by allowing the delivery of a more effective range of public services.

Implications for public services

The overall impact of these forces (particularly the economic forces) will place huge challenges on public services. It must be remembered that the UK and other countries face the scenario of growing demands for public services coupled with real terms reductions in the level of resources available, although it is not clear how large this level of reduction might be. This means that difficult choices will have to be made in many areas, and so this section describes some of the over-arching issues to be considered when looking at the future of public services.

Reconsidering the role of the state

Political scientists have often talked about the concept of the 'small state' with a much reduced involvement by the state in individual and corporate lives than under current arrangements. Although the small state idea may have politically gone out of fashion, the economic crisis may bring it back because of government inability to keep funding public expenditure at historic rates. Thus, consideration needs to be given as to whether the government can sustain its involvement in many areas of activity or whether it should draw back from certain areas of activity, which might be left to the non-state sector comprising the private sector, the third sector and the individual citizen. Governments may need to consider a number of issues, such as the balance between the roles of the state as:

→ an enabler;
→ a guarantor of services for those unable to pay;
→ a financier;
→ a regulator;
→ a direct provider.

Unfortunately, this seems to the author to be a non-starter. In the UK we now have a government and a legislature composed largely of what might be termed pro-fessional politicians. Such persons (of whatever party) generally have an activist tendency, to whom the idea of withdrawal from certain activities and areas of public life would probably seem an anathema.

Altering the levers of public policy

Governments have several levers at their disposal to implement public policy, includ-ing the following:

→ exhortation and leadership;
→ statute law;
→ regulation;
→ targeted taxes;
→ monetary incentives coupled with improved behaviours;
→ service provision – through public spending.

In recent years, in a number of countries, there have been substantial increases in overall public spending, which implies increased use of those levers of policy which require public spending. Given a lack of funding for public expenditure, governments may wish to consider how they might use other levers of public policy more effectively. This might include such measures as greater authoritarianism, soft paternalism, 'nudging', etc.

Shift from universal services to targeted services

Some public services (e.g. NHS services) are universally available to all citizens whereas others are targeted on certain sections of the community (e.g. free public transport for the elderly). The challenges described above may reopen a vigorous debate on whether some public services should continue to be universally available or whether they should be restricted to those in need. In some cases this may also rekindle the debate about the merits or otherwise of means testing for eligibility for public services.

Shift from service delivery to preventative services

Another area of debate concerns the balance between preventing the need for a public service and actually delivering that public service. These arguments can apply in a number of areas such as health, criminal justice, looking after children, etc. However, a key concern here will always be the question of how effective such preventative approaches can be at reducing future demands for public services.

Changing patterns of services

The effects of these forces could be to create pressure for a change in the pattern of public services. Under this heading would be included a number of issues, all of which imply changing the pattern of public services being delivered. Some examples of what could be done include the following:

➔ **Ineffective service** – elimination of public services where there is seen to be little or no effectiveness. It is a mistake to just assume that no such ineffective services exist.

➔ **Changing the service package** – an example here concerns refuse collection, which could involve reduced waste collections coupled with greater recycling and more civic amenity facilities.

➔ **Changing the means of service delivery** – although the basics of the service might remain unchanged, the means of delivery could alter. This could involve any number of things, such as the location of service delivery, the means involved or the type of staff involved.

→ **Greater prioritisation** – this would involve looking at the relative merit of services currently being delivered and attaching a degree of prioritisation to them. As a consequence the relative balance of provision between the different services would be altered.

Taxation versus co-payments

The vast majority of public services in the UK are financed through some form of taxation with some element of user charging, although clearly the contribution from charging will vary from case to case. A debate for the future is the extent to which tax levels can be maintained (or even increased) or whether there will have to be increases in what are termed co-payments. Whereas with tax-based services the idea is that the amount one pays is not related to the use one makes of the service, the idea of co-payments is that those who benefit from particular public services may have to pay a greater share of the costs in order to ensure that better public services can be afforded at a time of financial austerity.

Public versus private

Another debate concerns the public versus private issues. First, there is the issue of how services should be financed, and the economic climate may suggest that some services should no longer be financed from the public purse but should be paid for privately by individuals who wish to have the services. Again, some form of means testing could be applied. With regard to service provision, we have already seen in Chapter 3 how public services have achieved a greater plurality of provision over the last 20–30 years, with a greater role for both the private sector and the third sector. Clearly, the current economic recession will mean that many private sector organisations will wish to access public sector markets.

User-driven versus professionally driven budgets

Many public services involve some form of assessment of a potential service recipient by a service professional who will then prepare a schedule of services to be delivered. Examples here would be medical treatment prescribed by a doctor or social care prescribed by a social worker. The alternative approach to this is that the service recipient will be given a personal budget for care (from public funds) and they will have the discretion to decide what care to purchase and from where. In doing this they will presumably take professional advice about what to purchase. Such personal budgets in relation to adult social care are already being developed and similar personal budgets are to be developed for health care. Undoubtedly, there will be a vigorous debate about the merits of these two approaches.

Improved efficiency

One thing that is certain is that in the future the search for improved efficiency in the delivery of public services will continue. Clearly, efficiency improvements have been generated by public services over a period of several years and the easy approaches to making such improvements have long gone. Thus, in future it may be that efficiency improvements will be generated by major strategic changes in service provision rather than operational improvements. However, operational improvements will still be sought through the use of approaches such as Six Sigma, Lean, etc.

Reductions in services

Ultimately, significant reductions in public expenditure may be required and can only be generated through reductions in the levels and quality of public services. It is self-evident that such decisions will be painful but choices must be made as the current situation is unprecedented.

There are certain prerequisites that need to be agreed before addressing these challenges, including:

→ Accepting that expenditure reductions of this magnitude cannot be achieved by 'efficiency savings' alone under the current centralised UK model for planning and managing public spending.

→ There is a need to protect front-line services (such as nurses, doctors, teachers, police officers, etc.) as far as possible.

→ There must be recognition that large-scale job losses are inevitable and that it is not possible to make cost savings of the required magnitude by cutting non-staff costs alone.

→ There needs to be a balance between the short-term and long-term impacts of decisions made.

The tendency in identifying savings of this magnitude might be to try and spread the pain evenly with some crude savings targets which take no account of the relative priorities for public expenditure. It is suggested that some sort of framework is needed to address reductions of this magnitude by removing big chunks of expenditure which might be seen as being of lower priority and/or limited effectiveness. Some possible ideas to be considered include:

→ cut back substantially on capital expenditure programmes;

→ reduce levels of and entitlement to social benefits;

→ rationalise the range of regulatory services and regulatory bodies;

→ reductions and rationalisation in the number of quangos;

→ cut back on what might be termed 'social engineering' projects;

→ rationalise back-office functions and promote shared services;

→ facilitate more organisational mergers quickly;

→ cut out many service development projects;

→ rationalise managerial infrastructures;

→ reduce the maintenance costs of infrastructure;

→ constrain pay costs by, for example, freezing job evaluation or pay restructuring.

Financial management challenges

In light of the above, the question may be asked of what is the likely future impact on the practice of financial management in PSOs. In many ways it would appear that the future is a continuation of the past with continual improvement of basic financial management approaches. Looking more specifically, it is suggested that the following are key areas where significant improvements in financial management will be a priority for development:

→ **Capital investment appraisal** – the large budget deficit of the government and the difficulties of promoting PFI in the credit crunch era will probably mean that funds for capital expenditure will be in short supply. In such circumstances, approaches to the appraisal of capital projects need to become more robust in order to make the best use of funds available.

→ **Costing** – the developments described above are certain to mean that greater focus will be placed on considering the costs of various public services. This implies a need to develop more robust approaches to costing in public services and to be able to produce a wider range of high quality information about the costs of services.

→ **Strategic financial planning** – it would appear that the delivery of public services will become more complex and undergo radical change. It can be expected that in many parts of the public sector there will be a significant reconfiguration of service provision. This will be fuelled by the development of the service commissioning process and the use of partnerships rather than sole agencies. To ensure that such changes are managed effectively, there is a need for much improved approaches to strategic financial management.

Conclusions

Taken together, the forces described above (and particularly the economic forces) will create huge challenges for public services in the future and will require a rethink about matters such as:

→ what public services should be provided;

→ how they should be paid for;

→ how they should be provided and for whom.

These challenges will, in turn, produce what are probably unprecedented challenges for financial management in public services, remembering that public service financial management was largely non-existent at the time of the last similar economic crisis in 1976.

However, at this point the author would strongly suggest that, in order to achieve the necessary improvements in financial management, some of the isolationism that sometimes permeates public services may become a barrier to improvement. It is a mistake to regard public service management as something distinct and different from the management of any other type of organisation (e.g. private, not for profit), although clearly there will be differences in detail. Thus, for example, there are distinct similarities between managing a private hospital and an NHS hospital or between a private prison and a state prison. In attempting to improve financial management methods in public services it is vital both to look beyond one's own sector into other sectors and also outside of public services to best practices in the private sector.

Questions for discussion

→ How realistic is the analysis of forces described in this chapter?

→ Are the implications for public services fully analysed and are there other possible changes that might take place?

→ How well would our organisation cope with the financial management challenges which might flow from these changes?

References

Antony, R.N. (1978) *Financial Accounting in Non-business Organisations*. FASB.

Appleby, J. (2007) NHS: where's the money gone, BBC, January, available on-line at: www.bbc.co.uk/radio4/today/reports/politics/nhs_cake_20070118.shtml.

ASB (2007) *Interpretation for Public Benefit Entities of its Statement of Principles for Public Benefit Entities*. Accounting Standards Board, June.

Baumol, W. (1982) *Contestable Markets and the Theory of Industry Structure*. Harcourt Brace Jovanovich.

BBC (1998) All in the mind: mental health evolves, BBC, available on-line at: news.bbc.co.uk/1/hi/events/nhs_at_50/special_report/124368.stm.

BBC (2005) Home alone, BBC, available on-line at: news.bbc.co.uk/1/hi/magazine/4375030.stm.

Beveridge, W. (1942) *Report of the Inter-Departmental Committee on Social Insurance and Allied Services, UK*. HMSO.

Black, D. (1980) *Inequalities in Health: Report of a Research Working Group*. DHSS.

Cabinet Office (2001) *Satisfaction with Public Services*. Cabinet Office, available on-line at: www.cabinetoffice.gov.uk/media/cabinetoffice/strategy/assets/satisfaction.pdf.

Christensen, T. and Laegreid, P. (2007) *Transcending New Public Management*. Ashgate Publishing.

CIPFA (2003a) *The Prudential Code for Capital Finance in Local Authorities*. Chartered Institute of Public Finance and Accountancy.

CIPFA (2003b) *A Model Set of Financial Regulations for Further and Higher Education Institutions*. Chartered Institute of Public Finance and Accountancy.

Daily Telegraph (2009) Recession will fuel racial tensions, Hazel Blears admits, *Daily Telegraph*, 11 January.

Department of Health (2003) *Every Child Matters*, White Paper, Department of Health.

Department of Health (2008) *NHS Costing Manual*. Department of Health, available on-line at: www.dh.gov.uk/en/Publicationsandstatistics/Publications/PublicationsPolicyAndGuidance/DH_082747.

Drury, C. (2004) *Management and Cost Accounting*, 6th edn. Cengage Learning/EMEA.

Eccles, R.G. (1991) The performance measurement manifesto, *Harvard Business Review*, January–February, 131–137.

Elcock, H. (1996) Strategic management, in Farnham, D. and Horton, S. (eds), *Managing the New Public Services*, 2nd edn. Macmillan.

Enthoven, A. (1985) *Reflections on the Management of the NHS*. Nuffield Provincial Hospitals Trust.

ESRC (undated) *A Level Briefing*. Economic and Social Research Council, available on-line at: www.esrcsocietytoday.ac.uk/ESRCInfoCentre/Images/families_a-level_tcm6-11450.pdf.

FASB (1994) *Objectives of Federal Financial Reporting*. FASB.

Fletcher, A. *et al.* (2003) Mapping stakeholder perceptions for a third sector organization, *Journal of Intellectual Capital*, **4**(4), 505–527.

FRC (2003) *The Combined Code on Corporate Governance, July 2003*. Financial Reporting Council.

GASB (1998) *Financial Reporting Model*. Governmental Accounting Standards Board.

Gaster, L. (1995) *Quality in Public Services*. Open University Press.

Goldratt, E.M. and Cox, J. (2007) *The Goal: The Process of Ongoing Improvement*, 3rd edn. Gower.

Griffiths, R. (1983) *Report of the NHS Management Inquiry*. DHSS.

Guardian (2009a) Recession bites as thefts and burglaries rise, *Guardian*, 24 April.

Guardian (2009b) Tax rise warning as government borrowing soars to £75bn, *Guardian*, 19 March.

Hague, W. (2005) *William Pitt the Younger*. Harper Perennial.

HEFCE (2003) Model financial memorandum between HEFCE and institutions, HEFCE, October.

Higgs, D. (2003) *Review of the Role and Effectiveness of Non-executive Directors*. DTI.

HM Treasury (1994) Private finance: overview of progress, news release 118/94.

HM Treasury (1995) *PFI Private Opportunity, Public Benefit*. HM Treasury.

HM Treasury (2003) *Appraisal and Evaluation in Central Government (The Green Book)*. HM Treasury.

Hopwood, A.G. (1976) *Accounting and Human Behaviour*. Prentice-Hall.

House of Commons (2001) The Private Finance Initiative (PFI), Research Paper 01/117.

ICEAW (1999) *Internal Control: Guidance for Directors on the Combined Code* [Turnball Report]. Institute of Chartered Accountants in England and Wales.

IDeA (2008) The performance management cycle, Improvement and Development Agency for Local Government, available on-line at: www.idea.gov.uk/idk/core/page.do?pageId=4405789.

IDeA (2009) What is performance management, Improvement and Development Agency for Local Government, available on-line at: www.idea.gov.uk/idk/core/page.do?pageId=4405770.

IFRIC (2006) *IFRIC 12 Service Concession Arrangements*, November. International Financial Reporting Interpretations Committee.

IFS (2005) *The Tax Burden Under Labour*. Institute for Fiscal Studies.

IFS (2008) *NHS Spending – What Does the Future Hold?* Institute of Fiscal Studies, October.

IFS (2009) *Two Parliaments of Pain*. Institute of Fiscal Studies, April, available on-line at: www.ifs.org.uk/publications/4509.

IPPR (2001) *Building Better Partnerships*. Institute of Public Policy Research.

Jones, R. and Pendlebury, M. (2000) *Public Sector Accounting*, 5th edn. Financial Times/Prentice Hall.

Jones, T.W. and Prowle, M.J. (1997) *Health Service Finance – An Introduction*, 4th edn. CAET.

Kaplan, R.S. and Norton, D.P. (1996) *Balanced Scorecard: Translating Strategy into Action*. Harvard Business School Press.

Kaplan, R.S. and Bruns, W. (1987) *Accounting and Management: A Field Study Perspective*. Harvard Business School Press.

Koutsoyiannis, A. (1975) *Modern Microeconomics*. Macmillan.

Layfield, F. (1976) *Report of the Committee of Enquiry into Local Government Finance*. HMSO.

Lyons, M. (2007) Report of the inquiry into the future role, function and funding of local government, available on-line at: www.webarchive.org.uk/wayback/archive/20070329144919/http://www.lyonsinquiry.org.uk/index.html.

Maltby, P. (2003) PPPs in perspective, has the PFI grown up? *Public Finance Magazine*, 8 August.

Mitchell, R.K., Agle, B.R. and Wood, D.J. (1997) Toward a theory of stakeholder identification and salience: defining the principle of who and what really counts, *Academy of Management Review*, **22**(4), 853–888.

Monitor (2009) *Prudential Borrowing Code for NHS Foundation Trusts*, Monitor, April.

NAO (2001) *Managing the Relationship to Ensure a Successful Partnership in PFI Projects*. National Audit Office.

NAO (2002) *The PFO Contract for the Refurbishment of West Middlesex University Hospital*. National Audit Office.

Nolan, Lord (1995) Standards in Public Life: First Report of the Committee on Standards in Public Life. Chairman, Lord Nolan, May, 2 Vols.

ONS (2002) *Trends in Female Employment*. Office for National Statistics.

ONS (2008a) *Social Trends Report*. Office for National Statistics.

ONS (2008b) Work and family. Office for National Statistics, available on-line at: www.statistics.gov.uk/cci/nugget.asp?id=1655.

Parasuraman, A. *et al.* (1988) SERVQUAL: a multiple item scale for measuring customer perceptions of service quality, *Journal of Retailing*.

Phillips, M.S., Bradham, D.D., Williams, R.B. and Petry, M.L. (1986) Multiple regression hospitalisation cost model for pharmacy cost analysis, *American Journal of Hospital Pharmacy*, **43**(3), 676–681.

Pollock, A.M. (2005) PFI – you'll pay for it later, *Health Matters*, issue 38.

Prowle, M.J. (1988) Budgeting in a general management environment, Chapter 8 in Koch, H. (ed.) *General Management in the Health Service*. Croon Helm.

Prowle, M.J. (2007) Costs of imaging services in NHS Trusts, *Healthcare Finance*, April.

Prowle, M.J. (2008) Developing contestability in the delivery of public services, *Public Money and Management*, August.

Prowle, M.J. (2009a) Evaluating the PFI, unpublished paper presented at a staff seminar at Nottingham Business School, April.

Prowle, M.J. (2009b) Facing up to the 'D' word, *Public Finance*, March.

Public Audit Forum (2008) ICT indicators, available on-line at: www.public-audit-forum. gov.uk/ICTPI0708.pdf.

Randell, B. (2007) A computer scientist's reactions to NPfIT, *Journal of Information Technology*, **22**, 222–234.

SJPG (2006) *Breakdown Britain: Interim Report on the State of the Nation*. Social Justice Policy Group, December.

Smith, A. (1776) *An Inquiry into the Nature and Causes of the Wealth of Nations*. Electric Book Company [2001].

Smith, R. (2003) *Audit Committees – Combined Code Guidance* [Smith Report]. Financial Reporting Council.

Talbot, C. (2009) Public domain: Mandarin-tinted glasses, *Public Finance*, 27 February.

The Economist (2004) A survey of risk, *The Economist*, 24–30 January.

Warwick University (1995) Research summary – the scope for choice and variety in local government, available on-line at: www.jrf.org.uk/knowledge/findings/government/ G3.asp.

Wikipedia (2009a) Recruitment to the British Army during World War I, available on-line at: en.wikipedia.org/wiki/Recruitment_to_the_British_Army_during_World_War_I.

Wikipedia (2009b) Target costing, available on-line at: en.wikipedia.org/wiki/Target_Costing.

Relevant websites

Accounting Standards Board
www.frc.org.uk/asb

Audit Commission
www.audit-commission.gov.uk

Chartered Institute of Management
Accountants
www.cimaglobal.com

Chartered Institute of Public Finance
and Accountancy
www.cipfa.org

Eurostat
http://epp.eurostat.ec.europa.eu

HM Treasury (UK)
www.hm-treasury.gov.uk

Institute for Fiscal Studies
www.ifs.org.uk

International Accounting Standards Board
www.iasb.org

International Public Sector Accounting
Standards Board
www.ifac.org/PublicSector

National Audit Office
www.nao.gov.uk

Office for National Statistics
www.statistics.gov.uk

Organisation for Economic Cooperation
and Development
www.oecd.org

Public Management and Policy
Association
www.pmpa.co.uk

The Economist
www.economist.com

UK Cabinet Office
www.cabinetoffice.gov.uk

Further reading

Argyris, C. (1953) Human problems with budgets, *Harvard Business Review*, **31**(1), 97–110.

Armstrong, W. (1980) *Budgetary Reform in the United Kingdom*. Oxford University Press.

Barber, M. (2007) *Instruction to Deliver: Tony Blair, Public Services and the Challenge of Achieving Targets*. Politico's.

Barnett, J. (1982) *Inside the Treasury*. Andre Deutsch.

Bergmann, A. (2009) *Public Sector Financial Management*. Pearson Education.

Boyne, G.A., Farrell, C., Law, J. and Powell, M. (2003) *Evaluating Public Management Reforms*. Open University Press.

CIMA (1987) *Management Accounting, Official Terminology of the CIMA*. Chartered Institute of Management Accountancy.

CIMA. *Transparency and Accountability: Using Better Data to Drive Performance in the NHS*. Chartered Institute of Management Accountancy.

Checkland, P.B. and Howell, S. (1998) *Information, Systems and Information Systems: Making Sense of the Field*. John Wiley & Sons.

Christensen, T. and Laegreid, P. (2007) *Transcending New Public Management*. Ashgate Publishing.

CIPFA (1971) *Programme*. Chartered Institute of Public Finance and Accountancy.

CIPFA (2001a) *Risk Management in the Public Services*. Chartered Institute of Public Finance and Accountancy.

CIPFA (2001b) The use of benchmarking as a management tool in the public sector to improve performance – a discussion paper. Chartered Institute of Public Finance and Accountancy.

CIPFA (2003) *Financial Control and Budgeting for NHS Partnerships: A Practical Guide*. Chartered Institute of Public Finance and Accountancy.

CIPFA (2005) *Audit Committees – Practical Guidance For Local Authorities*. Chartered Institute of Public Finance and Accountancy.

CIPFA (2006a) *Code of Practice for Internal Audit in Local Government in the United Kingdom*. Chartered Institute of Public Finance and Accountancy.

CIPFA (2006b) *Integrated Planning: An Overview of Approaches*. Chartered Institute of Public Finance and Accountancy.

CIPFA (2006c) *Guide to Central Government Finance and Financial Management*, 2nd edn. Chartered Institute of Public Finance and Accountancy.

CIPFA (2007a) *Achieving Transformational Change – Reform, Efficiency and Lean Thinking in the NHS: A Comprehensive Guide to Success*. Chartered Institute of Public Finance and Accountancy.

CIPFA (2007b) *Accounting and Auditing Standards: A Public Services Perspective*, 3rd edn. Chartered Institute of Public Finance and Accountancy.

CIPFA (2008a) *Improving Budgeting: Modernising the Cycle*. Chartered Institute of Public Finance and Accountancy.

CIPFA (2008b) *Shared Services: Where Now? A Guide to Public Sector Implementation*. Chartered Institute of Public Finance and Accountancy.

CIPFA (2009a) *The Top Ten Tips for Delivering Efficiencies through Technology*. Chartered Institute of Public Finance and Accountancy.

Collins, P. and Byrne, L. (eds) (2004) *Reinventing Government Again*. The Social Market Foundation.

Coombes, H.M. and Jenkins, D.E. (2002) *Public Sector Financial Management*, 3rd edn. Thompson Learning.

Committee on Corporate Governance (1998) *Final Report* [Hampel Report]. Gee Publishing.

Department of Health, Definition: patient-level information and costing systems, available on-line at: http://www.dh.gov.uk/en/Managingyourorganisation/Financialplanning/NHScostingmanual/DH_080056.

Drury, C. (2004) *Management and Cost Accounting*, 6th edn. Thomson Learning.

Drury, C. (2004) *Management Accounting for Business Decisions*. Thomson Learning.

Ellwood, S. (1992) *Cost Methods for NHS Health Care Contracts*. Chartered Institute of Management Accountancy.

Ellwood, S. (1996) *Cost-based Pricing in the NHS Internal Market*. Chartered Institute of Management Accountancy.

Glautier, M. and Underdown, B. (1976) *Accounting Theory and Practice*. Pitman.

Goldratt, E.M. and Cox, J. (2007) *The Goal: The Process of Ongoing Improvement*, 3rd edn. Gower.

Hammer, M. and Champy, J. (1993) *Reengineering the Corporation: A Manifesto for Business Revolution*. Harper Business.

Heeks, R. (2001) *Reinventing Government in the Information Age*. Routledge.

Hendriksen, E.S. (1970) *Accounting Theory*. Richard D. Irwin.

HFMA, WHS finance in the UK-revised each year. HFMA.

Irani, Z. and Love, P. (2008) *Evaluating Information Systems: Public and Private Sector*. Butterworth-Heinemann.

Jones, R. and Pendlebury, M. (2000) *Public Sector Accounting*, 5th edn. Financial Times/Prentice Hall.

Jones, T.W. and Prowle, M.J. (1997) *Health Service Finance – An Introduction*, 4th edn. CAET.

Kaplan, R.S. and Atkinson, A.A. (1998) *Advanced Management Accounting*, 3rd edn. Prentice Hall.

Kaplan, R.S. and Bruns, W. (1987) *Accounting and Management: A Field Study Perspective*. Harvard Business School Press.

Kaplan, R.S. and Norton, D.P. (1996) *Translating Strategy into Action: The Balanced Scorecard*. Harvard College.

Kettl, D.F. (2000) *Global Public Management Revolution: A Report on the Transformation of Governance*. Brookings Institution.

Laudon, K.C. and Laudon, J.P. (2006) *Management Information Systems: Managing the Digital Firm*, 9th edn. Pearson Prentice Hall.

Milner, E. (2000) *Managing Information and Knowledge in the Public Sector*. Routledge.

Milner, E. and Joyce, P. (2005) *Lessons in Leadership: Meeting the Challenges of Public Services Management*. Routledge.

Monitor (2006) *Guide to Developing Reliable Financial Data for Service-line Reporting*. Monitor.

Monitor (2006) *How Service-line Reporting can Improve Productivity and Performance in NHS Foundation Trusts*. Monitor.

Osborne, D. and Gaebler, D. (1992) *Reinventing Government; How the Entrepreneurial Spirit is Transforming the Public Sector*. Addison Wesley.

P, 6 (2002) *Towards Holistic Governance: The New Reform Agenda (Government Beyond the Centre)*. Palgrave Macmillan.

Perrin, J. (1988) *Resource Management in the NHS*. Van Nostrand Reinhold.

Pidd, M. (2003) *Tools for Thinking: Modelling in Management Science*. 2nd edn. Wiley.

Pollitt, C. and Bouckaert, G. (2004) *Public Management Reform: A Comparative Analysis*, Oxford University Press.

Prowle, M.J. (2000) *The Changing Public Sector: A Practical Management Guide*. Gower.

Prowle, M.J. and Morgan, D.E. (2005) *Financial Management and Control in Higher Education*. Routledge Falmer.

Public Management and Policy Association (2002) *Accountability and Performance Improvement: Are they Complementary?* Public Management and Policy Association.

Public Management and Policy Association (2003) *Delivery: The Role of the Voluntary Sector*. Public Management and Policy Association.

Public Management and Policy Association (2005a) *The State of Britain: A Guide to the UK Public Sector*, 3rd edn. Public Management and Policy Association.

Public Management and Policy Association (2005b) *Why Are We So Badly Governed?* Public Management and Policy Association.

Public Management and Policy Association (2006a) *Modernizing Governance: Leadership, Red Flags, Trust and Professional Power.* Public Management and Policy Association.

Public Management and Policy Association (2006b) *Public Service Improvement: The Conditions for Success and the Scottish Experience.* Public Management and Policy Association.

Public Management and Policy Association (2008) *Evidence-based Policy-making.* Public Management and Policy Association.

The Prime Minister's Strategy Unit (2006) The UK government's approach to public service reform – a discussion paper. Crown Copyright.

Ward, J. and Peppard, J. (2002) *Strategic Planning for Information Systems*, 3rd edn. J. Wiley & Sons.

Wildavsky, A. (1974) *The Politics of the Budgetary Process*, 2nd edn, Little Brown.

Womack, J.P., Jones, D.T. and Roos, D. (1991) *The Machine That Changed the World: The Story of Lean Production.* Harper Perennial.

Index